A Tale of Two Cities

A Tale of Two Cities

SANTO DOMINGO AND NEW YORK AFTER 1950

Jesse Hoffnung-Garskof

PRINCETON UNIVERSITY PRESS

PRINCETON AND OXFORD

ISBN-13: 978-0-691-12338-7

Library of Congress Cataloging-in-Publication Data

Hoffnung-Garskof, Jesse, 1971–
    A tale of two cities : Santo Domingo and New York after 1950 / Jesse Hoffnung-
Garskof.
        p. cm.
    Includes bibliographical references and index.
    ISBN-13: 978-0-691-12338-7 (hardcover : alk. paper) 1. Dominican Americans—New
York (State)—New York—Social conditions—20th century. 2. Immigrants—New
York (State)—New York—Social conditions—20th century. 3. Dominicans (Domincan
Republic)—Migrations—History—20th century. 4. Santo Domingo (Dominican
Republic)—Emigration and immigration—History—20th century. 5. New York (N.Y.)—
Emigration and immigration—History—20th century. 6. Transnationalism—Case
studies. 7. Sociology, Urban—Case studies. 8. Santo Domingo (Dominican Republic)—
Social conditions—20th century. 9. New York (N.Y.)—Social conditions—20th century.
10. New York (N.Y.)—Ethnic relations—History—20th century. I. Title.
    F128.9.D6H64   2007
    972.93'75054—dc22   2007010934

British Library Cataloging-in-Publication Data is available

For my parents

Contents

Illustrations

Foreword

THIS IS A TALE OF TWO CITIES: Santo Domingo de Guzmán, Dominican Republic, and New York City, United States of America. In 1950, one was the capital of an overwhelmingly rural country, thrust suddenly into an uneven and often wretched modernity. The other was a world capital, a mature—to some eyes decrepit—manufacturing, commercial, and financial center with a long history of immigration and a recent explosion of black and Puerto Rican populations. Over the second half of the century, an unprecedented movement of people, money, goods, and ideas back and forth between these two cities transformed them both. Santo Domingo grew by more than two million residents, and more than a million Dominicans settled in the United States, mostly in New York City. The two cities grew into twin capitals of a Dominican society that was predominantly urban, deeply diasporic, and saturated with mass media and consumer products. The United States and the Dominican Republic already shared a long history of intimate and highly unequal exchange. But in the late twentieth century, this relationship took on a new form as the neighborhoods, politics, and culture of the tropical capital grew intimately intertwined with the neighborhoods, politics, and culture of the northern "inner city." Set in both cities, this book tells a single tale intended to be read in two directions: as an episode in the contemporary transformation of Latin America and as a key turning point in the reshaping of cities, immigration, race, and ethnicity in the postwar United States.

This book is my attempt to write a transnational history. It is based on archival research and oral history in working-class *barrios* in both cities, and is intently focused on the overlap between two national histories. While the current scholarly interest in this approach may benefit the reception of my book, I confess to some misgivings about the contemporary fascination with all things transnational. The wide popularity of the term in history and American Studies departments reflects a decades-old critique of nationalism's role in constructing historical knowledge. A growing body of fine transnational scholarship exists, as well as a long tradition of regional and global histories. Nevertheless, scholarship based on research in more than one national context is still relatively rare when compared to the proliferation of references to "transnational" in academic conversation. My goal is to contribute to the discussion of transnationalism by telling the intertwined histories of Santo Domingo and New York, rather than by engaging in a lengthy theoretical discussion or prescription. Yet it seems worthwhile, in the form of a foreword, to offer some of the scholarly context for the project in order to suggest the usefulness of my own methodology to rethinking familiar themes in Latin American history, U.S. history, and migration studies.[1]

Outside of the United States there is nothing new about attention to international contexts in the practice of national or local histories. Indeed, under the sway of dependency theory, many Latin American histories written in the 1970s carefully investigated the role of imperialism, international capitalism, and Latin American oligarchs (allied with international forces) in the region's history. The concern with dependency, however, encouraged scholars to focus mainly on factors external to the region. They often wrote more about the role of the United States than about the influence of local events and nonelite Latin Americans in shaping regional historical change. Beginning in the 1980s, historians worked to shift this balance, seeking to tell how Latin Americans, and particularly Latin American working classes, peasants, slaves, native peoples, and women, actually helped shape Latin American societies through conflict and negotiation with national and international elites. More recent scholarship expands this focus on protest and resistance to include ways that nonelites participated in the construction of social meaning, including the meanings of concepts such as freedom, citizenship, and national identity.[2]

Historians writing since the 1990s have also rethought the clear lines earlier Latin American intellectuals, and other critics of United States imperialism, generally drew between "national" and "foreign" cultures. Nations, they argued, are not natural objects but rather social inventions, constructed by nationalists in the course of their social relations with state actors, imperial powers, and popular sectors. Since both imperialism and nationalism sought to organize the world into coherent "peoples" and to argue that the racial and cultural characteristics of those peoples should dictate how they were governed, the two were not so much opposites as two sides of the same coin. The evolution of elite (and eventually popular) notions of a Dominican "self" relied heavily on the relationship with the United States as "other." And, albeit on more advantageous terms, the invention of a celebratory story of the United States' national "self" rested largely on the experience of intervention and imperialism in the Caribbean. Rather than accept the binary division of the Americas as the essential basis for evaluating hemispheric relations, it is necessary to see how this imagined binary arose out of these hemispheric relations, often serving to hide the real diversity of both Latin and Anglo America, as well as the overlap between the two.[3]

The combination of concern for the agency and intellectual productions of everyday Latin Americans and scrutiny of the presumed opposition of Latin America and the United States makes it possible also to rethink imperialism itself as something that happens not just between governments or uniform nations, but in countless local interactions. While in their totality these interactions enforce and reproduce the asymmetry of power between the two regions, individually they are not always predictable or unilateral.[4] It is in this context that stories about the relations among Dominican barrios in Santo Domingo and New York offer an opportunity for enriching the field of Latin American history. Urban migration and international migration are, arguably, the two most significant transformations in many Latin American countries in the past fifty years. The massive influx of Dominicans into barrios in Santo Domingo and New York are, furthermore, crucial examples of both nonelite participation in social change, including the production of social meaning, and of bottom-up, unpredictable, "close encounters" of empire.[5]

The question of international contexts and national history has a different trajectory among historians of the United States. While the predicaments of nationalism in Latin America made the region's historians aware of external influences as early as the nineteenth century, in the United States the nationalist origins of the historical profession laid the foundations for an inward focus on the exceptional nature of the United States. To the earliest practitioners of U.S. history and American Studies, the United States stood alone among nations as democratic, affluent, and averse to colonial expansion. In the 1970s, scholars began to critique this view by investigating U.S. imperialism and attempting to situate the United States in the context of a capitalist "world system."[6] Yet throughout the second half of the twentieth century, the primary narratives of U.S. history and literary analysis proved resilient to these insights. This meant that, at the turn of the twentieth century, calls for "new" attention to U.S. imperialism and international contexts made perfect sense, even if they were not wholly new. In the face of the apparently unchecked economic and cultural power (and renewed militarism) of the United States, attention to previous imperial practices took on uncanny resonance. International histories of the United States, scholars began to argue, could correct the blind spots created by the stubborn traditions of U.S. exceptionalism and insularity. Transnational American Studies encouraged new readings of historical moments or texts previously, inexplicably, interpreted as though the United States were not an imperial power.[7] Yet to write the history of the globe from the United States is a difficult business. Even after a decade of excellent work, transnational American Studies and international U.S. history still look to the world primarily for the purpose of explaining something about the United States.[8] Transnational histories that speak to the social history of the United States, but that begin and end outside of the United States, are still quite rare.

Yet if this book is different because of how it fits into Latin American and Caribbean history, it nevertheless also speaks to some of the major themes of U.S. history in precisely the ways proponents of international history imagine. To begin with, placing Dominican and other Latin American migrations in an international context can serve to revise the very idea, in United States history, of "post-1965" immigration. The categorization "post-1965" erroneously attributes the rise in Latin American immigration (by far the greatest proportion of arrivals since 1965) to the liberalization of national-origins restrictions in that year. In fact, after a brief lull in the 1930s, millions of Latin Americans came to the United States beginning in the mid 1940s—mostly as U.S. citizens from Puerto Rico, as guest workers or undocumented workers from Mexico, and as refugees from Cuba. Indeed the authors of the 1965 legislation aimed to reduce the number of Latin Americans coming to the United States.[9] Interestingly, Dominican scholars also see 1965 as the crucial turning point in the history of migration to New York, but not because of changes in immigration law. The United States invaded and occupied the Dominican Republic in 1965 (for the second time in the century), and although Dominican migration actually took off several years before, the prominence of the invasion in national memory serves as a symbol of the importance of imperialism to migration. Indeed, as I argue in this book, U.S. attempts to manage political opinion in Santo Domingo in 1961 and 1962 led directly to a policy speeding the processing of U.S. visas, unintentionally setting in motion the transformation of much of New York into Dominican territory.[10] The Dominican case is surely unique, but it may serve as a model for doing postwar or Cold War (rather than post-1965) migration history. Other leading sending societies, like Cuba, Haiti, Nicaragua, the Philippines, Vietnam, Cambodia, Colombia, Korea, and El Salvador (even Japan and Germany), all share the experiences of U.S. invasion and occupation or U.S. sponsored proxy wars.

Again, this international perspective on migration is not wholly new. As early as the late 1970s, sociologists argued that disparities in wages between the United States and Latin America, the driving force of postwar migration, were not natural outcomes of national differences, but rather the long-term result of the history of capitalism in the Americas—the "world system." When combined with the short-term effects of misguided development planning in the 1960s, this structural context created the boom in Latin American migration. These social scientists also noticed that labor migration had become a new form of unequal economic exchange. Poor countries exported cheap labor to rich countries and received remitted wages in return. Like the export of other raw materials, they argued, this commerce in labor reinforced the wealth of the United States and the poverty of Latin America. Migration was not simply an opportunity created by the history of political intervention; it was a part of the highly unequal economic relationship between the United States and Latin America as well. [11] The case of Santo Domingo and New York confirms many of these insights. Yet looking at the actions and beliefs of migrants themselves, rather than just at economic structures, shows how even this kind of imperialism was not monolithic or one-sided. Dominicans responded to—and helped to reproduce—economic inequalities when they moved to the United States. They also remolded nationalist and imperialist ideologies (such as the superiority of the "American way of life") to their own purposes, to pressure U.S. policy makers to meet their demands.

Here too a study of two cities, in two nation-states, offers an opportunity to push further, to see how the cultural and ideological aspects of empire (rather than just economic structures) shaped and were reshaped by the cultural and ideological aspects of migration. Even as Dominicans in New York faced the dilemmas of immigrant incorporation and ethnic definition, Dominicans in Santo Domingo continued to live in dialogue with the cultural, economic, and military influence of the United States. What is more, Dominicans living abroad conversed, compared, and debated their encounter with the United States with those living at home. This book is thus "transnational" in a final sense as well. It addresses the origins and nature of the ties between international migrants and their communities of origin. It attempts to tell how these ties came into being, and to interpret them in the context of already existing relationships among poor Dominicans, national elites, and the United States.

Two ideas drawn from the social science literature are particularly useful here. The first is a distinction some in migration studies have come to make between transnational transactions—such as travel, business, and family relations that cross national borders—and transnationalism. While these scholars first described transnationalism as the erosion or breakdown of the nation-state and the end of nationalism, they now argue that transnationalism is an ideology of group belonging parallel to nationalism. That is, transnationalism, or nationalism practiced at a distance, does not transcend, but is in fact part of, the history of nationalism and the nation-state. The second is the concept of the transnational social field. Again, some early accounts of transnational migration emphasized the radical mobility of Dominicans and other migrants, who in their travel and transactions seemed to move in the world as if national boundaries did not exist. Few scholars still think this is the case. Remarkable numbers of migrants actually circulate or regularly transact business with home, but they are still not the majority. Yet in Santo Domingo and New York, even those Dominicans who do not actually migrate (or who migrate and never return) participate in a world of ideas and symbols shared across national boundaries. People live in a transnational social field, without always taking part in transnational practices. Taking a historical approach offers an opportunity to enrich both of these theoretical perspectives. This book begins with the evolution of nationalism in the context of imperialism and state formation, and then examines how the novelty of migration reshaped that nationalism. It begins with the evolving "national" social field that Dominicans shared, unevenly, before the advent of migration, then seeks to explain how that field changed as it became, unevenly, transnational.[12]

A final scholarly consideration has to do with race. The history of Santo Domingo, as it overlaps with the history of New York, can add a crucial dimension to existing work on race in the postwar United States. A strong body of scholarship in U.S. history tells how, after World War II, white resistance, federal policy, and shifting economic structures effectively segregated metropolitan space in the United States between white suburbs and black inner cities, and how African American social movements engaged with this process. But if the fate of cities in the late twentieth century owed much to the painful legacy of slavery and emancipation in the United States—and the process by which Jews, Italians, and other European immigrants solidified their status as white Americans—it owed too to the history of hemispheric relations between the United States and Latin America. The conflicts over metropolitan space in the United States after World War II included not only whites and blacks, but also Latino citizens, and new Latin American immigrants (also Asians, Pacific Islanders, Native Americans, Arab Americans, and post-Soviet immigrants, each with their own histories of colonization or Cold War politics). Seeing how Dominicans, and other new immigrant groups, fit or did not fit into the history of African American social movements, white resistance, and urban politics in New York can add another dimension to the study of race in the United States. It also can situate the question of Dominican experience in the United States—in the "belly of the beast," as many antiimperialists would say—usefully within the contested terrain of urban racial politics. In the case of Dominicans, this untold story of race and the city is especially interesting, since Dominicans themselves are largely descended from Africans enslaved in the New World. The encounter between Dominicans and New York therefore requires attention both to the historical racial divide between Anglo and Latin America and to the comparative history of racial divisions operating within both Anglo and Latin America.[13]

The history of late-twentieth-century migrations produced a fascinating set of encounters between contrasting (yet overlapping) racial systems, as New Yorkers and Dominicans both struggled to determine what racial status the new arrivals would inhabit.[14] Attention to these encounters helps to break down the very notion of uniform and nationally contained racial systems—often described as the one-drop rule in the United States and a color continuum in the Caribbean—focusing instead on the tensions within these systems generated by highly localized interactions between them. Dominicans who migrated to New York, for instance, did not encounter an abstract or timeless U.S. racial system. They encountered the particular terms of neighborhood racial conflict in Upper Manhattan in the late 1960s and early 1970s. When stories of Dominicans' racial encounters in New York appeared in Santo Domingo, they in turn unfolded within the specific context of that city's urban crisis in the 1980s, and not within an abstract or timeless Dominican racial system. Thus the history of race in the context of postwar U.S. cities is enriched by attention to the comparative history of race in the hemisphere, and the reverse is also true. The social history of migrations helps fill out the broader history of racial formation in the Americas.

These, in brief, are the scholarly concerns that shaped the writing of *A Tale of Two Cities*. Yet these debates were not my original reason for writing the book, and many of my principal collaborators in writing were not scholars but friends and acquaintances in the Dominican barrios of Washington Heights, New York, and Cristo Rey, Santo Domingo. The book would never have been written if not for the years I spent, in the early 1990s, working as a social worker and parent organizer in a Head Start center in Washington Heights. There, a group of amazing neighborhood residents welcomed me with far greater enthusiasm than I could possibly have deserved. They fed me Dominican foods, taught me to Dominicanize my Spanish, and told me about Santo Domingo, a place that I had never been and that many of them had never fully left. I began writing about Washington Heights when my boss, Lenore Peay, asked me to contribute a neighborhood sketch to a grant application. I spent hours agonizing over how to provide a clear description of everything that was wrong in the neighborhood—poverty, drug selling, street violence, corrupt police, overcrowded apartments, failing schools—without falling in line with all the narratives of urban chaos and pathology that reigned in newspapers, television, and film. I tried to sort out whether the wonderful things about neighborhood life should be told through the dominant New York City narrative of the "good" older immigrants—people who had sacrificed everything to be American and who were busily contributing to national cultural diversity. This narrative seemed constricting even though it was sometimes true. I was amazed by the encouragement that the people I worked with gave me for these first feeble efforts at a story I have now spent ten years trying to tell. When I went back to university, I took up Latin American history mostly because of the many things about Washington Heights that I knew I could not understand without knowing something about Santo Domingo. My first thanks go to the people (mostly women) of the Fort George Community Enrichment Center, who taught me so much.

In the end, I found that the neighborhoods of Santo Domingo were worth writing about on their own terms, and not just in order to fit them into a story about the United States. Indeed, in a country that generally imagines itself as rural but is actually two-thirds urban, as little historical work has been done on Santo Domingo neighborhoods as on New York's Dominican neighborhoods. I am indebted to a wide range of scholars, activists, and intellectuals who met with me to explain aspects of local history, notably Father Jorge Cela, Marcos Villaman, and Amparo Chantada. But my deepest gratitude goes to the people I met at the Youth Center of the Parish of Cristo Rey. I spent nearly six months visiting Cristo Rey in 2000, during the remarkable time that the Center was run by Father Rogelio Cruz. Padre Rogelio, a charismatic young man who wore Lennon specs, a goatee, and Converse All-Stars, began working with parishioners to create an energetic space of community action, liberation theology, and social critique. Every morning dozens of *chiriperos*, neighborhood children who support themselves as street vendors, gathered at the church. The Youth Center lent them bicycles and coolers, and provided them with bags of purified water at cost, as long as they stayed in school and came to activities organized by teenagers from the church. Among the chiriperos the most popular game was hacky-sack, which the kids had picked up from hippie tourists in the city center and which local women made for them out of old socks and dry beans. In the late afternoons, as the shadows lengthened, the courtyard would again fill with children and adults from the neighborhood. A group of about thirty girls rehearsed a baton-twirling routine, accompanied by a battery of boys playing snare and bass drums. Adult students filled an evening literacy class. A women's group and youth groups met weekly and for special programs. And from June to August, volunteers ran a free summer camp for more than two thousand neighborhoood children.

When I asked Padre Rogelio if I could conduct an oral history project in Cristo Rey, he told me it was not a matter for him to decide. Instead he invited me to participate in church activities, to explain myself to the participants there, and to let them decide whether to work with me or not. Over six months I became a regular face at the Youth Center and in the nearby streets. One day I tried to organize a hacky-sack tournament with a group of chiriperos, which ended in a playful dispute over the rules of the game. On several occasions I filled in for the teacher in the adult literacy class. I accompanied a young woman who ran a program for the disabled and elderly as she made her rounds, walking through the most isolated parts of the neighborhood to check in on people too old or sick to take care of themselves. I helped sell drinks and fried chicken feet at the Easter fair. But mostly I sat in the shade and talked with people. Although no one ever took me up on my initial idea, which was to start a neighborhood-run history project, to my continued embarrassment people often acted as if my simple presence was an act of generosity. They cheerfully walked with me through the maze of paths and gullies in their neighborhood, some narrow enough that with arms outstretched you can touch the zinc-roofed shanties and houses on either side. Perhaps this reaction was an ingrained practice of deference to people with the trappings of "importance": white skin, a foreign passport, university degrees. Though I felt like a poor student with little power, they knew better. Yet I am convinced that the welcome offered by residents of Cristo Rey was also an extension of friendship, and I am profoundly grateful to all of them.

The personal relationships I developed in Washington Heights and Cristo Rey lend immeasurably to what I am able to tell about the cities of Santo Domingo and New York. Yet these relationships were conditioned by my own foreignness to these neighborhoods, and deserve a word of caveat. Not infrequently, in Cristo Rey, someone would pass me on the street and say, "Buenas tardes, Padre" (Good afternoon, Father), treating me as if I were a visiting priest. I was a white foreigner who wore plain clothing, who was often seen at the church, and who was evidently not interested in buying sex or drugs in the neighborhood. The idea that I was a visiting Padre made much more sense than the truth, that I was a graduate student in history. I tried to make the difference clear, but frequently found it hard to explain my life back home. Likewise, neighborhood kids often saluted me as I passed by shouting "Hipólito!" and breaking into laughter. The nickname had emerged during the contested hacky-sack tournament and, while friendly, was not exactly a compliment. Hipólito Mejía, at the time a candidate for president, is not an especially handsome man and is not known for his quick wit. He is white (pink, really) like me, bald like me, and wears glasses like me, but I prefer not to recognize any further resemblance. So while some residents assigned me the role of priest, others saw a humorous resemblance in me to another familiar figure in their world. It is sobering to wonder in what ways I must have misread them, made them fit into categories meaningful to me, seen humorous resemblances in them to things from my world. It is also troubling to imagine, remembering my own inability to explain what graduate school was like, the ways that the people I interviewed may have simplified what they told me, or accepted my obvious mistakes, out of politeness or because of what they expected I could not understand. If I console myself with the notion that an outsider's gaze can sometimes discover details that an insider's cannot, does that mean that I am more like a priest or like Hipólito Mejía than I have ever realized?

As will already be obvious, this book is intended primarily for an audience far from Cristo Rey, and even far from most residents of Washington Heights. Yet I hope it will someday be translated, and that some of the citizens of these barrios will read and approve of it.

I am grateful to the many other people who helped to make this project a reality. The Social Science Research Council, The Spencer Foundation and National Academy of Education, the University of Michigan, and Princeton University all provided funding. The Dominican Studies Institute at the City College of New York, especially Sarah Aponte and Silvio Torres-Saillant, provided materials and assistance during the research in New York. The staff at the Special Collections Division of Teachers College Archives provided access to the Ellen Lurie papers and New York City Board of Education collections. In the Dominican Republic, Raymundo González, Roberto Cassá, and Eddy Jáquez, as well as the reading room staff at the Archivo General de la Nación, helped in digging out dusty government documents and historical newspapers. Frank Moya Pons and OGM Base de Datos provided assistance with newspaper sources. The librarians at the UASD, COPADEBA, Ciudad Alternativa, CEDE, and the Centro Bonó all helped to locate clippings and other materials. Frank Báez, Carlos Dore, Isis Duarte, Blas Jiménez, Ciprian Soler, Mu Kien Sang, and Dagoberto Tejeda offered helpful guidance. Jacqueline Polanco and the other scholars at FLACSO provided feedback and encouragement. Nelsy Aldebot read to me from her childhood diaries. Lorgia García was tireless as a research assistant, tracking down images and permissions. I am grateful to them all.

I was fortunate to begin this project within an exciting intellectual community at Princeton University. I wish especially to thank my adviser, Jeremy Adelman, and committee members Daniel Rodgers, Arcadio

Díaz Quiñones, Richard Turits, and Kenneth Mills. Patricia Pessar graciously agreed to serve as an outside member of my dissertation committee, contributing crucial insights and encouragement. My thanks go also to William Chester Jordan and Alejandro Portes, who helped shape the initial dissertation proposal. Fellow graduate students at Princeton and the University of Pennsylvania, Eduardo Elena, Todd Stevens, Meri Clark, Sarah Igo, Barbara Krauthamer, Karen Caplan, Madeleine López, Anore Horton, Tony Lucero, Lorrin Thomas, Deirdre Brill, and Yanna Yannakakis, all read and commented on drafts and, generally made graduate school a fun place to be.

I was doubly fortunate to finish the project among wonderful colleagues at the University of Michigan. Rebecca Scott, María Montoya, Matthew Briones, Matthew Countryman, Matthew Lassiter, Phil Deloria, Sueann Caulfield, Richard Turits, Vince Diaz, Tiya Miles, Susan Najita, Michele Mitchell, Kevin Gaines, Julie Ellison, Sonya Rose, Larry LaFountain-Stokes, María Cotera, Catherine Benamou, David Pedersen, Rita Chin, John Carson, Kali Israel, and David William Cohen all took the time to read and comment on the manuscript as well. Many more friends and colleagues offered other kinds of support and advice. Graduate students Isabel Córdova, Sam Erman, and Lily Geismer all contributed with research, editing, and their own helpful comments.

I am deeply indebted to David Gutiérrez, Rosario Espinal, Dan Czitrom, Colin Wayne Leach, Christopher Mitchell, Robin Derby, Donna Gabaccia, Patricia Albjerg Graham, Carmen Whalen, and three anonymous readers for Princeton University Press, all of whom also read and commented on part or all of the manuscript. I am especially thankful to Jesse Heitler and Janice Nimura, who read it only out of friendship, and to John Mack Faragher, who read it twice and offered final editorial advice. Josefina Báez cheerfully discussed my documents with me at length. Adrian Kitzinger drew beautiful maps. John Paul Gallagher took photographs of Cristo Rey. Mariana Alberto helped conceive and design the cover. Christopher Rennie helped improve the quality of archival images. Brigitta van Rheinberg, my editor at Princeton University Press, supported the project from its very early stages and expertly shepherded it to completion. My thanks go to all of these talented and generous people.

My love and thanks go to Robert Garskof, Sharon Montesi, Gabriel and Emily Montesi-Garskof; Josh, Deb, Jeremy and Sam Garskof; Sarah, Brian, Arthur, and Oscar Aucoin; Ellen Lieberman, Jamie Garskof, Raychel Garskof; Dan and Rob Hoffnung, Deb Eldrich; Ana, Yayi, Mariana, and Cristina Alberto; Dave Kovel, Kira Kingren, Ben Waltzer, and many more friends than I can list here. Thanks too to Dan Garskof, in memoriam.

Paulina Alberto shared the darkest moments of this project: long, sweltering blackouts in Santo Domingo, sleepless crises of confidence in Philadelphia, and marathon editing sessions in Ann Arbor. She also shared the moments of sudden understanding, the thrilling discoveries, and the satisfaction of completion. She is my most careful critic, my most ardent advocate, and a more wonderful partner in life than I ever wished for. I cannot think how to begin to thank her.

Bert Garskof, Michele Hoffnung, and Johnny Faragher patiently taught me about social justice, history, and the importance of intellectual life from the moment of my birth. It is to them that I dedicate this book.

Maps

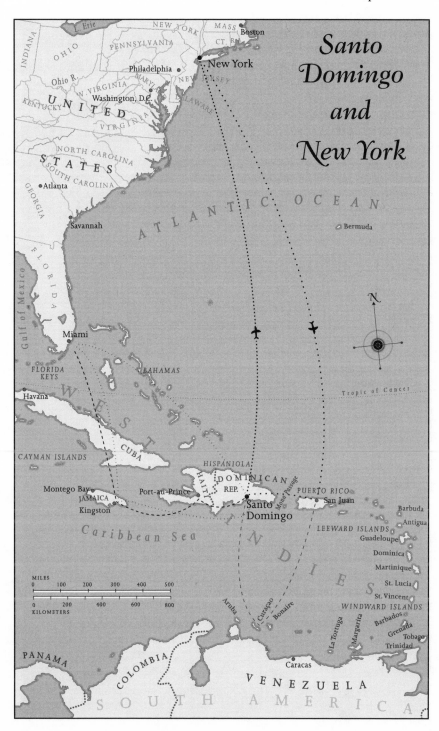

Santo
Domingo
and
New York

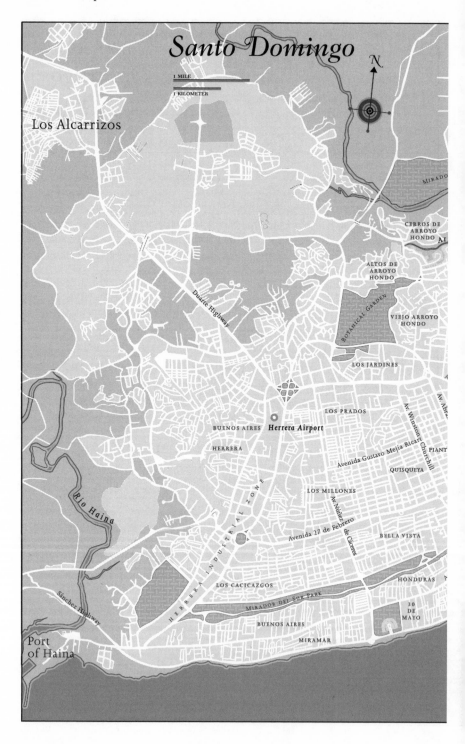

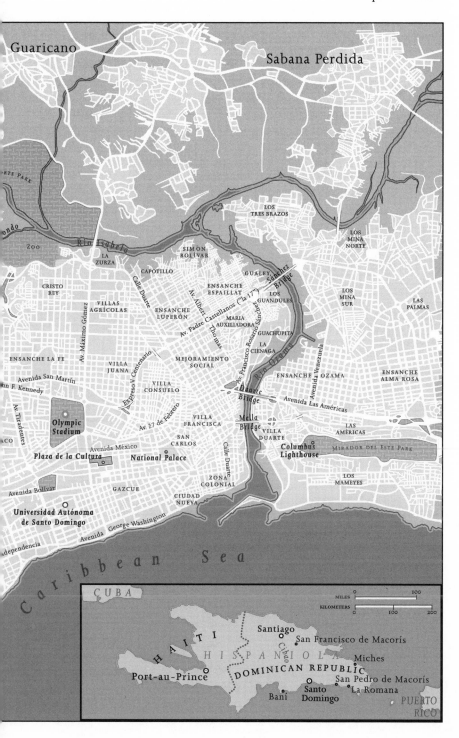

Guaricano

Sabana Perdida

RTE PARK

ondo

ZOO

Río Isabela

LA ZURZA

CAPOTILLO

SIMON BOLÍVAR

GUALEY

LOS TRES BRAZOS

LOS MINA NORTE

Sánchez Bridge

CRISTO REY

VILLAS AGRÍCOLAS

ENSANCHE LUPERÓN

Calle Duarte

Av. Máximo Gómez

ENSANCHE ESPAILLAT

Av. Albert Thomas

Av. Padre Castellanos ("la 17")

MARIA AUXILIADORA

LOS GUANDULES

Av. Francisco Rosario Sánchez

LOS MINA SUR

LAS PALMAS

ENSANCHE LA FE

Avenida San Martín

n F. Kennedy

VILLA JUANA

VILLA CONSUELO

Expreso V Centenario

MEJORAMIENTO SOCIAL

GUACHUPITA

LA CIÉNAGA

Río Ozama

ENSANCHE OZAMA

Avenida Venezuela

ENSANCHE ALMA ROSA

Av. Tiradentes

ACO

Olympic Stadium

Av. 27 de Febrero

VILLA FRANCISCA

Duarte Bridge

Avenida Las Américas

Plaza de la Cultura

Avenida México

SAN CARLOS

Mella Bridge

VILLA DUARTE

LAS AMÉRICAS

National Palace

Calle Duarte

Columbus Lighthouse

MIRADOR DEL ESTE PARK

Avenida Bolívar

GAZCUE

ZONA COLONIAL

LOS MAMEYES

Universidad Autónoma de Santo Domingo

CIUDAD NUEVA

Avenida George Washington

dependencia

Caribbean Sea

CUBA

MILES 0 100

KILOMETERS 0 .... 100 200

HAITI

HISPANIOLA

Cibao

Santiago

San Francisco de Macorís

Miches

Port-au-Prince

DOMINICAN REPUBLIC

San Pedro de Macorís

La Romana

Baní

Santo Domingo

PUERTO RICO

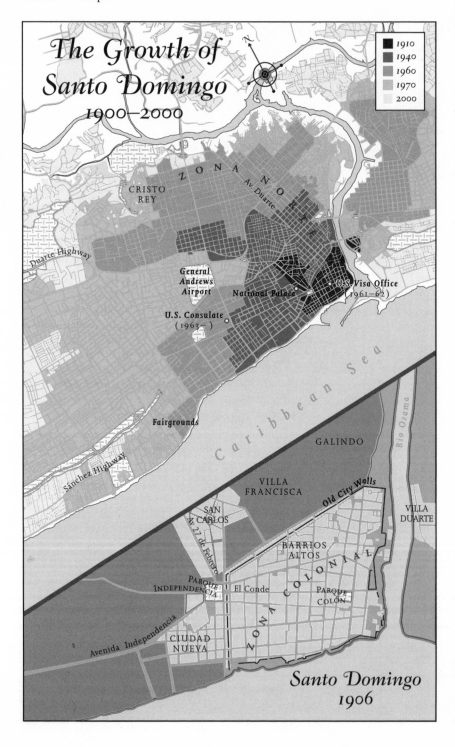

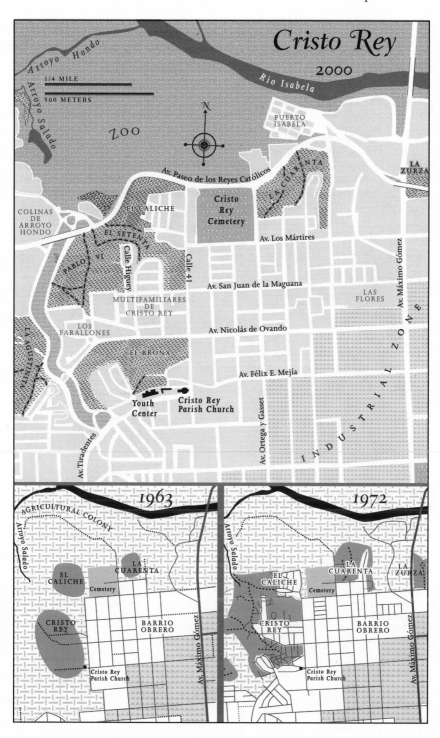

Cristo Rey
2000

Arroyo Hondo

Río Isabela

1/4 MILE
500 METERS

ZOO

N

PUERTO
ISABELA

LA
ZURZA

Arroyo Salado

Av. Paseo de los Reyes Católicos

LA CUARENTA

COLINAS
DE
ARROYO
HONDO

EL CALICHE

Cristo
Rey
Cemetery

Av. Los Mártires

EL SETENTA

PABLO VI

Calle Higuey

Calle 41

Av. San Juan de la Maguana

Av. Máximo Gómez

LAS
FLORES

MULTIFAMILIARES
DE
CRISTO REY

LOS
FARALLONES

Av. Nicolás de Ovando

LA AGUSTINITA

EL BRONX

Av. Félix E. Mejía

Youth
Center

Cristo Rey
Parish Church

Av. Ortega y Gasset

INDUSTRIAL ZONE

Av. Tiradentes

1963

AGRICULTURAL COLONY

Arroyo Salado

EL
CALICHE

LA
CUARENTA

Cemetery

CRISTO
REY

BARRIO
OBRERO

Av. Máximo Gómez

Cristo Rey
Parish Church

1972

Arroyo Salado

EL
CALICHE

LA
CUARENTA

LA
ZURZA

Cemetery

CRISTO
REY

BARRIO
OBRERO

Av. Máximo Gómez

Cristo Rey
Parish Church

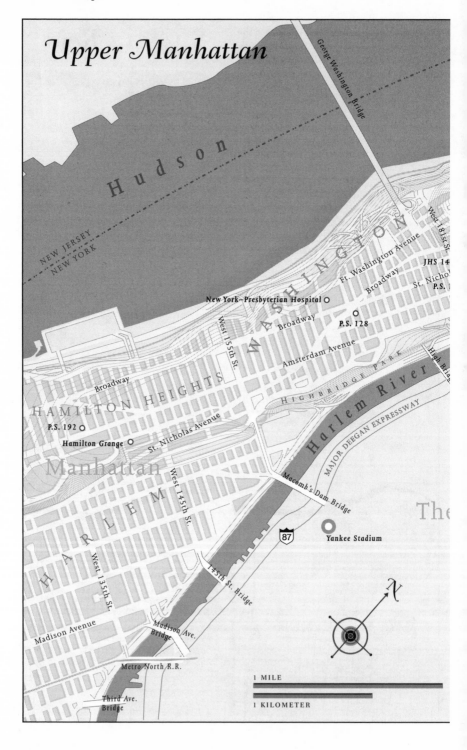

Upper Manhattan

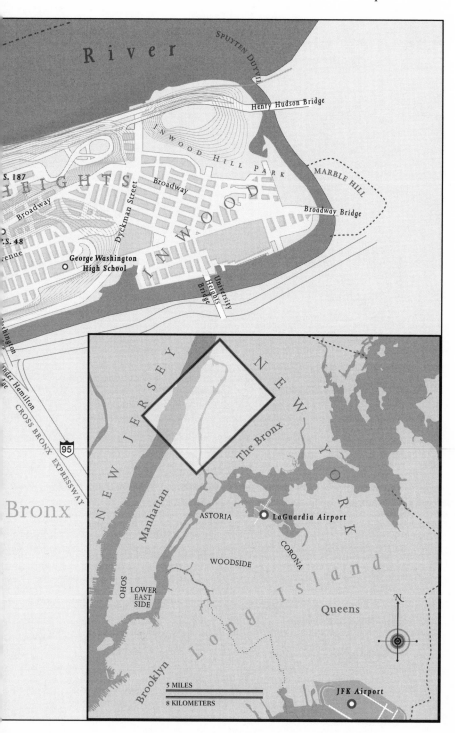

R i v e r

SPUYTEN DUYVIL

Henry Hudson Bridge

I N W O O D   H I L L   P A R K

MARBLE HILL

HEIGHTS

S. 187

Broadway

Dyckman Street

Broadway

I N W O O D

Broadway Bridge

Broadway

.S. 48

venue

George Washington
High School

University
Heights
Bridge

shington

CROSS BRONX EXPRESSWAY

nder Hamilton

95

Bronx

N E W   J E R S E Y

N E W

Y O R K

The Bronx

Manhattan

ASTORIA

LaGuardia Airport

CORONA

WOODSIDE

SOHO

LOWER
EAST
SIDE

L o n g   I s l a n d

Queens

N

Brooklyn

5 MILES

8 KILOMETERS

JFK Airport

ONE

From the Burro to the Subway

THE DOMINICAN REPUBLIC, like much of Latin America, has a history of uneasy relations between the city and the countryside. When the former Spanish colony of Santo Domingo gained independence, a handful of small cities and their tiny cadre of lettered elites found themselves profoundly burdened by the demographic and political weight of the countryside. The independent Dominican peasantry, and the regional strongmen it supported, resisted the imposition of a centralized state and commercial agriculture. To urban intellectuals, peasants represented the backward and barbarous legacy of centuries of Spanish neglect.[1] Yet in a republic that seemed perpetually threatened by external domination, from either Haiti or the United States, Dominican nationalists also frequently depicted idealized country folk as carriers of supposedly essential Dominican values like Spanish language, premodern simplicity, and Roman Catholicism.[2] The disorganized, and racially suspect, countryside was the main obstacle to the flourishing of the nation. But if it could be bent to the will of urban elites, it was also the ultimate hope for national salvation and the antidote to foreign influence.

In the twentieth century, attempts by urban Dominicans to domesticate and transform the countryside unleashed the transformation of their rural nation into an urban society, a process that quickly spun out of their control. The change began as early as the 1930s, when the dictatorship of Rafael Trujillo concentrated political power in the capital, renamed it Ciudad Trujillo (Trujillo City), and began to build it as a monument to the modernizing potency of the regime.[3] But the urbanization of the Dominican Republic sped after 1950 as rural Dominicans began flooding into the monumental city. Between 1950 and 2000, the proportion of Dominicans living in cities (defined as provincial capitals and municipal districts) grew from 23.7 percent to 62.4 percent.[4] In 1950, the population of Santo Domingo stood at 181,553.[5] By the end of the century the population of greater Santo Domingo, including the capital and contiguous urban areas, had reached about 2.1 million, or about 25 percent of the national population.[6] As in much of Latin America, the exodus from the countryside far outpaced construction in the capital and the demand for urban workers. Rural migrants built their own city of shantytowns in converted cane lands, steep canyons, and marshy riverbanks on the outskirts of the capital. They engaged in daily struggles to secure jobs, housing, sanitation, water, schools, and electricity: the unfulfilled promises of the modern Dominican capital. The center of everyday Dominican politics and culture thus migrated with the rural poor, from small villages, cattle ranches, and sugar plantations to sprawling expanses of concrete block, corrugated iron, and found materials.

Rural migrants in the capital became key symbols of this uneasy change. To critics of the government, migrants were victims of the development politics pursued by Dominican leaders. They were starved out of the countryside and crowded into slums to provide capitalists with a permanent pool of reserve labor, the key sign that national development strategies were out of balance. To intellectuals allied with the government, migration to the city was a symptom of overpopulation, which undermined the otherwise exemplary course of economic development. The growing urban slums, they argued, were the result of the cultural failings and misbehavior of the Dominican masses who crowded into "illegal and promiscuous" shantytowns at the city's edge.[7]

The rural exodus also became fodder for comedic commentary on the national condition. In the early 1970s, for instance, a character named Don Cibaíto appeared regularly in sketches on Radio Universal in Santo Domingo. Created by author Domingo Rodríguez Creus and comedian Julio César Matías, Don Cibaíto was a peasant who had ventured from the countryside to the Dominican capital. There, in comic monologues, he reported on the magnificent city to a kinsman in his remote village. "I am not going to send you the hundred pesos for your cataract operation, compadre," he related in an early episode. "For what you have to look at in Nabá Aentro, one eye is enough." A person would need "two eyes or more, if it were possible," to take in all the sights of the capital, he marveled. "I don't think even Nueva Yoi [a heavily accented pronounciation of New York] has as many houses and beautiful things. There must be almost three hundred houses, or maybe a few more."[8] In their tales of a man transported from the farthest reaches of civilization to the bewildering modern world, Cibaíto's creators offered an easy sort of humor at the expense of the rural poor. Yet the sketches were not without sympathy for the peasant. Rodríguez and Matías used Cibaíto's thickly accented voice to make sharp and unmistakably Dominican assessments of civilization itself, and especially of Dominican big-city life. "What's modern is modern, compadre," Cibaíto lamented, "even though it is ugly, expensive, and in bad taste. You have to be up to date because if you aren't they criticize you, they call you a hick, a rebel, and an illiterate."[9]

THE EMPIRE CITY

Cibaíto's creators deployed him as a symbol of the nation at large, a lovable island of backwardness suddenly afloat in the ugly and expensive sea of modern urban life. In this playful mockery, it was of no small significance that the mispronounced world capital, New York, was the yardstick against which Cibaíto measured the capital city he wandered. It was laughable, radio audiences surely expected, that anyone would think muddy Santo Domingo a bigger, more modern city than New York. But audiences likely shared Cibaíto's assumption that Dominican modernity ought to be measured by comparison with the United States—and that the comparison could be boiled down to the contrast between two cities, New York and Santo Domingo.

In the century before Cibaíto appeared on the radio, the Dominican Republic endured one of the most thorough experiences of United States imperialism of any country in the world. In 1870 the United States nearly annexed the nascent republic. When Congress voted the annexation down, U.S. trade representatives outmaneuvered their European rivals to monopolize Dominican imports and exports including the emerging sugar industry. In the 1880s and 1890s, a corrupt Wall Street firm purchased the entire national debt of the Dominican Republic, monopolized shipping to and from the island, and through its dealings with a Dominican dictator plunged national political life into chaos. In 1904 the United States seized direct control over the collection of Dominican customs revenue. In 1916, the U.S. Marines invaded Santo Domingo and for the next eight years governed the Dominican Republic by force. The U.S. War Department then supported dictator Rafael Trujillo's rise to power, lending his thirty-one-year regime both weaponry and legitimacy. After Trujillo's death in 1961, President John F. Kennedy sent the Alliance for Progress, the Peace Corps, and the Central Intelligence Agency to Santo Domingo in order to construct a stable, anticommunist government. Then, in response to a popular democratic uprising in 1965, President Lyndon Johnson invaded Santo Domingo again. By the time Cibaíto appeared on the radio, a new authoritarian patriarch, Joaquín Balaguer—elected while U.S. forces held Santo Domingo and backed by the U.S. Embassy and the CIA—was firmly in place.[10]

Open assertions of United States modernity and Dominican backwardness underwrote each of these imperial encounters, fundamentally shaping the ways that Dominicans imagined themselves. U.S. officials explained their aggression by claiming the role of tutor, helping a young, dark-skinned neighbor to learn the ways of civilized life. Dominicans responded with projects to imitate the United States and, as frequently, with rejections of everything about the United States as wholly opposite to a true Dominican spirit. But whether they inspired mimicry or nationalist resentment, appropriation or self-deprecating humor, comparisons with the United States became inseparable from attempts to define Dominican identity. New York took on a special role in this relationship. New York was where Dominican sugar went to market and where shippers loaded manufactured goods for the return voyage to Santo Domingo. New York was where the San Domingo Improvement Company had its headquarters, where the U.S. government deposited Dominican customs receipts before disbursing them to creditors. Meanwhile, urban reformers, architects, and city planners consciously redesigned the buildings, parks, and public works in New York to "prepare" it for its "imperial destiny." They built the Empire City on the theory that "the appearance of a metropolis will always be accepted as the index of the national character."[11] As the twentieth century progressed the iconic New York City skyline cast a shadow long enough to be visible to the distant subjects of the U.S. empire. When Cibaito appeared on Dominican radio, the Empire State Building, the new World Trade Center, and the subway system were akin to the moon launch in Dominican public opinion, undisputed symbols of Anglo-American achievement. The comparison with New York served as an easy shorthand for the general differences between the United States and the Dominican Republic.

Songwriter Mercedes Sagredo summed up this contrast in a popular dance tune about a Dominican traveler to New York, "Del burro al subway." "What a big change," the chorus repeated, "from the *burro* to the subway." New York was grand, Sagredo conceded, but it offered little comfort to the "typical" Dominican. "I prefer my little mule to riding the subway," the song concluded. "I won't trade my little hut, not even for the Empire State building."[12] Like tales of Don Cibaíto's endearing rural simplicity, this message may have been comforting as Santo Domingo was quickly transformed into a sweaty sprawl. But not all Dominicans preferred huts to skyscrapers. In fact, despite her nationalist sentiments, the author of the tune was among the first Dominicans to take up residence in New York City. When she arrived by steamship in 1929, she joined about 350 other Dominicans living in the city.[13] In 1962, when she published, "Del burro al subway," there were perhaps as many as 10,000 or 15,000, including many who had arrived in the year since Trujillo's death.[14] Then, in the four decades that followed, Dominicans became regular fixtures on the New York subway. By end of the century, conservative estimates put the Dominican ethnic population in the United States at about 1.12 million. By comparison, the total population living in the Dominican Republic at the time was only 8.27 million.[15]

NUEVA YORK

Nueva York, as Dominicans frequently called it, was the unquestioned capital of the new Dominican diaspora, home to more than two-thirds of U.S. Dominicans throughout the 1970s and 1980s. After 1990 smaller settlements in the cities of New Jersey and in Boston, San Juan, Providence, and South Florida grew in relative importance compared with the city. But fully one-half of U.S. Dominicans, more than 650,000 people, continued to live in New York City, and 200,000 more lived in smaller cities in the surrounding metropolitan area.[16] The extent of this primacy was reflected in everyday speech. Just as Dominicans often referred to all of the Dominican Republic as Santo Domingo, they commonly referred to the whole United States as Nueva York. As settlements outside New York grew more widespread, the conventions of Dominican Spanish simply incorporated the increasingly important territories west of the Hudson, north of the Bronx, and south of Staten Island as "the states of Nueva York" or "the countries of Nueva York."

"What a big change," Mercedes Sagredo unwittingly predicted. Not only did a nation long imagined as essentially rural rapidly become unmanageably urban. The distant Empire City, the universal standard against which Dominican identity could be measured, grew over four decades into the second-largest Dominican city.[17] Washington Heights, Corona, the Upper West Side, the Lower East Side, and the West Bronx became transplanted Dominican neighborhoods. Migrants brought their notions of racial belonging, their language, their political parties, their religious practices, their music, and their proliferation of street vendors to these newly Dominican spaces. They plastered the subway stations in their neighborhoods, once perfect symbols of the dissonance and distance between the United States and Dominican identity, with posters supporting various political parties in Santo Domingo. Some rose to leadership in Dominican political parties from their community activity in New York. Others, naming themselves the *dominicanos ausentes* (absent Dominicans), demanded the right to participate in Dominican national politics. After decades of delay, in 1994 the Dominican government allowed dual nationality for Dominicans who chose to naturalize as U.S. citizens. In 2004, for the first time, Dominicans voted for president of the Dominican Republic at polling places in New York, Boston, Florida, and San Juan. They helped elect Leonel Fernández, who himself had moved with his family to New York in the 1970s and spent summers working in the family *bodega* (corner store) in Washington Heights even after he returned to Santo Domingo to study law.[18]

Even as migrants carved out distinctive enclaves in their adopted city, transplanting homeland norms and institutions, and even as they created mechanisms for continued participation in homeland politics as dominicanos ausentes, they also became New Yorkers. Dominicans were the largest new immigrant group in New York after 1960, as the city once again became a patchwork of immigrant neighborhoods. They were among the poorest of all New Yorkers, crowding into small apartments and working in garment factories, as taxi drivers, as superintendents and janitors, as hospital workers, as nannies, and in countless small groceries or bodegas.[19] And among the many groups that came to be called New York Hispanics or Latinos, Dominicans were second in numbers only to Puerto Ricans. Dominicans were Spanish speakers descended, in large part, from enslaved Africans. Even as they negotiated identities distinct from blacks and Puerto Ricans, they often shared the neighborhood spaces, politics, and social fate of those other groups. In the process they became one of the "minority" groups to which the city was left as the descendants of earlier immigrants confirmed their white status by fleeing to the suburbs.[20]

This incorporation into New York, as workers, immigrants, and racialized minorities, reverberated profoundly in the national life of the Dominican Republic. More impressive than the prominent return of individual migrants, like Leonel Fernández, were the small sums of money sent home by hundreds of thousands of immigrant workers. In 1999, remittances sent home by Dominicans working abroad amounted to $1.75 billion, 10 percent of the country's gross domestic product. Remitted migrant wages provided three times more revenue than agricultural exports, including sugar, coffee, tobacco, and bananas. They also surpassed foreign direct investment, income from export processing zones, and international development aid. Only tourism contributed more foreign exchange to the national economy, and among the tourists who spent most freely in the Dominican Republic each year were thousands of Dominicans living abroad, visiting home.[21]

Much more complicated and controversial were the cultural changes migrants in New York began to transmit to the homeland. Becoming Dominican New Yorkers, migrants created new ways to imagine themselves and new ways to understand the world they inhabited. Like other immigrants they remade their gender and family practices, racial and ethnic identities, politics, music, and language even as they sought to define and preserve Dominican traditions. Given migrants' intimate ties to families and communities in the Dominican Republic, this process had an inevitable influence on national culture.[22] Dominicans tend to hold one of two sharply contrasting views of this influence. Those who see migrants as dominicanos ausentes or, more recently, *dominicanos*

en el exterior (Dominicans abroad) emphasize that these cultural transformations in New York were relatively mild, and generally brought
the benefits of modernization to the homeland. Migrants, according
to this view, transmitted technology and entrepreneurial spirit. They
fostered local development through private investment and hometown
associations. Some even argue that migrants brought home progressive
racial and gender consciousness, a new willingness to celebrate African Dominican culture and challenge Dominican machismo.[23] On the
other hand, those who refer to migrants with the widespread epithet
dominicanyork deploy a range of insulting stereotypes about migrant acculturation that emerged in the Dominican Republic over the 1970s and
1980s. They hold dominicanyork responsible for infecting the Republic
with modern social ills like materialism, perverse sexuality, crime, and
drug use.[24] These stock narratives offer no better portrait of Dominican
New Yorkers' influence on the homeland than the comic tales of Don
Cibaíto offered of the daily struggles of poor migrants to Santo Domingo. And they share a basic, unfounded presupposition that New
York steeped Dominicans in modern notions, for good or for ill, while
Dominicans who stayed on Dominican territory remained blissfully
isolated from contemporary affairs.

CONSUMERS AND CITIZENS

Perhaps the most dramatic, and most controversial, cultural change
blamed on the influence of international migrants was the transformation of Dominicans into consumers. After midcentury, Dominican
middle and lower classes learned of the practical allure of automobiles,
houshold products, electronics, and leisure goods. They grew attentive
to the symbolic value of brand names, hairstyles, clothing, and commercial media. What Dominicans, even those of modest means, owned,
wore, watched, or heard became progressively more important in defining their everyday lives. Often, understandably, they associated the
power to consume with New York. The old idea that New York represented the center of modern life persisted, now entangled with a new
idea that modern well-being amounted to mass consumption. Popular
musicians Pochy Familia y su Cocoband captured this entanglement in
"El hombre llegó parao" (The Man Came Back Standing Up), a thump-
ing 1995 dance hit, celebrating a Dominican who had left home on his
knees but returned from New York fully erect, in both senses of the
word. The song asked, "What is it about New York that makes people
more beautiful?" Then it answered, "he came with seven suitcases, the
man came back standing up." According to this logic, the products in

the suitcases represented migrant success, beauty, and even virility. "What did you bring me?" the chorus repeated. "A gold chain, a polo shirt, a bottle of whiskey!"[25] Things to buy and consume infused Dominicans' understanding of their evolving relationship to New York. Consumer objects like gold chains and fine clothes stood for the opportunities that New York offered Dominicans to remake themselves and return home standing up.

Yet the spread of mass media, consumer products, and consumer desires was not simply a consequence of Dominicans' brush with modern life in New York. It was also an important part of their transformation into city dwellers in Santo Domingo. Some twenty years before the Cocoband had its hit, Don Cibaíto had himself heralded the beginnings of this process. Advertisers deployed the character, on the radio and in print media, to sell "modern" products to the new urban populace. Migrants to the city, now far removed from land where they could grow the food they needed, encountered a barrage of messages diffusing the idea that civilization depended on consumption beyond mere sustenance. Advertisers told rural migrants that basic household products, from soap and detergents to margarine and gas ranges, were key measures of integration into modern urban life. Industrialists and merchants sought to transform shantytowns into markets for products manufactured by state-subsidized national industries.

Consumption was also crucial to Dominicans' relationship to world affairs, and to the shifting terms of international relations. After World War II, workers, employers, and governments in the United States and Europe created new forms of politics in which the categories of consumer and citizen increasingly overlapped. The rapid (if still uneven) expansion of mass consumption in both the United States and Europe created a new standard of civilization in the "White Atlantic," an idea of material comfort for purchase, against which the backwardness of the newly imagined Third World could be measured. Meanwhile, the U.S. State Department, in its efforts to best the Soviet Union, sought to spread an "American way of life" in Latin America as in Europe. Cold Warriors in the United States recommended rising living standards and expanding consumption to Latin Americans as the solution to social unrest and an alternative to revolution. So even as it sought to sell U.S. products to consumers in the region, Washington also cheered as state industries in the Dominican Republic began selling locally produced goods to the Dominican public.

Near the end of the century, however, the U.S. government and the international financial organizations it dominated changed tack, pressuring poor countries to dismantle national industries and throw their borders open to foreign goods. This flooded local markets with more and different things to buy, and sped the integration of middle classes into international practices of consumption. At the same time, the dismantling of state economies eroded the capacity of most poor people to buy these same products. Poor Dominicans, like much of the world's poor, lived in constant contact with a world of things, both foreign and domestic, that had become a standard currency of modern comfort (even citizenship) yet were, for the most part, far out of reach.[26]

Only the relatively well-off in Santo Domingo could afford Internet cafés, cable television, sport utility vehicles, cellular phones, food courts, and replicas of suburban midwestern steakhouses. But the new consumer society had a democratic side that helps explain its appeal to many poor Dominicans. Ideals of civilization based on mass consumption offered a contrast with the kinds of consumption that had previously distinguished urban elites from the rural poor. If a refrigerator or a gold chain marked a person's level of civilization, rather than skin color, university degrees, a box at the ballet, or membership in a hereditary oligarchy, then consumer triumphs, like those celebrated by the Cocoband, offered a new kind of hope in the barrios, a kind of consumer populism.

In these years, the spread of cell phones, pagers, NBA jerseys, and high-top sneakers in both the elite private schools and the barrios of Santo Domingo was a process common to cities around the world, from Johannesburg to Mumbai to Belgrade. All of these changes probably would have come to Santo Domingo too even if Dominicans had never begun to migrate to the United States. The New York celebrated by Pochy Familia in "El hombre llegó parao" was thus not simply a cause of the new consumerism—a source of information about what goods were possible, desirable, or fashionable to own in an otherwise innocent, rural country. It was also a reflection of Dominicans' already shifting relationship to consumption. Dominicans surely encountered a new kind of consumer society in New York, adapted to it, and helped speed and shape the spread of consumerism in homeland markets. But just as surely, Dominican migrants departed for the far-off city with the hope of shifting their relation, however marginally, to the things that already increasingly defined modern civilization, class, and status in the Dominican Republic. Dominicans in the barrios of Santo Domingo, like residents of many of the new global slums, made use of their ties to ghettos in wealthy countries in search of the new currency of international civilization. The chorus of "What did you bring me?" captured by Pochy y su Cocoband records the agile use that island Dominicans made of migrants, recasting the triumphant return from New York as an exhausting distribution of the consumer goods in demand in Santo Domingo.

A TALE OF TWO BARRIOS

This tale of two cities weaves between a broad view of the shifting international context and local stories of settlement and activism in two Dominican neighborhoods: Washington Heights, New York, and Cristo Rey, Santo Domingo. Washington Heights, the narrow strip of Manhattan north of Harlem, is the iconic Dominican neighborhood in the United States. It is the barrio where the largest number of Dominicans settled, where the most active Dominican community politics took shape, and where U.S. and Dominican media first discovered and described Dominican migrants. It is also a neighborhood where the presence of Afro-Hispanic Caribbean migrants complicated the tale of white flight, civil rights, and urban transformation familiarly told about relations between black and white New Yorkers. Cristo Rey, a mixed neighborhood of working-class homes, public housing projects, and makeshift shanties, is one of a string of barrios collectively known as the Zona Norte (Northern Zone) in Santo Domingo. These neighborhoods, constructed through a combination of informal land occupations, private development, and state construction, were the main sites of urban growth and social conflict between the 1950s and the 1990s (though newer shantytowns outside the municipal boundaries now absorb the largest proportion of new rural migrants). Washington Heights and Cristo Rey serve as the foreground for examining the sweeping changes in the Dominican Republic, New York City, and U.S.-Dominican relations.

In these barrios, local stories of settlement and community action most frequently center on youth and young people. As is common in migrant and immigrant populations, young people in families newly arrived in big cities were the most daring in their attempts to work out what it could mean to be Dominican American or modern, urban Dominicans. Young people played a special role in both the political rebellions and the great explosion of media and consumer culture that so deeply marked neighborhood life in New York and Santo Domingo after 1950, inventing and adopting new clothing and hairstyles and new music and dance in each city. Therefore young people were often in the crosshairs of local controversy about cultural purity and mixture. At the same time, young people were a potent political force in both cities. They were at the center of the national liberation struggles in the Dominican Republic in the 1960s and 1970s. And they were at the center of the antiwar and racial liberation struggles that shook New York City at precisely the moment that Dominican teenagers there were first testing what it might mean to be Dominican American. In Santo Domingo, the young antiimperialists who dominated student politics rejected U.S.

influences like rock and roll, hippie style, and disco dancing. In New York, the youth rebellions that surrounded young migrants reveled in these same styles. In each city, nationalist politics, generational rebellion, acculturation, ethnic definition, and style were tied together in the messy knot of adolescence.

PROGRESO AND CULTURA

Two concepts, *progreso* and *cultura*, prove particularly useful for understanding the histories many Dominicans tell about their neighborhoods and the young people in them. *Progreso* is an idea of historical change: over time, things get better. Although the histories of neighborhoods in New York and Santo Domingo are replete with tales of things getting steadily worse, the notion of progreso is close to the surface whenever residents talk about the changes around them. Progreso is how things ought to work. *Cultura,* on the other hand, is primarily a way of thinking about belonging. It measures who or what belongs to the Dominican Republic and who or what belongs to the United States or Haiti, the two defining "others" in the construction of Dominican nationhood. In particular, Dominican nationalists have long imagined *cultura popular,* the idealized practices and values of "the people," to be the source of national liberation. In this sense, even the most "primitive" of the poor can embody Dominican cultura as when Mercedes Sagredo's humble tourist prefers his little mule to the subway or Cibaíto adorably points out the flaws of the big city. But the fact that elite nationalists deploy the idea of cultura popular to represent national identity does not mean that they always accept and celebrate the actual cultural practices of the Dominican poor. It means rather that nationalist intellectuals on both the left and the right frequently regard the popular customs they like as truly Dominican and the ones they dislike as distasteful foreign influences. In particular they often describe "modern" cultural ills, such as materialism and delinquency, as the influence of the United States. They attribute "primitive" cultural ills, such as African Dominican religion, to the influence of Haiti, which shares the island of Hispaniola with the Dominican Republic.

Understanding the history of ideas about progreso and cultura is particularly important for understanding both elite and popular stories of urban migration, international migration, and consumption because these concepts are also ways of talking about social class. Progreso is not only an idea about social change. It is also an idea of social mobility. In Dominican vernacular, progreso describes the improving status of an individual or family, not just of the neighborhood or the nation.

Building a concrete house to replace a shanty, moving from the countryside to the city, moving to New York, sending children to school, and even participating in the kinds of consumer triumphs celebrated by Pochy y su Cocoband are all kinds of progreso. Likewise, cultura is a measure of national belonging but also a measure of class distinction. Despite the powerful idea of cultura popular, older notions of cultura as high, primarily European, refinement remain fully entrenched. Quite simply, cultura is a virtue that some people have and others do not. If the spread of consumer products as a measure of progreso has a democratic side, many elites use the notion of cultura (with both its national and its class meanings intact) as a way of reinforcing lost distinctions. The president of the Dominican Realtors' Association remembers, for instance, that when Dominicans began returning from New York, responsible agents kept them away from the best neighborhoods in Santo Domingo. This was not a matter of discrimination against dominican-york, she argues. It was simply that the economic progreso migrants had attained was not matched by the acquisition of cultura.[27]

Many of Santo Domingo's poor also see cultura as a mark of both national identity and refinement. Some barrio activists work tirelessly to enforce norms of proper behavior in their neighborhoods: to improve both the practice and the image of local cultura. Others attend university, against all odds, with the hopes of attaining cultura. And for others, cultura is merely the visible manifestation of progreso. Some people in the barrio of Cristo Rey, for instance, argue that Dominican New Yorkers return with "una cultura diferente." They offer as evidence of this different cultura that migrants are better fed, better dressed, have dollars in their pockets, and have lighter skin. "Different," in other words, is a euphemism for "better," and cultura is simply the outward expression of improved social status.

Ideas of progreso and cultura, in both their elite and popular formulations, are useful furthemore because they reflect Dominican thinking about color and race. In the early twentieth century Dominican intellectuals frequently used cultura in particular as a synonym for *raza*, a marker of shared national, Spanish, or Latin American traits. Wanting to insert themselves into a world that saw the capacity for progreso and self-government as tied to whiteness, they adapted international ideologies about African inferiority, about the beauty of white skin and features, and about the unity of national cultures and biological stocks to their own attempts to define Dominican nationality. When they wrote or spoke about cultura and raza, Dominican elites signaled the privileged place of European civilization in their idea of the Dominican Republic and dissociated themselves from Haiti, a "black republic" isolated by wealthy nations on the grounds that its leadership was barbaric and ridiculous. Still, generally, in the history of Dominican nationalism, *raza* did not mean quite what *race* has come to mean in the United States. Despite the racism inherent in most ideas of national cultura, and despite widespread prejudices against blackness and African culture, Dominican sources show little presumption that variation of color among Dominicans implied distinct racial communities or politics within the nation. As Silvio Torres-Saillant writes, the large majority of Dominicans who have some African descent have remained largely "indifferent to the Negrophobia of elites," and feel little drawn toward affirmations of black or mulatto* unity.[28]

In fact, many of the most prolific elite proponents of European cultura in Santo Domingo have been people who would be considered black in most parts of the United States. While little research has been done on how ordinary Dominicans received literary and political discourses about race and national culture, ethnographic observations show that in both the barrios of New York and the barrios of Santo Domingo, middle-class and poor Dominicans tend to express their identities in terms of race as cultura, rather than race as a social community determined by color. Most are highly aware of color and its social consequences. Many are openly denigrating toward blackness and Haitians. Few openly celebrate the African origins of their cultural practices. Still most describe their raza as Dominican, shared regardless of color. This is a difficult racial discourse for many people raised in the United States to accept. In the United States the rejection of openly racist language, skepticism about intermediate color categories, and celebrations of a black community and African roots are central aspects of mainstream racial politics. The challenge as Torres-Saillant puts it, is to understand Dominican racial identity on its own terms, not as a deviation from a racial baseline set by the United States; to identify Dominican racism without succumbing to the idea that Dominicans suffer from "collective dementia," that they deny what scholars can plainly see: that they are black.[29]

Cultura is a tool for racial oppression, and a strategy for racial inclusion based on the exclusion of others. But cultura cannot be reduced entirely to the question of race, as it will be understood by most English-language readers in the United States. Left untranslated, however, both cultura and progreso show how ideas about race, national difference, U.S. influence, and migrant assimilation fit together with the stories

---

*While the term *mulatto* is considered offensive in the United States and has passed out of use, it is commonly used in the Spanish-speaking Caribbean and the rest of Latin America. Although originally a derogatory term for people of mixed European and African ancestry (derived from the word for *mule*) the word lost its stigma in the period after slavery.

many Dominicans tell about changes in neighborhood and national life. They also show how Dominican thinking about national belonging and historical transformation overlapped with beliefs about social mobility and class hierarchy.

Finally, since progreso and cultura are concepts with origins in European colonialism, U.S. imperialism, and racist, elite nationalism in the Dominican Republic, they also help situate the recent transformation of the Dominican Republic in a much deeper historical process by which ordinary citizens came to use the same vocabulary as intellectuals, colonialists, and governments. The meanings of these words shifted, as they evolved from tools employed by a small, self-conscious elite into ideas that ordinary Dominicans used to understand their world and organize their lives. Indeed, while shifting economic and political structures help explain the major changes in Dominican society at the end of the century—urbanization, international migration, and growing consumer awareness—none of these transformations can be understood without tracing the evolving popular uses of progreso and cultura. Still, as important as it is to consider how progreso and cultura emerged as popular concepts beyond the control of elites, it is equally important to see how they never wholly left behind their origins as tools of exclusion. The remarkable durability of these old ways of thinking in the face of dramatic transformations helps also to highlight the persistence and reproduction of basic international inequalities and national predicaments in new contexts. Progreso and cultura show how different the world was in 2000 than in 1950, but also how strikingly similar it remained.

TWO

Progreso Cannot Be Stopped

AT THE BEGINNING OF the twentieth century fewer than 3 percent of Dominicans lived in Santo Domingo and the ideas of progreso and cultura belonged almost exclusively to a small group of educated urban men. These ideas underwrote their nationalist projects to make the countryside more productive, to beautify the capital city, and to transform Dominican peasants into a modern citizenry. The men held high hopes for the future of the nation, though they viewed its past and present with dismay. This was progreso, the idea that improvement was inevitable. They saw their own higher learning and patriotic moral sentiment—or cultura—as the most important resource for molding the universal march of progreso to the particular needs of the Dominican nation. At first the proponents of progreso and cultura could control little more than urban reforms. But in alliance with the powerful authoritarian regimes that ruled after 1930, nationalist intellectuals took charge of state development projects. This set in motion the rapid growth of Dominican cities and eventually the process of international migration. At the same time the state broadcast the ideas of progreso and cultura to explain its policies. As a result, at the end of the twentieth century, millions of Dominicans lived in vast urban barrios like Cristo Rey and Washington Heights. Many commonly used the words *progreso* and *cultura* to describe their own lives. The origins of these ideas and the history of how they became part of state construction projects together serve as the necessary historical backdrop for the histories of these barrios. For readers with little background in Caribbean history, these stories also offer the opportunity for a brief primer on Dominican history through the middle of the twentieth century.

COLONIAL LEGACIES

The men who first injected the words *progreso* and *cultura* into the center of Dominican political life at the end of the ninteenth century inherited the city of Santo Domingo, the basic contours of their civilizing project, and their notions of the proper relations between city and countryside from three hundred years of Spanish colonialism. Spain conquered the island of Hispaniola at the end of the fifteenth century. In the decades that followed, the newly founded city of Santo Domingo sat at the center of Europe's violent encounter with the Americas. Spanish governors, including Diego Colón, who inherited the title of viceroy from his father Cristóbal (known to English speakers as Christopher Columbus), presided over the early conquest and settlement of Spanish America from a palace overlooking the mouth of the Ozama River, in what is now Santo Domingo's Colonial District. Governor Nicolás de Ovando built Santo Domingo's perpendicular streets, sandstone plazas, fortified walls, a royal counting house, and by the 1530s, the first cathedral and university in the Americas. The physical structure of the city, laid out in a grid with specific neighborhoods set aside for residents according to their status, represented a model of urban order that was crucial to the Spanish imagination of conquest. Over subsequent decades Spanish conquerors would imitate the model of Santo Domingo again and again, often superimposing it on native urban spaces, in order to communicate colonial superiority and corporatist organization.[1]

The success of this symbolism depended on the city's military control over the surrounding countryside, which, at first, proved brutally effective. Spanish colonists in Santo Domingo experimented with the two great systems of economic exploitation that would define the hemisphere for the next four centuries. They divided up lands and native people for work in mines and food production, a system known as *encomienda*, and they built the first New World sugar plantations worked by enslaved Africans and captives from nearby islands.[2] Yet this preeminence was short-lived. After 1550, with mines exhausted, the native population exterminated, and new silver economies booming on the mainland, the colonial population of Santo Domingo dwindled. Colonists emigrated to Cuba, the Valley of Mexico, and Peru, and former slaves moved away from the abandoned plantations into the open countryside, along with scattered remnants of the native population and some poor European settlers. Santo Domingo receded from its early prominence in Spain's imperial experiment to become a secondary port, passed over by the great convoys that carried precious metals from New Spain to Europe. It became a modest, walled city with a military garrison, a local economy of food and goods, and a tiny merchant and ranching elite exporting small quantities of sugar, ginger, hides, meat, and timber. About a tenth of the population was still enslaved, but plantation slavery did not dominate society as in the nearby English colonies of Barbados and Jamaica, or in French Saint Domingue, with which the colony of Santo Domingo shared the island of Hispaniola.[3]

As a result, the power of the city over the countryside slipped dramatically. Outside the city, the Spanish territory of Santo Domingo developed along the lines of what historian Angel Quintero Rivera calls a *sociedad cimarrona*, a maroon society. The genocide committed against native populations left an abundance of open space where poor, largely African descended people fashioned themselves into an independent peasantry. The city remained an outpost of the Spanish colonial project—with a military garrison, church, and a tax collector. Near the city, ranches and farms relied on tenant or slave labor. But without a flourishing export economy, the city had little pull over most of the countryside. For the better part of three hundred years, *campesinos* (rural folk) lived independent and mobile lives, hunting free-range pigs and cattle and farming small temporary plots carved out of communal lands. When the production of one plot fell off, they simply moved on and burned down another section of forest.[4]

Because rural people lived outside the purview of the colonial bureaucracy and because they did not typically write about their own lives, there are few historical documents on which to base detailed descriptions of the society they created. Nevertheless it is clear that over the long centuries of independence from central authority, rural residents of Santo Domingo and the rest of the Spanish Caribbean practiced ways of life that relied heavily on African as well as Spanish and indigenous cultural resources.[5] Earlier generations of Dominican historians argue that the shared poverty of white and black Dominicans fostered an atmosphere of racial harmony in Santo Domingo. This almost certainly overstates the case, but the countryside of colonial Santo Domingo was a predominantly black and mulatto society. While the memory of plantation life and opposition to slavery persisted, along with African cultures, the idea of race—the notion that physical characteristics identifiable as African, European, or indigenous inevitably determine cultural and intellectual capacity and therefore serve as a useful basis for organizing society—probably had relatively little relevance to daily life in rural Santo Domingo. In the rural sociedad cimarrona, most likely, differences in color did not correspond to differences in social or legal status. Even in the city, social distance among Spaniards, white creoles, mulattos, and blacks shrank in the absence of strong ties to the outside world.[6]

Authorities in Santo Domingo did, periodically, attempt to assert their power over the rest of the territory, but to little avail. Spain eventually lost the western third of the island to French colonists, who founded a society rigorously subject to the dictates of the international trade in sugar and coffee. The French in Saint Domingue, as the colony was known, organized a lucrative plantation society worked by hundreds of thousands of African slaves. Awed by the wealthy French colony, landowners, clergy, and royal administrators in Spanish Santo Domingo hatched a plan to reassert the power of their city over its hinterlands.

They pleaded with the crown for the right to bring in more African slaves, drafted reforms to force rural populations back into plantation labor, and wrote laws to prevent further racial mixture. Dominican reformers did not, however, have the success of their counterparts in Cuba and Puerto Rico, who around this time set about vigorously rebuilding plantations left fallow for centuries. In 1791, a slave rebellion in Saint Domingue erupted into a full fleged anticolonial revolution, initiating thirteen years of warfare that engulfed all of Hispaniola. France took control over the Spanish side of the island during the conflict. Then control returned to Spain in 1814 at precisely the moment that the Spanish empire in the New World was collapsing. Creole elites in Santo Domingo joined in the revolt against Spain in 1821, declaring independence. But in 1822 Haitian president Jean Pierre Boyer invaded and unified the island under his government in Port-au-Prince, proclaiming an end to slavery in the whole of Hispaniola.[7]

A successful armed struggle against the Haitian government created an independent Dominican Republic in 1844. But urban creoles still faced the problem of their inability to control the countryside, now made worse by the growing power of *caudillos* (rural strongmen), who emerged as the military leadership in the anti-Haitian struggle. Confronting an armed rural populace committed to its traditions of independence, urban elites did not have much faith in their own ability to govern the new nation or to transform it along the lines they called civilization. They were not even convinced of their capacity to keep the Haitians at bay. Two main factions emerged in the cities: those who favored returning to Spanish rule and those who favored annexation to the United States. Each faction had its turn. President Pedro Santana sold Dominican sovereignty to Spain in 1861. Then, after another war of independence, President Buenaventura Báez signed a treaty with U.S. president Ulysses S. Grant, annexing the Dominican Republic to the United States. In 1870 a Dominican plebiscite confirmed the treaty, but the U.S. Congress rejected it.[8]

THE BIRTH OF DOMINICAN NATIONALISM

Only in the wake of this failed attempt at annexation did a new generation of thinkers emerge, liberals who set about transforming the long-standing ideology of civilization into a specifically nationalist ideology. The Dominican nation, they argued, not the great colonial powers, would conquer the backwardness of the former Spanish territory. These writers lived relatively comfortably compared to most Dominicans, and many had studied in France, Spain, or the United States. Still, simply to call them national elites would be to give a false impression of their power. Although liberal intellectuals were occasionally key allies, or employees, of ruling parties in Santo Domingo, the caudillos still generally held power through their ability to mobilize peasant armies. Nor were these intellectuals themselves wealthy beneficiaries of the growing sugar industry in the southeastern Dominican Republic in the 1880s and 1890s. Investors from the United States owned nearly all of Dominican sugar and monopolized shipping. The national projects proposed by urban intellectuals were therefore programmatic gestures rather than concrete political acts.[9]

The centerpiece of early nationalists' thought was the idea of progreso, of the gradual and inevitable improvement of the human condition. To unleash progreso in the Dominican Republic they hoped to centralize military and political power and reconstruct an export economy, projects that owed much to the old civilizing logic of the Spanish colonial period. But they coupled these plans with a new commitment to liberal principles of education, political democracy, and commerce. And while the Spanish defended the legitimacy of their rule through the traditional institutions of the church and the crown, these liberal nationalists saw progreso itself as a sacred and inevitable source of legitimacy. Every "nationality," essayist and politician José Ramón López declared in 1896, had the responsibility to take on "a productive mission, a transcendent destiny." Dominicans were obligated, he wrote, to transform their territory for the benefit of "civilization, for progreso, for that which is powerful, beautiful, and good."[10]

Dominican nationalist thinkers around the turn of the century generally lamented what they saw as the backwardness and barbarism of their rural countrymen. In particular they detested rural traditions of communal land tenure, slash-and-burn farming, and open-range grazing. Progreso required that land be cultivated with export crops and that rural people begin work in tobacco, coffee, or sugar production. Peasants who had free access to land and wild game had little use for the terms of labor in export agriculture.[11] López and his allies saw peasant independence as vagrancy and indolence. But peasants were also a key base of support for the caudillos who ruled the country. Urban intellectuals and statesmen had little power to force them to change their habits.[12]

Like their predecessors in the late-colonial period, the urban intellectuals often viewed their frustrated efforts to transform the countryside in terms of the hardening vision of racial difference and cultural distinction that circulated in the Atlantic World in the eighteenth and nineteenth centuries. They understood race to be the essential stock of the nation, and they understood some races to be superior to others.[13] They furthermore understood the rural majorities that resisted their projects to be an unfortunate mixture of races. The failure of the Dominican national project, wrote thinker and statesman Américo Lugo in 1916, was "[d]ue to the possession of a too fertile territory under a tropical climate, to the deficiency in nourishment, to the excessive mixture of African blood, to anarchical individualism, and to the lack of *cultura*."[14] As one solution to the problem of the countryside, liberals planned to negate the influence of African blood by encouraging white European immigration. In this project liberals did not seek to create a distinct immigrant majority, but rather hoped that Europeans might intermingle with Dominicans. Dominicans would remain a mixed race, but immigration would lighten, and "improve," the mixture.[15]

Yet Lugo's inclusion of cultura in his list of complaints was as important as his concern with blood. López, Lugo, and their generation of Dominican nationalists saw differences of cultura, created by environmental, nutritional, and racial factors, as a central dividing line between the civilized urban few and the barbaric rural many. The superiority of their own intellectual and moral enlightenment (often gleaned from universities in Europe) was, for urban thinkers, the primary justification for their claims to national leadership. Given their unimpressive wealth and their weak influence on state power, their contact with European high culture was, in fact, the only thing that qualified them as national elites. At the same time their view of cultura reflected their liberal faith in the perfectability of human beings through public, secular education. Dominican campesinos, they argued optimistically, could be enlightened beyond their present state. They could be taught the basic elements of civilized life. Public education in the hands of the cultured elite would be the key to creating a productive rural population, which in turn was the key to progreso and to national glory.[16]

Dominican liberals in the nineteenth century did not typically look to Spain as a model for the education they wished to offer. They regarded Spain as a source of a tragic colonial legacy: cruel and obscurantist.[17] Advocates of progreso saw much more to admire in English industry, French politics, and U.S. democracy.[18] Indeed, many initially celebrated the arrival of U.S. sugar investments and the San Domingo Improvement Company in the 1880s. The arrival of U.S. investors produced the construction of railways, the coming of electric light, and other idealized signs of progreso. Yet Dominican intellectuals soon developed misgivings about foreign economic control. U.S. sugar trusts solved the problem of rural labor by forcing peasants off the land and importing laborers from Haiti and the West Indies. Far from helping to create a modern, enlightened citizenry, this brought in new black workers and pushed Dominican creoles into rural banditry. The boom and bust cycles of the sugar markets, and the obvious machinations of the "Improvement," which helped President Ulises Heaureaux push the national treasury into paralyzing debt, also soured Dominican thinkers on the United States.[19]

In the early years of the twentieth century it became clear that the United States intended to be a formal colonial power in the Caribbean. U.S. forces invaded Cuba and Puerto Rico in 1898 and stayed on, claiming the superiority of Anglo-Saxon over Latin or mongrel races. Only white races were capable of self-government. And Caribbean whites, with their Spanish Catholic traditions, childlike innocence, and feminine passions, needed the civilizing hand of the United States before they could be left to their own devices.[20] This logic soon spread to Santo Domingo as well. In 1904, President Roosevelt seized control of the Dominican customs house, proclaiming the United States' right to enforce civilized behavior among neighboring states. In 1907 a treaty formalized U.S. control over Dominican state revenues. The United States collected customs receipts and deposited them in a New York bank, which paid out 45 percent to the Dominican government and 55 percent to international creditors. The Dominican Republic, hopelessly indebted and no longer in control of its own finances, proved increasingly impossible to govern. Between 1899 and 1916, seventeen presidents held office in the Dominican Republic. Some came to power in revolutions consisting only of several hundred armed men. Although this instability was, in large part, the result of the growing influence of the United States, it eventually served as a pretext to formalize Washington's control over Santo Domingo. In 1916, President Woodrow Wilson sent in the Marines, took control of the Dominican Republic, and ruled the country with a military government for eight years.[21]

In response, early-twentieth-century Dominican intellectuals began to use cultura and its frequent synonym raza to express the distinctiveness of *Latin* America in its resistance to the influence of the United States.[22] In Dominican letters cultura grew especially to mean nostalgia for Spanish heritage. As Pedro Henríquez Ureña put it, what unified the Latin "race" in the Americas was not racial stock, since Latin populations were of European, African, and indigenous ancestry. What unified the race was "the community of *cultura*, determined principally by the community of language."[23] For Henríquez Ureña, the renewal and preservation of lettered society, the elaboration of a national culture on Hispanic foundations, the defense of beauty, and the imposition of morality were the duties of the Dominican intellectual. Reaching back to the initial civilizing logic of Spanish conquest, he imagined Santo Domingo as a repository of faded glory inherited from a distant golden age, a dormant seed of ancient moral order that might redeem the rocky soil of rural anarchy and foreign influence.[24]

Dominican intellectuals, and their allies among traditional urban elites, also turned to cultura as a tool to critique those Dominicans who had recently become wealthy by working with U.S. corporations. As new sugar administrators took advantage of trade with the United States to buy and flaunt imported consumer goods such as automobiles, nationalist intellectuals attacked those goods as markers of a foreign and hostile society. The modern world had given birth to two kinds of civilization, they argued (largely following Uruguayan author José Enrique Rodó). One was aggressive, Protestant, materialist, democratic, and culturally mediocre. The other was gentle, Catholic, spiritual, hierarchal, and culturally refined. The United States, and certain inauthentic nouveaux riches in the Dominican Republic, glorified what was useful. True Dominicans glorified what was beautiful and moral. By arguing that their own spiritual and intellectual qualities were nobler and more *Dominican* than the material success of their rivals, they again used cultura to stake their claim to the exclusive status of national elites.[25]

The idea that the bearers of true Dominican cultura—comprised principally of Spanish heritage—were the rightful representatives of the nation also fit rather comfortably with these thinkers' ideas about African influence in the Dominican Republic. For Dominican writers, Spanish heritage acted as a kind of sleight of hand, directing attention away from the largely African origins of the Dominican population. The breach between North and South in the Americas was not a frontier between white civilization and black barbarism, or between white global leadership and colored dependency.[26] It was rather an extension of the conflict between Anglo-Saxon and Latin races in Europe, reaching back to the time of the Protestant Reformation. In this sense, cultura simultaneously defined the Dominican Republic in opposition to U.S. materialism *and* the African-ness of most Dominicans. In their claims to Spanish or Latin cultura, Dominican intellectuals thus joined Cubans and Puerto Ricans in their efforts to "perform their own civilization" for the benefit of the imperial powers. Representatives of the United States could rest assured, they suggested, that an independent Dominican Republic would be "responsibly" governed by a culturally European elite.[27]

In the Dominican Republic, the focus on cultura, rather than biological race, was especially important, since Dominican nationalists could hardly describe the citizenry they hoped to create as white. Indeed, some of the intellectuals who formulated the ideas of progreso and cultura were themselves men of color, notably José Ramón López and Pedro Henríquez Ureña. As the poet Juan Antonio Alix teased in 1883, even the enlightened and illustrious in Santo Domingo were "black behind the ears."[28] Thus while their counterparts in the United States

Ngoc Tran Le

HON 102

9/10

Add Research Question

McCarty, D., Argeriou, M., Huebner, R., Lubran, B. "Alcoholism, drug abuse, and the

homeless." *American Psychologist.* Vol. 11. American Psychological Association, 1991.

1139-1148. Print.

List the authors' names

"Alcoholism, drug abuse, and the homeless." *Sources upon the relationships between alcohol and* many factors, the first of which is the loss of low-income housing. This is common but not

limited to minority populations. The research shows that both drug and alcohol use may largely

increase the chances for a person to become homeless, but the factor of losing one's home can in

turn cause substance abuse as well. This source analyzes the effects of public actions upon the

homeless population, causes that lead to homelessness, and methods that have been taken to treat

what this research deems as a social problem in Maryland and Massachusetts.

[handwritten annotations:]

re?

how does this apply to your idea/research question?

good

J. I never planned
To open my hands
So take it or let it go

check out films

Feb 23
Morning. Conference

developed a racial ideology that sought to limit white privilege only to the purely white, Dominican intellectuals and statesmen focused rather on the rejection of the purely black, which they conflated with Haiti. By focusing on the question of cultura, not color, they emphasized the possibility of an alliance between whites and people of color who were willing to claim Spanish culture.[29] "We are not racially pure whites," President Buenaventura Báez (himself the mulatto son of an enslaved woman) admitted in a letter to the French government. Yet, he argued, the "center of civilization must convince itself that Dominicans currently constitute the only check against the cruelty and the incursions of the black race." By the black race, he meant Haiti, a nation the French regarded as barbaric to the extreme because of its blackness.[30] Dominican men of color were not unusual in this regard. It was common for mixed-race intellectuals in the Caribbean, even in French Saint Domingue, to oppose prejudice based on color but to adopt notions of civilization that belittled Africa and Africans.[31]

Cultura was, in this sense, a tool for elite Dominicans with varying degrees of African heritage to avoid exclusion from the civilized world, by asserting their *Latinidad* and by disdaining both Haitian and Afro-Dominican practices. Whether or not this strategy actually improved the status of white and mulatto intellectuals, it undeniably helped to exclude the vast majority of Dominicans, who lacked this kind of cultura, from symbolic belonging in the nation. Cultura, rather than biology, became the expressed basis of class and racial exclusion. Yet many turn-of-the-century intellectuals were optimistic about the possibility of transforming the mixed-race Dominican stock into a modern citizenry. They hoped to ease this project through an injection of white immigrant blood. But they also attributed to racially mixed peasants the capacity to be the bearers of civilization. Pedro F. Bonó, for instance, argued in the 1880s that the Spanish legacy of mixture and peaceful race relations had made Dominican mulattos and blacks into potential Hispanics. He imagined this *mestizaje* (mixture) in contrast to what he saw as a French legacy of race hatred. He believed that mixed peasants needed to be uplifted. But Bonó saw brown Dominicans in the countryside, not just mulatto elites, as the potential allies of civilization, the potential bearers of cultura. It was language and cultura, not racial stock, that defined the Dominican everyman.[32]

Bonó was an unusually early defender of the Dominican peasantry, but as nationalists chafed against U.S. imperialism, more and more came to imagine peasants, whom they idealized as culturally Hispanic, as crucial elements of the national character. Even Américo Lugo, who had earlier despaired that a nation could never be formed out of racially and culturally suspect Dominican campesinos, came to argue that campesinos were essentially Dominican. For this reason, he argued, Dominican peasants could not be civilized by foreign forces, only by a Dominican leadership.[33] Under U.S. occupation, nationalists began as well to seek out elements of rural folklore, most notably the dance music called *merengue* (a creole mix of African and European influences, which they nevertheless proclaimed to be pure Spanish folk music), as resources for expressing national cultura.[34]

PROGRESO AND URBAN BEAUTIFICATION

Most nationalist intellectuals in this period, even as they came to idealize a certain vision of the peasantry, still imagined urban space as the civilized, modern core of the national organism. As a practical matter, most of their political energies went into urban reform projects. Liberal intellectuals were, after all, generally urban residents themselves. And given the power of rural military captains, urban writers had decidedly more influence over town councils than they did over the national government. They could not transform land tenure in the countryside, but they could beautify and modernize the capital. There was much to be done. In 1893 Santo Domingo was a town of fourteen thousand, with a core of about three hundred multistory masonry structures surrounded by smaller buildings of concrete, wood, and thatch. Many urban residents farmed food in open lots, and pigs and chickens roamed the streets. The open spaces of the city were known for traditions of collective drumming and African Dominican street dance. Between 1880 and 1916, the town government embarked on an urban reform campaign to eliminate agriculture and animal husbandry, prohibit or hide wooden shacks, regulate hygiene and public morals, build parks, light the streets, and place children in schools. Liberals sought, in short, to make the city reflect their notions of urban progreso, and to make its residents follow codes of proper urban behavior.[35]

In the course of their projects to beautify the city, urban intellectuals invested the physical space of the city with the idea of cultura as well. As newly wealthy sugar administrators began to build expensive villas in the neighborhood of Gazcue, west of the city walls, intellectuals portrayed the colonial vestiges of the old city to be the sites of true Dominican cultura. The Parque Colón, a public square facing the Spanish cathedral, was in the words of one commentator, "an oasis where talent, *cultura*, delicacy, gallantry, love and proper etiquette were concentrated."[36] At the same time that they glorified the old Spanish heritage, they saw the city, where foreign visitors arrived, as a crucial site for performing the civilization of the Dominican nation. It was therefore no place for African Dominican drumming or religious ceremonies. "[R]agged peasants carrying saints and stones and singing strange psalms," another writer complained, seemed to be "African scenes" and undermined the *"cultura*, decency, and civilization" of the city.[37]

In 1916, when the United States took over the government of Santo Domingo, Marine commanders proposed largely the same goals: hygiene and moral uplift, civic education, urban reconstruction, and rural transformation. These were the benefits that a friendly democracy would bestow on its weaker neighbor. In practice, the United States achieved only anemic results in most of its projects. But the occupation did succeed in laying the foundations for liberals' long-desired shift in power from the countryside to the city. The creation of a new national constabulary shifted military might from independent regional caudillos to the central authority of the national police, later renamed the national army. And a new system of roads, particularly the Duarte Highway between the Cibao Valley and Santo Domingo, finally linked the bulk of the rural population to the capital city and its government. At the same time, the continued spread of U.S. investment shifted the Republic's economic center of gravity from the northern Cibao Valley, a center of tobacco production for European markets, to sugar plantations linked to the southern ports of Santo Domingo, San Pedro de Macorís, and La Romana.[38] As a result the population of Santo Domingo grew at a rate two or three times that of the population as a whole. Between 1893 and 1920 the population of the capital doubled to 30,943. This still amounted to only about 3.5 percent of the total Dominican population.[39] But the capital city now had the means to dominate the nation as never before, and was poised to assert this control.

CIUDAD TRUJILLO

Within a decade of the U.S. withdrawal from the Dominican Republic, a new political force emerged, seized hold of Santo Domingo, and began to transform it into a sprawling symbol of state power. Along with the army and new roads, Rafael Leonidas Trujillo represented perhaps the most significant contribution of the U.S. military occupation to Dominican society. U.S. Marines recruited and trained Trujillo, a guard on a sugar plantation outside of Santo Domingo, as part of their efforts to create a national constabulary. The new police force was supposed to protect the elected government that took power after the United States withdrew. Democratic rule, however, lasted a mere six years. In 1930 Trujillo, risen to command of the armed forces, took control in a military coup.[40] In a country where governments were traditionally toppled and replaced yearly, Trujillo erected an unparalleled apparatus of terror, political guile, and economic monopoly that kept him in place as *el jefe* for the next thirty-one years.[41] Trujillo proclaimed that he would finally convert the chaotic Dominican Republic into a vigorous and orderly nation. In the language that dominated political discourse in the Dominican Republic, he offered both progreso and cultura, predicated on a strong central state, order, and the forcible incorporation of the rural population.

The generation of intellectuals that came of age in the 1930s, steeped in the traditions of Dominican nationalism, joined the regime, helping to design its social projects. First and foremost, they sought the final transformation of the Dominican countryside into the kind of productive landscape long imagined by men like Bonó and others, a landscape settled by yeoman farmers industriously bringing their goods to market. They also proposed the reconstruction of the city of Santo Domingo, the cradle of the Americas, as a source of national regeneration. To domesticate the countryside, the regime imposed a tax on all citizens, forcing peasants into the cash economy. It instituted a system of forced labor to build roads and irrigation canals. It punished vagrancy, which it defined as farming fewer than 10 *tareas* (about 1.5 acres), the amount considered necessary to support a family. In exchange, the regime gave peasants access to land and distributed seeds, fertilizer, and information to rural people. By 1958 Trujillo's land reform had distributed 500,000 hectares (more than 1.2 million acres), 22 percent of the nation's farmland, to 140,717 peasants, 31 percent of landholders. The state also settled campesinos in agricultural colonies and, frequently, protected squatters from encroachments by private interests and large capitalist enterprises.[42]

True to the traditions of Dominican nationalism, Trujillo promised to bring cultura to the countryside along with progreso. This was not the high cultura of the city, but rather the imposition of "basic civilization." In the words of Manuel Arturo Peña Batlle, one of the most important intellectuals associated with the regime, Trujillo taught the populace everything "from the most basic necessities, like eating, bathing, wearing shoes and clothing, to the adoption of a *cultura* consonant with the *progreso* of this epoch."[43] This idea of cultura included a heavy dose of nationalism and regime worship. The Dominican people had to be taught to behave according to "national" values such as Roman Catholicism, patriarchy, and hard work. They had to be taught to respect the presidency, the hymn, Columbus, the Virgin of the Altagracia, and other symbols of national pride. Yet the regime also made crucial populist gestures. "My best friends are the men of work," the president told rural citizens on his periodic tours of the countryside. And Trujillo officially elevated merengue to the status of national dance, a demonstration that he was a man of the people willing to impose popular forms on snobbish elites.[44]

Regime intellectuals saw no contradiction between their campaign to civilize campesinos and their celebrations of campesinos as the representatives of the true national spirit. In forcibly changing the habits of the poor, Peña Batlle explained, Trujillo was simply protecting a peasantry that was essentially Hispanic from the threat of "cultural penetration" from Haiti. That is, the cultural deficiencies that men like López and Lugo had long bemoaned were not characteristics of Dominican peasants at all. They were deformations of Dominican cultura due to Haitian influence. Cleansing the countryside of this barbarism was therefore a defense of true Dominican popular cultura. This logic took on its most brutal form in the hands of the regime's other chief intellectual, Joaquín Balaguer. Balaguer described the threat of Haitian influence to be biological as well as cultural. A "pacific invasion" of immigrant Haitians was spreading physical blackness as well as cultural blackness, which in Balaguer's view justified the 1937 massacre of tens of thousands of Haitian Dominican people living near the border as a defense of national purity against outside attack.[45]

Although Peña Batlle and Balaguer were virulent white supremacists and were given a relatively free hand in cultural policy, they worked for a man, Trujillo, who was both mulatto and of Haitian ancestry. Hispanism served to exclude blackness from national life while, just as crucially, it set the restrictive conditions for the inclusion of dark-skinned Dominicans in the nation. They had to accept Hispanic, Dominican identities. The regime applied this logic when it came to counting and classifying citizens according to color. Census enumerators assigned the great majority of citizens to intermediate color categories such as mestizo and mulatto. On national identity cards, officials similarly applied the intermediate category *indio* to most of the population. In its literal meaning the use of *indio* instead of *black* or *mulatto* conformed to a broad Caribbean tradition of celebrating indigenous cultural and racial traits at the expense of African ones. In practice though, indio (with its variants "burnt indio," "toasted indio," and "light indio") was a color term. It operated like the other popular color term *trigueño* (wheaten), not as a description of an imagined indigenous cultural group or community. It signified the wide range between black and white for people presumed to have Hispanic cultura. Even some African Dominican cultural forms became national symbols through this ascription of Spanish-ness. In the case of merengue, for instance, regime intellectuals insisted that it was Hispanic folklore with no identifiable African influences.[46]

Although the Trujillo regime proclaimed the Dominican Republic to be a nation of agriculturalists, it nevertheless followed in the footsteps of nineteenth-century reformers and U.S. military governors in viewing the urban landscape as representative of the process of national development. "To govern," Trujillo told the Dominican people, "is to build." His building campaigns began just months after he took control of the government in 1930, when the hurricane of San Zenón razed the city of Santo Domingo, leaving thousands dead and tens of thousands homeless. In Trujillo's first feat of widely publicized heroism, and a grand allegory for his rekindling of the national spirit, Trujillo piled tons of concrete and steel into rebuilding the capital city. The dictator, his loyal biographers wrote, worked tirelessly among the huddled masses of the capital to alleviate their suffering and to restore the most ancient outpost of civilization in the New World to its rightful glory.[47]

To further cement the physical construction of the capital to the person of the dictator, in 1936 Trujillo's supporters orchestrated a plebiscite to rename the city after him, out of thanks for his efforts to restore it. They constructed a forty-foot obelisk to commemorate the reconstruction of Ciudad Trujillo. And they reveled in double entendres that further confused the shape of the changing skyline with the potent body and patriarchal mien of the man it honored. At the 1937 carnival, inaugurating the obelisk, the head of the "Pro-Erection Committee," Vice President Jacinto Peynado, remarked that the edifice was an apt tribute to a man of "superior natural gifts."[48] More than a half-century later the phallic reference lives on. Dominicans still refer to the building as the "male obelisk" and to a second, V-shaped, monument as the "female obelisk." Buildings, bridges, roads, and monuments in the city were evidence of Trujillo's manly vigor, and they were also allegories for his role as *sembrador* (planter) and father of the new nation. For those who could not attend the parades or read the newspaper, the regime sponsored official merengue tunes. The lyrics of the 1930 merengue "The Hurricane" told Dominicans the central story of the dictator's relationship to the city. "There is Trujillo, every bit a man, ordering the ruins to be cleared. And from the ruins Trujillo raises a new city."[49]

After the initial fanfare of hurricane relief in Santo Domingo, perpetual building in the city, especially in the western neighborhoods along Avenida Independencia, Avenida George Washington, and Avenida Máximo Gómez, remained a central public theater for rehearsing the dictator's power. The inaugurations of buildings provided constant opportunities for demonstrations and speeches. And urban growth had a further virtue: busy construction sites, like the massive fairgrounds that nearly bankrupted the regime in the late 1950s, were a kind of drama in and of themselves. They told condensed stories of the government putting Dominicans to work, introducing new technologies, and imposing progreso on empty space. Once finished, roads and buildings stood as permanent advertisements for the regime. A 1958 merengue called "The Great Deeds" told listeners

> Every good Dominican who has any sense
> Cannot help but see the *progreso* that we have.
> There are highways and bridges, there are buildings, models of perfection,
> And there are so many modern works that make Quisqueya* great.[50]

In one very important respect this propaganda worked. Although in fact Trujillo left the actual design of the city almost entirely to his trusted architects and engineers, Dominicans in Santo Domingo, including many historians, still recall the construction of particular buildings or neighborhoods as the solitary acts of presidential heroism. "Trujillo built that," they say. "Balaguer built that."[51]

True to the intellectual roots of the regime's principal thinkers, the dictatorship represented Ciudad Trujillo as a balance between the power of urbane Spanish tradition and the rush of modern advancement, a city imbued with both cultura and progreso. Trujillo-era architects and urban planners were wary that modernization might bring the uncontrolled growth of slums, an upsetting of the proper division between refined urban space and a rural citizenry.[52] In the wake of the San Zenón hurricane, urban intellectuals clamored for Trujillo to do something for poor families who, after losing their homes in the storm, built shanties in the Colonial District. The regime evicted the settlers, reasserting the importance of well-ordered urban space. The ancient repository of cultura and the modern capital of the nation was no place for rustic encampments.[53] The regime sought also to control the movement of rural people to the city. In 1937 Trujillo told the National Congress that "in a rural country like ours" the unemployed in the city "should be considered delinquents."[54] In 1953, he issued a decree making it illegal for campesinos to move to cities without the permission of district governors and mayors.[55] One elderly resident of Santo Domingo recalls that if a man was caught in the city without the "*tres golpes*" (three blows)—a national identity card, proof of military service, and a proof of membership in the official Partido Dominicano—"they

---

*Quisqueya is an indigenous word for the island of Hispaniola, used by Dominican nationalists to refer to the Dominican Republic much like the word Borinquen is used in Puerto Rico.

FIGURE 2-1. The Fairgrounds, built in 1955–1956 to host the International Fair of Peace and Brotherhood. This was the apogee of Trujillo's monumental urbanism, an attempt to create a modern city to show off to foreign visitors. It nearly bankrupted the government. (Photograph by Hank Walker, courtesy of Getty Images)

sent you away and applied the ten tareas law" defining men who did not work plots of at least 1.5 acres as vagrants. "It was *pa' fuera, pa'l campo, al trabajo!*" Get out, go to the countryside, get to work![56]

Yet modernization and monumental building in the city also required the growth of urban working classes to meet the demand for construction workers. After World War II, the regime also sponsored a brewery and bottling plant, factories to produce basic foodstuffs, construction materials and other basic goods that had previously been imported.[57] These plants also needed workers. The state therefore began to encourage the migration of some laborers to the capital, but sought to regulate their incorporation into an idealized, harmonious, orderly, modern city. Beginning in the 1940s, the regime began construction of the northwest course of the Duarte Avenue and the rudimentary creation of the neighborhoods on either side of it: Villa Consuelo, Mejoramiento Social, and Barrio Obrero (as well as Los Minas on the far side of the Ozama River). Adjacent to the old working-class settlements on the rise of land inside the city's old northern wall, this would become the crucial backbone of the Zona Norte (Northern District), the popular and marginal neighborhoods of Santo Domingo in the half-century that followed.[58] Indeed, as working-class settlements grew northward, many Dominicans continued to refer to them as the Barrios Altos (Upper Barrios), referring to those original hillside settlements inside the city walls.

Concrete, single-family bungalows in these neighborhoods, doled out by a lottery, served to build loyalty for the regime among beneficiaries. The merengue "El Progreso no se detiene" (Progreso Cannot be Stopped) translated the old idea of progreso for a popular audience in terms of these new homes. According to the song, progreso meant "building beautiful *barrios* for the humble folk."[59] The creation of urban working-class neighborhoods also conformed to an ideology of social control, which sought "the social, cultural, and moral perfection" of the new working class.[60] At the inauguration of several hundred homes in a neighborhood named Mejoramiento Social (Social Improvement), Trujillo told the new settlers that his regime's orderly project of urbanization protected them from "the universal crisis that tortures all humanity and inverts noble and ancient values." The construction of well-ordered working-class neighborhoods in the capital, Trujillo told his subjects, would protect the Dominican people against the unraveling of modern social life. The regime would bring outward progreso, but also "a purification of the inside that will move men and change their materialist, skeptical attitudes into a vibrant emotional energy."[61] Well-built and well-policed neighborhoods were a means for protecting the symbols of high cultura in the center city from the exodus of rural people, and for imposing the rudiments of a more basic cultura on the new urban working class.

In truth the modernization and expansion of the capital became something much more unruly than this rhetoric admitted. Thousands of miles of roads built ever deeper into the Dominican backlands pushed state power and capitalist economic relations into previously independent lands. But those roads also encouraged new kinds of mobility. By 1950, 18 percent of Dominicans lived in a province other than where they were born.[62] Then, in the 1950s, the promise of rural modernity based on peasant access to land began to crumble as Trujillo's rural land distribution policies ran up against the limits of arable lands. Without directly attacking the large holdings amassed by prominent Dominican families, the regime could no longer meet peasant needs for more plots. At the same time, Trujillo shifted his economic focus from encouraging small commercial farming to building a sugar monopoly. He bought out foreign sugar producers and began to acquire vast personal holdings. A regime that had protected peasant access to land now actively dispossessed peasants, especially in the cane lands of the San Juan Valley and in the southern province of San Cristóbal.[63]

FIGURE 2-2. Building new working-class housing in the Zona Norte, 1959. The government built "chalets" like these in the neighborhoods along Calle Duarte and Avenida Máximo Gómez. Alongside them migrants continued to build makeshift wooden structures. (Photograph by Hank Walker, courtesy of Getty Images)

As the exhaustion of land reform and the romance with sugar foreclosed rural alternatives, and as Ciudad Trujillo gained economic, political, and symbolic power, more and more Dominicans made their way to the capital city.[64] By the 1950s, thousands of migrants, most from the rural areas near the capital and the provinces of the southwest, settled informally on the edges of the working-class neighborhoods, on open lands near the river, or on the edge of the airport. Technically these settlements were illegal, but the regime was complicit in the process. For instance, when the authorities cleared several poor neighborhoods to build the Duarte Bridge, they permitted residents to resettle in shanties on the slopes east of María Auxiliadora, in a neighborhood called Guachupita. Urban building projects often produced mass evictions like these. But evicted families were not sent to the countryside. They were dumped in unoccupied lands with building materials or a few pesos to compensate for the destruction of their neighborhoods. At the same time, administrators on Trujillo's cane lands north of the city began parceling off and "selling" small lots to settlers, who built shacks and planted small garden plots. The sales did not transfer ownership of the land. They were tacit permission to build a squatter colony. These precarious settlements on the hillsides and steep fingerlike canyons that extended north from the working-class neighborhoods toward the

FIGURE 2-3. A woman and several children near a sewing machine, in an informal settlement of Santo Domingo, 1959. (Photograph by Hank Walker, courtesy of Getty Images)

Ozama and Isabela Rivers would become the neighborhoods of Simón Bolívar and Capotillo.[65]

The growth of shantytowns worried intellectuals in Santo Domingo. In 1958, geographers and planners attending a conference on natural resources convened a session to discuss the "problem" of the "rural exodus."[66] Panelists proposed stricter application of restrictions on migration and a survey of poor city neighborhoods to see if migrants would be willing to return to the countryside in exchange for grants of 100 tareas (15.5 acres).[67] In reality urban planners could not offer such large plots because land in the countryside was increasingly scarce. In 1960 the regime instructed rural police to register all residents of their districts who lacked the means to sustain themselves. The police should provide them with work, since the jobless and landless were likely otherwise to move to the capital and "create problems of housing, live unhygienically, and *malpasar* (suffer) too." The central authorities advised rural police to discourage peasants from migrating to Ciudad Trujillo "through conversations and friendly advice."[68] It is not clear whether the official who drafted the directive was being intentionally or unintentionally ironic when he suggested that advice from Trujillo's brutal rural police could ever be "friendly."

In any event, none of this had much effect. In 1936, when regime syco-phants overcame the dictator's self-effacing protests to rebaptize Santo Domingo as Ciudad Trujillo, its population was close to 71,091. By the last years of the regime, its population had grown to 367,053.[69] National-ists had long imagined the city as a bastion of cultura, apart from the ru-ral nation. But now poor Dominicans increasingly lived clustered at the edge of the city walls, poised to assert themselves in new ways within national politics. This tinder received a spark in May of 1961 when a group of disaffected military men and civilian officials, with some as-sistance from the CIA, successfully plotted to assassinate Rafael Trujillo. The plan was for anti-Trujillo officers in the army to take charge. But the plan went terribly awry. Trujillo's brothers and sons retained control of the military and unleashed a reign of vengeful terror on the capital. Meanwhile, large crowds began to assemble downtown in the capital. They demanded a response to their hunger and poverty, the departure of the surviving Trujillos and of Joaquín Balaguer, who happened to be the constitutional president of the Republic (very much a figurehead po-sition as long as Trujillo was alive) at the time of the assassination. They tore down statues of the dead dictator and clashed with police, armed forces, and bands of thugs armed by the government.[70]

The Kennedy administration in Washington took these demonstra-tions very seriously. The young president had stumbled badly at the Bay of Pigs only six weeks earlier and wanted to prove that he could prevent the region from going communist. Kennedy and his liberal al-lies, steeped in a New Deal ideology of social peace, hoped that moder-ate reform and rapid economic development could be used to outflank revolution.[71] The Dominican Republic was to be the crucial first test of this new strategy. The U.S. Embassy in Santo Domingo pressured Balaguer and the Trujillos into leaving the country. Kennedy sent John Bartlow Martin, a journalist and speechwriter, to Santo Domingo as ambassador to coddle "moderate" anticommunists, create a "Domini-can Tennessee Valley Authority," and generally manage the situation. Washington also hurriedly put a novel array of tools at Martin's dis-posal: the newly created Alliance for Progress, imagined as a kind of Marshall Plan for Latin America, and the Peace Corps.[72]

Juan Bosch, a populist democrat with broad rural support, won the presidency in a competitive election held in 1962. But Bosch made some early missteps, and his rural popularity did little to protect him when the business sector and the church turned against him, denouncing him as a communist. In the end a stable, anticommunist regime was more important to liberals in Washington than a democratic one. They stood by as the armed forces easily deposed Bosch in 1963, establishing a Tri-umvirato, or military junta. Yet even the military dictatorship could not ensure stability. In 1965, a democratic wing of the military and the leadership of Bosch's party, the Partido Revolucionario Dominicano (PRD), tried to put Bosch back into power without new elections. Young PRD activist José Francisco Peña Gómez took to the radio to call the new urban working-class to the streets. Over the course of four days in April, the residents of the working-class neighborhoods and shantytowns in the Zona Norte took control of the city, blocking the advance of the loyalist military. In the early part of the century, national governments had been at the mercy of rural strongmen. Now after three decades of urban growth, the government found itself at the mercy of residents of the Zona Norte, who lived a stone's throw (or sniper's shot) from the national palace.[73]

Just as rural rebellions had eventually inspired the United States to invade and pacify the Dominican Republic in 1916, in the summer of 1965 the alliance between disaffected military officers and barrio residents in Santo Domingo triggered a new U.S. intervention. Determined to show his mettle as a Cold Warrior, President Lyndon Johnson invaded Santo Domingo on April 29, sending a message to congressional leaders that he had "just taken action that will prove that Democratic presidents can deal with Communists as strongly as Republicans."[74] It soon became clear that the accusation of communism was gravely overstated. Many in the volunteer forces in Santo Domingo and some in the barrios were members of unions or left-wing parties, but the military and civilian leadership were hardly radicals. The uprising was an alliance between a fairly moderate sector of the political class, who merely wanted a larger share of power, and a starving urban population, who wanted the return of a president who had promised them fuller citizenship. Johnson shifted his public explanation for the invasion. The United States, he said, had landed only as a neutral peacekeeper, seeking to prevent civil war and assist in the return to democracy.[75]

Despite this supposed neutrality, representatives of the U.S. government took the opportunity to deal with the strategic threat of mobilized urban barrios, which they saw as an obstacle to stable government in the Dominican Republic. They encouraged a terror campaign against leftists, unionists, and armed neighborhood leaders. U.S. troops held the pro-Bosch forces pinned down in the Colonial District but allowed Loyalist forces to roam the city waging a severe campaign of repression in the Zona Norte. "Operation Cleanup," as it was called, put the lid back on the urban crisis in Santo Domingo. Meanwhile Joaquín Balaguer, returned from exile in New York, pieced together a new party, the Partido Reformista (Reformista Party), from the fragments of the old regime and launched a bid to regain the presidency. His opponent, former president Bosch, was afraid to leave his home for fear

FIGURE 2-4. Barrio residents join the Constitutionalist forces, stopping a Loyalist tank from entering the city on the first day of the uprising, April 24, 1965. (Photograph by Juan Pérez Terrero)

of attack by Loyalist forces. Balaguer told voters that the United States would never permit his opponent, Juan Bosch, to take power. The only way to end the conflict was to elect him. Although the urban poor voted overwhelmingly for Bosch, Balaguer won the presidency in 1966.[76]

THE POLITICAL ECONOMY OF URBAN GROWTH

Once in office Balaguer made urban construction, based on the twin ideologies of progreso and cultura, the centerpiece of national political life as never before. Balaguer's allies in the U.S. State Department and Agency for International Development pushed for investments in rural projects. But the new president defied them.[77] Big projects in the city were a form of easily understood propaganda carried over from the Trujillo years. Cement mixers and trucks carrying steel rods were a public theater proving that Balaguer was doing something. "One cannot live in the Dominican Republic a single day," one observer remarked, "without seeing an active, personable president opening up a new housing development, presiding over the ground-breaking for a new school, inspecting a dam project, handing out a land deed to an appreciative peasant."[78] But Balaguer also used urban construction as an economic and political resource in negotiating his relationship to various sectors of Dominican society, including eventually the urban poor.

His government enjoyed a temporary boom in public wealth, generated by confiscated Trujillo sugar holdings and abundant international aid. Ballooning contracts for road and neighborhood construction, investments in industrial zones, land grants, and the rising private property values that resulted from public investment helped to transfer this wealth to industrialists, construction companies, real estate speculators, financiers, and bureaucrats of all levels.[79] The result was rapid growth and sharpened spatial segregation in the city, as wealthy provincial families and the rural middle class moved into the capital, joining the expanding urban elite and a growing class of public employees. The beneficiaries of the urban boom also inhabited the newly constructed city, moving out of the old center city—which had been easily overrun by the poor in the early 1960s—into new modern neighborhoods to the west. Beginning with the site of the old General Andrews Airport, Balaguer's growth machine transformed the western suburbs—inherited by the state from Trujillo holdings—into a landscape of large avenues, quiet streets, parks, fancy social clubs, high-rise hotels, and air-conditioned commercial plazas. In the place of Parque Colón, the former preserve of cultura that was now a site for popular protest, Balaguer sponsored a Plaza de Cultura as center of the new Santo Domingo. There, in newly built museums, a library, and a national theater, Hispanic traditions had pride of place alongside the key symbols of political power. Around the Plaza de Cultura stood the Central Bank, the U.S. Embassy, the Embassy of the Holy See, and the family mansion where Balaguer conducted the bulk of state business.

Pushing still farther west, new *urbanizaciones* (a Spanish word similar to *subdivision*, meaning a neighborhood planned and urbanized by engineers) and exclusive condominiums, built with a combination of private and public capital, spread wide across the landscape. Among these urbanizaciones, public investments created multifamily housing projects and *ensanches* (another word for a formal neighborhood that comes from the verb *ensanchar*, to widen or improve a street). These grids of small, concrete one-family homes housed government employees, military families, and others in the Balaguerista lower-middle class. The new city monopolized land, government resources, and most of the cars, telephones, and indoor toilets in the entire country, for the use of the new government and its political base.[80] Trujillo's personal control over much of the Dominican economy had prevented the formation of a fully independent business elite. In Trujillo's day, administrators might get rich, but they would get rich working for Trujillo. Balaguer, by contrast, used public investments in the city, incentives to industry, and official corruption to create new private wealthy and middle classes and to secure the loyalty of an increasingly independent elite.

Yet the city continued to attract poor Dominicans as well. The consolidation of large landholdings and the dispossession of peasants proceeded apace between the fall of Trujillo and the end of the 1970s. The Balaguer regime continued Trujillo-era land colonization programs and proposed its own rural reforms in 1972. But Balaguer's rural policies were designed to boost production of foodstuffs to feed urban workers and to extract surpluses from state holdings to fund transfers to urban sectors, not to meet the needs of the rural poor. The few rural landholders who agreed to sell their lands to the state for the purposes of redistribution to peasants seem to have understood this. They requested compensation in the form of lands in the outskirts of Santo Domingo, exchanging their status as rural landowners for a more lucrative foothold in the regime's urban growth machine. These policies favoring the urban sector contributed to a rapid and calamitous consolidation of landholdings in the countryside. In 1960, even after Trujillo's romance with sugar, small- and medium-sized farmers held 70 percent of occupied land in the Dominican Republic. By 1980, the percentage had shrunk to 36 percent. Even as the national population grew by more than 2.5 million, less and less land was available for campesinos to grow food. This brewing subsistence crisis emerged at the same time that the state relaxed legal restrictions on internal migration. The result was an explosive growth of poor neighborhoods at the edges of the new capital.[81]

In the 1950s Trujillo had celebrated a harmonious, orderly capital, a rhetoric that contrasted with the creeping reality of informal settlements and abject poverty. As the city grew still further, Balaguer identified the informal settlements that could no longer be hidden as an affront to civilized living. The Barrios Altos, he said, were *caseríos vergonzosos*, "shameful little towns," disorganized, unhealthy, promiscuous, and illegal settlements "on the margin of *progreso* and civilization."[82] Promiscuity was a crucial aspect of his invective. At the time, most Dominican demographers believed that the problem of urban poverty was related to the problem of overpopulation, favoring birth control measures and instruction in family planning. Balaguer tried to shift focus from birthrates to the promiscuity of the city's barrios. The problem, he said, was not how many Dominicans there were. To the contrary, population growth was essential for protecting the nation against Haitian incursions. The problem of the barrios was rather the sexual immorality of the Dominican women who engaged in serial consensual unions and the irresponsible character of Dominican men who did not recognize paternity. The solution was not birth control, but rather a revitalized

Roman Catholic patriarchy. The regime did, however, participate in international efforts at population control in the 1970s, many of which similarly identified the sexuality and fertility of poor women as a primary obstacle to development.[83]

It was no coincidence that many of the "shameful little towns" against which Balaguer inveighed stood on lands he coveted for his ambitious urbanism. Balaguer explained projects for public housing, sewers, street construction, or local schools in the Zona Norte as a charitable distribution of progreso to citizens portrayed as "defenseless." At the same time the very rurality, anarchy, illegality, and promiscuity of these neighborhoods was justification for tearing some of them down to make way for new construction. In the 1970s the president orchestrated mass evictions in Cristo Rey, La Fe, Honduras, Las Américas, and other settlements in order to build public housing projects. The new units were distributed to political allies and public employees, and the original settlers relocated to some other, more perilous shantytown.[84]

It was also no coincidence that the targets of Balaguer's harsh tirades, and eventually some of the most aggressive building projects, were the neighborhoods where the popular uprising began in 1965 and where the bulk of his political opposition lived. The church and Dominican elites loyal to the military dictatorship had denigrated the constitutionalist uprising, which sought to reinstate Juan Bosch in 1965, as a rebellion of *tígueres*, dangerous young men from the barrios threatening Christian civilization in the city. After the uprising, the remnants of civilian commando forces went underground, forming revolutionary cells in the barrios. The Dominican police, retrained by U.S. advisers in tactics of counterinsurgency and riot control, worked with bands of "anticommunist" thugs to arrest, beat, and assassinate thousands of constitutionalists, leftists, students, union organizers, and other local leaders in the Zona Norte. These abuses continued well into the middle of the 1970s, long after the disappearance of clandestine commandos. Rhetorical attacks on the neighborhoods as festering dens of illicit and dangerous activity helped cloak political repression under the banner of fighting "delinquency" and imposing order in the capital.[85]

Still the Barrios Altos grew northward and westward, as the frontier of informal urban settlement in Santo Domingo spread to spaces unclaimed by official development. Piecemeal, a rudimentary process of urbanization spread behind this frontier as new migrants arrived, until informal settlements filled the empty spaces in official working-class barrios and the entire arc of bluffs, canyons, and marshes along the riverbank. Marginal and popular neighborhoods also grew up in Buenos Aires near the new industrial zone in Herrera to the far west of the city, and in Los Minas on the eastern bank of the Ozama River. By the time Balaguer gave up office in 1978, nearly 74 percent of the city's population lived crowded into these neighborhoods.[86]

How the Other Three-Fourths Lived

In Balaguer's speeches, the poor neighborhoods that housed three-fourths of the city appeared as uniformly chaotic, promiscuous, and dirty. Similarly, by long-standing tradition, elites viewed the urban poor, whether migrant or city born, as an undifferentiated mass of campesinos who, unfortunately, happened to occupy the city.[87] But when a team of Dominican and international researchers undertook a census of the city's neighborhoods in 1977, they found that the barrios that had evolved under the regime were anything but uniform. They were, in fact, a jumble of different social groups, housing types, and spatial organizations. This heterogeneous experience, and the distinctions barrio residents made among themselves, helps to explain the ways that ideas about progreso and cultura came to operate within the barrios.

At the core of the Zona Norte were the old neighborhoods built by the state along Duarte Avenue and Máximo Gómez Avenue in the 1940s, and a newer string of urbanized settlements and ensanches along the east-west course of Nicolás de Ovando Avenue and Avenida Diecisiete (officially called Avenida Padre Castellanos). (See maps 2, 3.) These had acquired a basic outline of regular blocks, street names, and wooden or concrete houses in an unbroken line facing the street. In a few of these neighborhoods, Ensanche Espaillat, 24 de Abril, and María Auxiliadora for instance, substantial numbers of residents legally owned their homes. In Villa Juana, Villa Consuelo, Barrio Obrero, and Mejoramiento Social most rented, but their landlords held legal title to their homes. Although Trujillo's architects built the bungalows or "chalets" in these areas intending to impose nuclear-family arrangements on rural migrants, multiple families often shared the homes. Often, too, relatively stable working-class families would bring poor relatives, especially girls and young women, to provide domestic labor in exchange for the right to live in rear patios. Others sublet small constructions in the back patios on the open market. This led to a gradual filling of the interior spaces of these orderly neighborhood blocks with ramshackle constructions and footpaths.[88]

In a ring around this core lay a sprawl of informal settlements where residents owned only the structures they built, not the land. The blocks and homes often had no regular aspect, just a jumble of wooden and concrete structures along muddy alleys, known as *callejones*, with constant streams of filthy water running through them. These neighbor-hoods started out as shantytowns, but over time had acquired piecemeal and uneven modernization. Sometimes neighbors created their own basic grid of numbered streets hoping that someday the city government would pave them. Residents also tapped informally into city power lines, creating a tangled web of electric cables from rooftop to rooftop.[89]

In a still wider ring outside these settlements, and in the rocky ravines that cut through them, the terrain sloped steeply downward toward the river. There the informal settlements continued, now clinging precariously to the sides of deep canyons or soggily to marshlands at the river's edge. Rural migrants and victims of the mass urban evictions occasioned by the construction of the Francisco del Rosario Sánchez Avenue built the most famous of these settlements, La Ciénaga (The Swamp), in the shadow of the Duarte bridge in the middle of the 1960s. To reach the more regularized, but still informal, neighborhood of Guachupita, residents of La Ciénaga climbed from their homes in the mud and marshes at the river's edge on a narrow path up the steep unstable bluffs. Guachupita, in turn, bordered on the officially constructed neighborhood María Auxiliadora. By the late 1970s all of the poor neighborhoods on the northern rim of the city, and many of the newer middle-class neighborhoods, contained large pockets of extreme poverty like La Ciénaga, usually linked to neighborhood life by steeply plunging pathways or alleys referred to as *cañadas* (ravines). But because it was visible to anyone crossing the Duarte Bridge, La Ciénaga became emblematic to Santo Domingo residents who commonly referred to any marginal settlement as "under a bridge."[90]

Neighborhoods with different histories of settlement, geography, patterns of ownership, and kinds of construction also had differences in income and employment. These differences were smaller than one might imagine. In 1977, all the neighborhoods shared a common backdrop of economic misery, distinguished only by pockets of still worse abjection in some neighborhoods and clusters of better-off families in others. When the city was surveyed in 1977, modal incomes in all of the neighborhoods in the Zona Norte ranged between 100 and 150 pesos per month, well below the line of extreme poverty determined by the Dominican Central Bank. Still, in the most precarious settlements, like La Ciénaga, 15 percent of families earned fewer than 50 pesos a month. Only 7 percent of residents in these settlements earned between 300 and 600 pesos per month, enough to be considered "popular" rather than "marginal" by the Central Bank. By contrast, in the more established neighborhoods, which often bordered on middle-class areas, 24 percent of families earned enough to be considered "popular." This income distribution mirrored the local built environment, with better-off families living in concrete homes, with legal titles, on paved roads, and their neighbors renting or squatting along the dirt callejones behind.

Typically, differences in income level reflected different relationships to the formal economy. Construction was the primary source of employment for working-class men, as the city grew rapidly outward, although some men found employment in industry or small crafts shops. Women worked in domestic service, commuting to middle-class and wealthy neighborhoods to fulfill a wide range of gendered tasks from cooking and cleaning to washing and ironing. In better-off families, at least one member had formal employment—either for the state or in the private sector—or operated a small business. Other household members supplemented this income by organizing informal neighborhood economies. These activities recirculated the few wages that came into the neighborhood. Women, men, and children made, rented, sold, transported, or built anything that could bring in a few pesos. Sometimes these odd jobs led to long-term employment or street peddling grew into a small business, a fruit stand, or a *colmado*, as local markets were called. But more frequently odd jobs remained *chiripa*, constant economic improvisation with no safety net beyond the credit offered by the colmado on the corner. If the best-off families combined formal employment with informal work, poorer families relied exclusively on chiripa. The poorest of all were the sick, elderly people without the support of adult children, and orphaned children.[91]

In newer barrios, settlers from older barrios often arrived with ties to local Catholic parishes and appointed themselves the role of organizers and leaders. As neighborhood lands came open for settlement, military personnel and police, who were well positioned to defend claims and secure prime plots, frequently settled in the barrios. When the state tore down shanties, evicted their residents, and built public housing projects called *multifamiliares*, popular and middle-class enclaves formed in marginal barrios. Likewise, in the core working-class neighborhoods and at the stable edges of all the informal barrios, lower-middle-class students from the provinces, attending university on meager budgets, rented rooms and lived among the city's poor. And while opportunities for schooling were notoriously scarce, a minority of local barrio youngsters did push their way into public high schools and even the Autonomous University of Santo Domingo (UASD). In 1975 for instance, La Ciénaga, that perilously marginal settlement of several thousand homes in the marshlands under the Duarte Bridge, was home to some fifty students at the UASD.[92] This diversity in the barrios helped bring the official concepts of cultura and progreso into local usage.

After the urban reforms of the early twentieth century, the U.S. occupation, three decades of Trujillismo, and a dozen years of Balaguerismo, a nation dominated by the city—something Dominican nationalists had pined for since the conception of the Republic—had become an unruly reality. In a few more years, urban citizens would outnumber rural citizens. And as the city grew, its growth not only supported new elite and middle classes, linked to urban construction, imports, and industry, but also new popular classes. The Dominican population no longer consisted of rural producers far from the center of power, but of barrio residents who engaged with the state and each other over the terms of their claims to central urban space, resources, and respectability. Individual barrios, like the Zona Norte as a whole, were internally diverse and closely packed. They were home to residents of different backgrounds, of different status, and with different relationships to elite ideas about progreso and cultura. But these ideas, borrowed from above and reconfigured for use in the barrios, emerged as central themes of popular social life in the now increasingly urban Dominican Republic.

THREE

Beautiful Barrios for the Humble Folk

SOCIAL SCIENTISTS and politicians typically tell two kinds of stories about the vast and heartbreakingly poor neighborhoods that grew up on the outskirts of Santo Domingo and other Latin American cities in the middle of the twentieth century. One story explains rural-to-urban migration almost exclusively in terms of the changing structures of the national economy. The other tells of the ideas and politics of the poor themselves, as they descended upon the city and made its forgotten corners their own. Unfortunately, from the 1930s through the 1980s, the authors most likely to include the ideas of poor Dominicans in their accounts typically assessed popular ways of thinking from afar, and deplored what they thought they saw. The Trujillo regime, for instance, blamed the rise in migration on the mistaken ways that migrants imagined the city. In 1937, the dictator told the National Congress that campesinos moved to the capital because they were "bedazzled by the mirage of the city." The solution was to force them back to the countryside.[1] In the Balaguer years, official explanations for urban poverty tended to fixate on the problem of overpopulation, which similarly led policy makers to bemoan the worldview of the poor. Urbanization was a natural part of development, but in the Dominican Republic (as in Latin America as a whole), uncontrolled fertility in the slums threw it out of balance. Some development experts proposed measures to change the values of the promiscuous poor. Others favored birth control. Still others favored a program of investment and development that would eventually incorporate surplus population. In all of these views, modernization would eventually teach the poor not to have so many children.[2]

In response, Isis Duarte, Jorge Cela, and the other social scientists (influenced by Marxism and dependency theory) who first conducted research in Santo Domingo's barrios in the 1970s argued just the opposite: economic structures and government policies drove the growth of urban slums, not the grandiose expectations or profligate sexuality of the poor. In a country governed by an alliance between local elites and representatives of the U.S. State Department, these scholars pointed out, the consolidation of large landholdings expelled an unwilling population from the countryside. Displaced campesinos then served as a permanent pool of reserve industrial labor in the cities.[3] The solution to the problem of the slums was not convincing the poor to behave in ways that were more sensible; the solution was to use the state to shift the benefits of development from foreign investors and domestic capitalists to peasants and workers. In these structural accounts, migrants' unfulfilled hopes, especially their shattered dreams of rural self-sufficiency, served to highlight the injustice of the social order, but they did not have any causal effect on urban growth and poverty.[4]

At the end of the 1980s, proponents of market capitalism in Latin America responded in turn, seeking to focus the study of migration to cities like Santo Domingo once again on the ideas and aspirations of migrants. The widely influential Peruvian economist Hernando de Soto, for instance, argued that rural people moved to the city because of what they hoped to find there. In contrast to Trujillo and Balaguer, de Soto celebrated such aspirations and the vast settlements they seemed to inspire. Informal shantytowns and economic improvisation were examples of migrants' inherent desires to participate in modern urban capitalism. Urban populations, de Soto argued, were not poor because they jumped foolishly, or were pushed unwillingly, into the maw of capitalism. Nor were they poor because the state failed to act on their behalf, as the structuralists contended. They were poor because the state, for supposedly populist reasons, intervened *too actively* in Latin American economies, squelching the natural workings of the market.[5]

In the 1990s many anthropologists and sociologists of migration in Latin America joined de Soto's shift back to migrants' own ideas, though not his extreme antagonism to government programs. Although economic and political structures were fundamental, migration could not, scholars like Sherri Grasmuck and Patricia Pessar argued, be wholly understood by studying those structures. People moved because of the ways that they perceived the world, not because of individual rational economic calculations. The ideas, social relationships, and aspirations that drove decisions to migrate were related to structures of economic and political domination, but not in a straightforward way.[6] Poor people frequently held high hopes for the city and often viewed the countryside as backwards. The collapse of the rural economy unleashed not just an exodus of migrants but a process of learning and appropriation that made the ideas of modern social change and proper behavior broadcast by the state into popular claims for urban citizenship. Variations on the ideas of progreso and cultura became central to the ways that many poor Dominicans understood their migration to the city and especially the politics they engaged in once there. The adoption of these ideas was, to be certain, uneven, just as the barrios were diverse and heterogeneous places. Yet it is impossible to understand the massive mobilization of Dominicans that created modern

Santo Domingo without considering the ways that progresso and cultura became part of urban popular culture.

BARRIO HISTORIES

All local tales of the neighborhood of Cristo Rey start when it was still open countryside. Except for a few landmarks, including one of Trujllo's stables and the infamous prison La Cuarenta, the area was still a mix of agricultural land and *monte* (undisturbed forest) into the 1950s. Older residents, most of whom lived first in other parts of Santo Domingo, remember walking through the area that later became Cristo Rey. They took footpaths on their way to the swimming beach at the salt springs called Arroyo Salado (now part of the National Zoo). Doña Pirín, who runs a small concession at the Parish Youth Center in Cristo Rey, selling candy and cold drinks, remembers that when she first arrived, in the early 1960s, there was "one house *way* over here, and another house *way* over there."[7] Yet the emergence of a city neighborhood in this open space holds different meanings for different residents. Don Marcelino, an elderly mason, grew up in an agricultural family on the land that became Cristo Rey. "Only thirteen families lived here," he remembers. "There was no *barrio*, all of this was *monte*. Back then we worked together at agriculture and raising animals." For Don Marcelino, the coming of the city meant the extinction of a life of "abundance" and independence. "Here there were groves of *plátanos*, *yautía*—yellow, white, and brown— those good yams that are for frying . . . the only thing we had to buy was rice, not meat, not grains of any kind, beans, *guandules*, we had it all."[8]

Don Marcelino remembers that things deteriorated after the death of Trujillo. New "groups began to take over pieces of land, and in this way it all filled up with *barrios* wherever you looked; this made it difficult for us." He gave up agriculture to work as a security guard, preventing new migrants from settling on plots claimed by several military officers. Then he worked in a cement block factory owned by a general, then as a mason, building houses for new arrivals, and finally as a caretaker for the gravestones and crypts in the local cemetery. His successive employment is itself a story of transformation, from agriculture to the free-for-all of settlement, to construction, to the permanence of death and burial. Don Marcelino never chose to leave the countryside, though. The countryside simply dissolved around him. He bitterly recalls the changes in the neighborhood as a process, not of his choosing, that transformed him from an agricultural producer, with the symbolic backing of a dictator whose "best friends" were the "men of work," to an urban consumer with little independence and no status. "Those

times were better, *ay sí.*" Back then "everything was in abundance."
Now, "you have to buy everything, and everything is expensive."[9]

Don Marcelino's view is common among elderly Dominicans born in
the countryside, many of whom remember rural life under Trujillo as a
bygone golden age. Trujillo succeeded in finally overcoming rural resistance to commercial agriculture in part through fear and violence and
in part by protecting peasant access to land. The dictator made it a practice to tour the countryside on horseback, meeting with local officials
and speaking to assemblies of campesinos. The regime also sponsored
hundreds of popular songs to broadcast its ideology, provided the text
of speeches to local Dominican Party officials, and deployed new technologies like sound amplification, inexpensive photographic reproduction, and radio to create an image of the dictator and a symbolism of
the regime that could be personally consumed by even the physically
distant and desperately poor. In the process, Trujillo introduced the
powerful, if contradictory, concepts of progreso and cultura to his new
rural constituents. The regime offered rural people a new vision of citizenship in the countryside based on hard work, respect for authority,
and self-sufficiency. Yet, by the 1960s, this promise of rural citizenship
began to prove hollow. The state ceased to protect campesino access to
land while investing in massive urban construction.[10]

In this context, the rise of urban migration can be seen, in part, as a
return to the old patterns of mobility, informality, and cultura cimarrona that Trujillo's land policies had sought to eradicate. Despite the
dictatorship's attempts to domesticate peasants and affix them to rural
plots, Dominicans continued to find space outside of the purview of
the state, or in covert interactions with the state, in order to survive. But
tales like Don Marcelino's also reveal the remarkable success that the
Trujillo regime had in convincing campesinos of the message of rural
citizenship. The rural crisis of the 1960s and 1970s did not, in this sense,
interrupt a centuries-old set of social arrangements. The fully independent peasant life of the seventeenth through nineteenth centuries had
already come to an end in the 1940s and 1950s. The crisis, rather, interrupted a specific social compact constructed in the rural modernization
projects in those earlier decades. The language of rural modernization
therefore helped barrio residents explain their settlement in the city.
Indeed the first group of researchers to survey urban migrants in Santo
Domingo about their experiences found, in 1975, that many residents of
the barrio 30 de Mayo thought the move to the city owed to "the impossibility of *progreso* in agriculture."[11]

Yet if some remember bygone days of rural abundance, many in the
barrios tell a history of the city itself as an unfolding promise of progreso. The evolution of the neighborhood from monte to shanties to

cinderblock houses, from alleyways and open sewers to paved streets was a narrative of gradual improvement, of progreso made concrete, literally and figuratively, in the practice of orderly urban life. In Cristo Rey, Señora Polanco tells this kind of neighborhood history. She is a shopkeeper who grew up in an older working-class neighborhood in the capital and arrived in Cristo Rey as a Carmelite nun and teacher in the 1960s, before marrying and raising her family there. Starting her tale where everyone starts, when Cristo Rey was monte, she describes trees and clear brooks. One hot afternoon, looking at the heat waves shimmering off concrete and garbage near the public market, she is surprised when asked if the neighborhood was more beautiful in its natural state. "No, it is much more beautiful today." Señora Polanco, like many in the neighborhood, subscribes to a view of progreso in which the city, for all its flaws, is fundamentally superior to the country-side.[12] Many residents of 30 de Mayo, responding to a 1975 survey, also saw the move to the capital as a function of "the attractions of the city" rather than the crisis in the countryside. These attractions included "the variety of jobs," the "possibility of having fun during free time," and the "fact" that "women could dedicate themselves exclusively to household and family labor in the city."[13]

There is some evidence that the urban born, like Señora Polanco, were more likely to attribute urban growth to "the attractions of the city" and that those born in the countryside were more likely to explain "that life was becoming impossible" in the campo.[14] In other words, it seems likely that many migrants heard the perspective on the city offered by Señora Polanco, or government officials, *after* arriving in the city. On the other hand, the Trujillo regime broadcast messages about progreso in the capital even as it celebrated its rural modernization programs. Official songs and speeches recalling the marvels of Ciudad Trujillo, as well as invitations to select groups of provincial citizens to visit the city to participate in parades celebrating the regime, all brought the message of urban progreso to rural citizens. Recalling his own first trip to Ciudad Trujillo in 1956 to attend one of these parades, Walter Cordero remembers that "moving toward the city, even fleetingly, was a step forward, a clear sign of differentiation from those who only saw it in their imaginations, through the prism of a fragmented and confused oral culture."[15] He returned to Baní from that first visit, poised to contribute his own observations of the capital to the oral culture of the provinces. As more and more migrants moved to the city, they too contributed to the evolving idea of the city as a "step forward" circulating in the countryside. Don Cibaíto's fictional dispatches to a compadre in his hometown were caricatures, but they nevertheless reflected a real set of conversations. At the very least it is clear that both kinds of explanations for urban growth—those in dialogue with the idea of the collapsing promise of rural progreso and those adhering to a vision of evolving urban progreso—circulated in the newly forming barrios.

Still others in Cristo Rey explain the course of neighborhood transformation in ways that resonate little with state projects for either rural or urban modernization. One afternoon, in her small concrete-block home perched on the steep hillside called la Agustinita, Doña Francisca is among the elderly neighborhood residents who have no adult children to support them. She is still relatively able and survives with help from the church and by selling hand-sewn hacky-sacks to neighborhood children. When asked if things in the neighborhood are getting better or worse, Doña Francisca catalogues the vandalism, delinquency, and poverty around her. In her view things are obviously getting worse. "What is lacking," she says, "is love." Why is the neighborhood in decline? "The Bible predicts the end of the world," she explains. "This is it." According to Doña Francisca, political parties, presidents, the preservation of traditions and the march of progress are not the engines of history. Biblical prophesy is.[16]

Indeed, many residents of Santo Domingo (including some in the middle class) frequently turn to spiritual explanations for both collective and individual improvement or decline. These explanations rely on African Dominican spirituality as well as popular Catholicism like Doña Francisca's. Anthropologists describe the popular concept of *desenvolvimiento* in Santo Domingo, an idea of unfolding, or spiritual health that guides communal and personal fortunes. It is possible to manage this desenvolvimiento by addressing and appeasing spirits through the mediation of local priestesses, or *servidoras*.[17] The aspirations that shape Dominicans' migration to cities and to foreign lands may well be related to the secular idea of progreso. But they seem also frequently to rely on this notion of desenvolvimiento. Some people in the barrios leave their passports on the altars of local servidoras, asking saints or *guedes* (African Dominican deities) for help in getting visas.[18] Some international migrants later return to cemeteries in Santo Domingo, to thank both spiritual practitioners and spirits for their triumphs abroad. Even those who will not participate in rituals that they consider "witchcraft" often organize *horas santas*, or Catholic prayer circles, to ask for the intercession of saints or the Virgin on matters of migration, health, or economic fortune.[19]

The intellectual history of Cristo Rey is no different from any intellectual history in that these distinct viewpoints live more comfortably together in practice than they would seem to on paper. Often a single person will espouse elements of seemingly contradictory worldviews in different contexts. Yet the interaction among rural nostalgia, urban aspiration, and popular religiosity is not wholly haphazard or idiosyncratic. These various perspectives seem, at least in part, to operate in terms of local social hierarchies in the barrio. As the barrios grew in the 1960s and 1970s, artisans, factory, construction, and port workers, and shopkeepers—many born in older city neighborhoods or middle-class rural families—lived in close quarters with poor and desperately poor rural folk. Under Trujillo, local elites in the classic working-class neighborhoods often served as officials in the Dominican Party. It was their role to bring the message of the state into the neighborhoods and, within certain bounds, to bring neighborhood complaints to the state. Similarly, it seems that a local leadership emerged in Cristo Rey after 1960, actively constructing its own history of neighborhood progress in attempts to wrest the promise of "beautiful neighborhoods for the humble folk" from the state. These local leaders' influence could not dictate that their neighbors accept their conceptions of progreso in the neighborhood. But their status, and their alliances with important people outside the barrios, helped to lend power to their vision of popular urbanism.

The Struggle for Progreso in Two Barrios, El Caliche and Cristo Rey

In the early 1960s, the Dominican government began the process of up-rooting a group of families living on the site of the decommissioned General Andrews Airport. The airport stood on the site for a planned Municipal Park (now the Olympic Stadium) and adjacent high-status residential areas. The residents of the site were rural migrants. According to Rafael Tobías Genao, subsecretary of the Police and the Interior, who toured the area "incognito" in 1969, they had built about "300 to 350 little shacks out of pieces of cardboard, pieces of wood, and a few planks of zinc, in other words, out of trash."[20] These migrants survived, he noted, by working in "landscaping and gardening, as street vendors, selling charcoal, lottery tickets, as domestic workers, and a few with small fruit and vegetable stands with which they earn their daily sustenance." That is, they survived through chiripa and domestic labor. The conflict between settlers at the empty airport and state officials planning to build on the site lasted for most of the 1960s. According to the memories of one neighborhood activist the first *desalojo* (eviction) at the airport actually took place around 1963.[21]

There is no written record of the 1963 desalojo at the airport, but its outlines were likely similar to one reported a year later not far away at the corner of Máximo Gómez and Calle 38. An assistant district attorney, two engineers, and a detachment of combat police destroyed a group of shanties and several businesses standing on a parcel privately owned by a third engineer. A twelve-year-old boy meanwhile berated them with epithets like, "'You ARE THE KINGS AND THAT IS WHY YOU ARE DOING THIS!'" The engineers believed his intent to be "provoking us to a state of agitation." Nevertheless, they loaded the residents of the homes onto trucks, then deposited them on another open piece of land along with the materials from their destroyed homes. In their letter the engineers described the evicted residents as "women with underage children, and some who were pregnant, who alleged that they had neither husbands nor anywhere else to live."[22]

Similarly officials dumped the first families removed from the airport, in 1963, at an abandoned mine about a mile to the north. Because the mine had provided the Trujillo cement monopoly with lime, or *caliche*, before passing to the state, these families called the new treeless encampment on the hard, chalky clay El Caliche. Settlers carried water into the neighborhood in buckets from public spigots in nearby subdivisions. In rainy weather the mud was so thick that residents walked barefoot to the single path that led up to Calle 41 and put their shoes on at the bus stop there. To the east lay a public cemetery and the abandoned site of Trujillo's notorious prison, La Cuarenta, which later became a neighborhood as well. To the south were the recently formed hardscrabble settlements of La Cuadra (The Stables), Corea (Korea), and Jarro Sucio (Dirty Jar).[23]

It was not long before a neighborhood leadership, intent on bringing a semblance of religious organization, material progress, and culture emerged in all of these settlements. In fact religious missionaries and social activists from the older popular neighborhoods in the city began to spread the project of religious and social development to the vicinity a few years before the first settlers arrived in El Caliche. In 1960 and 1961 young volunteers in the Juventud Obrera Católica (Catholic Workers' Youth) group, based at the Parish of San Juan Bosco in María Auxiliadora, began visiting La Cuadra, Corea, and Jarro Sucio. In Father Andrés Menem's small Chrysler, they navigated the winding footpaths west of Avenida Ortega y Gassett and built a wooden chapel that served during the week as a one-room school. Some of these young evangelists, like Señora Polanco, eventually settled in the neighborhood, leaving their crowded barrios for the open space and promise of the new settlement. By the mid-1960s, a second priest, Father Ignacio, organized the construction of a parish house and baptized the whole district with the new name Cristo Rey (Christ the King). The name initially referred only to the areas immediately around the church, but eventually included El Caliche, La Cuarenta, and other nearby settlements. For those in the neighborhood who remember Father Ignacio, his Christian baptism of the neighborhood was a turning point in the course of local history. With the help of local activists, who traveled downtown to collect donations on street corners, and powerful allies outside the neighborhood, the parish built a larger grammar school and organized a mutual aid society, youth groups, and a protest campaign demanding water from the city aqueduct.[24]

A similar development project emerged in El Caliche in 1964, with the arrival of a young couple named Ramona Báez and Luís Reyes. Through a connection in the government, Reyes and Báez had procured a piece of land and transplanted their family from Villa Juana, one of the older neighborhoods along Duarte Avenue, to El Caliche. There, the two urbanites, surrounded by rural migrants, became leaders in a local movement to urbanize the district. In late 1964, they staged a series of protests outside the headquarters of the Dominican Electric Company, demanding that electrical service be brought to the neighborhood, and finally prevailed.[25] Reyes, Báez, and their allies in El Caliche received an offer of help from the activists at Cristo Rey Parish in 1964. But for reasons that are not entirely clear, they maintained their distance from Father Ignacio. Perhaps the difference between the two groups stemmed from national politics. Ignacio, like the church higher-ups, opposed President Juan Bosch as a communist and relied on an alliance with the Reformista Party to bring resources to the neighborhood. Báez and Reyes opposed the presidency of Joaquín Balaguer and relied on their ties to Bosch's Dominican Revolutionary Party to bring resources to their neighborhood.[26]

These political tensions continued after the civil war and U.S. invasion in 1965. The group in El Caliche found new strength in an alliance with a young leftist minority in the Dominican church. Though the church hierarchy supported Balaguer, many younger clergy, influenced by the experience of the French "worker priests" in the 1950s, supported the pro-Bosch revolution and chose to risk their relations with the church in order to do organizing work in the barrios.[27] Two pioneers in the new social gospel, the Cuban priests Miguel Domínguez Paula and Antonio Cabeta, created the Institute for Social Promotion in the Zona Norte, to train local leadership and organize construction projects in the string of neighborhoods on the northern extreme of the city: La Zurza, La Cuarenta, El Caliche, and La Puya de Arroyo Hondo. The community organization in El Caliche that successfully staged protests for electrical service before the war, now with the help of Brothers Miguel and Antonio, created the Comité para el Desarrollo Social de El Caliche (Committee for the Social Development of El Caliche), sometimes also called the Neighborhood Citizens' Committee. Reyes was elected president. Local high school and college students created a youth club called The Seven Diamonds. Women in the neighborhood elected Báez to lead the newly formed Mothers Association of El Calvario. This group unsuccessfully sought to rebaptize El Caliche as El Calvario (Mount Calvary). Just as their neighbors had done in Cristo Rey, they saw a proper Christian name as a mark of formalization and organization in the barrio. In 1967 these groups secured pipes from private donors, dug up the streets, connected to the public water supply, and installed running water to some homes in the neighborhood and to two public faucets. In March of 1968, the neighborhood held a parade and block party, with the participation of Monseñor Hugo Polanco Brito and the official band of the Fire Brigade, celebrating the arrival of water. Residents paraded to martial music, danced to merengue, and chanted, "The first step has been taken. Justice and truth are the cause!"[28] The local development organizations also collaborated to rid the neighborhood of an open sewer, build a school taught by members of the youth club, and create several nutritional centers attached to the Roman Catholic charity, Caritas.[29]

The work of social missionaries like Father Andrés and his young volunteers, the builder priests like Father Ignacio, committees like the one started by Reyes and Báez, and dozens of other neighborhood organizations in the Zona Norte made repeated attempts to turn official messages of urban construction and progress into claims against the state. They demanded the basic elements of modern urban citizenship: water, paved roads, electricity, schools, sanitation, and clinics. And indeed the Balaguer regime dispensed schools, playgrounds, sewers, and other crucial resources, in attempts to build loyalty among certain barrio activists and promote its image of paternal benevolence. Symbolic gestures of social assistance were part of the governing strategy. Still, Doña Ramona Reyes remembers mostly the Balaguer government's antagonism to independent, radically tinged social organizing in poor neighborhoods. Balaguer deported Brother Miguel and Brother Antonio in 1971, along with a cohort of other foreign-born progressive priests. This state hostility, the scarcity of resources, and the constant influx of new, desperately poor migrants meant that local development projects would always be dwarfed by local underdevelopment.[30]

Despite the limits of its periodic gifts of modernization, the Balaguer regime played a disproportionate role in neighborhood expectations for development. The government had inherited ownership over the huge estates left behind by the Trujillo family, including much of the territory occupied by informal barrios. And its many projects for clearing and developing the barrios usually brought promises for new housing, paved streets, or other local development. Although they were unequal contests, desalojos were grounds for interaction between the state and

Figure 3-1. Children in El Caliche play in newly inaugurated public faucet, 1968. Neighborhood activists organized residents to dig and install the pipes that brought water to the neighborhood for the first time. (Photograph by Héctor Herrera, courtesy of *Listín Diario*)

shantytown dwellers, rare opportunities to pressure, negotiate, connive, or simply plead for resources. The several thousand residents of the old airport that Undersecretary Rafael T. Genao visited in 1969 resisted repeated efforts to remove them far from the center of the city, where there would be no electricity, water, or access to employment. In the wake of the 1965 uprising, such resistance could rely on government concerns about surly urban populations. The engineers responsible for building the new park asked the government to lend them its "moral power, and if necessary its power to compel." Genao, though, wrote to Balaguer that "a precipitous solution would be much worse, politically, for the Honorable Señor Presidente of the Republic" since its "only consequence would be to cause an uproar" and because the opposition would use it for their campaigns against the government.[31] Some officials also jumped at the chance to intervene to "protect" urban citizens from desalojo in the name of the benevolent president. When a sugar manufacturer forcibly removed several hundred fired workers from company-owned lands in the city of San Pedro de Macorís, local officials stopped the desalojo, considering that such actions did not conform to the "policy of protecting the needy classes" put in practice by "the Most Excellent Señor Presidente of the Republic."[32]

It seems that the local leadership that emerged in these informal settlements also knew how to speak the state's language. The officials in San Pedro reported that many of the families rescued from desalojo "showed signs of lively jubilation," cheering the president and his beneficence. Likewise Undersecretary Genao reported that a group of representatives from the settlement at the General Andrews Airport visited a sympathetic official stating that "they understand that *progreso* cannot be stopped" and that they acknowledged they did not really own the land on which they lived. They simply wanted the government to find them a better place to resettle, so they would not be "sent to die, abandoned."[33] Perhaps this is a case of an intermediary putting words into the mouths of residents to make them seem more amenable to state rhetoric, and less oppositional. Yet, if the residents indeed used this language on their official visit, they were quoting directly from the Trujillo-era merengue "Progreso Cannot Be Stopped." That song, among other things, described progreso as "beautiful barrios for the humble folk." In other words, this is an instance of shantytown residents and their allies using the exact language the Trujillo regime broadcast in its musical propaganda, to support a claim for space to live in the center of the city.[34]

The give and take between barrio residents and the government over the right to occupy city space—the most basic element of urban citizenship—continued to shape Cristo Rey in the decades that followed. In the 1960s the neighborhood still lay outside of the regularized development of the Trujillo-era working-class barrios. West of Calle 41, where the city sloped off into farmland and monte, settlers established a maze of footpaths and ranchos. Starting in about 1970, though, the government began pushing official urban construction west into the neighborhood as well, destroying many of the original settlements to extend Avenida Ovando and build the Cristo Rey multifamiliares (see map 4). Dominga Ogando remembers these desalojos from when she was a child living in Cristo Rey. "My mother had a house there on Calle 41, but they evicted her. President [Balaguer] ordered them to knock down three houses, then about forty more, and they left us in the street." After staging a small protest, she remembers, the residents received small plots in Sabana Perdida, a shantytown far outside the city limits. Ogando's mother sold her rights to settle in Sabana Perdida and returned to Cristo Rey, where she occupied a plot in a newly settled ravine that ran west toward Arroyo Salado, a cañada now called El Setenta (1970) after the year of the first desalojos in Cristo Rey. She built a small wooden shack from a fallen tree.[35] At around the same time, Epifanio Tejada, known as Chulín, led the settlement of the deep ravine on the north edge of La Cuarenta, which came to be known as the Hoyo de Chulín (Chulín's Ditch). "I first lowered myself down here with ropes, my wife went ahead with a light, and I came behind with a machete," he later told reporters. "What a lot of work! No one knew what we were doing here. We had to throw the zinc for the roofs over the ledge, and then carry them up from the bottom."[36]

As the government claimed the center of Cristo Rey for official urban construction, displaced residents and new migrants occupied the western and northern edges, especially in uneven terrain and flood-prone arroyos. But claiming this space was not easy. The government had plans to extend the Avenida Ovando further, to construct a parkway servicing the zoo along the western edge of Cristo Rey, and to build a second parkway along the northern edge of the neighborhood, part of a beltway around the whole city. These roads ran straight through El Setenta, the northen edge of El Caliche, and the northern edge of La Cuarenta, including El Hoyo de Chulín. Engineers kept pressure on the police to prevent new settlement in these areas, hoping to avoid the hassle and costs of future desalojos. One architect later wrote that the competition between the official construction projects and the informal occupations in El Setenta was, in his view, a "race between order and disorder."[37] Ogando remembers, "It was a lot of work, because she [my mother] would build a house and they [the police] would knock it down, and she would build it again." Political and economic crises stalled the road building in the late 1970s.[38] An overpass, half built, stood pointing at the increasingly dense shantytowns of El Caliche and La Cuarenta until 1987, when the government finally evicted Chulín and hundreds of other residents to build the Avenida Paseo de los Reyes Católicos, and the Puerto Isabela housing projects.[39] At around the same time the government evicted the residents of Los Farallones to extend the Avenida Ovando and build another cluster of housing projects.

Although officials represented these projects as necessary social assistance and modernization for the residents of "suicidal and promiscuous" barrios, barrio activists and intellectuals remember them as a pretense to reclaim and develop valuable lands.[40] They point out that many fewer new homes were built than families evicted. Frequently, too, the new apartments in housing projects went straight into the hands of the city's growing middle class, especially middle-class families with ties to Balaguer's party. Most of those evicted therefore never received an apartment in exchange for their lost homes. They ended up in some other informal settlement, either outside the city limits or in some precarious corner of the neighborhood not yet occupied. Chulín, for instance, received a plot in Guaricano, a growing shantytown north of the Rio Isabela. Ogando's mother received a plot in Sabana Perdida, then built and rebuilt her home in El Setenta many times in defiance of police. Neighborhood leaders like Ramona Báez organized residents to protest and resist desalojos.

At the same time, however, many residents of the Zona Norte clamored for desalojos. Projects to tear down neighborhoods and build public housing provided opportunities for neighborhood dwellers seeking to wrest small benefits from official urbanism. Many of those evicted ended up starting over in new shantytowns farther from their places of work. But a few lucky ones exchanged their insecure shanties and steep cañadas for safe, permanent housing. People in the barrios therefore invested remarkable energies trying to position themselves for desalojo and for apartments in the new housing projects. The government compensated residents the value of their *mejoras* (the word used to describe the homes of squatters who did not own their land, only the improvements or mejoras they had made on it). The larger and more permanent the structure, the more likely it would be valued highly enough to serve as a down payment on a new apartment. Residents therefore often intentionally moved into and built up areas slated for eviction, hoping for the eventual right to a new apartment. Those who owned multiple mejoras in the path of announced desalojos sold their second and third properties and invested the proceeds in the principal property. Or they moved friends and relatives into secondary homes, signed over ownership, and split the compensation with them. Officials did their best to clamp down on local real estate speculation. They conducted surveys of housing at the time they announced a new eviction, then assigned police detachments, as Undersecretary Genao suggested at the airport in 1969, to "maintain a permanent watch, so that no new shacks are built."[41]

Real estate maneuvers in the context of a desalojo required a level of income above mere subsistence and reliable information about what the government planned. This helps explain why many of those who ended up with keys to new apartments were not original residents of the area. The process of urban beautification removed the poorest and most vulnerable residents. Furthermore, attempts to game the system were not always successful. Many residents who moved into Pablo VI, *buscando desalojo*, looking for an eviction, are still waiting in wooden shanties after more than two decades. Evicted residents of Los Farallones lived for more than a decade in plywood bunkers called *barracones* (the old term for slave quarters) before some of them finally received apartments.[42] By the same token, those desalojados who did receive apartments in exchange for their old homes often sold or rented their rights to live in them. The most desperately poor residents of Santo Domingo's Zona Norte, if they somehow managed to end up with a public apartment, could not afford the luxury of living in middle-class housing. They cashed out the capital in their new apartments, relocated to some other neighborhood, and invested the proceeds in some crucial element of survival: a fruit cart, a taxi, or a passport.[43]

Like collective projects for social development, and group resistance to displacement, widespread improvisation to secure resources provided by state incursions reveals how urban ideals of construction permeated the consciousness of many barrio residents. So too did the generalized use of the word *progreso* to describe small, piecemeal improvements to homes and blocks, accomplished independently of state resources. Progreso might mean the construction of a new national identity as Trujillo declared. It might mean the transformation of urban space, new buildings, roads, and bridges, as President Balaguer proclaimed. Or it might mean the gradual transformation of a neighborhood from a muddle of shacks to a concrete grid with sewers, a school, and a church, as barrio leaders argued. But in everyday language progreso became something that pertained to individual households. It became shorthand for urban permanence, and for social mobility.

Typically, even in the worst neighborhoods, improvements or mejoras inched forward as families occasionally secured unexpected resources. One year, members of a household might put a single row of concrete blocks around their shanty. Two years later they might add several more courses. Over time they built a permanent structure. Laying a row of concrete blocks, starting a colmado or other small business, moving to a paved street, getting indoor plumbing and electricity, receiving a public housing unit, getting a degree and becoming a professional, were all examples of this kind of progreso. This is perhaps the best explanation for Señora Polanco's view that the neighborhood is much more beautiful in its present state than in its rural past. The Polancos were early church activists helping to construct a school and a basic infrastructure. They managed the desalojo in order to get an apartment in the public project called Multifamiliares de Cristo Rey. They built a business on one of the busy streets near the public market. That dirty concrete is better than mud is self-evident to people who have spent their lives struggling toward a vision of urban citizenship, fighting for beautiful barrios for the humble folk, and working to accumulate small elements of progreso.[44]

Although thousands of individuals like Chulín and Ogando cleared and constructed Cristo Rey, two groups led the gradual transformation of the neighborhood from rural land to a semiformal urban space: government officials and neighborhood leaders. Both groups were usually

FIGURE 3-2. Woman and child in front of a concrete block home in Cristo Rey, 2005. Over time even the poorest of residents gradually accumulate the resources to replace shanties with concrete constructions. (Photograph by John Paul Gallagher)

urban born, better educated, and more economically successful than the neighborhood at large. This helps to explain how urban permanence, concrete homes, paved streets, and running water evolved into broadly desired marks of social status. It would be unjust to suggest that barrio activists sought simply to impose elite urban prejudices on a neighborhood that otherwise resisted urban modernity. This would reduce their frequently selfless community organizing and care to a kind of snobbery. Still, a conversation between two residents provides an example of how the personal status of the neighborhood residents who most consistently espoused this developmental view of local history, one that prized urban progreso, gave it a certain power over alternate explanations seen as rural or low class. Marcelino, the elderly caretaker at the Cristo Rey Cemetery, explained why campesinos had begun to migrate to the city and fill up the monte with barrios according to his memory of how rural society dissolved around him. "The grandes (important or big families) took over the best lands." Doña Ramona, a Santo Domingo–born leader of innumerable social development projects in El Caliche interjected that many migrants also came to the city, not because they lost their land, but because they were looking for "comfort," including the promise of electric lights and even television. The agriculturalist robbed of his independence saw migrants as reluctant participants in the project of the city. The long-time activist for community progreso saw campesino aspirations for urban life as central to the settlement of the barrio. This difference in view is predictable.

Yet the disagreement does not take place on equal footing. Faced with Doña Ramona's correction, Don Marcelino professes ignorance, "Oh really, *comadre*? I did not know that." The gesture is subtly deferential. It helps to explain why an uneven process of social learning, an uneven incorporation of ideas about progreso, might come to look like a universally held "popular" perspective on the city. It is easy to see why ideas that resonated with elite and state visions of progreso were more likely to find their way into official documents and newspaper articles, since their proponents were the most articulate and well-documented residents of the neighborhood, while popular spirituality and even nostalgia for the countryside were silenced by the written record. But here, even in casual conversations in the neighborhood, Doña Ramona's ideas enjoyed the backing of her reputation as a person dedicated to the betterment of the community, as well as her education, her urbanity, and her social standing.

CULTURA, COLOR, AND CORRUPTION

This implicit hierarchy of values imbued not only neighborhood discussions of progreso, but also local notions of cultura, especially the idea of Dominican cultura that demoted widespread African Dominican cultural practices to the status of Haitian influence. If nostalgia for an earlier era in the countryside subtly defers to aspiration for the promises of urban life in the discussion between Marcelino and Ramona, popular religiosity and its multiple explanations for social change are silenced altogether. The conversation takes place while sitting on gravestones in the public cemetery on a Friday evening. Part of the small crowd that has gathered to watch may well have been waiting for sundown to visit local spiritual practitioners who work among the gravestones. But no one speaks of the guedes or the Baron (the spirit of the first person buried in a cemetery).[45]

This silence is notable since many residents of Cristo Rey practice a full range of Dominican popular religiosity. Vitico, who runs the program for chiriperos at the church, widens his eyes in reference to the neighborhood cemetery, "¡Hermano, allí se montan!" ("Brother, they take the spirit there!"), a reference to the practice of spiritual possession common in Dominican *vodú* and in many Afro-Atlantic religious traditions. Young church activists are, on occasion, pleased to talk about the peculiar beliefs of some neighbors, and even their own chance encounters with spiritual healers. But the older churchgoers are silent on these matters. This silence is probably a mark of the uneven success of elite Hispanism and white supremacy in controlling certain aspects of Dominican popular culture. On the one hand an informal and marginal existence and the long legacy of independent rural society bestowed a regime of relative cultural tolerance on the barrios. On the other hand, the interplay between officially sanctioned views of cultura and unofficial, but widely shared, cultural practices placed the latter at an extreme symbolic disadvantage. The African Dominican aspects of popular religiosity are widespread but hushed up, especially in the presence of foreigners and friends of the local priest. One intellectual and longtime neighborhood activist in the barrios of the Zona Norte explains: neighbors in popular and marginal neighborhoods all know where local spiritual practitioners live, but when they need a consultation they go to a practitioner in some other barrio, where they will not be recognized.[46]

Color consciousness without a corresponding notion of races as social groups, another crucial element of elite Dominican views of cultura, appears similarly to have permeated the barrios by the end of the twentieth century. In their own accounts, people in Cristo Rey describe themselves as poor, as Dominican, as Roman Catholic. These descriptions, it seems, express a notion of belonging to a collective. On the other hand, while they often refer to themselves and each other according to a range of color categories—blanco, indio, trigueño, and *moreno* (brown)—they infrequently call themselves *prieto* (black), and they do not seem to view themselves as members of distinct white and black communities. Nor do they organize their politics around race. This is not to say that color does not matter in Cristo Rey. One frequently sees examples of everyday racism. Light-skinned children are generally held to be more beautiful. Tightly curled hair is simply "bad hair" and straight hair is "good hair." A white, foreign researcher videotapes an interview with a young church worker and another, light-skinned church worker interrupts to "joke" that such an ugly black face will ruin the picture. A mother teases her adult dark-skinned son that he refuses to drink coffee because he worries that it would turn him even blacker. This young man later explains that he experiences discrimination when he ventures downtown, both because of his color and because he is from Cristo Rey. At certain nightclubs, if he could afford them, he would be denied service because of color. Applying for jobs, he is turned down when he gives his home address in the barrio.[47]

The hushing up of popular African Dominican practices and the widespread practice of color prejudice were, however, only two aspects of the concept of cultura as it evolved among urban thinkers since the late nineteenth century. Cultura was also a crucial element of state projects to instruct rural people in the basics of organized, civilized life. It was a counterpart to rural and urban reform projects, the fundamental behavior that Dominicans had to exhibit in order to participate in the project of national modernization. To be sure, many in the barrios resisted the pressure to conform to abstract notions of respectable urban behavior, either by maintaining their secret rituals or loudly playing the shantytown musical style known scornfully by the middle class as *bachata*.[48] Given the many spaces in the barrios that were off-limits to police and other representatives of the state, it is possible that in many instances the actual pressure to behave according to the norms of cultura was so slight that barrio residents simply did not feel it. Nevertheless, some among the poor learned and appropriated the idea that certain kinds of public behavior, or cultura, properly belonged to the city. As it had been for urban elites since the founding of the republic, cultura was a tool for barrio residents to exclude others and a tool many used in seeking to avoid their own exclusion. Beginning in the early 1960s, the same local leadership in the barrios that had turned state messages about progreso into demands for social development turned official rhetoric about cultura into campaigns against noise, especially amplified music, and against moral turpitude, especially gambling, drinking, homosexuality, and carousing at local nightspots.

Although this idea of cultura clearly has overtones of snobbery, these decency campaigns had their roots in practical concerns generated by the close quarters and social organization of the Zona Norte. Since there were no supermarkets and few public street markets, the barrios supported hundreds of small colmados, or corner stores, tucked in among the houses, with a door or window opening onto the street or alleyway. Money was scarce, so most residents made separate trips to the colmado to buy supplies for every meal. Merchants accommodated their clientele by selling on credit or *cheleando*, selling a few *cheles* (cents) worth of any item—a scoop of tomato paste from the can, a slice of salami, or a half-cup of oil. Men and boys also gathered outside the colmados to *hacer esquina* (do the street corner)—that is, to talk, gossip, watch neighborhood activity, drink, and play dominoes. In the 1950s, one of Trujillo's brothers-in-law imported thousands of used 78 rpm jukeboxes from Puerto Rico, and distributed them to colmados in the capital in exchange for half of the proceeds. Along with nightclubs and cabarets, which also began pumping amplified music into neighborhoods, by the middle of the

1960s the colmados and their jukeboxes had turned the barrios into exceptionally noisy places.[49]

It might be tempting to idealize the rowdy, and frequently bawdy, popular culture in these as resistance to the rigid norms of elite and middle-class society. But neighborhood improvement associations and church groups were not simply attempting to approximate middle-class abstractions when they regularly appealed to the police to clamp down on jukeboxes and radios in the colmados. Frequently, they claimed, they were trying to get some sleep between long days of struggling to eke out a living. In 1964, for instance, a group of representatives from the established working-class barrios Villa Juana, Villa Consuelo, Villa Duarte, Villa Francisca, Gualey, San Carlos, and Mejoramiento Social wrote to the government that some corners in the neighborhoods had two or four jukeboxes playing simultaneously; "it is something like the entranceway to hell." What was worse, they wrote, in the "early morning some aggressive neighbors, who live separated only by a wooden barrier, put their radios on so loud that they wake the whole neighborhood."[50] Likewise residents of Cristo Rey complained, in 1973, of a jukebox that played so loud that "it is impossible for us to find relief from our exhaustion."[51]

Complaints about the constant nuisance of noise and insecurity in the barrios blended, however, into denunciations of the drinking, dancing, gambling, sexual liaisons, and prostitution that, some barrio residents claimed, were taking place in neighborhood cabarets. In 1973, residents of Cristo Rey wrote to the secretary of the Interior complaining of prostitutes occupying a house on Avenida de los Mártires, who offended "public decency and *buenas costumbres*" and "corrupted the social environment of the whole sector."[52] A separate neighborhood group from El Caliche wrote to the secretary of the Interior, also in 1973, complaining of cabarets in their midst. They called on the state to live up to its celebrations of action on behalf of decent humble folk. "We are confident," they wrote, "that you will manage to bring tranquility to our humble and hard working families." And indeed a later report suggests that the police did shut down several cabarets on Calle 49 in El Caliche.[53] These kinds of complaints appear throughout the police archives in Santo Domingo, from the early 1960s through the middle 1980s. In 1964, letters from barrio residents in Santo Domingo and provincial cities demanding government action against cabarets were so common that the secretary of Public Health and Welfare released a statement to be read on local radio, denying that his office was responsible for intervening in neighborhood cultura.[54]

Such objections to cabarets used the language of public decency, good behavior, and corruption, all familiar to the state. *Buenas costumbres* (which might be translated as good customs, good behavior, or decency) was an official designation of moral and legal behavior. Dominicans needed a certificate of *vida y costumbres* (life and customs, or manners) from the police, for instance, in order to apply for a passport. More significantly, the Dominican constitution officially limited the right to free speech, free association, and freedom of religion in order to protect "the dignity and morals of persons," "public order," and "buenas costumbres."[55] In neighborhood cultural politics, as in the cultural politics of the patriarchal state, the threat to buenas costumbres seemed to come principally from the sexual behaviors of women. In a few instances, however, neighborhood activists described homosexuals as sources of local corruption. Residents of Calle Enriquillo complained of a building that rented rooms to both gay men and lesbians (although it is not clear if these rentals were for purposes of habitation, brief romantic liaisons, or prostitution) and residents of María Auxiliadora complained of a "center of homosexuals" in their midst that was "corrupting the youth and an embarrassment for the neighborhood."[56]

Although these campaigns against corruption, allied with desperate pleas for quiet, were likely the work of small groups of neighborhood activists, residents of the Zona Norte eventually conformed to a general rhetorical convention that described certain neighborhood spaces as "centers of corruption" and other opposing spaces as "centers of cultura." Nightclubs, cabarets, pool halls, and certain colmados were centers of corruption. Schools, churches, and youth clubs were centers of cultura.[57] Neighborhood cabarets in the 1970s and 1980s were, in fact, the sites of a vibrant culture (as anthropologists understand the word), including the evolution of bachata. Scholars see this music as part of rural migrants' widespread resistance to the prejudices and cultural impositions of elite and middle-class Dominicans.[58] Yet local activists did not agree. They sought to enlist the police in efforts to secure what they saw as an appropriate level of urban decorum and public decency. While they rarely had much long-term success in controlling cultural expressions in their neighborhoods, their success in defining these spaces of alternative cultural creativity as nothing more than festering sores of moral decay is another mark of the process of learning by which the idea of cultura seeped into barrio life. Neighborhood leaders, and eventually common linguistic practice, denied that what went on inside the cabarets was a kind of cultura. It was, to the contrary, corruption or *incultura*—lack of culture.

In a sense, cultura remained what it had been for Dominican thinkers in the early part of the century, a kind of exclusion that was also, paradoxically, a means of belonging. If a poor resident of Santo Domingo, even one with dark skin and "bad hair," managed her desenvolvimiento right, if she attained a measure of progreso, she might, in rare cases, be able to move from a shanty in a marginal neighborhood to a home in a popular or middle-class sector. To *belong* in that new space, she had to behave according to certain norms of cultura. Neighborhood public opinion in middle-class neighborhoods would not accept those perceived as bringing noise and other barrio ways with them.

In the barrios themselves, activists tried similarly to impose basic standards of behavior, and when they could not, they used the concept of cultura to distinguish themselves from the corruption around them, and, when possible, to inscribe decency into the social geography of their barrios. They were, after all, likely to suffer social discrimination based on the reputation of their neighborhood, with geography and cultura standing in for broader categories of color or class. For instance, the street named Calle Barahona in the neighborhood known as Borojól suffers a reputation for its tradition of cabarets and prostitutes stretching back its designation as a "tolerance zone" in 1917 under U.S. occupation. At the time of the ordinance, residents of the barrio wrote to protest "in the name of morality and *cultura*," pleading with the government not to "damage the interests of hardworking and honorable families."[59] Although residents lost this battle, they did not give up on the effort to separate themselves from the ill repute of their surroundings. More than eight decades later, researcher and educator Miguel Angel Moreno writes that residents of Borojól "understand themselves to be part of Villa Francisca," a more respectable urban space. This kind of local distinction he interprets as "yet another attempt not to be excluded." One group of women in the neighborhood went so far as to name their street Las Honradas, the honest women, hoping to distinguish their own decency from the bad costumbres associated with nearby Calle Barahona.[60]

While cabarets, with the taint of prostitution and homosexuality, represented specifically female or queer threats to public decency, barrio residents wrote groups of young unemployed men "haciendo esquina" into local geographies of respectability and danger too. Residents of Villa Francisca, for instance, identify nearby Guachupita as a source of political protest and conflict with the police. And, borrowing from the racial iconography of Hollywood films, they refer to one corner in particular as Zona Apache (Apache Territory) because of the "ostentatiously aggressive" behaviors of the boys who cluster there.[61] Barrio residents in the Zona Norte adopted, as their neighborhoods grew, local conventions of speech for describing the spaces identified as *caliente* (hot), patrolled by tígueres (literally tigers, a description of streetwise neighborhood toughs). In Cristo Rey, residents take pains to warn foreign guests about certain corners or cañadas that are occupied by tígueres.[62] Yet this language did not appear in the letters neighborhood leaders wrote to government officials. *Tigueraje*, straight male misbehavior, was a prominent aspect of local cultural geographies—and a practical threat to women in these neighborhoods—but was never mentioned in official complaints to the police. Those complaints were limited to the threats posed by female and homosexual misbehavior.

In practice, however, barriers of cultura between the neighborhood and the corrupt or violent individuals next door were never as firm as these attempts at distinction made them seem. Local activists in El Caliche connected their attempts at local development with their attempts at patrolling local culture. They tried to change the name from its "antiquated" association with mud and chalk to a new Christian name, El Calvario. And they asked the police to clear cabarets from their midst. But even the official celebration for the opening of the water faucets in the neighborhood, with the bishop and a marching band, was not fully regulated. Youths ran shouting through the streets with fists raised one minute and threw their arms around a local police commander the next. Then the party "for the goddess, water" stretched into the night, one reporter noted, with its attention turned to "the god, rum." Similarly, a scholar and activist who grew up in Borojól remembers that the women on Las Honradas actually coexisted peacefully with the prostitutes nearby. Many earned their living washing clothing for their disreputable neighbors and many consulted them for advice in love. And in any neighborhood of the Zona Norte, when rival neighborhoods, the police, or U.S. Marines threatened the neighborhood from the outside, everyone understood that the tígueres were the first line of defense.[63]

As a practical matter, the sense Dominicans made of their lives as they moved to the sprawling barrios of the capital often resonated with, or explicitly appropriated, the language of progreso and cultura. Whether or not audiences in the largely migrant barrios chuckled when they heard the tales of Don Cibaíto on the radio, they understood the message that the city was the center of civilization and the countryside a morass of backwardness. They also understood the regret with which Cibaíto left behind the earlier promise of rural progreso. They accepted the idea of cultura as a hierarchical ideal, even as they continued to use a range of actual cultural practices that conformed little to this ideal. And they deployed both progreso and cultura in attempts to wrest resources from the state, to claim urban citizenship, to organize their barrios, and to avoid social exclusion. As it first settled on small plots, then moved to, and settled in, the city, a rural populace that had lived independently for three hundred years incorporated ideas conceived by a handful of lettered elites and empowered by the extraordinary rise of an authoritarian state.

Over four decades of explosive urban growth, cultura, and progreso—ideas that had long served to differentiate the city from the countryside, rich from poor, and Dominicans from outsiders—entered the intellectual life of the barrios, creating murky detente rather than a consensus. The adoption of these notions, whether to make claims for the resources of the state, to organize collective action, or merely, as Moreno puts it, "to avoid exclusion," never fully erased the practical tolerance for a variety of ideas and expressions that rural Dominicans brought with them from the countryside. Yet progreso and cultura enjoyed a privileged symbolic status as the ideas of the elite and of neighborhood elites. They shaped neighborhood ideas about who belonged where and what sorts of people were respectable. And neighborhood residents turned them into the basis of local political activism. The United States invasion of 1965 added a final piece to this complicated puzzle of cultura and progreso in the barrios. Suddenly that other important meaning of cultura—the difference between the Dominican Republic and the United States—regained its urgency in Dominican politics. At the same time, shifting international politics helped direct Dominican aspirations for progreso, and their carefully managed desenvolvimiento, from the Dominican capital to a distant world capital, New York City.

FOUR

Yankee, Go Home . . . and Take Me with You!

IN 1968 AN ANTHROPOLOGIST studying rural-to-urban migration in the Dominican Republic found, to her surprise, that reaching Santo Domingo was not the ultimate goal of the campesinos she interviewed. Those who planned to leave their villages might first stop in the capital. Indeed, for many, Santo Domingo was as far as they would ever travel. But, she found, a great many peasants saw the route to progreso in the eventual prospect of reaching New York.[1]

That Dominicans might imagine a world in which movement from rural backwardness to urban modernity had its logical conclusion in the United States is, in retrospect, no surprise. From the middle of the nineteenth century, relations between the two countries were both intimate and brutally lopsided. The United States and its representatives sought persistently to buy, bully, occupy, or govern the Dominican Republic. And representatives of the United States occasionally made earnest, if self-serving, attempts to alleviate poverty, build a modern state, and establish a democratic polity in the neighboring Republic. A strident rhetoric of friendship and tutorship, and an open assumption of the superiority of North American society accompanied these wildly asymmetrical arrangements. The image of the United States as the epitome of modern life overshadowed the projects of national modernization begun under its condescending tutelage.[2]

In short, the Dominican Republic was a primary target of U.S. imperialism as it evolved in the nineteenth and twentieth centuries. As a result, the United States held a powerfully ambivalent grip on the imaginations of Dominican elites, who both admired and deplored the neighbor that so dominated them. And as popular sectors began to incorporate the idea of progreso into their own lives in the middle of the twentieth century, it is little wonder that the United States lured them as well. The United States was in many ways a more convincing symbol of power, modernity, and well-being than the intrusive Dominican state. Films, newspapers, and the frequent presence of U.S. companies and troops on Dominican soil diffused images of the United States widely in Dominican popular culture. This deep historical influence of U.S. imperialism on Dominican imaginations makes peasants' unexpected desire to travel to the United States wholly understandable.[3]

What was surprising was that, by the middle of the 1960s, the prospect of reaching the most famous city in the heart of the imperial system suddenly came within reach for many thousands of Dominicans. In preceding decades the number of Dominicans moving to the United States grew slowly. In the 1930s, 1,150 Dominicans immigrated to the United States. Another 5,627 joined them in the 1940s, followed by 9,897 in the 1950s. But between the death of Rafael Trujillo in 1961 and the U.S. invasion of Santo Domingo in the spring of 1965, the number of immigrant visas granted to Dominicans jumped to nearly 10,000 a year. With slight fluctuations, immigrant visas averaged about 10,000 a year for the next decade, then grew steadily for the rest of the century. Also beginning in the period between 1961 and 1965, 20,000–30,000 Dominican tourists and students received permission to travel to the United States each year.[4] This increase in tourism persisted throughout subsequent decades, providing still more opportunities for migration, as many Dominicans overstayed their nonimmigrant visas in order to work.[5] In the span of a decade Dominicans, starting from almost zero, became the largest new immigrant group in New York, and New York became one of the largest Dominican cities.

Conventional wisdom in U.S. history holds that the boom in new immigration from the Third World in the 1960s resulted from the passage of the Immigration Reform Act in 1965. The 1965 act is usually seen primarily as its liberal sponsors intended, as a repeal of national origins restrictions originally put in place in the 1920s to keep out "undesirable races." The reform granted a set number of immigrant visas to the Eastern and Western Hemispheres, without discriminatory national origins quotas. This change in policy spurred the transformation of New York into an archipelago of new ethnic neighborhoods, home to hundreds of thousands of migrants from the Third World and former Soviet Bloc. New York's largest group of newcomers after 1965, Dominican migrants led this remarkable ethnic explosion. But the Immigration Reform Act does not help to explain the sudden jump in Dominican migration. The immigration restrictions of the 1920s exempted the Dominican Republic, like all the republics of the Western Hemisphere. While often imagined as a removal of restrictions, the 1965 reform actually placed the first numerical restriction on the number of visas that could be granted to Dominicans and other Latin Americans. In any event, the legislation passed in 1965 could not have been a condition for the explosion in Dominican migration. By the time the reforms were enacted in 1968, Dominicans' colonization of New York was already well under way.[6]

A shift in international politics, not the reform of immigration laws, produced the sudden opportunity for migration and a massive displacement of Dominicans to New York. To be precise, the sudden surge in Dominican international migration began as Washington stepped up its intervention in Dominican affairs after the death of dictator Rafael Trujillo. The intricacies of this opening reveal much, not only about the nature of migration to the United States in the period after World War II, but also about the nature of U.S. imperialism. Ironically, even as thousands of Dominicans began settling in New York, adopting and experimenting with local culture, the intensity of U.S. meddling in Dominican affairs produced a resurgence of cultural nationalism in Santo Domingo. Just as the question of assimilation—the proper mixture of Dominican and U.S. cultures among Dominican New Yorkers—emerged on the horizon of New York barrios, activists in Santo Domingo barrios turned their attention to weeding out U.S. influences from local cultura. The new imperialism of the 1960s was not just a cause of the burst in Dominican settlement in New York—it was also the context in which Dominicans first experienced and interpreted international migration.

Put another way, Dominicans' experiences of contact with the cultures of the United States in New York and Santo Domingo were two faces of the same pervasive relationship, both radically reconfigured in the 1960s. Understanding this story therefore requires turning again to the tense moments after Trujillo's assassination, to see how imperialism, international migration, and ideas about Dominican cultura all began to shift.

THE VISA MESS

Under Trujillo, Dominicans suffered severe restrictions on their rights to international travel. As a result, in the 1950s, as wealthy families in many Latin American countries began flying to the United States to vacation, to shop, and to form middle-class immigrant enclaves, and as working-class Mexicans and Puerto Ricans settled in ever larger numbers inside the United States, Dominicans lagged behind. For many, the cost of passports was the primary obstacle to traveling abroad. In 1961, a bottle of milk cost .13 pesos in the Dominican Republic. One hundred plantains cost 1.27 pesos. By contrast, passport applications and processing fees amounted to 125 pesos.[7] The government also denied passports to many of those who could afford the application.[8] One reason for this stinginess was the belief that the Dominican Republic was underpopulated, and that an outward flow of citizens would be economically damaging. At the same time, controlling and restricting passage in and out of the Republic was a way of ensuring loyalty to the regime (since there could be no escaping) and blocking access to the flow of information from dissidents abroad.[9] Trujillo's control, however, was never airtight. Only weeks before the dictator's death, the Dominican consul in San Juan wrote to the Foreign Ministry that some Dominican citizens returning from Aruba were using the stopover in Puerto Rico to defect. "[T]hey disappear into Puerto Rican territory," he wrote, "and some have reappeared asking for political asylum."[10] By this and other means, exile communities grew over the course of the regime.[11]

Although his control over international travel had never been absolute, Trujillo's death brought a dramatic relaxation of Dominican restrictions on international travel and a rapid reshuffling of border controls in the Caribbean. Trujillo was killed on May 30, 1961. By July 5, the Dominican senate approved President Balaguer's proposed reduction of the taxes charged for passports and the yearly certification of "buenas costumbres." The price of a passport dropped from 125 to 40 pesos.[12] In late summer the Dominican Congress officially announced a new guarantee of the freedom of travel.[13] By March 1962, the Civil Governor of Santo Domingo wrote to the Council of State expressing his commitment to the principle "that we should extend every facility for Dominicans to travel abroad."[14]

The government most likely reduced fees on passports, along with many other burdens imposed by the state, in order to curry public favor. In the same week, President Balaguer put an end to mandatory military service, and Congress proposed amnesty on taxes owed for national identity cards.[15] But the new passport policy was also a response to specific demands for freedom of travel, beginning with calls from exiles for permission to return to the Dominican Republic.[16] In July 1961 El Caribe's Foro Público (a letters to the editor section that under Trujillo had been a key site of political denunciation, often planted by the regime) published a call on behalf of those inside the Republic, decrying government slowness in issuing passports. Inspired by the article, a Dominican citizen named Luciano Torres wrote to the government arguing that the freedom of travel was a fundamental element of the democratic transition: "Is there not a Democratic Plan? Is there no freedom of conscience and of free transit? . . . If there is democratization, then it should be easy to leave and enter, without being submitted to investigations, which unnecessarily consume time and money."[17] This letter is unusual in its clear written articulation of a demand for passports. Most Dominicans expressed this desire in administrative fashion, at state offices. By winter of 1961, the Dominican government reported as many as 75 to 150 new passport applications per day, a pace that would continue throughout 1962. In January and February of 1962 alone, the state issued 5,000 passports.[18]

That the thousands of requests for passports were granted probably reflects the interest that government decision makers themselves had in traveling abroad. Bureaucrats and politicians had been the most actively constricted by Trujillo-era passport policies, since they had the resources to travel, but not the right. They also had the most to gain from new freedoms. And as political tides ebbed and flowed, no one, not even members of the Council of State, could be sure that he or she would not be the next in line to flee the country. In fact, many of the first Dominicans to avail themselves of the new right to passports were members of the old regime themselves. Under pressure from popular demonstrations and the U.S. Embassy, members of the Trujillo family, prominent figures in the old regime, themselves sought passports and visas to flee the country in August, September, and October of 1961.[19] Likewise, over the following months dozens of police officers began to make internal requests to the Ministry of the Interior for passports. Some wished to travel to the United States for training courses, at the invitation of the State Department. Others requested permission merely to visit relatives in New York.[20]

The Human Rights Commission of the Organization of American States, sent to Santo Domingo in 1961, gave added leverage to calls for a more liberal passport policy. The OAS demanded progress on human rights as a condition for lifting economic sanctions, and clearly saw the right to travel as a crucial human right.[21] The United States, by contrast, opposed any guarantee of the freedom of travel. Throughout the early 1960s, the U.S. Embassy saw forced exile as a strategy for getting rid of remnants of the Trujillo military or, more frequently, young nationalists and leftists. In October of 1961, a secret "background paper" for President Kennedy reported, "Our Consulate in Ciudad Trujillo would continue to urge that Communists and Pro-Castro elements be deported . . . [A]nother agency . . . has forwarded to Ciudad Trujillo a list of such undesirable persons, which, after local checking, the Consulate is to transmit to the Balaguer Government." In his memoir Ambassador Martin also admitted to collaborating with Dominican officials to deport young leftists under the protection of U.S. visas, but he left out the role of the "other agency" that sent lists of names to the Dominicans. Martin recalled that Dominican military officers "would simply send a man's passport to our Consulate for a Visa." Some of these exiles went through the United States to Europe. Others remained on U.S. soil, unable to return home. By the end of 1962, Martin estimated, the United States held 125 Dominicans against their will in this fashion.[22] The United States did not want a generalized right to travel. But the State Department expressed no objection to increasing the number of passports issued to ordinary citizens. To the contrary, since the idea was to push the troublesome actors out of the country, an efficient flow of passports probably pleased U.S. Embassy officials.

Given the pressure they felt from the public, given their own interest in traveling abroad, given pressure from the OAS to guarantee human rights, and given U.S. enthusiasm for sweeping political dissidents out of the country, it is easy to see why Dominican politicians so quickly reversed decades of stinginess with passports. As thousands of Dominican citizens joined exiles, members of the old regime, and police officials in requesting travel documents, state bureaucrats also recognized yet another reason for maintaining the easy flow of passports. There was good money to be made in the transactions. Tomás Báez Díaz, civil governor of Santo Domingo, complained to the Council of State that the reduced taxes on passports left too little margin. "A just increase in the cost of dispensing passports would constitute an important income, much needed by the public coffers in these moments of grave economic crisis."[23] It is hard to judge Báez's figures or to find evidence about whether the state ever received a windfall from the boom in passport applications. It seems sure, however, that state officials saw opportunities to line their pockets with bribes, the unofficial processing fees required by virtually all government bureaucracies in the Dominican Republic. A new, complicated, and lengthy administrative procedure, a new government document that thousands of Dominicans desperately wanted, must have seemed like manna from heaven.[24]

With the exception of overland crossings into Haiti, the new airport at Punto Caucedo, completed in 1958, was the principal way out of the Dominican Republic.[25] As Dominican officials loosened the reins on Dominican international travel, officials of countries with direct routes arriving from Santo Domingo saw a flood of Dominican travelers. Within four months of Trujillo's death, the Dutch colonial government of Curaçao reported that "numerous" Dominicans were arriving "without sufficient economic resources," including a few who were "invited to leave Dominican territory because of Communist activities." The government in Curaçao banned the entry of Dominicans without visas and subjected all Dominican passengers to humiliating searches in the airport.[26]

Yet attempts to enter the United States surpassed attempts to travel to Curaçao by many orders of magnitude. Each time the Dominican government issued a new batch of passports, the U.S. delegation in Santo Domingo saw a sudden surge in visa applications.[27] As has already been suggested, the dominating presence of the United States in Dominican life, and the widespread assumption of U.S. superiority, shaped Dominican aspirations. Also, the existence of an exile colony in New York numbering in the thousands exerted a pull northward to that city. Friends and relatives wanted to be reunited with exiles. The historical relationship with the United States also created a transportation infrastructure that pushed Dominicans along specific routes.[28]

Although it was possible to reach Curaçao, Haiti, or Jamaica without passing through the United States, returning required a stopover in Miami. In practice, in the age of air travel, San Juan, Miami, and New York were the necessary portals between Santo Domingo and the rest of the world.[29]

These combined factors put more pressure on U.S. immigration officers to accept Dominican passengers than the relatively smaller route to South America put on officials in Curaçao. But the ways the U.S. government publicized its role in managing Dominican internal affairs (something the Dutch, for instance, had never done) sharpened this problem. As anti-Yankee sentiment began to spread across Latin America in the early 1960s, and as urban unrest shook Santo Domingo, the representatives of the United States saw themselves forced to respond carefully to Dominican public opinion. As Latin American students and workers began turning their ardent nationalism against the United States, putting on a friendly face, even while intensifying attempts to interfere in Latin American affairs, became all the more important to Washington's aims. Claims of friendship and attempts to project the United States as eminently able to solve the development problems of its weaker allies were the new justifications for empire. And, in the particular crucible of the political crisis in Santo Domingo, claims of friendship had to be backed up with the free flow of visas, the documents Dominicans needed in order to reach the outside world. In other words, Washington politicians' unique desire, even among the world powers, to manage Dominican public opinion gave Dominican visa seekers considerable leverage in getting admitted to the United States.

From the point of view of Ambassador John Bartlow Martin, the political crisis in Santo Domingo thus quickly created a visa crisis. By 1962, the sudden increase in visa applications was much more than the small staff could manage. Lines grew to more than five hundred applicants daily, clogging the stairway and stretching around the corner on the hot pavement. The wait for an application to be processed stretched to as long as sixty-four weeks. As Democrats in Washington grew increasingly jittery about the constant unrest in Santo Domingo, Ambassador Martin worried that the visa backlog had "taken on political importance, and the public image of the United States is being impaired."[30] How could U.S. officials advertise themselves as the friends of the Dominican people and the American way of life as the pinnacle of world civilization, but turn away Dominicans wishing to travel to the United States? How, especially, could they refuse to admit Dominicans while tens of thousands of Cuban refugees received such warm welcome and Puerto Rican citizens, if not warmly welcomed, flew unimpeded to the mainland?

The political geography of Santo Domingo further aggravated what Martin called the "visa mess." Between the death of Trujillo and the election of Juan Bosch, varied opposition forces gathered huge crowds of students and youths (including not a few tígueres) from the poor barrios in the north of the city. Smaller spontaneous disturbances, or *turbas*, broke out periodically in the capital as barrio residents hunted down the thugs and spies who had long patrolled on behalf of the dictator, and crowds tore down the many statues of Trujillo erected about the city. Though the provinces of the interior and most of the capital remained peaceful, these demonstrations had disproportionate symbolic power because they took place in the old Zona Colonial. Usually they began at Parque Colón, proceeded down El Conde, and ended at Parque Independencia or the Presidential Palace several blocks farther on. This sliver of Santo Domingo was the same area that nationalists had idealized in the 1920s and 1930s as the center of refined cultura and elite power. Under Trujillo it had also been the terrain of the powerful, home to banks, airlines, government offices, and stores. More important to Martin and his Visa Officers, the United States Visa Office also stood on El Conde. As groups of young demonstrators reached this easy target for antiimperial gestures, they invariably met an angry queue of visa applicants, suffocating on the hot pavement and ready to vent their frustrations.[31]

The mingling of frustrated visa applicants and protesters, Ambassador Martin later wrote, produced frequent "full-fledged anti-American riots" in front of the consulate. "On some days it almost seemed that the young vice consuls spent more time throwing tear gas out the windows than issuing visas."[32] It is impossible to know precisely the logic that joining an anti-Yankee riot had for Dominicans seeking permission to fly to, and even settle in, the United States. Beyond sheer frustration, perhaps the demonstrators perceived that protests against the United States were an effective way to force the embassy into solving the visa backlog. Dominicans were surely aware that the United States feared unrest and the spread of communism, and that it hoped to lure the Dominican public into sympathy with Washington. Members of the Council of State, like most Latin American politicians of their generation, spent their lives warning and threatening that unless the U.S. delegation met one set of conditions or another, the country was sure to go communist. In fact, one member of the Council of State specifically threatened Ambassador Martin that he would speak out to the Dominican public against the United States if the United States did not quickly resolve the visa backlog.[33] Maybe the riots were a way for the crowds outside the consulate similarly to twist the arm of the ambassador with the most powerful weapon available: Washington's fear of unrest.

FIGURE 4-1. Protesters in the Zona Colonial calling for the departure of Joaquín Balaguer, November 1961. By 1962, demonstrations frequently turned into riots at the U.S. Visa Office. The United States responded by building a new Consulate outside the Zona Colonial and by streamlining visa processing. (Photograph by Lynn Pelham, courtesy of Getty Images)

But whether the rioters in Santo Domingo understood themselves to be pressuring the United States to grant more visas or simply expressed their immediate outrage at the long lines, the riots outside the Visa Office did inspire Kennedy and Martin to quick action. By April 1962, Martin, Kennedy, and the State Department agreed to contract two Mexican American officers from the Los Angeles Police Department to advise Dominican police on riot control. They appointed a Puerto Rican public relations firm to work on improving the image of the Council of State and the United States. And they agreed to "take immediate steps to reduce Embassy Santo Domingo's visa backlog to the point where it is no longer a political liability."[34] By September, they built a new and larger consulate in the western suburbs far from the troubled center city, a second consulate in the city of Santiago, and two temporary visa processing centers in Manzanillo and La Romana.[35] Kennedy and Martin increased the consular personnel, sending in a "planeload of visa experts" and hiring more local staff.[36] The United States responded to Dominican protests, in short, by making it much easier for large numbers of Dominicans to get quickly into the United States. The resolution of the visa crisis created a strong flowing current from the Dominican Republic to the United States where only a small channel had existed before. The number of U.S. immigrant visas issued in the Dominican Republic rose quickly, from 464 in 1960, to 1,789 in 1961, to 3,680 in 1962, to 9,857 in 1963, when the new consulates were fully functioning. With some fluctuations, the number of immigrant visas granted would remain at this level, averaging just over 10,000 a year over the next decade.[37] Employers in New York undoubtedly enjoyed the influx of a new, vulnerable workforce.[38] But employers did not need to send labor recruiters to round up these workers. Dominicans took hold of the opportunity created in 1962 and quickly laid the foundations of what would become the largest immigrant enclave in the city of New York over the following twenty-five years.

Ambassador Martin did not change the rules governing visa eligibility. Existing immigration law placed no limit on the number of visas he could grant to Dominicans, as long as the applicants passed their literacy tests, could convince consular officials that they would not become public charges, and satisfied basic health requirements. Also they could not be polygamists, prostitutes, homosexuals, or communists. Local officials enjoyed considerable leeway in interpreting these rules, and could tighten or loosen the flow of visas in response to political considerations or individual whim. But since there had never been anything resembling the flood of applications that reached the Visa Office in the early 1960s, there is no precise way to compare how officers interpreted the regulations before and after the death of Trujillo. What is clear is that the consulate continued to turn down applicants it deemed unworthy in the early 1960s, even as it sought a way to resolve the problem of the visa backlog. According to confidential reports, the Visa Office rejected close to 40 percent of applicants in the months of January and July of 1962.[39] This suggests that Martin's goal was improving public perception without lowering the bar for immigration. Martin's solution was to apply, effectively and expeditiously, the existing U.S. immigration laws to all who requested visas. His hope was that by increasing bureaucratic efficiency he could take the politics out of the visa process. Of course, in his efforts to influence Dominican affairs, taking the politics out of migration was, in itself, a political objective.[40]

At the very same time U.S. representatives continued to use their de facto control over Dominicans' right to travel abroad as an expressly political tool. After the coup in 1963, with the military firmly in control in Santo Domingo, the United States revoked the visas of known leftists like Manolo Tavares. This policy forced members of the opposition back into the Dominican Republic and into the hands of the military junta.[41] Then, in the negotiations to end the 1965 conflict, the United States again clashed with Dominican liberals on the question of freedom of travel. Sensitive to the recent history of forced exile, the Constitutionalists negotiated hard, in 1965, for guarantees of the freedom of travel for all Dominican citizens, and for the reintegration of rebel soldiers into the Dominican army.[42] The U.S. Embassy, anxious to pacify the country and exclude the far left from the upcoming elections, "vigorously" made the point that a no-deportation provision in the Act of Reconciliation was "unworkable."[43] But policy makers in Washington and Santo Domingo finally contented themselves by reasoning that none of the guarantees of freedom need apply to any Dominican citizens labeled communists. In the summer and fall of 1965, the embassy officials implored interim president García Godoy to round up and imprison communists and to transfer rebel military leaders out of the country along with a few military figures on the far right.[44]

In some cases, the embassy intervened directly to remove individual Dominican radicals to the United States or to pressure the Dominican government to do so. U.S. "agencies" presumably continued to pass lists of suspects to the Dominican police, and presumably its visa officers continued to process passports sent by the police. But many cases of political exile required no such direct diplomatic action; in the early years of the Balaguer regime, installed in 1966, it was rarely necessary actually to round up and deport dissenters. Fearful of repression and suffering economic strangulation, former combatants in the Constitutionalist struggle themselves appealed for visas through whatever channels they could find. One high-level Constitutionalist official remembers that Sacha Volman, a Bosch confidant and some-time CIA operative, worked as a go-between with the U.S. Embassy to help many escape.[45] Constitutionalists used their ties to Volman to avoid falling into the hands of Dominican police who, with the help of *their* CIA allies, carried out a violent "cleanup" operation in the city. In other instances, clergy or journalists acted as go-betweens to arrange exile for members of the opposition.[46] Often too, the middle-class families of many young radicals took the lead role in promoting the exile of their sons and daughters.[47] This protected both children and parents from reprisals at the hands of the authorities. After the coup in 1963, Leonardo Tapia, a young radical at the university, decided to go into exile. His parents made the arrangements for him to live with an aunt in New York. Sulley Saneaux, a student radical from Ensanche La Fe, ran away from home when his parents used family contacts to arrange to send him to a military academy in Florida in 1965.[48]

Frequently, young radicals found themselves in "exile" because their parents and families migrated to New York for reasons wholly unrelated to the political evolution of their children. Union leader Agustín Vargas-Saillant remembers those who experienced this kind of exile as the *llevados* (those taken along). Llevados, he recalls, were torn between feelings of responsibility to the Dominican Republic and family responsibilities.[49] In a serialized memoir, "A Family That Emigrated to New York," published in 1974, María Ramos remembered being taken along just as the civil war unfolded in 1965, just as she began to experience the political "transformation imposed on us by a changing society."[50] As she prepared her bags, the prospect of leaving behind the "possibilities, the risks, and the consequences of these ideas and of this great mobilization of men" produced a deep anxiety.[51] New York felt like exile to young radicals like Ramos, even if the proximate circumstances that brought them there had little to do with politics or the calculations of the U.S. Embassy.

Exact statistics are impossible to provide, but all indications are that "migrants," who benefited from their own ingenuity and the increased efficiency of U.S. visa processing, far outnumbered "exiles," including those manipulated out of the country with the help of the embassy, those who escaped through the intervention of family or other contacts, and the llevados. In the early 1960s, the embassy collaborated in deporting only several hundred Dominicans. Even in the peak years of 1965 and 1966, there were probably never more than a few thousand Constitutionalist exiles, voluntary or involuntary.[52] Once in New York even the most expressly political exiles, veterans of the fighting in 1965, blended seamlessly into the hundreds of thousands of Dominicans who had fled unrest or unemployment. Neighborhood and university activist José Enrique Trinidad recalls, for instance, that his older brother was a commando fighter from Villa Juana. After disappearing from the barrio in 1965, he reappeared in the Bronx, to the great relief of his family. There he gave up politics, working as a mechanic and saving money to eventually open his own auto-repair business.[53] Revolution was one way of looking for progreso. Migration was another.

Still, the widespread use of exile as a political tool by both Balaguer and the United States, and the painful irony of migrating to a country that many saw as responsible for the suffering in Santo Domingo, had a deep impact on the way many Dominicans *understood* the growth of Dominican barrios in New York. Exiles, and especially llevados, had a disproportionate influence on the formation of the first Dominican political organizations in New York. And the compañeros they left behind were key figures in the evolution of Dominican intellectual life. For both groups the involvement of the Visa Office in the exile of Constitutionalists became the foundational moment of the New York settlement. The experience of exile, though numerically small, had a profound influence on the way that Dominicans expressed their national identity in New York, and on the ways that leftists and intellectuals left behind in Santo Domingo would perceive their missing comrades.

Imperialism and Cultura

More generally, many Dominicans viewed migration primarily in relation to still another aspect of life in Santo Domingo in the early 1960s: the flood of new commercial influences from the United States. They viewed migrants' dreams of progreso in New York as part of a broader imperial threat to Dominican cultura brought on by the fall of Trujillo and the burst of U.S. intervention. This idea of national cultura threatened from the outside harkened back to the cultural policies of the Trujillo dictatorship. The regime often portrayed Haitians as the primary threat to Dominican cultura. It even waged a brutal massacre of Haitians in the name of "Dominicanizing " the countryside. At the same time, Trujillo set a cultural policy directed at the enforcement of cultura in the sense of "buenas costumbres" and public decency. The Public Spectacles Commission prohibited music considered "prosaic," "having double meaning," "indecorous," or "in no way edifying for public morality." This ban included Dominican songs like "Menéame los Mangos" (Shake Your Mangos) and "Por Arriba y Por Abajo" (Up Above and Down Below). In practice too this often meant blocking the entry of commercial music or films from the United States. In 1957, the commission banned movies depicting rock and roll, considering it "a frenetic way to excite the spirits which leads to a departure from moral character to the detriment of the whole of society."[54]

These pronouncements probably had less effect than the practical monopoly over Dominican television, radio, and recorded music held by one of Trujillo's erratic and vicious brothers. Petán Trujillo favored live performances of Mexican and Cuban music. Rafael Trujillo himself favored an ornate form of orchestral merengue (including many songs with lyrics celebrating his rule). So that is what Dominican audiences heard and saw. The danger of interfering with a Trujillo monopoly effectively prevented competitors from importing music or television programming from the United States. Toward the end of the regime, even listening to foreign radio broadcasts was prohibited.[55]

Thus just as Trujillo's death provided an opening for people to begin moving to New York, it also opened the door for film and music to arrive from the United States. Radio broadcasts like "Willie con la Juventud" (Willie with the Youth) on Radio Santa María suddenly made foreign songs and dances available to young Dominicans.[56] Those dances reflected the meteoric rise of commercial youth culture in the United States and Europe. A generation of Dominican youngsters, many of whom would later condemn the influence of imperial cultura, welcomed these songs and dances in the early 1960s as modern, cosmopolitan, youth-driven symbols of everything the former regime had denied them. The *twi* (twist), *ye ye* (from the Lennon and McCartney lyric "Yeah, Yeah, Yeah"), and *go go*—collectively known as the *nueva ola* (new wave) or simply *música moderna* (modern music)—provided a soundtrack to the hopes of a democratic transition and the perilously high expectations for the new era of openness.[57] Middle-class Dominican musicians formed their own bands to re-create these styles, giving them names like "Los Happy Boys" and "Los Manhattan Boys."[58] Meanwhile young working-class musicians like Johnny Ventura, to the horror of traditionalists, incorporated aspects of Elvis Presley's newly popular rhythms, dance steps, and performance styles into their merengue acts. They played electric instruments and put dancers in front of the musicians, grease in their hair and sexual innuendo in their hips. Ventura had the first great hit of the post-Trujillo era with "La Agarradera" (The Handle), a raucous, sexually provocative song—intentionally the opposite of the ponderous and sycophantic Mexican bands or merengue orchestras sponsored by the old regime. Dominicans did not need foreign inspiration to write sexual double meanings into their lyrics. But the music and the stage show were, in Ventura's words, "a mixture of classic merengue, rock, and twist."[59]

Like music, the clothing and hairstyles associated with North American youth subcultures spread in the Dominican Republic during the middle 1960s. Homegrown hippies and mods began to attract attention from the press, appearing outside nightclubs on the historic main street of Santo Domingo and in secondary schools across the country. In San Pedro de Macorís, several hundred makeshift hippies staged a demonstration in 1968. They started out on motorbikes and horses from the Casa Puertorriqueña and marched through the city carrying signs that opposed chaperones, beauty pageants, and in one instance, baths. "No queremos ni agua ni jabones" (We Don't Want Water, We Don't Want Soap) read one sign.[60] It seems that these were middle-class rebels, perhaps with ties to the Puerto Rican enclave in San Pedro. They directed their complaints at the restrictive pressures of respectable family life, not at the broader injustices of the society around them. Middle-class youngsters also had greater access to styles that depended on the consumption of expensive imported clothing than did most Dominicans. Some of the local hippies were probably among the tens of thousands of tourists and exchange students who traveled each year to the United States.

However limited in their class appeal, these audible and visible signs of spreading North American cultural influence among Dominican youths produced an array of commentary, not least from those who inherited the state from Trujillo and the U.S. invasion. Cassandra Damirón, a well-known singer allied with the Balaguer regime, waged a campaign to protect merengue from incursions from morally suspect foreign dances. President Balaguer himself attacked "the insubordination of children against their parents' authority and . . . *extremely licentious* customs. . . . Nothing in the world today is free from this wave of paganism, of pathological aberration and of sensuality, and it is logical that these evils, which belong to societies in decadence, would dampen even the shores of lands that had been immune to them."[61] Resuscitating the idea of a national essence threatened by contact with the modern world, Balaguer used attacks on cultural corruption to deflect criticism from the well-founded accusations of *political* corruption against his regime. What is more, the fight against delinquency and corruption, the viruses of modern life, justified government repression of young people in the opposition.[62] This conservative cultural politics was not limited to friends of the regime. The magazine ¡Ahora!, generally critical of Balaguer, published the assertion that rock and roll, like other "lascivious movements" and "exciting rhythms, full of sensuality and even insanity," fostered "sexual immorality" in the Dominican Republic.[63] Still, before 1965 Dominican public opinion held the United States in high regard and música moderna seemed, generally, to be a harbinger of democratic change.[64]

The U.S. intervention profoundly reoriented how the bulk of Dominican students and intellectuals perceived the United States and its cultures. Lyndon Johnson's invasion made enemies of a generation of Dominican youth who, only a few years earlier, had openly admired John F. Kennedy and had danced the twist to mark the new era of freedom. Dominicans in the opposition to Balaguer looked back at the conflict and remembered it as the "Revolution of April," a heroic stand-off between the Dominican *pueblo* and Yankee imperialism. Although Goliath triumphed in the conflict, David stood his ground for several months, testing the limits of U.S. power. This sentiment was captured in the most important visual image of the intervention, Juan Pérez Terrero's Pulitzer Prize–winning photograph of an unarmed Dominican civilian confronting a fully equipped U.S. Marine.[65] The shift in attitude toward the United States, most prominent in the university, was also notable in those parts of the Zona Norte that had sent sons to join the Constitutionalist commandos, and had lost many in the subsequent cleanup operation. Tony Estrella was a young boy in Capotillo in 1966 when Dominican authorities assassinated his father, a labor leader and commando chief. Now a cultural worker in Cristo Rey, he recalls his own sense that the Yankee was "the worst thing in the world."[66]

In "The Last Stand," a poem Estrella wrote as a teenager, the poet holds the U.S. responsible for its contributions to hunger, war, and exploitation in the Dominican Republic and pledges "though it is with my last breath, I stand against you, damned Yankee!"[67] Along with their righteous indignation in the fever of antiimperialism, some critics shot wildly, blaming Yankee interference for almost anything distasteful in local culture and seeing something distasteful in every Yankee interference. A student interviewed by the weekly magazine *¡Ahora!* argued, for instance, that the "problem" of *brujería*, or popular religiosity, in the Dominican Republic was a result of "agents of world reaction."[68] An article in the same magazine accused *Sesame Street*, produced in Spanish in Mexico City, of serving as a form of imperial capitalist propaganda. Setting one of the scenes in a commercial establishment (a neighborhood store), the argument went, taught children to value ideals of consumption and individualism. This meant that it encouraged them to value North American society at the expense of national liberation. Besides, the author wrote, "[T]he Yankees are not capable of creating anything for 'purely educational' purposes, much less things as 'cultural' and monstrous as Sesame Street."[69]

In this context, many early devotees of the twist radically changed their perspective on "modern music," joining the "defense" of national cultura from the left. It was Balaguer, these critics argued, who conspired with the U.S. Embassy to flood the Dominican Republic with U.S. advisers, investors, and products. It was he who had forged the hundreds of new millionaires and the thousands of new upper-middle-class

FIGURE 4-2. Confrontation between a Dominican man and a U.S. Marine during the United States intervention in 1965. This image was part of a trilogy that won the Pulitzer Prize. It is the most widely circulated image from the intervention, often seen as an icon of Dominican resistance to imperialism. (Photograph by Juan Pérez Terrero)

teenagers who studied in elite American schools and who frequently traveled as tourists to New York or Miami. The new music and hairstyles, left-leaning nationalists argued, were a clear symbol of the "servile imitation, for reasons of snobbery, of foreign styles and manners" that defined Balaguer's constituency.[70] When, in the summer of 1970, police in Santiago arrested more than fifty students from the fancy private Evangelical Institute for using drugs, this was more proof of the unholy alliance between native elites and a corrupt foreign power. Wealthy students returning from exchange programs in the United States, the press reported, had brought most of the drugs for the "veritable orgies" of these "children of moneyed families."[71] One left-wing activist who studied at the school saw it differently. The problem was the *gringos*, Dominican students who had traveled abroad with their families and were sent home to finish high school. They not only used drugs and listened to rock music; they also openly defended the United States, a position for which the local student culture had little tolerance.[72]

In addition to their general resentment over United States intervention and control, activists in the student movement and the left-wing parties were also deeply influenced by the cultural renaissance under way in Cuba. In step with critics of cultural imperialism in Latin America and Europe, these young people appropriated the Trujillista idea of "cultural penetration" and the long-standing Dominican antagonism toward North American materialism. It was not Haiti that was using culture as a sinister weapon of denationalization and external control, they argued. It was the United States, "through its agents, the Peace Corps, 5-D Clubs, AID, and other organizations."[73] The imitation of North American commercial culture, the desire to consume new styles, and drug addiction were palpable threats to local popular culture. This was reason enough for patriots to oppose them. But worse yet, cultural penetration was a conscious strategy to erode the revolutionary potential of Dominican young people. Why would students or workers struggle against U.S. imperial power if they were enamored of U.S. culture, if they believed in the image of North American prosperity, if they preferred to work for material items, new clothes or new appliances, rather than for national liberation and communal well-being? Materialism was not only a sign of North American vulgarity; it was a force eroding the communal spirit of the Dominican people.[74]

As the government cracked down heavily on oppositional unions and political parties, cultural activism became the primary outlet for young antiimperialists who joined church-sponsored youth groups, cinema clubs, and poetry societies. At the University in Santo Domingo, students of anthropologists Fraidique Lizardo and Dagoberto Tejada organized a group named Convite to study rural traditions, including African Dominican traditions, and to perform them for urban audiences. Like-minded musicians like Sonia Silvestre, Luis Díaz, and Expresión Jóven began recording and performing a style known throughout Latin America as *nueva canción*, or new song. The nueva canción movement, like North American folk music in the same period, sought to transform popular and indigenous musical styles into protest music. Silvestre and others engaged, in the words of musicologist Deborah Pacini Hernández, in a battle of the airwaves, presenting themselves as an alternative to commercial popular music. Anthropologists, performers, and others in the cultural resistance organized a massive public concert in 1974 known as Seven Days with the People. A related form of spoken word performance, known as *poesía coreada*, or chanted poetry, also gained popularity among cultural activists. Performers recited homespun poems in the traditional *décima* form with didactic messages written in stylized rural accents. In this way, the opposition created its own idealized rural national character to challenge both the elite Hispanism of the Balaguer administration and the growing popularity of imported, urban, and commercial cultures. Calls for the defense of national cultura, for instructing Dominicans in their own traditions, became a coded language for opposition to the Balaguer regime and U.S. imperialism. In this context it is easy to see how cultural activists and intellectuals could construe widespread Dominican desires to travel to the United States as a conspiracy hatched in Washington, an attempt to tie Dominican aspirations to the United States.[75]

CULTURA WARS IN THE BARRIOS

This reinvigorated cultural struggle found its way into the barrios as well, as they emerged from the violence of 1965. After the Loyalists finished their cleanup operation, the remnants of neighborhood commandos, including some left-wing militants and many unemployed young men, went underground. "Clandestine commandos," as they were called, undertook sporadic attacks on police and banks and intense sectarian confrontations among themselves.[76] The police, meanwhile, recruited groups of neighborhood toughs into a terror squad called the Anti-Terror and Anti-Communist Youth Front of the Reformista Party. In exchange for freedom from arrest and other payments, these youngsters attacked opponents of the regime in schools, social clubs, unions, newspaper offices, and especially on the streets of marginal and popular neighborhoods where the police themselves had little control. When human rights groups criticized the policy, Balaguer denied the group existed, then denied any government responsibility for them. They were *incontrolables* (out-of-control elements), and in any event the terror in the barrios was the fault of delinquents and terrorists on the left. Still, no one was fooled; these gangs attacked opponents of the regime and enjoyed the protection of the police. Dominicans called the group the Banda Colorá (Red Gang), in reference to their loyalty to Balaguer's Red Party. Even friends of the Balaguer government, like Father Ignacio in Cristo Rey, lifted their voices in protest over the regular mistreatment of neighborhood youth.[77]

With the open repression of most kinds of social organization in the barrios, simmering neighborhood opposition to the regime and the simple desire for sociability both found refuge in neighborhood-based "cultural and sporting clubs." In the most radical neighborhoods, these clubs began to appear almost as soon as the U.S. troops withdrew. In María Auxiliadora, for instance, young revolutionaries founded the Club María Trinidad Sánchez in 1966. From these early, highly politicized beginnings, the clubs spread across the Zona Norte. By the end of the 1970s, 93 percent of residents in the string of barrios closest to the river, stretching from La Zurza to Gualey, told interviewers that they knew of club activities in their neighborhoods. In the rest of the Zona Norte, club activities were interspersed with church-sponsored youth groups. The clubs' initial radicalism was largely tempered by the early 1970s, but club leadership in the barrios remained closely allied to the University Cultural Movement and, as at the university, the ostensibly apolitical defense of national culture often stood in for a broader critique of imperialism and the Balaguer regime.[78]

Whatever club members said in muffled tones, they constructed a public politics that overlapped closely with the regime's own bases for authority. This did not save them from police brutality. In May of 1971, for instance, forty members of La Banda set fire to the Club Mauricio Báez. They kidnapped a handful of club members and then delivered them to the police, who held them for questioning.[79] Still the focus on cultura rather than more explicit political struggles helped club members frame the repression in ways that could embarrass the state. In El Caliche, when the police broke up a meeting of the Club Capotillo in 1971, club members told the press that the police had disrupted a reading of verses written by Dominican founding father Juan Pablo Duarte. El Caribe reported the incident under the headline "Ideas of Duarte Are Considered 'Political Agitation.'" This was meant to embarrass Balaguer, who publicly promoted veneration of Duarte. The president himself wrote a book about the early Dominican intellectual with the understated title The Christ of Liberty. Several years later the charity organization run by his sister, Emma Balaguer, sponsored performances of a play based on Balaguer's biography in the poor neighborhoods of the capital. Many in the barrio club movement interpreted Duarte differently from Balaguer, seeing him as a revolutionary icon. But because the regime invested heavily in promoting Duarte, neighborhood activists could couch their activities as neutral celebrations of a national hero. Recounting the raid, members of the Club Capotillo described the police as "an impediment to the diffusion of national cultura."[80]

In fact, despite the undercurrent of radicalism and resistance in the clubs, the police tolerated many club activities that fit with government cultural policies promoting Roman Catholicism, Hispanism, nationalism, and public decency. In 1973, for instance, local activists in Villa Consuelo requested official permission to close off the streets of their neighborhood to "raise a cultural platform" for musical and other performances from local groups. The organizers explained that their goal was to infuse the Easter holiday with "profound and heartfelt Christianity and reflection" and to provide an alternative to the tradition of public drinking. Later that year, the leaders of the Club Cultural Federico Bermúdez, in María Auxiliadora, proposed to close the streets of their barrio for a "lyrical and cultural act" to celebrate the Día de la Raza (calling

Columbus Day the "day of the race" is a tradition across Latin America, referring to the idea of a Hispanic race forged from the meeting of the old and new worlds). Police files in the early 1970s also record dozens of requests by barrio clubs to hold *verbenas* (block parties) and *aguinaldos* (Christmas celebrations) as well as festivals in honor of Juan Pablo Duarte. Even the radicals at the Club María Trinidad Sánchez received official permission to close the streets of their neighborhood for an aguinaldo in 1973. Adopting official symbols of cultura, such as Columbus Day, Christianity, and Duarte, may merely have been strategic moves intended to preserve spaces for independent neighborhood social life. More than anything, neighborhood poets and musicians may simply have hoped for an opportunity to perform. But these efforts also reflect the ways that young activists continued to promote long-standing ideas about neighborhood cultura as a counterpoint to disorganization and corruption.[81]

Like their allies in the university, neighborhood club leaders often linked this old question of cultura and corruption to the problem of Yankee cultural penetration. They took it as an established fact that U.S. troops had introduced drugs and other aspects of counterculture into the barrios, and that U.S. intelligence agencies were intent on diffusing these corruptions still more. The clubs saw themselves, the leaders of the Club Mauricio Báez told a reporter in 1971, as the enemies of "cultural penetration, which perverts our essence as Dominicans." The clubs, they reported, "have prevented the vices of decadent societies— ye ye rhythms, hippies, etc—from soaking deeply into the Dominican youth."[82] This sometimes meant offering "healthy" alternatives to delinquency such as sports teams, folklore troops, or block parties. But in some instances, clubs imagined themselves literally defending local territory against the incursions of immorality and cultural penetration, as the commandos had defended against the incursions of Marines. Isidro Torres, then an activist in the Club Enriquillo in the neighborhood called 24 de Abril in those years remembers, "The clubs took care of those who were delinquents, for instance, those who we defined as lumpen or degenerates. . . . In our territory strange elements with connections to drugs were not likely to show themselves. If they did they learned their lesson. I remember they would be tied up, beaten, and if not later we would speak with their families. And if the family did not intervene they would have to move out of the area. That happened in many places."[83] At the Liceo Paraguay, for instance, in the spring of 1971, a group of revolutionary classmates captured a sixteen-year-old hippie, accused him of being a member of La Banda, and nearly threw him out a third-floor window.[84]

In matters of personal style, neighborhood cultural activists largely agreed with the regime they so detested. Like club members, the Dominican police (under the direction of Balaguer and his U.S. military advisers) targeted *extraños* (weirdos) and *melenuses* (longhairs) for repression. One man, a teenager in Cristo Rey in the early 1970s, laughs when asked if local club members discouraged him from using hippie styles. "No," he says, the police discouraged him. "You would be arrested if you had long hair."[85] The ideological difference between the leftists and the regime on these matters was clear. The police sought to crack down on subversion and the left on cultural penetration. But practically the difference only revealed itself in the treatment of styles gleaned from third world resistance movements: olive drab pants, black T-shirts, beards, and berets. Club activists had no problem with these styles, but the police treated them as harshly as long hair, blue jeans, and peace symbols.

Paradoxically official repression targeted at strange clothing and hairstyles ended up confirming barrio activists' suspicions that such styles belonged only to their enemies. Given special dispensation by police to mark themselves as extraños, and with little to fear from the cultural clubs, it seems the neighborhood boys who most consistently adopted hippie styles in the early 1970s were members of La Banda. A young man named Tony el Pelú (Hairy Tony), known for his unusually long hair, became the most famous leader of La Banda in the capital. In Ensanche La Fe, accounts described La Banda leaders Radhamés el Flaco (Skinny Radhamés) and Chuchi el Pelú (Hairy Chuchi) as "hippie ne'er-do-wells" and "ominous hippies." Luís Germán Frías, accused by his own parents of membership in La Banda, appeared in a newspaper photograph with an afro and wearing a T-shirt decorated with drawings of peace signs and iron crosses. It is not always clear that La Banda members identified themselves as hippies, but they seem in many instances to have adopted, brazenly, styles viewed as foreign and dangerous in the charged cultural politics of the moment. It is not clear, however, exactly what they were up to. They may have adopted imported cultural signs principally to demonstrate their power over the cultural activists in the neighborhood. Perhaps their stylistic choices were broadly representative of an emerging subculture in the barrios that played on the terrors of the middle class and flaunted the norms of cultura and buenas costumbres in the barrios. Perhaps, as cultural activists feared, they were actually largely in step with a society that increasingly saw goods from and migration to the United States as a mark of social achievement. In other words, maybe the only thing that distinguished La Banda from others in the barrios was the indiscriminate right to use controversial styles without fear of repression from the police.[86]

THE GOLDEN DOOR

The year 1965 was a watershed for Dominican settlement in New York, but not because of any relaxation in immigration policy. In fact, even as the new consulate churned out visas, even as the intervention revived anti-Yankee sentiments in some sectors in the Dominican Republic, domestic politics in the United States began to turn darkly against Latin American immigrants. Already by the 1950s powerful voices in Congress began warning that the United States was becoming a "dumping ground" for surplus Latin American populations. The most dramatic immediate effects of this antiimmigrant politics were the massive roundups and deportations of Mexican workers known as "Operation Wetback" beginning in 1954 and the end of the Bracero Program in 1964. Then in 1965, the same year that he authorized the invasion of Santo Domingo, President Lyndon Johnson made a deal with anti-immigrant legislators. He accepted a fixed limit of 120,000 immigrant visas for the Western Hemisphere in exchange for an end to national origins quotas and relaxation of limits on Europe, Asia, and Africa. This deal imposed the first numerical limit that the United States had ever placed on Latin American immigration. The new law also required all Latin Americans wishing to immigrate to obtain certification by the Department of Labor that a labor shortage existed in the region and occupation in which they proposed to work. This meant applicants needed to find an employer willing to sponsor their immigration months or years before moving to the United States, a practical impossibility for most visa seekers. Although it is often remembered only as a relaxation of immigration, the intent of the landmark immigration reform in 1965 was to restrict new Latin American immigration.[87]

Dominicans perceived this reversal as demand for visas continued to grow and the new law artificially limited the number of visas granted. By the end of 1971 the visa backlog in Santo Domingo (as in Mexico and Jamaica) had returned, now numbering more than 12,000. Regular processing for qualified candidates took more than a year and a half. But the restrictions did not bring Dominican migration to a complete halt because they exempted immediate family members of already admitted immigrants from labor certification rules. The reasons behind this provision had nothing to do with Dominicans, but it unintentionally put them, with their recent surge in settlement in the United States, in a relatively privileged position to apply for now-scarce Western Hemisphere visas. The family exemption also had the effect of magnifying the importance of the family networks that already formed the basis of Dominican international migration. While U.S. foreign policy helped to create the conditions for Dominican settlement in New York, Dominican extended kinship networks proved exceedingly resourceful and tenacious in orchestrating their own migration. Secundino Díaz, for instance, moved from San José de las Matas to New York in 1959 when a friend "arranged my trip for me," he later recalled. The friend, already in New York, helped him to get a visa, a plane ticket, an apartment, and a job at the Westbury Hotel. Then Díaz did the same for his friends. "We went on bringing relatives and helping relatives," he recalled. "I brought eight of my brothers."[88]

While some Dominican families learned how to work within the increasingly restrictive system for granting immigrant visas, others invented ways to settle in New York that undermined the control of the immigration authorities or skirted them altogether. Some Dominicans exploited the fact that the visa officers who interviewed them had too little experience with Dominican culture reliably to separate "deserving" from "undeserving" applicants based on speech or appearance.[89] Consular officials could not read the symbols of Dominican cultura, so they relied on bank statements or other documentation. Dominicans responded by creating a system of short-term borrowing, or "show money," for the visa application process. Others made a steady business out of falsification of documents.[90] These tricks usually worked best to get tourist or student visas, which were not restricted by the 1965 reforms, but Dominicans also quickly learned that immigrant visas were not strictly required for moving to New York. It was quite easy, actually, to violate the terms of a nonimmigrant visa. Once inside U.S. territory, such misdocumented migrants earned less, received few government services, and had no legal protections, but they could live and work without much complication. Despite frequent harassment of immigrant workers by authorities, widespread fear in immigrant communities, and an escalating political fervor surrounding the supposed "illegal alien" crisis of the 1970s, the INS never consistently apprehended or deported enough Dominicans to make a dent in the growing misdocumented population.[91]

Dominicans also made their way into the United States despite the new restrictions through an opportunity created, unintentionally, by the history of U.S. colonialism in Puerto Rico. For complex reasons, including an intentional policy by local politicians and U.S. officials aimed at shifting "surplus population" to the mainland, Puerto Rico already had a swift current of migration to New York City. As U.S. citizens, Puerto Ricans did not need passports or visas to enter the mainland, and by the 1960s, Puerto Ricans flew back and forth to New York in astounding numbers. Because North American eyes could not distinguish one Spanish-speaking Caribbean from another, all Dominicans had to do was get to Puerto Rico (which they did by boat or by plane). Then they simply boarded airplanes to New York, blending in as if they were Puerto Rican. In this fashion, tens of thousands of Dominicans managed to float unnoticed on the great stream of humanity between the United States and Puerto Rico.[92] By 1969 Ambassador Crimmins and U.S. Consul General McLean knew that many Dominicans were using nonimmigrant visas and other extralegal means to settle and work in New York. They complained bitterly in the Santo Domingo press that the Dominican government did not crack down on falsification of documents and other "dishonest" practices."[93]

Yet the two officials had markedly different responsibilities at their posts in Santo Domingo. The ambassador had to manage public opinion, bolster the authoritarian regime, and encourage exchange between the two countries, while the consul sought to enforce unpopular and restrictive immigration policy. Increasingly, that is, the State Department's foreign policy objectives ran counter to the immigration restrictions imposed by Congress. In 1973, as Congress considered tightening restrictions on Latin American immigration still further (by closing the family reunification loophole and setting aside a portion of Western Hemisphere visas for Canadians), State Department officials testified against the proposed measures. Barbara Watson explained that Latin American governments had come to rely on immigration to the United States as a "safety valve," a way of funneling the unemployed and other disaffected citizens out of the country. In the Caribbean, she added, many viewed the favoritism shown to Canada and Europe as a form of racial discrimination. Another State Department representative, John Hurwitch, testified that the 1965 law had already "caused us a fair amount of problems with our Latin American friends." With Allende in office in Chile and a civil war in Argentina, he warned, this was no time to alienate anticommunist Latin American allies. As Hurwitch put it, "[W]e need all the friends we can get."[94]

A few months later Hurwitch arrived in Santo Domingo as the new ambassador and met a local press corps eager to press him on the question of immigration. Many in the consulate wanted to stem the tide of illegal migration by turning down a higher proportion of nonimmigrant visa applications. But Hurwitch "winced," one staffer later remembered, whenever "gung-ho consular types talk[ed] about getting the refusal rate up."[95] In order to shut down illegal migration, the delegation would have to restrict the normal flow of travel between the two countries. That would be a serious political problem. Though the long backlogs in the early 1970s never brought a return to riots at the Visa Office, the control that the U.S. Consulate exerted over Dominicans' right to travel abroad remained a prominent sore spot in Santo Domingo. In the exercise of this power, visa officers poked into financial records, inquired about intimate family arrangements, judged applicants' honesty, and made decisions that frequently split husbands from wives and parents from children.[96] A Dominican political cartoon published in the late 1960s depicted the U.S. Consul as an ogre, standing in a doorway wielding a large wooden club. On the ground before her sat a Dominican visa applicant nursing a welt, obviously administered to his head as part of his rejection.[97] This cartoon reflected the general tenor of Dominican resentment over the power of the Visa Office. Journalists and politicians were quick to criticize any suggested crackdown on illegal migration. Though somewhat embarrassed by the growing phenomenon of illegal migration, the left-leaning editors of ¡Ahora! for instance, responded angrily when Consul McLean complained about the surge in forgeries. Given the image the United States broadcast of openness and plenty, the tricks invented by Dominicans to skirt visa restrictions were an understandable result of "our growing desperate march towards the blinding light of disenchantment, when we discover that the Golden Door . . . can also be slammed shut in anyone's face."[98]

As a result of these tensions, and a likely desire to keep the flow of unemployed and disaffected citizens moving out of the Dominican Republic, U.S. officials tacitly accepted Dominicans' efforts to skirt the new immigration restrictions. No longer able to keep up with demand for immigrant visas, consular officials provided an ever-growing supply of tourist and student visas, with the certain knowledge that many of the "tourists" intended to settle and work in New York. In fact, the number of Dominican nonimmigrant admissions to the United States peaked in the decade after the immigration reform went into effect. Between 1970 and 1978 Dominican "nonimmigrants" legally crossed into the United States a total of 1.2 million times. It is impossible to know exactly how many worked in the United States or overstayed their visas, but Dominican border guards recorded a net loss of tourists traveling to the United States each year in the decade after 1965. By the end of 1975, these losses added up to 180,000 people. The 1965 immigration reforms were a watershed, but not in the way that either liberal sponsors or antiimmigrant opponents intended. When combined with Dominican initiative and the continued imperatives of Cold War foreign policy in Santo Domingo, the new restrictions merely shifted a large portion of Dominican settlement in New York into misdocumented or undocumented status.[99]

And Take Me with You

The imperatives of U.S. foreign policy, rather than the much-heralded 1965 immigration reform, provided the opening for new migration from the Dominican Republic. Contradictions between the limits imposed by the 1965 reforms and the continued political significance of the free flow of visas in Santo Domingo helped, then, to create a second flow of misdocumented migrants. Yet it would overstate the case to say that the U.S. government planned Dominican migration for its own strategic purposes. From an ethical standpoint, the White House and the State Department were certainly capable of this kind of manipulation in pursuit of perceived national interests. But the evidence from the 1960s rather points to a tale that has become familiar to historians of colonialism, of the long-term unintended consequences of decisions made by colonial "men on the spot" in the course of crisis management.[100] Dominicans themselves, consciously or not, put pressure on the United States to open the gates and keep them open. The unequal relationship with the United States made travel to the United States the only option. But the logic of that relationship offered them the leverage they needed to press the issue, to make claims against the United States. Gradually, unintentionally, the management of a crisis on the periphery of the imperial system led to a shift in the relationship between the United States and the Dominican Republic, a profound, if at first little-noticed, transformation at its heart: the Dominicanization of neighborhoods in the Empire City.

That applicants looking for permission to move to the United States would join with crowds chanting "Yankee, go home!" and other anti-imperialist slogans, and that these demonstrations would inaugurate a massive settlement of Dominicans in New York shows the deep irony of the relationship between imperialism and migration. The only place for many Dominicans to go, and the place many preferred to go, was a country deeply implicated in the sustenance of an oppressive regime in the Dominican Republic. The flow of migrants to the United States therefore coincided with a resurgent nationalist movement intent on stanching the flow of commercial and cultural influences from the United States. Ambassador Martin did not see this as irony, but rather as a form of hypocrisy among the antiimperialists and a mark of the shallowness of anti-Yankee feelings. Likewise, U.S. Embassy officials weathering the storm of anti-Yankee protests during the long summer of 1965 found comfort in the lines of applicants outside the Visa Office. The embassy wrote triumphantly in a cable to Washington that the fighting between neighborhood commandos and U.S. Marines seemed to have no impact on the views of visa applicants. "USA STILL 'LAND OF PROMISE' HERE."[101]

In a sense, the embassy officials were right; the stream of hopeful migrants reflected Washington's astounding success in tying the ambitions of everyday Dominicans to the attractions of the U.S. system.

Nevertheless, given the difficulty of bare survival in Santo Domingo in the early 1960s, the opportunities for work in the United States, and the lack of alternatives, there was nothing hypocritical about Dominicans feeling both anger at the United States and desperation to get there. Without hypocrisy, Dominican visa seekers could angrily blame the United States for its contribution to the crisis in the Dominican Republic and still understand that moving to the United States was an opportunity for salvation. Faced with the reluctance of the United States to provide visas, and aware of the power that any threat of anti-Americanism lent a demand, they could lead a riot against the very nation they wished to join. They could use U.S. visas to escape repression at the hands of police trained by the United States. And they could imagine themselves as exiles, although they did not migrate for political reasons and lived together with thousands of economic refugees. A bit of graffiti that appeared in Santo Domingo in these years expressed the predicament. To the slogan "!Fuera Yanqui!" someone added the phrase "y llévame contigo!" Yankee go home, it read, and take me with you![102] This tension explains much about the immigrant identities and ethnic politics that Dominicans would later create in the United States.

The success of the demonstrations outside the Visa Office and the subsequent reluctance of Ambassador Hurwitch to enforce immigration restrictions show the susceptibility of a U.S. imperial regime, predicated on the ideology of friendship, to certain kinds of demands. Just as oppressed citizens of the United States have often used the idea of citizenship to demand redress, oppressed subjects of the United States used the theories of U.S. friendship and global leadership to demand other forms of redress. Ironically, the United States, no historic friend of social advancement or political power for the Dominican poor, became a place for unprecedented social mobility and even for a measure of democracy. Representatives of the U.S. government opened the doors to Dominicans as part of an attempt to control politics in Santo Domingo. But if anything, the massive, largely unanticipated, and difficult-to-contain flood of Dominicans into New York shows just how difficult the prospect of imperial control was in the Dominican Republic.

If imperialism, with all its twists and turns, helps explain the origins of Dominican settlement in New York, it must also be understood as a crucial context for that experience. The clumsy and often cynical meddling of the United States helped create a wave of cultural activism in the Dominican Republic even as it opened the door for Dominicans to travel to the United States. The counterpoint between imperialism and antiimperialism helped sharpen Dominican views about cultural encounters with the United States just as Dominicans began creating new hybrid cultures in New York. The influence of U.S. culture on young

Dominicans became a matter of grave import, and considerable controversy, at precisely the moment when the migration of people to the United States emerged as a new social reality. Dominicans therefore inevitably interpreted their migration and acculturation in New York in terms of the cultural struggles—involving questions of class status, civil behavior, and national belonging—already under way. Political exiles and radical youngsters "taken along" by immigrant parents would play a crucial role in injecting this notion of cultura into ethnic politics in New York. And Dominican intellectuals in Santo Domingo would find it all too easy to fit the phenomenon of migration into their narrative of a social revolution undone by the unhappy fondness poor Dominicans had for the United States.

Migration to the city of Santo Domingo forced Dominicans to contend with who they were and where they belonged in certain ways. Were they campesinos or *capitaleños*? Were they part of the modern city or marginal to it? Were they decent humble folks or promiscuous, illegal tígueres? In the 1960s, the renewed experience of imperialism changed the terms of the question of who belonged where, resurrecting the idea of an impermeable wall between what was Dominican and what was the United States. This reconfiguration of the idea of cultura would pose a challenge for Dominicans who began traveling to New York seeking progreso in the 1960s. But this proved only half of the challenge in New York. For when New Yorkers asked the question "What are you?" in their own direct fashion, they meant something completely different. In New York this question had little to do with the divide between rural and urban, backward and modern, or colonizer and colonized. It had everything to do with racial and ethnic definition, something Dominicans did not discuss much in the barrios of Santo Domingo, but that dominated the politics of belonging in the neighborhoods of New York at the moment Dominicans arrived there.

FIVE

Hispanic, Whatever That's Supposed to Mean

DURING THE FIRST CENTURY of Dominican independence, businessmen, political representatives, soldiers, goods, and media images from the United States regularly crossed the border into the Dominican Republic. Then, in the political turmoil after the death of Trujillo, the border gates swung open in the other direction. Over the following decade, more than one hundred thousand Dominicans filed through the Visa Office, rode the escalators to baggage claim at John F. Kennedy Airport, and settled in a handful of neighborhoods in Manhattan and Queens. In so doing, they transplanted the long encounter between the two societies, in large part, from Dominican to U.S. soil. Dominican ideas of urban life and belonging in the modern world, ideas that had been fashioned in the shadow of the United States, would be transformed by a new experience of living inside the United States. But, most accounts agree, Dominicans first arrived in New York with little plan to refashion themselves into "American" ethnics. In 1969 an elderly journalist reporting on Dominican life in New York for a Santo Domingo magazine wrote that Dominican migrants dreamed of nothing but their homeland, "and long for the happy day of their return."[1]

Dominican plans to return to their native land distinguished them little from earlier generations of immigrants to the United States. Despite the common presumption that immigrants have always sought to become Americans, a great many of the foreign workers who flooded into New York City in the early decades of the twentieth century saw the city as a temporary stopover before returning to the old country, whether it was Italy, Russia, Bulgaria, Turkey, or elsewhere. Dominican migrants in the 1960s expressed similar desires to work abroad only long enough to return to the Dominican Republic with the savings to invest in a small home, a colmado (corner store), a beauty shop, or some other business. They called their settlements the *colonia,* or colony, emphasizing the relationship between colonists and their home territory. Some saw themselves as political exiles, paying dues in the Dominican opposition parties in New York until the Balaguer regime could be overthrown. Some saw themselves as "economic exiles," who had escaped from the misery and unemployment created by their government. When the regime finally changed in the Dominican Republic and new economic policies were implemented, these economic exiles would return to the Dominican Republic triumphantly, and there enjoy the fruits of their hard sacrifice. Migrant *progreso* would eventually be measured in terms of the social and political geography of Santo Domingo, not New York.[2]

Documents from the early Dominican experience in New York suggest that two ideas rarely occurred to migrant Dominicans: that they were a social group that would become a permanent fixture of Dominican social life, the "dominicanos ausentes," or that they were "domínicans" (with an accent on the second syllable, as it is pronounced in English), a new ethnic or racial minority with a permanent role in the economic, political, and social life of New York City. Yet in the years between the U.S. invasion in 1965 and the return to electoral democracy in Santo Domingo in 1978, Dominican identities and politics in New York evolved in both of these unexpected directions. Many Dominicans came to be, by the end of this period, simultaneously incorporated into both local and homeland politics. They reorganized their families, business, and culture, as well, to span the distance between New York and the Dominican Republic.[3] Despite their focus on returning home, by the late 1960s, temporary Dominican exiles and economic sojourners began to peer out at the city where they lived and to rough out their relationships with their new neighbors and with the society at large.[4] They began too to build institutions for participating in the politics and society of the Dominican Republic from abroad. Again, the simultaneous engagement with both homeland and neighborhood did not distinguish Dominicans dramatically from many earlier immigrant groups to the United States. But what was new about this process, and what has received very little study, is *how* these new migrants became New Yorkers and dominicanos ausentes in the specific contexts of the late 1960s and early 1970s.

Most dramatically, in adjusting their sense of self to this new neighborhood, Dominican migrants confronted an uncomfortable reality. Moving from the periphery of the imperial system to the center meant coming to occupy the position of a racial minority inside the United States, even for Dominicans who viewed themselves as white or mulatto, or simply Dominican. This meant confronting the differences between the racial identities they carried with them and the ones proposed to them by New York racial politics, in particular the politics that pitted black community activists against a white backlash in Washington Heights. As one Puerto Rican resident from Washington Heights observes, the outcome of this encounter was predictable in some ways and inconclusive in others. "Don't call a Dominican black. . . . He is Hispanic, whatever that's supposed to mean." Indeed, while the new migrants took many paths to local racial identities, it is fair to say that Dominicans, as a group, became New Yorkers who, while held to be racially distinct from whites, were not simply collapsed into the existing categories of African American and Puerto Rican. Dominican became a kind of person one could be, in its own right. It also became a subset of both the broader category of Hispanic (or Latino) and of the even broader category of racial minority. Judging what it meant for Dominicans to be or not to be black, to be or not to be Hispanic, to be or not to be minorities requires turning to the particulars of the city and neighborhood they settled in the late 1960s.[5]

WASHINGTON HEIGHTS, NEW YORK, 1900–1960

The first decade of mass Dominican settlement in New York did not definitively settle the complex alliances and boundaries among white, black, Puerto Rican, and Dominican New Yorkers. It was merely an early act in the drama of Dominican ethnic and racial identity, with crucial scenes played against a backdrop provided by the turbulent racial politics of the city in the late 1960s. In particular, Dominicans worked out their new status as New Yorkers in the context of the northern Manhattan neighborhood called Washington Heights, which grew into the largest Dominican settlement outside the Republic. With the benefit of hindsight, it is clear that the Dominicans settling the neighborhood were an early wave of the new migration that would return New York to its age-old status as a city of racial and ethnic multitudes. But when they arrived, the neighborhood was fully engrossed in midcentury processes that were seemingly erasing the city's immigrant origins. The exclusion of new immigration from Europe in 1924 and the participation of the U.S.-born children of immigrants in the New Deal, World War II, and the postwar economic expansion had helped transform the many foreign races catalogued by Congress in 1911 into a new, white, ethnic American middle class. At the same time, the decline of ideas about Anglo-Saxon racial superiority after the fall of Hitler had repudiated the notion of inferior Hebrew, Celtic, and Italian races and confirmed the notion of a unified Caucasian race marked by relatively mild variations in ethnicity. But the very process that consolidated a supposed Caucasian race reinforced a notion that race relations in the city were defined by the "problem" of black and Puerto Rican New Yorkers. The transformation of off-white racial multitudes into ethnic Americans left the city increasingly divided between white and nonwhite.[6]

This shift from a city of many races to a city with a white majority and two racial "minorities" reached a dramatic climax in neighborhoods like Washington Heights in the 1960s, just as Dominicans began arriving. A narrow, hilly strip of land at the northernmost tip of Manhattan, Washington Heights was the last area of undeveloped farmland and country homes on the island. When the elevated train arrived in the early twentieth century and developers first built apartment buildings there, the neighborhood became a preferred residential area for second- and third-generation Jewish and Irish families eager to move out of the old working-class sectors of the Lower East Side and Harlem. During World War II, African Americans too began moving across the border of overcrowded Harlem into neighboring Washington Heights. By 1946, nearly 60 percent of residents in southeast Washington Heights (east of what is now Jackie Robinson Park) and almost a third of residents in the southwestern corner, an area known as Hamilton Heights, were black (see map 5). By 1950, more than half of residents in Hamilton Heights were black. Black families in Washington Heights had better jobs and higher incomes than their counterparts a few blocks south and east in Harlem. They generally saw the move north and west into middle-class Washington Heights as a move up in social status.[7]

Similarly large numbers of Puerto Ricans began moving into eastern Washington Heights—an area roughly bounded by 160th Street, 190th Street, Broadway, and the Harlem River—from other city neighborhoods in the decade after the war.[8] This new influx joined the handful of Puerto Rican, Cuban, and Dominican settlers who had settled along upper Broadway in the 1930s.[9] Scattered evidence suggests that Puerto Ricans also saw the neighborhood as a space for upward mobility. A Spanish-speaking pastor, the Reverend Mr. Pérez, helped place many Puerto Rican families in apartments in Washington Heights in these years. He told interviewers in 1953, "[T]his is one of the few nice places left in the city where relatively poor people can live."[10] One longtime Puerto Rican resident of the neighborhood remembers that his parents moved the family from El Barrio (as Puerto Rican East Harlem was known) to an apartment near Riverside Drive in the 1950s for three reasons: because they wanted to get out of a slum, because they wanted to buy their own apartment, and because George Washington High School, the district school in Washington Heights, had a reputation for excellence.[11] Puerto Rican residents, like African Americans, told investigators that they saw a clear boundary line between Harlem and the higher-status Washington Heights. While white residents often saw the arrival of people of color as a shifting of neighborhood boundaries, Puerto Rican and black residents argued that the boundaries were the same and that they had crossed them.[12]

In response to the influx of black and Puerto Rican families, over the course of several decades, the Irish of Washington Heights retreated

northward, finally clustering in eastern Washington Heights and Inwood, the northernmost tip of the neighborhood, above 190th Street.
The Jews of Washington Heights moved north and west into central
Washington Heights and the relatively secluded section of Fort Washington Hill (at the northern end of Fort Washington Avenue), protected
by high bluffs and parkland from the changes taking place to the south
and east.[13] The Jews and Irish of Washington Heights interpreted the
shifting color line as a shift northward in the boundary between Harlem
and Washington Heights. They also responded to the arrival of African
Americans and Puerto Ricans of various complexions with considerable anxiety and frequent hostility. Where Irish blocks abutted newly
Puerto Rican blocks, Irish youth gangs targeted Puerto Rican children,
who formed their own gangs for self-protection and retaliation. Ethnic
attacks by children reflected widespread adult sentiments as well. In the
early 1960s, city social workers out on streets near the border between
East Washington Heights and Inwood witnessed open hostility toward
Puerto Rican kids from Irish adults as well as youth.[14] In 1953, a woman
living in the Irish areas near the border between Inwood and eastern
Washington Heights told interviewers, "Puerto Ricans are coming into
the neighborhood like cockroaches and are breeding like bedbugs."[15]

Jewish resistance to the integration of Washington Heights was often
less violent and more anguished. Through the 1940s and 1950s Jews in
New York often viewed their own racial status as whites ambivalently,
often seeing themselves as natural allies of other oppressed minorities
even as they started to accept the protections of whiteness. After a series of anti-Semitic incidents in Washington Heights during the Depression and war, in 1946 Jewish community leaders requested a study on
racial violence in the neighborhood. Two Jewish sociologists from the
City College of New York conducted the study, concluded that Jewish
children were the most frequent victims of attacks and that Jews saw
Catholics (seemingly Irish more than "Spaniards") as the primary ag-
gressors. That is, in the immediate aftermath of the war, Jews still saw
Irish Catholics as a more pressing threat, in everyday practice, than African Americans. Probably given the social pressures to be antiracist in
their own communities, Jews were also reluctant publicly to express
negative attitudes about African Americans but felt no such compunc-
tion when it came to white gentiles.[16] Nevertheless the alliance between
Jewish antiracism and African American civil rights struggles in Washington Heights often broke down around Jewish decisions to defend
their own privileges. As early as the 1930s, while Jewish civil rights organizations still fought to dismantle restrictive covenants against Jews
in city housing, many Jewish property owners in the blocks between
Amsterdam Avenue and Highbridge Park signed restrictive covenants

against black tenants. The neighborhood associations led by non-Jews had offered a share in the benefits of whiteness in the name of protecting property values, and many Jewish landlords accepted.[17] Relations also broke down when black activism or protest identified and targeted the privileges of local Jews in their struggles for equality. Jewish shop owners felt threatened both by the Harlem riots of 1935 and 1943, and by African American consumer activism such as the 1948 protest against "unscrupulous" merchants on 125th Street, 90 percent of whom were Jewish.[18]

That Jews had moved north into Washington Heights from Harlem was already a sign of the contradiction between their philosophical antiracism and their desires to enjoy the benefits of white middle-class status. Once there, they participated in a shift in city racial politics, seeing the problem increasingly as a problem of black and Puerto Rican juvenile delinquency. In 1956 the neighborhood went into an uproar over the slaying of a member of one multiracial gang by members of another multiracial gang in a fight over a stickball game. A subsequent trial of black, Puerto Rican, Dominican, and white defendants convicted all but the whites and one of the Puerto Ricans.[19] Contemporary social science, furthermore, offered a new set of theories that allowed Jewish residents to blame racial minorities for neighborhood "change" without resorting to the distasteful conventions of biological racism. Social scientists, by the early 1960s, began to describe the problem of racial minorities not in terms of innate inferiority or violence but rather in terms of the deleterious effects that race relations had on minority cultures. Racial prejudice and poverty, the theories went, distorted family relations and made black and Puerto Rican children culturally disadvantaged. That "culture of poverty" explained their difficulties in school and their presumed propensity to violence. As Puerto Rican leader Joseph Monserrat put it, "When I was raised in East Harlem, I was frequently called a 'spik.' I am now referred to as being culturally deprived, socially disadvantaged and a product of the culture of poverty."[20]

In 1963, just as the new consulate in Santo Domingo began issuing thousands of visas to new Dominican migrants, the break between black civil rights activism and Jewish community politics came to a head in Washington Heights. Hamilton Heights parents proposed desegregating neighborhood schools by busing students among the ethnic enclaves, north, south, east, and west. In 1964 Puerto Rican parents in Washington Heights joined with the African American school reformers in a one-day citywide school boycott. Black and Puerto Rican parents kept an estimated 360,000 students home from school to protest segregated and inferior schools in their neighborhoods. The boycott gave birth to an alliance between Puerto Rican and African

American civil rights activists in Washington Heights. But the school system, under pressure from white constituents, responded with weak voluntary busing programs. The bulk of Jewish residents opposed the idea. Despite continued goodwill toward civil rights measures, protecting their own children from the inferior schools in black districts and from the violence they feared at the hands of black and Latino children was paramount. As Jewish leaders successfully flexed their muscles in local politics, these expressions of white privilege, no matter how anguished, became ways to resist neighborhood change that were no less potent than the open hostility practiced at the borders between Irish and Puerto Rican blocks. [21]

Not all of the Jews in Washington Heights opposed busing. Ellen Lurie, a Jewish social worker, broke with her neighbors as they migrated toward the politics of white backlash, becoming a fiery leader in a continued alliance between radical whites and black liberation struggles. She supported desegregation in the early 1960s, sending her own children across districting lines to majority black schools. This decision served a dual purpose. It was a rejection of her neighbors' commitment to white privilege. It also allowed her to run for seats in the parent associations in mostly black schools, where she hoped to help organize black parents into a social movement. She also took a job as a parent educator and organizer at United Bronx Parents, a service agency led by Puerto Rican community activist Evelina Antonetty. Lurie kept voluminous notes and files on these efforts, now stored at the Teachers College Library Special Collections. Her papers provide invaluable insight into the dynamics of neighborhood politics in the years just before Dominicans arrived. [22]

The defeat of the desegregation movement in Washington Heights (as in the rest of New York) set the terms for conflicts that would even more violently divide the neighborhood and city along racial lines at the end of the decade. In 1966 and 1967, as the newly installed Balaguer government "cleaned up" the remnants of political opposition in Santo Domingo and many thousands made the decision to move to New York, civil rights leaders in New York gave up on desegregation (and more generally on the liberal allies who had proved so unreliable) and issued a new call for local control of neighborhood schools. This idea of community self-determination had strong roots in New York's black neighborhoods, stretching back especially to the movement led by Marcus Garvey in the 1920s. Among mainstream civil rights leaders the ideal of integration eclipsed the ideal of self-determination in the decades after World War II, but the two were always in tension. By 1966, as the desegregation movement floundered, the appeal of community control grew. If black students were going to be stuck in segregated districts, proponents reasoned, at least the educational and budgetary decisions should be made locally. This would undo the sort of "internal colonialism" that put white social service workers and teachers in tutelary positions in black neighborhoods. And it would also reverse the damage done by the new theories of cultural impoverishment, which, according to proponents of community control, subjected black children to bourgeois white cultural prejudices masquerading as universal cultural values. Furthermore, community control would allow experimental methods and minority hiring. Advocates of community control argued that traditional merit-based promotions, enshrined in teacher contracts, did not always measure competency or serve the interests of students. As Rhody McCoy, one of the leaders of the movement, put it, "If you go into your classroom with a string of Ph.D.s and all sorts of other 'qualifications' and still you're convinced that this kid is doomed by nature or by something else to lead a shrunken and curtailed life, then you're basically incompetent to teach that child."[23]

The Ford Foundation decided to fund an experiment in local control in the Ocean Hill–Brownsville section of Brooklyn in September 1967, granting a locally elected school board, with McCoy as superintendent, the same power to decide about curriculum and personnel that elected boards in comparably sized suburban districts already enjoyed. The United Federation of Teachers under the leadership of its president, Albert Shanker, opposed local control and quickly mobilized its mostly Jewish and white Catholic membership to block the experiment. UFT leadership especially objected to the forced transfer of a dozen teachers and a handful of administrators in the Ocean Hill–Brownsville school district. These union members had lost their classrooms because they had crossed the local authorities, openly voicing their opposition to community control. In the eyes of many teachers, the incident proved that the experiment was not about increasing parent involvement or improving education at all. To the contrary, it smelled suspiciously like an attempt by black power activists, with no professional credentials and a decidedly Jacobin spirit, to wrest control of the schools and expel any white teachers who disagreed with their politics. Herman Benson, a teacher and longtime civil liberties activist, described what he perceived as "a hovering atmosphere of moral and political intimidation" in many neighborhood schools. "In the mood of frustration, demagogues in and around the ghetto point to what is close at hand and make teachers the scapegoat for its ills."[24]

Quite apart from their resentment at being blamed for social inequalities that they did not create, teachers saw the questions of culture, merit, and professionalism in terms wholly different from the reformers. Many teachers had come from working-class, immigrant origins. A system of promotion based on ostensibly neutral assessments of merit was crucial to the process that had brought them to the middle class despite prejudice against their social backgrounds. This was the flip side of the emerging social science of race that had exchanged a focus on biological inferiority into a focus on cultural deviance. To white teachers, cultural accomplishment had been the tool of their success. Their own commitment to education and culture, now under attack as "white" culture, was exactly what black and Puerto Rican students ought to emulate to overcome their social disadvantage. It was the lack of, or deformation of, such culture that explained the problem of juvenile delinquency. These teachers vehemently resisted the notion that racial privilege, rather than individual effort, was responsible for their ascent. To their opponents, white teachers' belief in meritocracy and "culture" seemed a convenient cover for a widespread belief that a "culture of poverty" rather than the failure to teach was responsible for the low achievement of black and Puerto Rican students.[25]

New York's teachers, including many Jewish residents of Washington Heights, walked off the job in 1968 to protest the forced transfers in Ocean Hill–Brownsville. The seemingly irreconcilable positions of "community control" and "due process"—and a deep divide over the meaning of culture—became a weather vane aligning dozens of local conflicts over neighborhood boundaries in places like Washington Heights. President Shanker decided, Teachers Union vice president John O'Neill wrote disgustedly, "that the way to solidify his power within the union and to project himself into prominence on a national scale was to become the leader of a substantial backlash movement—the symbol of the leadership needed to contain the black thrust for a share of power."[26] The UFT leadership played up the Jew-baiting of some community control activists, seeking to tie the battle about the professional assumptions of the new Jewish middle class to an evolving fear that blacks targeted Jews in their rebellions against the broader society. Many Jewish teachers and civil rights activists broke with the UFT, working with black teachers to cross picket lines and keep the schools open. But the idea that black politics was rife with anti-Semitism and the belief that Jewish teachers were unfairly being blamed for the low motivation of black students helped many Jews to imagine a position for themselves as victims in a struggle that was confirming them as white Americans, part of the racial majority.[27]

Although participants in these conflicts did not anticipate the arrival of Dominicans (and often did not even recognize the presence of Puerto Ricans and Dominicans who already formed part of the "community"), the racial conflicts bred during the teacher's strike helped define local politics in Washington Heights for nearly a decade. In 1968, Mayor John

Lindsey created a locally elected Community School Board in the neighborhood (a test case for the local boards he would later create in all the city's neighborhoods). This was not the victory for community control that it might seem. The central School Board and United Federation of Teachers retained the basic prerogative of negotiating teacher contracts. But local boards had control over limited local hiring, districting, and budgetary decisions. The decentralization project channeled the citywide conflict that had emerged during the strike into local struggles to control a shrinking set of resources. Community control activists in Washington Heights entered the competition at a disadvantage. The new district boundary lines guaranteed a large black majority in Harlem, but removed some largely black schools and many vocal black parents from Washington Heights school politics.[28] They codified the contested northward shift of the border between Harlem and Washington Heights, to the benefit of power blocks on either side of the boundary, and weakened the voices of black parents in Washington Heights.

In the new Community School District number 6 elections, as in dozens of other mixed neighborhoods, the local UFT chapter squared off against community control activists, including Gwen Crenshaw and Ramona Morris and their handful of radical Jewish allies, including Ellen Lurie. The UFT relied on religious congregations and neighborhood civic associations quickly to mobilize the few thousand voters needed to swing local elections. The white backlash captured the very "community" institutions that were supposed to offer black activists traction in their battles with the UFT. What was more, according to opponents, the Jewish leaders who took control of Community School Board number 6 diverted funds, gerrymandered feeder patterns, created protected college-bound and honors programs, prevented public school construction near the Yeshiva elementary school, and otherwise insulated Jewish children from a widely perceived decline in city schools, and from contact with black and "Spanish" children.[29]

By the end of the 1960s, when Dominican children arrived in neighborhood schools in Washington Heights, school politics were aligned along the same racial fault lines that had emerged in the city as a whole. Yet in Washington Heights, earlier than in other city neighborhoods, the enrollment of what were known in school board documents as "other Spanish" disrupted the three-way racial division of black, white, and Puerto Rican even as it took hold.[30] First Cubans and then, much more profoundly, Dominicans reshaped the terrain of ethnicity and race in the neighborhood, and changed what it meant to be Latino in the city. Conversely, this moment in New York City history played a crucial role in shaping Dominicans' own experiments with their new role as ethnic New Yorkers. To the extent that other New Yorkers noticed newly arrived Dominicans in the early 1970s, they saw them in terms of the racial category "minorities," and the panethnic categories "Spanish" or "Hispanic," rather than viewing them in terms of what they shared with other immigrants, other Catholics, or other workers, or primarily in terms of the divides between modern and marginal, urban and rural, decent and indecent that were common in Santo Domingo. Being a racial minority meant something specific as the tide of antipoverty programs begun in the early 1960s began to recede and school elections became the central terrain for dividing up scarce resources. When New York politicians and activists first sought Dominicans out, it was to enlist them in school politics. And when Dominican activists and politicians began running for public office, it was in local school elections.[31]

LOCAL POLITICS

Finding out exactly how Dominicans first experienced this heated politics of race in the neighborhood is no easy task. Ellen Lurie's personal papers are, again, an invaluable source. In the early 1970s Lurie became convinced that the only way to unseat the UFT from the local board in Washington Heights was to build a "black-Spanish" parent coalition. Lurie's early political formation in the settlement houses of East Harlem and in Washington Heights during the remarkable 1964 school boycott, jointly organized by black and Puerto Rican parent leadership, gave her hope for the possibility of a citywide minority alliance. Yet this project ran aground, leaving her increasingly frustrated and motivating her attempts to keep a record of the movement. In September of 1972 she wrote in her diary, "[M]y one absolute self discipline this year will be to keep this record. For if I remain as cynical and down and hopeless as I am currently, I should at least record why."[32]

The drama of Lurie's attempt to document this political movement, now stored in thirty-odd boxes of unsorted documents at Columbia University, holds great value for any project on Dominican settlement in New York. It is rare to find such complete and subtle records of local political life, and still more fortunate that these records exist for the very neighborhood that would become synonymous with Dominican New York. Yet Lurie's papers provide a highly partisan window onto politics in Washington Heights. The United Federation of Teachers and allied Jewish groups were, for Lurie, absolute enemies. Only occasionally did she consider what might have motivated their politics, beyond racism. In a telling moment she once admitted that some of her black and Puerto Rican allies used anti-Semitic language that made her uncomfortable: "I'm not saying we don't deserve to be hated—I'm only recording what

I feel—I cannot make any of this public because it is all half formed thoughts—and besides some of these thoughts would betray the people and causes I believe so much in."[33] And if she granted only rare moments of insight into Jewish views contrary to her own, Irish and Greek leadership in the neighborhood is wholly absent in her documents. They are therefore underrepresented in this account, leaving the question of how much the categories "white" and "Jewish" eventually came to mean the same thing in the neighborhood unanswered.

A separate problem emerges from depending on Lurie for information about black, Puerto Rican, and Dominican politics in the neighborhood. She was a committed ally of these groups but not *one* of them. This sometimes produced wide gaps in her understanding, as when she commented that Dominican reluctance to show identity cards in order to vote in school elections was "silly!"[34] No one familiar with Dominicans' experiences with authorities in their own country and with immigration officials in the United States could have thought such a thing. Lurie also did not speak Spanish. This especially made it difficult for her to distinguish between the mostly Puerto Rican leaders with whom she negotiated and the Puerto Rican and Dominican parents whom she frequently lumped together as "Spanish." Beyond the inevitable limitations of her status as an outsider, her deep conviction that grassroots community politics was the one true politics deeply influenced her otherwise subtle insights on the problem of coalition building. In this sense, her notes on building community politics often harken back to old-school socialists who deplored ethnic differentiation in the United States because it seemed to interfere with the formation of a true working-class consciousness. From her perspective, differences among black, "Spanish," and progressive white neighbors constituted a failure. "The whites are afraid of scandal and UFT more than they are of losing elections," she wrote in frustration. "The Blacks want to win no matter how—the Sp[anish] want to screw the Blacks no matter if they lose—and none of them really knows how to work hard!" It is difficult not to root, along with Lurie, for the success of this coalition. Opportunities missed are important for social historians to recount. But the presumption that a particular kind of coalition politics is where Dominicans *ought* to have ended up seriously clouds any attempt to describe how they actually negotiated their belonging in New York given the conditions they faced.

Nevertheless, Lurie's documents are a gold mine for reconstructing the earliest episodes of Dominican political engagement with local politics in New York. In 1970 and 1971, Lurie worked with black parent activists Gwen Crenshaw and Ramona Morris to build an alliance with Latino parents Isabel Navarro, Ruth Rivera, and Helen Torres and the leaders of a loose umbrella called the Concilio Hispano. Together black and Latino parents, Puerto Rican organizations, dissident Jews, and Roman Catholic priest Tom Marino proposed a joint slate for local school board elections to oppose the UFT. Crenshaw, Morris, and Lurie also organized campaigns in Parent Association elections, school by school. Their guiding philosophy was twofold: that parents themselves should govern the schools and that black and "Spanish" parents were natural allies against the teachers union. In its efforts to recruit allies, the group attracted a few Dominicans into its ranks. Socorro Rivera, who had been part of a parent movement at a vocational school in Santo Domingo before migrating, ran for Parent Association at George Washington High School on a slate supported by Lurie and her allies. Víctor Espinoza, a Dominican civil engineer and a member of the Concilio Hispano, was president of the Dominican Parent Association at JHS 192. He was an unsuccessful candidate for Community School Board number 6 in May of 1973, on a joint Parent Association–Concilio Hispano ticket. In 1975 Dominican lawyer and community activist Víctor Espinal also ran for school board on the Parent Association slate. The Parent Association coalition was thus the political movement that propelled Rivera, Espinoza, and Espinal to become three of the first Dominican candidates for public office in New York.[35]

Still, as powerful as the logic of a minority coalition was in the wake of the teacher strike, in practice this alliance often broke down into competition and animosity between black and Spanish factions. In 1972 the Concilio Hispano and the citywide Puerto Rican Community Development Project (PRCDP) broke their ties with the Parents Association coalition and ran an "all Spanish" slate in Washington Heights. Their message was, "*Hermanos Hispanos* . . . vota por los tuyos": Hispanic brothers, vote for your own.[36] According to Lurie, the PRCDP pressured its local employee, Juana López, to abandon the Parent Association alliance and to attend rallies against black control in other city neighborhoods.[37] The PRCDP also deployed fifty or more workers from all over the city at neighborhood schools for the week before school elections, mustering real electoral power in school board elections that were decided by a few thousand votes, enough to win crucial swing seats on the board. In 1972 and 1973, the Concilio played each side of the conflict between black parents and UFT board members against the other. According to Lurie's notes, for breaking with the Parent Coalition, Concilio leader Ben García was given a key position in district bilingual programs, allowing him to distribute jobs to specific activist parents or community leaders. Another Concilio leader, Frank Nieves, himself a recent graduate of Washington Heights public schools and an accounting student at Baruch College, also received a job in the district offices.[38] In 1973, the district stripped García and Nieves of their posts, and the Concilio rejoined the Parent Association coalition, demanding that black allies accept three Puerto Rican candidates and Espinoza on the joint slate.[39]

Although the Concilio moved back and forth in its allegiance, the UFT and allied groups consistently included other Latino candidates on slates in school elections. The Cuban publisher Julián Gallastegui, for instance, ran for Parent Association president at George Washington High School in the early 1970s, leading a slate of Jewish parents. Gallastegui and his allies pronounced themselves in opposition to "the tactics of violence and confrontation" that in their view characterized radical black activism (and Lurie's influence) at the school.[40] For Gallastegui, the alliance with the white backlash movement was probably heartfelt as well as strategic. His newspaper *El Tiempo* had served as a propaganda machine for two staunch defenders of law and order, Rafael Trujillo and Fulgencio Batista, in the 1950s. The case of Ramón Pedraza, a Puerto Rican factory worker and the president of Local 222 of the International Ladies Garment Workers Union, is somewhat more complicated. He won a seat on the board with the support of the Concilio in 1972, but in 1973 when Nieves and García rejoined the Parent Association slate, he ran on the UFT slate and again won a seat on the board. His campaign literature in Spanish proclaimed that teachers deserved "dignity, *respeto*, and consideration" as professionals and that "chaos should disappear from the schools."[41] This was an expression of solidarity with unionized teachers as a progressive value, but it also seems to have been in tune with the sentiments of many Puerto Rican and Dominican parents. In Spanish, *respeto* is used to mean respect, public order, and rightful obedience to authority. It has a conservative and nostalgic ring, as when Dominicans lament the erosion of respeto since the death of Trujillo. Yet respeto is a deeply held value for many people from Puerto Rico and the Dominican Republic. Many parents from these backgrounds saw "order," "vigilance" and "respeto" as the most important qualities for judging a school. And they often viewed other children, particularly *morenos*, as they called African Americans, as undisciplined threats to their children.[42]

Many Dominicans, in particular, also harbored deep prejudices about African Americans that presumably influenced their view of neighborhood problems and their view of the conflict between white teachers and black parents. María Ramos, in a 1974 memoir about her family's migration to New York, complained that Dominicans propagated "a series of myths about other people." Dominicans believed that "morenos" were poor, she reported, because "they had no education" (which can be read as schooling, as it would be in English, but also as "falta de educación" or bad behavior, lack of cultura as it would be in Spanish) and because they were lazy. These stereotypes resonated with the racist stereotypes common in U.S. media, as well as the arguments of the UFT. But they may well have formed before Dominicans began moving to the United States. The U.S. origins of much of Dominican television programming and nearly all movie distribution in Santo Domingo, Armando Almánzar observed in ¡Ahora! in 1974, helped promote the idea that "North American blacks are lazy, stupid, naïve, and drug addicted pimps, murderers, and thieves."[43] Informal channels of contact between the Dominican settlement in New York and Santo Domingo brought back legends about black criminality and danger, too. In an example of the ways that racial concepts sometimes moved between the distinct racial contexts of Santo Domingo and New York, by the middle 1970s, Dominican newspapers found it easy, when reporting on the murder and robbery of a Dominican woman in New York, to assert offhandedly that the culprit was "presumably a black man."[44]

That is, despite Lurie's disappointment in Pedraza and Gallastegui because they did not stand up for the "community" when these leaders allied with the UFT, they were not necessarily out of tune with the perceptions of a large portion of the Puerto Rican and Dominican grassroots. Lurie and her allies saw the board members supported by UFT as absolute enemies with whom there could be no compromise, but there is no reason why Puerto Rican and Dominican leadership should have shared this view. A "Spanish parent" named Gloria Rodríguez wrote a letter to this effect in the local newspaper Heights-Inwood in 1975. When black leaders deployed the concept of community, she wrote, they really meant themselves: unity was a polite way of saying Puerto Rican support for a black movement and black control. The attacks against "Spanish" UFT candidates, she complained, were the work of "three or four black parents filibustering the meeting to form a coalition, or to better put it, to use the names and integrity of the Spanish candidates to obtain a majority in next May's election."[45]

Nor was it always obvious that there was room in the community control movement for Latinos to participate on their own terms, rather than simply as supporters of a "community" politics that had already been defined by black activists. Lurie herself noticed the ways that the movement she supported could be inhospitable to the Latino allies it needed to recruit. In one instance she commented in her journal on the prejudices she heard black allies express against Latinos, which worried her just like the racism she saw among Jewish neighbors. In 1971, Lurie wondered, "[D]o jews think all blacks are welfare? do blacks think all spanish are welfare?"[46] Lurie also described a painful episode in July of 1972, when three "Spanish" parents accompanied a group of fifteen black parents downtown to testify against the Washington Heights

School Board. The Spanish contingent, including a Mexican woman named Isabel Navarro who would later become a local board member, testified particularly to the fact that the board did not provide translation at the meetings. Inclusion of their language into local schooling and school politics, they argued, was a crucial civil rights issue. When the group stopped for dinner at a restaurant in Chinatown they were told by a Chinese-speaking waitress that there was no room for a party of eighteen. One of the black parents suspected a racial slight. "This is America," she snapped at the waitress. "You'd better speak English if you want to have anything to do with us."

To Lurie, this was merely a depressing obstacle to solidarity. "It is a long struggle," she remarked.[47] But this kind of nativism made sense given that black activists were engaged in a long fight for full recognition of their citizenship. That new immigrants would come quickly to own businesses, and would then seemingly deny services to black citizens based on their race, was understandably a source of unease for black participants in any minority coalition. Dominicans and Asian Americans, like Irish, Jews, and Puerto Ricans before them, sometimes attempted to assert distance between themselves and blacks as a way of avoiding exclusion. Rather than attack racism, they deflected it. Likewise, African Americans sometimes made the claim to citizenship, language, and nativity a way of claiming to belong at the expense of foreigners. Still, if the outburst is understandable, one can only imagine what Puerto Rican and Dominican allies made of it.

African American parent activists also sometimes sacrificed the ideal of a minority coalition to assert their own power, in some instances to protect their own gains specifically against the threat of growing Latino power. According to Lurie's notes, in 1972, just as the Concilio Hispano made deals with the UFT to gain control over districtwide bilingual programs, black parents in Washington Heights flexed their muscles in local Parent Associations. At PS 192, where nearly half of students were reported as "other Spanish" in 1970 (along with 25 percent U.S. black and 22 percent Puerto Rican), the hiring of Alex Rodríguez, a Puerto Rican principal with ties to the UFT, motivated black parents to consolidate their control over the Parent Association. They then maintained control through a bureaucratic election process and a system of dues that, Rodríguez complained, amounted to a poll tax.[48] At JHS 143 (30 percent U.S. black, 22 percent Puerto Rican, 25 percent "other Spanish," and 20 percent "other"), the principal blocked proposals by Lurie and others to hold a parent meeting in Spanish, for fear of angering mobilized black parents.[49] At PS 128 (35 percent U.S. black, 18 percent Puerto Rican, and 38 percent "other Spanish"), the all-black Parent Association, including Gwen Crenshaw, sought to exert "community" control over the selection of a new principal in 1971. A group of Spanish parents argued that new Parent Association elections should be held first, but the standing leadership pointed to bylaws and election rules to defend their position. In the midst of the controversy, serious budget cuts hit the school. Bilingual programs took the hardest blow. Rumors started that the black members of the parent association were responsible for getting rid of Spanish-speaking staff.[50]

It is quite possible, as Crenshaw, Lurie, and their allies asserted, that white members of the school board consciously created competition between programs serving black and Latino students in order to spark this kind of dissension. In fact this strategy seems to have reached the highest levels of government in the early 1970s. The Nixon White House instituted bilingual education, despite its general resistance to civil rights programs, precisely in order to peel Latinos away from black social movements. Nonetheless it would be a grave underestimation of the intellectual and political capacities of black and Latino factions in local schools to imagine that white politicians planned and controlled all their disagreements.[51] What seems clear is that neighborhood parents and school administrators all understood that dollars could be targeted either to bilingual programs, serving Spanish-speaking students and likely to hire Puerto Rican or Dominican staff, or to traditional antipoverty programs, targeted at black students and likely to hire black staff. Parent Associations were crucial in determining where these marginal resources would go, and Parent Association officers were the most likely to be hired as paraprofessionals to work in these programs. The new system of local control over scarce resources raised the stakes for leaders to mobilize group identities, black against Spanish and Spanish against black. The structure of rewards for ethnic leadership left little reason to encourage ideas of belonging in which categories of Dominican-ness and blackness were fluid, or overlapping.

What Are You?

That Dominicans arrived in New York as the city increasingly saw itself divided between black and white and as the structure of neighborhood politics revitalized the boundaries between black and Spanish provides a window into the complicated question of exactly where Dominicans fit in New York's racial landscape. In an important essay written in the 1980s historian Frank Moya Pons argues that experiences of racism and "contact with blacks and other minorities" in the United States caused Dominicans to "discover their black roots."[52] Indeed, by the year 2000, some 10 percent of Dominicans reported their race as black on the U.S.

census, and they were considerably more likely to do so if they lived in New York than in the rest of the country. This figure likely reflects some persons who are children of "one Dominican" and "one black" parent (and who nevertheless still see those as distinct social categories). But it is also likely the reflection of lived experiences of blackness, in New York as well as the Dominican Republic. One Dominican informant told a researcher, for instance, that he chose to consider himself black because "when they beat me up they call me a nigger, not a spic." It makes little sense to see a changing racial self-concept as an awakening to an underlying racial reality, since Dominicans were not "really" any race outside the social contexts that define racial identity. Some Dominicans adopted new racial identities in New York that reflected the *social* realities they perceived there, especially the racism they experienced and the potentially liberatory celebration of black as beautiful. Nonetheless, as Silvio Torres-Saillant notes, most Dominicans, like many Mexican Americans, Puerto Ricans, and Cubans, remained profoundly ambivalent toward the prospect that their national or ethnic identities marked a racial difference in the United States. For each of these groups the category Hispanic has sometimes seemed to offer an escape, an ethnicity rather than a race, and a clear alternative to being black. Indeed, although Dominicans generally recognized that many in the United States perceived them as black, on both the 1990 and 2000 censuses, nine out of ten Dominicans in the United States reported themselves as either "white" or "some other race," most frequently Dominican or Hispanic. In other words, "Don't call a Dominican black. . . . He is Hispanic, whatever that's supposed to mean."[53]

Structures of neighborhood ethnic politics encouraged the deployment of Hispanic as an alternative to blackness. But at the same time, tensions over Dominicans' reluctance to identify as black probably help explain some of the conflicts within minority coalitions. In the United States, the radical affirmation of blackness and a deep skepticism of categories such as mulatto and practices such as "passing" were crucial elements of the politics of black liberation by the late 1960s. Looking black without thinking black was a serious offense. A movement with this kind of assumption at its core was not likely to attract Dominicans who, among themselves, did not imagine distinct racial communities, recognized intermediate color categories such as indio and trigueño, celebrated light skin and Spanish cultura, and associated blackness with ugliness. By the same token, if Dominican discussions of color were ever translated, they would likely have offended and alienated black neighbors and spoiled the possibility of coalition. African American leaders were also understandably sensitive to the possibility that Latinos, like Jews and Irish before them, would seek to improve their own social status by joining in a movement of racial backlash against blacks. Perhaps all of these elements were in play when Eric Illidge, a black community leader in Washington Heights and sometime candidate for school board, explained the basic problem he had with the Spanish (in this case Puerto Rican) leadership to Ellen Lurie. He "had to get it off his chest," she wrote in her journal after the two drove home together from a fractious meeting in 1972. "They think they're white!!"[54]

Yet for Dominicans, being Hispanic was more than a simple effort not to be black. It was also a complicated negotiation about the relationship between Dominicans and Puerto Ricans. Dominicans arrived in New York with a notion of their own Hispanic national identity already intact. Hispanism in Santo Domingo encompassed class, cultural, and racial distinctions from both Haiti and Anglo-America. It is easy to see how this notion could be turned into a tool for simultaneous differentiation from whites *and* blacks in the United States. But if in Santo Domingo being Hispanic meant an abstract affiliation with Spain and an abstract unity with the rest of Latin America, in New York it meant close practical association with Puerto Ricans. In fact the idea of *Hispano* took on meaning in Washington Heights specifically when leaders sought to mobilize concerted political action including both Dominicans and Puerto Ricans. The message "*Hermanos Hispanos,* vote for your own," offered by Concilio Hispano candidates in the 1973 school board elections, would have made little difference in neighborhoods without a growing Dominican population. There Puerto Rican leaders, if similarly reluctant to recognize the centrality of sisters and mothers in the school movement, would simply have appealed for Puerto Rican *hermanos* to vote for their own.[55]

Social and familial ties between Dominicans and Puerto Ricans helped in the political mobilization of Hispano unity. Leonardo Tapia, president of the Club Deportivo Dominicano and a resident of New York since the early 1960s, remembers that Puerto Ricans were the group that Dominicans most depended on in New York before they had institutions of their own. He describes, in particular, institutions like the one he presided over: softball leagues, dance halls, and other precursors to the Dominican social clubs.[56] Puerto Ricans and Dominicans also formed family alliances with each other far more frequently than with any other ethnoracial group in New York. In 1975 about 20 percent of Dominican brides and 25 percent of Dominican grooms who got married in New York married Puerto Ricans. By 1991, those proportions had risen to 34 percent of Dominican grooms and 28 percent of brides. Meanwhile, very few Puerto Ricans *or* Dominicans married New Yorkers of other Latin American origin, and even fewer married non-Latino New Yorkers. In this sense, when Dominicans acculturated in New York, they did so in large part by sharing the social space and the fate of Puerto Rican neighbors.[57]

Yet as the categories of Puerto Rican and Dominican began to blend into a single category variously called Spanish, Hispanic, Hispano, Latin, or Latino, attempts to assert clear boundaries between the two groups became central to defining what it meant to be Dominican in New York. A group of American Civil Liberties Union observers reported a telling incident at George Washington High School in 1969. A security guard called out to a student, "Hey, Rican, come over here." When the student replied, "I'm not Puerto Rican, I'm Dominican," the guard told him, "You're all spics to me, boy."[58] This dialogue seems a bit too well scripted to be taken literally. But, as a part of a political indictment of the school administration, it was likely intended as a parable reflecting both anti-Hispanic prejudice *and* insensitivity to Dominican distinctiveness, both of which, the observers noted, bothered Dominican students. The episode also highlights the most problematic aspect of answering "Hispanic" when asked the inevitable question "What are you?" Being Hispanic might help you escape the social prejudice associated with being black, but in exchange it exposed you to the social prejudice associated with being Puerto Rican.

Often the key signs of distinction between Dominican and Puerto Rican were obvious to Latinos themselves but too subtle for other New Yorkers. This is the case with the plate lunch of meat, rice, beans, and plantains known tellingly as the "Dominican flag," and the perpetual competition between salsa and merengue dance music on the radio. Meat, rice, beans, and plantains are also eaten in Puerto Rico, but the color of the beans and the seasoning of the meat and rice are different. Salsa and merengue both sound like "Latin" dance music to unsophisticated listeners, but the lyrics, the rhythms, and the dance steps are quite different. Dominican and Puerto Rican linguistic practices are also different in ways that are obvious to speakers themselves, but elusive to English speakers and even to many Spanish speakers from other parts of Latin America. Such contrasts, while seemingly trivial to outsiders, could provide important cleavages in the idea of a single Hispano community in Washington Heights.

Beyond this constellation of cultural distinctions, the relationship to U.S. colonialism and citizenship were the crucial symbols that many Dominicans used to distinguish themselves from Puerto Ricans. The flag, shield, and constitution of the Dominican Republic, and most especially the 1965 uprising and the commandos' stand against U.S. Marines, served as symbols that Dominicans were nationalists and fiercely resistant to U.S. imperialism. By contrast Dominicans often represented Puerto Ricans as passive before the political and cultural forces of Americanization. Even as many Dominicans pretended to be Puerto Rican in order to enter the United States, some Dominicans told demeaning stories about Puerto Ricans, who "have no flag, have no country."[59] In this sense ethnic difference among Latinos in New York was intimately linked to the political geography of the Caribbean. Different histories of colonization provided the basis for social differentiation as ethnic New Yorkers. (The Cubans in the neighborhood also fit into this system, viewed by other groups as upper-class exiles and anticommunists, favored by U.S. immigration officials.)

Dominican attempts to dissociate their own identities from Puerto Rican–ness also responded to the low status of Puerto Ricans in New York. The challenge was not simply to distinguish Dominican food from Puerto Rican food, or Dominican nationhood from Puerto Rican colonization; it was to avoid becoming a "spic." By the early 1970s, this meant distinguishing oneself from the supposed Puerto Rican culture of poverty. In 1971, Ubi Rivas, a Dominican social worker in New York, informed reading audiences in Santo Domingo that he had the "honor" to report that Dominicans did not accept welfare. This, he pointed out, distinguished Dominicans from Puerto Ricans, "who most of the time are irresponsible, using the slightest ache or pain to excuse themselves from work and request that they be placed on the long list of those who beg for the charity of the state." Nor were Dominicans, whom he described as humble people of rural origins, drug users—rather, their colony in New York was "distinguished by healthy living."[60] Spokesmen from the Partido Revolucionario Dominicano in New York told the *New York Times* that since Dominicans were not citizens, and therefore not eligible for public assistance, they were "harder working and more serious than Puerto Ricans."[61] Vilma Weisz, a sociology student in Santo Domingo, conducted fieldwork in New York in the early 1970s. Eager to defend the nation against imperial penetration, Weisz expressed horror that Dominicans pretended to be Puerto Rican to enter the United States. She feared that they might, like the Puerto Ricans, be corrupted by their interactions with the United States, growing lazy, welfare dependent, drug addicted, and, in the case of young women, sexually careless.[62] Here the ideas of some Dominicans about their own national integrity (symbolized by the honest, if simple, campesino) and about Puerto Rican passivity in the face of imperialism resonated with U.S. social scientists' characterization of Puerto Ricans' supposedly failed experience of assimilation. The lack of cultura, compounded by imperial cultural penetration, translated literally into a "culture of poverty."

For their part, many Puerto Ricans made their own distinctions between themselves and Dominicans, especially when faced with the problem of Dominicans passing for Puerto Ricans. These distinctions operated simultaneously in New York and in working-class districts of San Juan, where Dominican migrants also began to settle in these years. Ethnic jokes and the popular press in Puerto Rico represented Dominicans as physically darker, illegal, foreign, and criminal, assigning Dominicans many of the same prejudicial stereotypes that had long been deployed against black Puerto Ricans.[63] Puerto Rican nationalist author Magalí García-Ramis, for instance, described a Dominican "who passed for a Puerto Rican and was able to seek a better life," as having "caramel colored, Puerto Rican, skin," revealing a generalized assumption that Puerto Rican identity was related to light brown color and that Dominicans were usually darker. To appear Puerto Rican, the vignette further explained, the man had to learn to speak like a Puerto Rican, and even to walk differently. Dominicans, the narrator noted, walk straight up and down, as if they have "sticks up their asses," but Puerto Ricans walk in a relaxed fashion, which in her estimation derived from "not living in a Republic," from being colonized.[64]

Puerto Rican community leaders in New York also sometimes sought to distinguish between deserving Puerto Ricans and undeserving Dominicans. In New York in 1971, a group of Puerto Rican leaders from Upper Manhattan and the Bronx complained to the mayor's task force on immigration that illegal Dominicans, with forged Puerto Rican documents, were undercutting Puerto Ricans economically and committing crimes for which the law-abiding Puerto Rican community was being blamed. Then, when the *New York Daily News* published a deeply offensive exposé on "illegal aliens" in New York, the Puerto Rican leaders contributed harsh testimony against Dominican newcomers. Luis Suárez, of the Upper Columbus Avenue Community Association, argued that Puerto Ricans in New York were mostly mainland-born and upwardly mobile. He said, "because of the influx of illegal aliens, crime is on the upturn. . . . But it is not the Puerto Rican citizens of New York who are responsible."[65] In their simultaneous efforts to avoid exclusion, some Dominicans relied on an image of Puerto Rican citizens racialized as lazy and welfare dependent. Some Puerto Ricans deployed an image of Dominicans as illegal aliens, racialized as criminal and foreign.[66]

If these sorts of generalized distinctions were a countercurrent to the mobilization of Hispanic unity, the parochialism of individual members of Puerto Rican and Dominican leadership also frequently disrupted coalition building. At the same time that Puerto Rican leaders in Washington Heights appealed to "hermanos Hispanos," the Concilio Hispano pressured Juana López, an employee at the Puerto Rican Family Institute in Washington Heights, not to work on "programs for Dominican kids."[67] Parochial tensions also flared up in crucial symbolic moments. Dominicans were not allowed to create their own float in the annual Puerto Rican Day Parade in the early 1970s (though a Dominican choreographer helped to produce the Club Ponceño float).[68] When a group of Dominicans displayed their flag at one Puerto Rican Day Parade in Boston in the early 1970s, the gesture sparked a violent confrontation between Puerto Ricans and Dominicans.[69] In New York, in the early 1970s, Dominicans participated in a broader Hispanic Day Parade and "Dia de la Raza" parades, in distinction with the Puerto Rican parade and in reflection of the Hispanism many had celebrated on the island. Finally, in the early 1980s, Dominicans began their own parade. These parades were crucial symbols of ethnic difference designed for the consumption of the city as a whole, understandable in ways that distinctions of food, music, and speech were not.

Hispanic coalitions were both elements of and alternatives to broader minority coalitions, imbued with tensions over just how much the categories Hispanic and black overlapped. Likewise, Dominican ethnic politics emerged both as an element of Hispanic politics and an alternative to it, imbued with tensions over the difference between Dominicans and Puerto Ricans. Just as they organized their own parades, Dominican leaders also began organizing their own efforts to win school elections as a way of asserting Dominican power rather than simply supporting broader minority or Hispanic coalitions. At the local level, Víctor Espinoza had already claimed the presidency of the "Dominican Parents Association" at JHS 153 (where Dominicans were already the biggest group of students) when he joined the Concilio Hispano in 1972. By the late 1970s Dominican parents, under the leadership of Rafael Estévez, won outright control of the Parent Association at IS 132.[70] Similar movements at several neighborhood schools, in turn, helped propel the election of Dominican schoolteacher Guillermo Linares to Community School Board number 6. Although his political formation came largely in the context of a minority coalition and Latino unity politics at City College, Linares became a leader in a Dominican power movement. He then helped lead a movement to create a majority Dominican city council district in Washington Heights and won the seat, becoming the first Dominican city council member.[71]

ANTIIMPERIALISTS IN THE EMPIRE CITY

Some Dominicans entered the fray of school elections and sought to define community politics in what was becoming a majority Dominican neighborhood. But in the early years of the 1970s, ethnic and racial boundaries in Washington Heights, and the dangers associated with

becoming a minority, provided dubious attractions to all but a few
Dominicans. Dominicans' plans to return home and the symbolic opposition between Dominican nationalism and U.S. imperialism also
helped to push the center of Dominican politics in Washington Heights
away from questions of local schooling. Whatever was transpiring in
the streets, schools, and community meetings of Washington Heights
seemed a distant reality to many Dominicans, who, by contrast, felt
deeply immersed in daily events in Santo Domingo. The Partido Revolucionario Dominicano (PRD) particularly infused the Dominican colonia with the sentiments of an opposition faction exiled by Balaguer's
authoritarian regime.[72] This pattern stretched back several decades.
Many of the exiles who had escaped Santo Domingo in the final years
of the Trujillo regime settled in New York. Then after the coup deposed
PRD president Juan Bosch in 1963, and especially after the defeat of
the Constitutionalists at the hands of the U.S. Marines in 1965, the opposition again set up shop in New York. Several thousand Constitutionalist combatants made their way to the city that was the historic
home to their party. They found work in factories, taxicabs, and restaurants. Public employees and bureaucrats allied with the opposition,
and therefore shut out of Balaguer's spoils system, also joined this exile
community piecemeal as a means for economic survival.[73]

The emergence of the opposition PRD as the most active political
and social institution in the colonia shaped Dominican public life in
Washington Heights around a particular symbolism of frustrated social revolution. The PRD, for instance, organized annual celebrations
and demonstrations to commemorate the anniversary of the April 24
uprising in Santo Domingo. Each year, thousands marched up Broadway from 139th Street to the party headquarters at 159th Street, where
they chanted, debated, listened to speeches by party leaders, and even
tussled with onlookers suspected of being FBI agents. An image of the
march, published in Santo Domingo's El Nacional in 1971, shows a pha-
lanx of young Dominican women, dressed in black shirts, military pants,
cavalry hats, and ammunition belts, carrying dummy rifles against the
backdrop of upper Broadway.[74] The performances of the PRD, captured
especially well in the tableau of nubile female guerrilla fighters marching among the ragged storefronts and fire escapes of Upper Manhattan,
lent a combative flare to the project of Dominican identity in New York.
Dominicans in New York were not immigrants or minorities, the image
proclaimed—they were an active resistance against Joaquín Balaguer
and against Yankee imperialism, only temporarily displaced to the
"belly of the beast." Paraded female bodies, which had long been used
as vessels for Dominican nationalism, provided a perfect canvas for this
message in New York.[75]

FIGURE 5-1. Dominican women dressed as guerrilla fighters march along Broadway, 1971. The parade, a commemoration of the uprising of April 1965, shows the importance of Dominican antiimperialism in shaping early expressions of Dominican ethnicity in New York. (Courtesy of Publicaciones Ahora, C. por A.)

Side-by-side with the PRD, with its essentially transplanted leadership and institutional base, a scattering of left-wing Dominican parties and groups flourished in the colonia. Some of these were cells of island-based revolutionary movements reconstituted by students or labor leaders who had been deported or fled the repression of the regime since the early 1960s. But many of the most public left-wing activists were middle-class immigrants in their teens or early twenties, who were not political refugees. They were llevados, the young radicals taken along to New York when their families migrated for reasons unrelated to politics. Some were veterans of the growing revolutionary student movement in the Dominican Republic and some were not. In New York, largely under the guidance of quirky left-wing militant Ramón Bodden, these llevados became a vociferous intellectual and political elite in Washington Heights.[76]

Bodden and his cadre of young radicals first formed the Frente Unido de Revolucionarios Dominicanos (United Front of Dominican Revolutionaries), which included militants from the Movimiento Popular Dominicano (Dominican Popular Movement, MPD), the 14th of June Movement (1J4), the Dominican Communist Party (PACOREDO), and some younger members of the PRD. These radicals saw the leadership of the PRD as too moderate. They heckled when leaders like José

Francisco Peña Gómez spoke in New York, tussling with the "white guard," the PRD security committee, at demonstrations. The Frente Unido was then reborn in the early 1970s as the Comité de Defensa de los Derechos Humanos en la República Dominicana (Committee in Defense of Human Rights in the Dominican Republic), under the leadership of several Dominican high school students in Washington Heights, Bodden (still an uptown activist), a Brooklyn College student named Scherazada (Chiqui) Vicioso (now a prominent Dominican poet and intellectual), and a young middle-class woman named Dinorah Cordero (now a longtime community activist in Washington Heights). They set about organizing international public opinion against the assassinations, disappearances, and general brutality of the regime, and debating heartily the proper interpretations of Marx, Mao, Fanon, and Juan Bosch. But most notably, their constant vigils and protests in front of the Dominican Consulate and the United Nations became a familiar part of Dominican youth social life in Manhattan.[77]

These marches, debates, and vigils took place only blocks from the heated school protests and contested elections that dominated Washington Heights politics in these years, and many of the young Dominican revolutionaries attended schools in the neighborhood. But these militant groups neither required nor desired that Dominicans become involved in U.S. politics, except as critics of foreign policy, and occasionally as aggrieved victims of police or INS abuses.[78] Since they believed that the revolution back home, and the end of exile, was "just around the corner," the Frente Unido, the Comité de Defensa, and even the PRD put little or no energy into organizing around local issues in New York. In fact, in the words of one journalist, their politics called for "a patriotic attitude and conduct, the systematic rejection of that which is North American."[79] This homeland-centered politics also required skepticism about what the left increasingly saw as the formality of elections. The dubious demonstration elections that the United States had sponsored in 1966 and the fraudulent Dominican elections that followed convinced Juan Bosch and many of his admirers that formal democracy was a sham designed to prevent real social change. In the years between 1966 and 1975, the suggestion that Dominicans should participate in the electoral process in Santo Domingo was enough to elicit cries that one was an "agent of yankee imperialism."[80] The idea of participating in elections in New York was farther still from the ideals of revolutionary exiles. Calls for naturalization and forays into New York City electoral politics were met still more harshly with denunciations such as *vendepatrias* (sellout).[81]

When it came to organizing apolitical Dominican migrants in New York, as one young revolutionary in New York wrote to the Dominican

newspaper *El Nacional* in 1971, the role of the politically active left in
New York was not to encourage migrants to take on local ethnic struggles. It was rather to "go about raising the consciousness of the hundreds of thousands of Dominican residents of New York . . . so that they
will return to their humiliated and exploited homeland."[82] Left-wing
parties and young llevados distributed leaflets at subway stations and
tried to politicize the social clubs, like the Dominican Sporting Club on
173rd Street and Amsterdam Avenue, where migrants gathered to play
dominoes, organize softball leagues, participate in beauty pageants,
drink, listen to *son* or merengue, and catch up with the news from Santo
Domingo. They did their best to give institutions the kind of political
edge that Sporting and Cultural Clubs had in Santo Domingo. "Always
in the leadership of the clubs we had a representative," recalls Juan
Daniel Balcácer, a veteran of the Comité de Defensa. The job of these
activists was to "make sure, at least once a month, that there was a
discussion or something about cultura."[83] Cultura, in this version, was
an expressly nationalist tool as well as a project of uplift led by middle-
class students.

The Dominican left in New York also forged an easy alliance with the
growing local movement against U.S. foreign policy in Latin America
and Vietnam. In fact, the Dominican left enjoyed a minor celebrity status in radical circles between 1968 and 1975. A range of political group-
ings in New York, from white antiwar radicals to proponents of Black
Power, were entering a period of romance with anticolonial heroes like
Che Guevara and Ho Chi Minh and were beginning to model their own
politics on these exotic images of martial discipline and self-sacrifice.
In the late 1960s and early 1970s these revolutionaries saw Dominicans
as "third world brothers."[84] The activists in the Comité de Defensa, for
instance, mingled happily with the luminaries of the North American
left: Norman Thomas, Stokely Carmichael, and the young intellectuals
of Students for a Democratic Society and the North American Conference on Latin America (NACLA), all of whom recognized the young
Dominican radicals as veterans of an actual popular revolution for
national liberation. Dominican leftists joined demonstrations against
the war in Vietnam. They used ties with the Socialist Workers Party to
publish a newsletter called *La Trinitaria*. Their friendships with the organizers of NACLA pushed liberal North Americans into a much more
critical stance on U.S. foreign policy and helped publicize the worst
of Balaguer's human rights abuses (indeed, the 1966 elections in Santo
Domingo were the first touchstone issue for NACLA). As a result, a
full spectrum of left-wing groups, from the Young Lords to antiwar
organizations, began attending anti-Balaguer rallies and signing anti-
Balaguer petitions.[85]

In a sense, this was a form of political integration and acculturation. The Dominican immigrant left mingled with the native left in the
student movements and antiwar rallies of the city. Eventually, this alliance would lead to deeper ties between veterans of the Dominican
left and progressive student and community politics in New York, especially in the context of the student movement at City College and
other City University of New York campuses. But in the late 1960s and
early 1970s, the Dominican left generally exhibited what one Dominican author described as "a lack of a political strategy . . . based on the
concrete reality of the different sectors *among whom we work and live
in this city* [italics mine]."[86] This meant that, despite the strong thirst
for social justice among these revolutionaries and a theoretical sympathy with any group that opposed the U.S. government, they had little
interest in the kinds of neighborhood politics practiced by black and
Puerto Rican neighbors. One Dominican revolutionary who worked in
a factory in the Bronx, attended George Washington High School, and
spent his evenings in Marxist discussion groups remembers thinking
that "the Puerto Ricans at that time had levels of political consciousness far below the Dominicans, meaning that they did not have a clear
consciousness of the national question." According to the view of the
Dominican left, the black militants "also had a very localist vision of the
problem, and did not have a very international view."[87] When pressed,
the Dominican left saw itself as a sympathetic ally to black and Puerto
Rican militants in *their* local struggles for civil rights and social power.
And it accepted the support of the U.S. left in its *own* international
struggle. But the young revolutionaries did not imagine any unified local struggle about schooling and other resources in the neighborhood.
To radical Dominican leaders, Dominicans were exiles with a properly
international vision, not an ethnic constituency with a local one.

How much this small group of activists managed to instill their nationalist political vision within the much broader community of migrants is hard to judge. Yet, despite themselves, these young activists
laid the foundations for the subsequent emergence of ethnic politics
in New York. The PRD began providing basic legal services to migrants and economic assistance for needy party loyalists in New York
and mobilizing public opinion about the injustices against Dominican
New Yorkers committed by both the United States and the Balaguer
regime. In particular, PRD leaders protested antiimmigrant abuses by
the INS and police, and they pointed out the abuses of Dominican police and customs officials during the annual Christmas vacations many
New Yorkers took on the island. From Santo Domingo, party leader
José Francisco Peña Gómez argued that the rights of migrant workers
should be part of the bilateral negotiations between the United States

and the Dominican Republic. PRD leaders in Santo Domingo traveled to New York and Washington and met with Democratic members of Congress about the problem of INS abuses against Dominican New Yorkers. That is, despite the argument that the colonia was a space of temporary exile, the main institution of the Dominican opposition began to advocate for the rights of Dominicans as long-term members of both U.S. and Dominican polities.[88] Activists on the far left also eventually turned to Dominican community politics, waging the first successful campaign to put a Dominican on the community school board, working to elect a Dominican to the city council, and creating some of the first neighborhood-based assistance organizations funded by the city government.[89]

Duarte in New York

The parties of the Dominican right, especially the Reformista Party, also emerged as major centers for political mobilization in New York. Joaquín Balaguer had founded the Reformista Party (later the Social Christian Reformista Party) out of the ashes of Trujillo's Dominican Party during his exile in New York between 1962 and 1965.[90] When he returned to the island, he left behind a core of conservative, Catholic, anti-Haitian, anticommunist, and highly patriotic allies, who remained loyal to the symbols and precepts of Trujillo-era nationalism. The center of gravity of this network was the Consul General, appointed personally by the president. The consul was the de facto leader of the Reformista Party in New York and a perpetual target for opposition activists in the colonia. With help from Santo Domingo, the Reformista Party maintained social clubs and domino tables in its various headquarters and, through the consulate, created its own network for distributing charity and patronage in New York. But aside from these basic elements of party building, the Reformistas' political objectives were to defend their president from criticism and to project to a North American public a positive image of the nation as civilized, well mannered, and possessed of a high level of cultura. Whenever possible they sought to blur the two efforts, acting as if criticism of the regime was slander against the national community. With the exception of some statements on INS abuses, Reformistas, like activists on the left, resisted any notion that the Dominican colonia was a minority in the United States with specific racial and ethnic grievances. This consular politics meant mostly ignoring the social needs of Dominican neighborhoods and keeping a safe distance from the black and Puerto Rican school politics that shook the foundations of the city around them. Still, the Reformistas' symbolic projection of national cultura laid the foundations for the later evolution of ethnic or community projection in the colonia.

The Dominican Consulate in New York, while always a plum posting in the Dominican Foreign Service, grew in size and importance in direct proportion to the growing colonia. The office handled thousands of visa and passport transactions, charging fees that provided an operating budget for other services, for Reformista Party activities, and, according to critics, for the personal enrichment of consular officials.[91] It was also the consul's job to construct a public face for the Dominican Republic in New York City. Often this meant explaining to the press why it should pay no heed to the protesters who lined the streets outside the consulate denouncing human rights abuses in Santo Domingo. In 1970, for instance, Consul Quisqueya Damirón del Alba explained that the vigils outside her office were a sign that the opposition in New York was desperate because of the overwhelming popular support that Balaguer enjoyed. She claimed that there was no repression in the Dominican Republic, that only those who broke the law were punished.[92]

To project their vision of the Dominican Republic as a civilized nation, the Reformistas in and around the consulate created a small civil society in New York with the participation of professional and artistic associations and the patriotic society called the Club Juan Pablo Duarte. Often this society seemed simply a re-creation of Trujillo-era banquets. The consulate and the Club Juan Pablo Duarte hosted "lyrical and cultural" events in hotel ballrooms around the city. The Reformistas also collaborated with the world of Dominican artistic promotion to bring representatives of Dominican high culture, like classical pianist Carlos Piantini, to New York for both performances and dinner parties. They also brought commercial artists like Papa Molina, who had been the leader of one of the great official merengue orchestras of the Trujillo era. Despite its elitist trappings, this form of pageantry appealed to factory workers as well as professionals. The party rewarded loyalty with invitations to participate in these exclusive expressions of cultura. Journalists too were always on hand to ensure that the events were indeed public projections, not simply private occasions, although they reached Dominican audiences in New York and Santo Domingo much more successfully than non-Dominican New Yorkers. In this reporting, banquets could be cast as a form of patriotic politics. This idea of national cultural projection was common among Latin American consuls in New York, and was familiar to a Dominican public that knew it well from the cultural politics of the later Trujillo years.[93]

The consulate and its attendant civil society also worked with the Dominican Tourism Office, which had its own reasons for "projecting" national culture, including folklore. The Tourism Board in Santo Domingo

(Turismo) was a high-profile part of Balaguer's national development plan. Balaguer gave Turismo responsibility for fomenting an "industry without smokestacks" in the Dominican Republic. In this capacity it became, in the late 1960s, the primary governmental body attending to the promotion and marketing of Dominican popular identity.[94] In search of tourist dollars, hotels, resorts, restaurants, and even the airport were rebuilt and embellished with symbols of Dominican folk kitsch. As in much of Latin America, the concept of the "typical" was tweaked and manipulated to provide just the right balance of familiarity and exoticism for an imagined international audience. Often the results were disappointing. Manuel Mora Serrano complained in *El Nacional*, "[I]n the famous typical places they put a pair of lazy women, a skinny mule, two or three large baskets, and a pair of hats . . . and they call it typical X."[95] Turismo also helped to fund and organize carnivals, merengue festivals, parades, beauty contests, and folklore troupes. This meant support for a wide range of cultural presentations based on Dominican folklore, even some that diverged from Balaguer's own starkly negrophobic nationalism. At the Tourism Parade, held in 1969, officials awarded first prize to a group from San Pedro de Macorís who performed "las Guloyas," a Dominican dance of black West Indian origin.[96]

In New York, the Tourism Office worked with the consulate to present much the same version of Dominican popular culture to potential tourists. It organized and funded the Dominican contingent in the "Día de la Raza" (Columbus Day) Parade, a parade organized by various Latin American consulates. Photographs of the parade show white Dominican ladies marching in conservative suits, a Dominican beauty queen representing the Oficina de Turismo, dressed in "typical" clothing, and floats depicting the tourist attractions in the colonial section.[97] This was a striking symbolic contrast to the PRD's parade of young female guerrilla fighters. In the logic of the consulate, positive or alluring images of the nation, from piano concertos to pretty women to ancient buildings, were patriotic in and of themselves. But they were particularly patriotic because they would bring tourist dollars and development to the homeland. Nor were they separate from the question of where Dominicans fit in local racial categories. José Jiménez Belén, an old Trujillista journalist who socialized with the crowd at the Consulate and wrote society columns for the right-wing Spanish language newspaper *El Tiempo*, explained the national pride that he felt as a Dominican when other New Yorkers saw a photograph of a Dominican beauty queen.[98] Belén, whose own skin was dark brown, harbored no apparent irony in writing that the image of a white Dominican beauty queen proved the civilization of the island and would probably help to foment tourism.[99]

Despite the claim that Dominican cultural life in New York would attract a North American public to the beaches of the Dominican Republic, Turismo never found a significant market among non-Dominican New Yorkers. When the Dominican tourism industry finally did begin to take off a decade later, Dominican New Yorkers and Northern Europeans were the bulk of passengers arriving at national airports. But that does not mean the efforts of the Tourism Office and the consulate were trivial. Just as the new focus on outward projections of popular culture reshaped the cultural productions consumed by Dominicans on the island, in New York the parade and its successor, the Dominican Day Parade, though planned for other purposes, became fixtures of ethnic self-expression. The commercialization and promotion of Dominican culture and traditional efforts to project the Dominican Republic as a civilized and cultured nation provided resources for an emerging ethnic politics of pride and projection.

One of the key figures in this overlap was Normandía Maldonado, a dancer and choreographer who lived in the heart of the Dominican settlement on Amsterdam Avenue and 167th Street. Maldonado's father sent her to the United States from Santiago in the immediate aftermath of Trujillo's assassination. She worked for a time in a clothing factory and studied nights at George Washington High School. Still a teenager, she began an artistic career as a dancer and singer in the early 1960s in a popular music group called the Mambo Girls. She worked too as an administrator in a commercial music venue, the Teatro Colón, where Puerto Rican, Cuban, and Dominican musicians performed. But her big break as a performer came in the context of the events planned by the Consulate and the Tourism Office. Turismo needed a folklore troupe in New York and Maldonado created the Ballet Quisqueya, which would become the most consistent disseminator of Dominican folklore in New York for the next twenty-five years. Like Cassandra Damirón (whose sister, Consul Quisqueya Damirón, was Maldonado's mentor in New York politics), and like other regime-friendly folklorists on the island, Maldonado established a group that would "elevate" the folklore of the Dominican Republic. The research of anthropologist René Carrasco and others into rural dances and rhythms became the inspiration for stylized choreography.[100]

Along with Alfida Fernández, Rafael Paulino, and several others, Maldonado also helped to found the Club Juan Pablo Duarte. A patriotic society dedicated to the memory of the nineteenth-century Dominican liberal and independence leader, the Club Juan Pablo Duarte promoted the abstract symbols of Dominican nationalism, especially the popular artifacts of nationalism under Trujillo. Their activities as "Duartianos" were an extension of Balaguer's cultural politics. Balaguer, author of

FIGURE 5-2. Dominican women in the Día de la Raza parade in New York, Columbus Day, 1966. They ride on a float depicting the Alcázar de Colón, the Columbus Castle, in the Zona Colonial. The use of the landmark reflects the importance of the symbols of elite nationalism and of the emerging tourism industry in shaping early representations of Dominican ethnicity in New York. (Courtesy of Publicaciones Ahora, C. por A.)

The Christ of Liberty, donated a bronze bust of Duarte to the leadership of the Club Juan Pablo Duarte in New York. And the club made it their cause to have the statue erected along with Bolívar, Martí, San Martín, and other Latin American liberators in Central Park. Eventually, the statue was erected in a small triangle park on Canal Street at the opposite end of the Avenue of the Americas.[101]

Patriotic symbols were, to the Duartianos, of self-evident value. An editorial in the Santo Domingo newspaper *El Sol* in 1975 titled "Dominicanidad" (Dominican-ness) captures the spirit of this heartfelt commitment to patriotic abstractions. The fall of Trujillo, the editors wrote, brought a new generation who, in their rejection of Trujillismo, had begun to threaten the "nation's morale" with lack of "respeto" for "the national symbols and values." Defense of the flag, crest, and hymn would help "Dominicans recover their roots and the Republic recover the most legitimate of its hopes for *progreso* and permanence."[102] As Reformista activist and Club Juan Pablo Duarte ally Rafael Estrella put it, this kind of nationalist cultura was a "benefit to the Dominican home, a way for young people to get sustenance, to reunite with their own history."[103] As a folklorist, Maldonado's first inspiration was a joy in performance and artistic excellence. But as a founding member of the Club Juan Pablo Duarte and eventually an officer in the Reformista Party, she also believed that the good of broadcasting national folklore or culture was as self-evident as recognizing the hymn, the flag, and the Founding Father.[104]

This idea of patriotic projection, at first, had little to do with a conscious immigrant identity. But Reformista civil society eventually turned to the process of ethnic integration too, shifting the function of symbols that had served the Trujillo regime in its attempt to regulate the relationship between the state and the nation to the project of defining ethnic identity in a multiethnic city. Normandía Maldonado and many other individual activists in this group would begin to see themselves as promoters of the Dominican "community" in New York through the same means that they had promoted the Dominican nation. When they began to participate in immigrant rights activities and the Dominican Day Parade, the dances and floats were the same, but the idea was to make a showing for the Dominican community in New York. The symbols of national belonging produced by Turismo, the Club Juan Pablo Duarte, the Consulate, and the Día de la Raza Parade Committee, while political in origin, were abstract enough to be equally useful to the project of marking ethnic projection in the everyday experiences of neighborhood life. The flag, the parade, the bust of Duarte were all quickly appropriated in New York as markers of ethnic difference. In the late 1960s, Dominican teenagers began sewing small flags on their jeans, not because they favored national independence, nor because they necessarily saw the flag as a symbol of morality and national progreso, but because they tired of answering the perpetual question "What are you, black or Puerto Rican?"[105] Similarly, when social workers went into lower Washington Heights to work with street gangs, they found that the gangs displayed Dominican, Puerto Rican, or black nationalist flags at a block party organized to promote neighborhood peace.[106]

Abstract national symbols, from the flag to Juan Pablo Duarte, eventually also proved crucial to Dominican forays into local politics in Washington Heights. Under the leadership of Club Juan Pablo Duarte member Rafael Estévez, for instance, Dominican parents took over the Parent Association at PS 132 on Wadsworth Avenue in the late 1970s from the black parents who ran it. In its first act the group renamed the school after Juan Pablo Duarte.[107] This was, the nationalist symbol made abundantly clear, not a Hispanic movement, but a Dominican one. Although in the late 1960s the Reformistas never imagined contributing to a lasting ethnic identity and stood pristinely aloof from neighborhood school politics, the nationalist symbols they erected provided crucial resources for an eventual Dominican leadership that made community visibility and pride a cornerstone of their ethnic politics. And these symbols also proved quite useful to Dominican politicians who entered the fray of neighborhood struggles as competitors to black and Puerto Rican leaders.

When New Yorkers asked Dominicans, "What are you?" they sought an answer that would fit Dominicans into the racial divides they perceived in their city. Yet they did not always wait for an answer, judging for themselves based on Dominicans' color, their accents, and their class status. Migrants might have found this shocking even if it merely repositioned them to a slightly darker position on the continuum of color that underwrote Dominican ideas of white supremacy. But in New York the evolving divide between white and nonwhite was an active seismic fault, not a gradient of prejudice. This racial divide organized labor and housing markets, practices of law enforcement, and especially local politics and ideas of community. The encounter between Dominican ideas of their own racial status and other New Yorkers' ascriptions offers a fascinating example of contact and dissonance between different racial systems. Yet the evolution of Dominicans' status in New York emerged not from an abstract meeting of national racial concepts nor primarily from an interaction between Dominican migrants and mainstream, white Anglo-America. Day-to-day alliances and antagonisms with African Americans and with the category of blackness structured Dominican ethnicity in New York, as Juan Flores writes of Puerto Rican ethnicity. Day-to-day alliances and antagonisms with Puerto Ricans and with the category of Hispanidad or Latinidad further structured Dominican ethnic identity.[108] And the ongoing conflict among black, Puerto Rican, and Jewish community leaders over local resources in the neighborhood where most Dominicans lived deeply conditioned relations with each of these groups and categories.

SIX

To Have an Identity Here

EVEN WHEN CONTENTIOUS school politics held little attraction for Dominican adults, who shuttled between long hours in factories and crowded apartment blocks, their children had already entered the fray simply by attending neighborhood schools. Here, again, to the extent that separate "Dominican" and "U.S." racial systems met in New York, they did not produce a conflict between abstract national ideologies, but rather an interaction between a specific generation of Dominican youngsters and their schools. As large numbers of Dominicans began enrolling at George Washington High, for instance, they walked into the crossfire of still more conflicts over community control. Between 1968 and 1972, the sole comprehensive high school in Washington Heights was home to student rebellion, teacher intransigence, fires and vandalism, gang violence, and repeated police brutality against students. The main players in these standoffs understood them as yet another skirmish in the citywide conflict over race, a conflict into which they imagined placing Dominican teenagers and into which Dominican teenagers sometimes placed themselves. Yet if it is useful to highlight the particular and unusual ways that history unfolded at George Washington High in order to understand questions of comparative and transnational racial formations in their local contexts, the story of George Washington was nevertheless emblematic of a broader transformation in U.S. society. As politics, real estate markets, and a shifting regional economy re-shaped the metropolitan region, good schools in good (mostly white, suburban) neighborhoods became synonyms for high property values and social opportunity. And a vicious circle of fearsome reputations and troubled fates in big-city high schools helped translate the growing income gap between skilled and unskilled workers into a breach between the black and Latino "inner city" and the rest of the region. This process racialized city schools and city youth with little concern for the complex ways local teenagers erected boundaries and coalitions among their ethnic communities. By the end of the 1970s, the geographical term "inner city" referred only to a subset of the children and schools actually located in the city. It meant children who were not white and not middle class and schools that were in institutional collapse.

Schools like George Washington were thus the fulcrum of a remarkably effective response to the civil rights movement by white citizens, city governments, federal policy makers, and real estate developers. These forces allied to reconstruct segregation in both the North and South at the end of the twentieth century. The course of events at George Washington can be told as a dispiriting coda to a long, discordant symphony of race in the United States, stretching back to slavery and emancipation.[1] Yet the reshaping of schools and metropolitan space in this period was simultaneously a process of incorporating new foreign populations into city neighborhoods and the nation: a process of creating new racial minorities, not simply isolating the old ones. To be sure, the emergence of Washington Heights as a Dominican barrio was scarcely on the minds of the teachers and students who, in the early 1970s, engaged in pitched battles over questions of white and black (with Puerto Ricans often a presumed silent partner of black politics). Yet for precisely this reason, at George Washington the settlement of new immigrants became intermingled with the ongoing history of struggle over black and Puerto Rican citizenship and white privilege. There, earlier than in any other school in the city, the uneasy mix of black, Puerto Rican, and "other" (as white students were counted on school censuses) was interrupted by the new ethnic multiplicity that would become common in city schools in the rest of the century (with Dominicans and Latin Americans eventually joined by Africans, Middle Easterners, and Asians). Already by 1970 more than one in five students at the high school was listed as "other Spanish." Thirty percent were black and 24 percent were Puerto Rican.[2] Indeed, by the end of the decade, George Washington would, like Washington Heights, be a largely Dominican territory, and in the 1980s being a Dominican school would be enough to mark it as "inner city" in local understandings. The terms on which Dominicans participated in these battles, or avoided them, help in examining the contradictions of a process of ethnic definition that drew (often furious) distinctions among blacks, Dominicans, and Puerto Ricans, without slowing the evolving racial and geographical divide between white and nonwhite.

GEORGE WASHINGTON HIGH SCHOOL

Located on 196th Street, in the borderlands between East Washington Heights and Inwood, George Washington High School drew students from all of northern Manhattan and reflected the patchwork character of the area. Historically well-regarded for a strong academic program, as George Washington absorbed new migrants from the South, Harlem,

El Barrio, and the Caribbean, the school maintained pockets of excellence through a rigorous tracking system that directed academic and extracurricular resources to the few students who were prepared to take advantage of them. Administrators funneled the best of what the school had to offer into the "college bound" program. At the other end of the spectrum, in 1970 the school set up truancy classes to house the nearly eight hundred students who had missed at least 60 percent of the school days in the previous term. Truancy programs were supposed to identify and help troubled students, but an investigating team discovered that the school had no social services program for truants and did not even attempt to contact the parents of absent children, though the district provided funding for both. School administrators largely ignored the growing problem of drugs and petty crime in the school as well. In the breach between the college-bound classes and the truancy bullpens, students fended for themselves. The lucky or exceptionally motivated ones found courses, sports, art, music, and other resources still largely intact. But guidance counselors handled caseloads of nearly fifteen hundred students each. The sheer size and institutional torpor of the school made it difficult for students to enroll in specific courses, make changes on program cards, or ask questions about which courses to take. Many discovered only late in their senior years that they did not have the requirements for graduation, adequate preparation for work, or the necessary credits to apply to college. Only about 30 percent left the school with academic diplomas.[3]

Academic tracking at George Washington and in neighborhood junior high schools worked in concert with local opposition to desegregation at the elementary level to insulate and protect white students. At Junior High School 143, a feeder for George Washington located only a few blocks away, department heads addressed the "SP," or college-bound, classes on the first day of school in 1971. The mostly white students there came from protected elementary schools in the north and west of the neighborhood, and the deans warned them to beware of blacks and "Spanish" with whom they would now cross paths between classes. The department heads explained that these other students were jealous of the SP kids and would beat them up in the halls.[4] A group of about thirty black (and a few Puerto Rican) students from George Washington interviewed by researchers in 1971 saw the matter of tracking differently. They believed "that colleges were meant for only white students and that white teachers [at GW] made sure that blacks do not go to college."[5] Administrators also admitted that the tracking system provided different educational experiences to different racial groups. Referring to the influx of black and "Spanish" students at George Washington in 1970, one supervisor candidly admitted to a *Times* reporter, "Whether it's our fault or theirs, or maybe both, we don't or can't reach many of these youngsters."[6]

Still, the school continued to function well enough for enough students to remain a magnet for black, Puerto Rican, and Dominican students with high aspirations. Washington Heights was "one of the few decent places left" where poor people could live, in part because George Washington was a place where working- and middle-class people of color could send their children for education. Despite the tracking system and segregated elementary schools many blacks, Dominicans, and Puerto Ricans negotiated their way into the academic and college-bound courses. A Jewish student who graduated in those years, now a physician, recalls that while there were two separate schools, "we had everyone in academic courses."[7] Political documents of the 1960s and 1970s depicted a school scarcely functioning, with resources wholly limited to whites, but many of the black, Puerto Rican, Dominican, and Cuban graduates remember the place fondly for the quality and caring of its teachers. "Those of us in the college-bound program," recalls Miguel Franco, a Puerto Rican man who graduated in 1971 and is also now a physician, "were bonded by academic interests and race was not a factor."[8] Even though the Washington Heights school district divided up resources unfairly, some black and Latino students found meaningful opportunities to learn at George Washington. Alumni registries, although hardly representative, list many black and Latino professionals educated at the school in the late 1960s and early 1970s.

Dominican migration during the period provided the school with an especially large crop of highly motivated and often well-prepared students. Many of those moving to New York came from the mobilized Dominican lower-middle classes, for whom access to education was a cornerstone of ideologies of social advancement: progreso by means of cultura. While many Dominican families chose to push teenagers directly into the labor market or to use their labor in family business ventures, George Washington became an extension of the eager rush of the children of rural middle classes and the urban lower-middle class into the public schools and universities formerly reserved for the Dominican Republic's elite.[9] Some, but by no means all, came from private schools and public liceos in the Dominican Republic that were more academically rigorous than most New York City middle schools. Several Dominican professionals educated at George Washington in these years remember commitment to education as a shared ethnic characteristic among Dominicans who "had the most drive" and "got the most out of the experience."[10] These claims seem to confirm what sociologists call the "immigrant optimism hypothesis," that new immigrants arrive with a cultural predisposition toward learning that distinguishes them from U.S.-born "inner-city" classmates. These claims, though, should be viewed with some caution. They likely ignore the class privileges, and even the lighter skin color, of the most successful Dominican students, emphasizing instead an ostensibly uniform national attitude toward education. Such memories also probably underestimate the extent to which the school failed many Dominican immigrants, even ones eager to learn. They also reflect broader Dominican ethnic prejudices against blacks and Puerto Ricans, particularly Dominican uses of the idea of a "culture of poverty" to distinguish themselves from blacks and Puerto Ricans.

Still, there is a productive tension between seeing the reality of the ways that some Dominican students energized George Washington High School and accepting as fact a rhetoric of ethnic pride that makes Dominicans out to be worthier, harder working, and more serious than other minority groups. Apart from student memories, other evidence shows that Dominicans surprised local school officials by simply signing up for all available resources. In the summer of 1969, when Dominicans were still a little-known, relatively small group in the school, a group of well-meaning teachers and parent volunteers planned a summer enrichment program for black students with high motivation and potential but low educational achievement. The organizers planned to enroll students identified and referred by teachers. But because of a glitch in the planning, school administrators allowed student volunteers to fill the slots. Much to the surprise of the teachers, none of whom spoke Spanish, all of the volunteers were Dominican. In another episode several years later, Dominicans were the first to sign up when some teachers at JHS 143 put up sarcastic announcements advertising extracurricular activities that the school did not offer—that no struggling city school could offer: "Join our Varsity Teams, fishing, basketball, rowing, etc." According to Ellen Lurie's diary, Dominican students were the only ones who did not get the "joke." They tried to sign up for the activities.[11]

In neither case did the schools reward this eagerness to volunteer for activities. At a loss for how to teach Spanish-speaking children or even assess their grade levels, the summer school teachers "reacted that this was truly a pathetic group" and turned the class over to two neighborhood Peace Corps volunteers who taught English as a Second Language. There is something fitting in this anecdote. The school relied on two young ambassadors of U.S. foreign policy to deal with changes in the neighborhood that had, in many ways, been created by invasive U.S. foreign policy. Yet there is also something deeply discordant in the ways that well-meaning teachers related the question of race and educational motivation, especially when compared with Dominican accounts of their own high motivation. The teachers had signed on to teach students whom they believed to be deserving of their help at a time of citywide conflict between white teachers and black critics over educational values. In this context, the concern with finding the "good" black students was so strong that teachers chose not to recognize *volunteering for summer school* as evidence of high motivation among Dominicans. Reflecting on what they regarded as a total failure, organizers suggested that the program for deserving black students be attempted again the following year with a better system in place for filtering out the "pathetic" Dominicans. They neatly excluded the challenge of educating Spanish-speaking students (and black students with low motivation) from what they regarded as their central responsibility in dealing with educational inequality.[12] Like the Visa Office in Santo Domingo, George Washington High School offered Dominican students opportunities for progreso, but also frequent reminders that the Golden Door could be slammed in one's face. If, indeed, the high motivation of Dominican children began to erode as a result of their time at George Washington, this was likely due to the cold shoulder offered by the school.

Student Politics

Even as experiences in the classrooms at George Washington began to shape the lives of young Dominicans in Washington Heights, the rush of events outside classrooms provided a still more unusual context for acculturation. A few years behind the rise of student politics in the Dominican Republic, students in the United States in the late 1960s began to see themselves as actors who could protest and reshape the world around them, including their own school. In the Dominican Republic the student movement carried the banner of antigovernment protest tinged by antiimperialism and sectarian leftism. In New York, school politics first revolved around students' rights to freedom of speech and expression, the right to dress and groom themselves as they chose, the right to participate in school governance, and the right to due process in suspension cases. The Vietnam War, into which many students could expect to be drafted after graduation, and the massacres of students at Kent State and Jackson State, also mobilized student sentiments at city schools. But at George Washington, students organized the bulk of their politics around reforming the school itself. They sought to address the inequalities in the way the school treated students, to improve counseling, to make classes more relevant, and to create drug treatment programs. These issues perhaps shared more similarities with student politics in Santo Domingo than it would seem. Beneath their heartfelt radicalism, student protests at the liceos and the Universidad Autónoma de Santo Domingo often revolved around demands for increased state funding to public education to satisfy the aspirations of students themselves. Radical student politics were in large part a fight by student radicals for their own social mobility, entangled with resistance to authoritarianism and imperialism.[13] In New York, students wound almost identical calls for educational opportunity, for access to middle-class lives, into struggles for ethnic self-definition and racial liberation. As radical students confronted teachers and administrators, the school saw repeated demonstrations, wildcat teacher strikes, police occupation, severe beatings of students, and eventually riots and school closings. If the particular changes in the classrooms of George Washington in these years shaped the evolving identities of immigrant children, so too did the unique moments under way in the hallways, lobby, and cafeteria.

Like the struggles to control the local school board, the student reform movement at George Washington had its immediate roots in the teacher strike of 1968 and its deeper origins in earlier efforts to undo "de facto" segregation in the schools in Washington Heights through busing. At George Washington, dissident teachers, community activists, and a growing number of disaffected students crossed picket lines and set up classes during the strike, invoking the ire of union members. "The people who opened up" George Washington High School, reported the *New York City High School Free Press* in 1968, "were really hassled but now have 2–300 students in attendance."[14] Nearby, police arrested, handcuffed, and beat three teenagers, two Latino and one Jewish, caught trying to break into Inwood Junior High School (JHS 52) in order to allow protesters to set up alternative classes inside.[15] This incident helps show how the cleavages of the strike so profoundly divided the city as a whole. Local neighborhood activists and local teachers drew battle lines and articulated the themes of the broader struggle. They fought these issues out in the context of local schools, spaces intimately entangled with daily family life and the central aspirations of city residents: their children's success. Once inside George Washington the pro-community-control coalition spent its time in "rap sessions." These meetings then gave birth to a new harvest of antiwar groups, underground newspapers, and African American student clubs.[16]

When school reopened, the confrontations left festering resentment on both sides. On December 2, 1968, an estimated 35 percent of city students boycotted schools to protest the "make-up time" clause in the strike settlement, arguing that it was merely a ploy by teachers to avoid losing pay for missed days. Thousands of high school students took to the streets and subways, throwing rocks, breaking bottles and

FIGURE 6-1. Students and dissident teachers hold classes inside a New York City school during the teacher strike, 1968. These class meetings gave birth to dozens of student reform groups in the subsequent year. (Photograph by Bob Gomel, courtesy of Getty Images)

windows, and shouting.[17] More and more antiwar clubs and black student associations sprang up across the city, on the model of the groups founded during the strike. Hundreds of students, with the help of the New York Civil Liberties Union (NYCLU) students' rights project, began to challenge school dress codes, restrictions of freedom of speech, and unfair suspensions, articulating a cultural politics wholly imbued with new styles of dress and grooming. At George Washington, nearly five hundred girls broke the dress code in January of 1969, wearing slacks to school instead of skirts during an extended cold spell.[18] With so many students wearing political buttons, long hair, afros, and dashikis, it looked to one beleaguered New York City principal as if suddenly "everyone" was a militant.[19] Principals and teachers loyal to the union felt besieged by groups they viewed as enemies, and began preparing for an all-out war against the emerging student movement. The High School Principals' Association drafted an analysis of student protest in 1968 and 1969 calling the student movement "part deeply committed black nationalist, part alienated white liberal and part elite corps of left fascism." There was no middle ground, the principals concluded, no possible collaboration with the student radicals. Absolute unity in opposition to the student movement was a vital necessity. "To confuse confrontation politics with traditional adolescent high jinks, to identify the student protest movement as simply reformist, an expression of deeply felt aspirations and traditional youthful idealism, is either naive or perverse."[20] The Principals' Association favored singling out student troublemakers and punishing them summarily. They denounced the NYCLU, which offered legal services to students in free speech and suspension cases, as a group of "professional agitators [who] are fueling the tensions in our schools."[21]

In one respect the Principals' Association got it right: the student movement at George Washington was an odd mixture of different kinds of politics, including committed black nationalism and alienated white liberalism. By the early 1970s, remembers Russell Jacquet-Acea, a graffiti artist and activist in the school, there were white groups that became enamored of the prospect of violent guerrilla action, after the model of the Weathermen. There were also black groups that saw themselves as preparing for an inevitable racial conflict. Their attitude, Jacquet-Acea recalls, was more or less "get whitey."[22] But the major impetus of the student movement, he remembers, was precisely the reformism, deeply felt aspirations, and youthful idealism that the Principals' Association was at such pains to deny. The NYCLU and other allies of student groups made the same point. The UFT accused "militants" and "outside radicals" of encouraging violence and disruption in student protest politics and represented student activists as violent hoodlums. But the absolute recalcitrance, and frequent foul play, of administrators and many teachers also provoked disturbances (often of unknown origins), which opponents then used to discredit the protesters in the media.[23]

At first, not many Dominican students jumped into the fray at George Washington. One Dominican student laughed when asked about her memories of the 1968 strike, remembering that she got a temporary job in a swimwear factory in Chinatown until the strike was over.[24] Even the most active revolutionary Dominican intellectuals at George Washington remained aloof from the student movement there. In 1967 and 1968, for instance, a handful of Dominican students at George Washington High School, led by Luis Simó, Juan Daniel Balcácer, and Aristides Vidal organized a "study group" to read and discuss social theory, philosophy, politics, and literature and to explore the intellectual life of the city. With their sharp black turtlenecks, dark leather jackets, and lunchtime debates about Tolstoy, Camus, and Trotsky, they earned the nickname of *filósofos* (philosophers) from the other Dominican kids in the school. Outside of the school, the filósofos published *La Trinitaria*, helped to organize the Frente Unido and the Comité de Defensa, and mixed with the luminaries of the North American left. Like the broader movement that they helped to organize, the filósofos paid little attention to the strike or to the subsequent student movement at George Washington High. Though they attended the school as the conflicts unfolded, their energies were invested in the campaign against Joaquín Balaguer and in protesting U.S. foreign policy.[25]

Still, this remarkable cultural and political context corresponded nearly exactly to the period between the appearance of the first Dominican students at the school and the emergence of Dominicans as the most populous ethnic or national group in the school. When Dominican students, on the one hand absorbed by the project of progreso and on the other bursting with political energy transplanted from the student movement in the Dominican Republic, set about fitting into their adopted society, they faced the challenge of fitting into this thrilling and sometimes chaotic politics and youth culture. Some did join the student struggles. In the spring of 1969, for instance, one Dominican student found her way, almost by accident, to the heart of the new conflicts. Nelsy Aldebot was one of the well-prepared Dominican students for whom the school worked best. She spoke English and enrolled in the academic track at the school. But, she remembers, she was shocked to find that the school offered no information about graduation requirements to the friends she made in the cafeteria, mostly Dominican and Puerto Rican. Most students had no sense of what resources were available in the school. After a series of discussions around the lunch table, Nelsy and another Dominican named Virginia Roca founded an Asociación de Estudiantes Hispanoamericanos (Spanish-American Students Association). The goal of the group, she recorded in her diary in Spanish, was "to have an identity here in the United States, to demand our rights, and to prevent discrimination against Latino youth."[26] That is, these two schoolgirls decided to address the very issue that most Dominican adults on the left and the right shied away from: their status as an ethnic and racial minority. To their great surprise, the first meeting was packed with interested students. Nelsy was nominated to be president, but declined. A Puerto Rican boy with better English was elected, and Nelsy became vice president.[27]

This direct engagement with the question of an "identity here in the United States," though unusual in Dominican politics at the time, was consonant with the attitudes of the transplanted Dominican Catholic youth circles in which Nelsy moved.[28] Social Catholics like the priest Porfirio Valdez and the local editorial office of the magazine *Amigo del Hogar* early advocated the creation of local social organizations to address the needs of Dominican migrants and their children.[29] Nelsy's close friend Scherezada Vicioso, known as Chiqui, had been a member of the Juventud Estudiantil Cristiana (Young Christian Students) and a contributer to *Amigo del Hogar* before her family moved from Santiago to Queens. Chiqui brought Nelsy, whose family lived in Inwood, into the Juventud Obrera Cristiana (Young Christian Workers) in New York.

There Nelsy met Father Valdez, who became her spiritual adviser during her political gestation at George Washington.[30] Engagement with local social projects may also have grown more easily out of the gendered experience of young, middle-class Dominican women in New York than out of that of their male counterparts. New York, Aldebot later recalls, offered freedoms to study, travel unaccompanied, participate in politics—in short, to have a public life outside the four walls of her home. Each new political gesture brought on both exhilarating self-fulfillment and terror. As they grew into young adults in the 1970s, many young Dominican women in New York found their voices in the confrontational world of Marxist reading circles and revolutionary partisanship. They proved themselves just as comfortable with homeland politics and theoretical abstraction as their male counterparts, and introduced socialist feminist politics to the Dominican left. But as teenagers in the late 1960s, they stuck closer to the politics of church and school groups while the filósofos participated in rows with Cuban boys in the neighborhood, socialist meetings in Greenwich Village coffeehouses, and secret revolutionary party activities.[31]

Still, if the first tentative steps toward creating an "identity" for Latin American students at George Washington began as a relatively mild-mannered political gesture, it was quickly subsumed by the heady swell of black protest on campus. In April 1969, a few months after the strike against gendered dress codes, a group of African American students formed a group called Umoja at George Washington. The name, the Swahili word for *unity*, was a symbol of black nationalism. Elizabeth Rich, a black substitute teacher who had opposed the UFT during the strike, served as a faculty adviser to the group. If the hint of nationalism and the involvement of a dissident teacher were not threatening enough to white teachers, the group immediately called for the hiring of more minority teachers and the teaching of minority group studies, suggesting that values of racial community could trump "merit," seniority, and even established curriculum. Umoja made these calls, threatening as they seemed to the UFT, as part of a broad student politics focused on the undeniable flaws of educational practice in the school. Umoja favored an end to tracking, more guidance personnel, a narcotics prevention program, and a student-faculty commission to resolve problems and implement programs.

A week after the first meeting of the Asociación de Estudiantes Hispanoamericanos, before the new group had begun to define its own agenda, a black classmate, Lena Riggs, invited Nelsy to address a meeting of Umoja, and the members of the Hispanic students group saw themselves "forced to act," deciding boldly to join the rising tide of student protest.[32] "There are only a few of us" wrote Nelsy in her diary, "but the protests and demands that are taking place have required us to help and participate with Umoja."[33] School principal Frank Sacks responded with the intransigence recommended by the High School Principals' Association. On Tuesday May 6, Sacks refused to allow a general assembly to discuss the matters. Umoja, with the participation of the Asociación, organized a gathering in the school auditorium anyway. During the rally, some of the students symbolically tore a school mural that depicted black slaves kneeling before George Washington. Still the administration did not respond. By late morning, about two hundred of the student protesters took to the hallways, shouting and disrupting classes. As a result, the city heard of the calls for reform for the first time in the context of reporting on the disruptions. The *Times* reported, in the passive voice, that windows *were broken*, fire alarms *were pulled* at least fourteen times, and, one school official alleged, three small fires *were set*, forcing classes to be dismissed early. No one knew who set the fires, but the incidents strengthened the administration's hand, making calls for reform seem to be a step toward anarchy. On Friday, student leaders planned an unsuccessful strike, hoping to get the student body to back them in a peaceful walkout. Tensions remained high for several weeks, as student groups and school authorities jockeyed for position and negotiated over student demands.[34] Nelsy became part of the team that— along with representatives from Umoja, the student government, and the local chapter of Aspira (a citywide, mostly Puerto Rican educational reform group)—spent two harrowing weeks negotiating with school officials over their demands for reform. Along with Umoja's call for better advising, more black teachers, and black studies courses, Aspira and the Asociación negotiated for better Spanish-language advising, more academic courses in Spanish, and Spanish-language assemblies, changes that new principal Louis Simon promised but quickly forgot.[35]

While Dominican ethnic politics in Washington Heights in the 1960s and early 1970s rarely adopted the idea of negritude or even allied with black activism, Nelsy Aldebot provides an example of how some Dominican students made precisely these moves. Nelsy lived in Inwood, she had a light complexion, she spoke English, she was college bound and had good relations with teachers at George Washington. She might easily have viewed her own success in the school as evidence that Dominicans were harder workers than blacks and that the school would serve anyone who really wanted to learn. But an early recognition of the deeper discrimination felt by her Dominican and Puerto Rican friends inspired her to create a Hispanic organization. Then, pushed along by the course of protest in the school, she forged an alliance with the most academically successful and politically astute black students in the school in a struggle to secure educational opportunity for all. In a remarkable diary entry, she interpreted this political evolution as a kind of blackening: "my skin is turning black, real black," she wrote, "and my heart is filled with love."[36] She continued in this politics of minority alliance at Hunter College, in the fight for open enrollment, before her own life history gradually pulled her into the world of exile politics, and finally back to Santo Domingo in the late 1970s.[37]

CONFRONTATION

George Washington was only one of the many schools where bitter and violent confrontations erupted between students and authorities in the two years after the UFT struck. In the spring of 1969, demands by the UFT chapter for "racial balance" at Franklin Lane High School led to the transfer of seven hundred black and Puerto Rican students, sparking unrest and violence. Racial conflicts between students and teachers followed at Eastern District High in Williamsburg, David Wingate and De Witt Clinton High Schools in the Bronx, and Bushwick High in Brooklyn, sometimes culminating in fires, destruction of school property, and police occupations of school buildings.[38] Lingering nastiness from the strike and resistance to the integration (and presumed decline) of schools in white neighborhoods made city schools seem like powder kegs. But the rise of common criminal violence in the hallways also contributed to a creeping sense of fear and disorder at George Washington when classes began again in the fall of 1969. According to city comptroller and mayoral hopeful Mario Procaccino, police received reports of seventy-four robberies and thirty-one muggings and assaults at George Washington during the first six weeks of the school year. The security guards at the school, Procaccino alleged, were ineffective due to their "lateness and absence and their lack of professionalism." A report on narcotics in the schools concluded that student drug addicts and abusers at George Washington "often extort, assault, intimidate, and rob fellow students." One teacher complained, "there is an absolute atmosphere of fear at G.W." Black student organizers agreed. "For every one straight student in this school, you will find at least two dope fiends," an unnamed student leader later told the *Amsterdam News*. "When they get uptight for money, some of us have to suffer."[39]

In this context, a group of parents and community activists, including Ellen Lurie, Parent Association vice president Jackie McCord, and welfare rights activist Juanita Kimble, took the student reform movement at George Washington under its wing, proposing to help the overloaded guidance system by setting up a "parent table" in the school lobby. The table, staffed by parent volunteers, would screen outsiders trying to get into the building, offer advice on student scheduling, and direct complaints to the school administration. The local chapter of the United Federation of Teachers opposed the idea as "a power play" by Lurie and other proponents of community control "to gain control of the school."[40] Little interested in waiting for teachers' endorsement, in February the parent activists began gathering complaints outside the school and accompanying students to see school officials to report the problems. School administrators objected to any adults entering the school except on business related to their own children. As parent activists, school board officials, and UFT representatives met to negotiate the situation, a group of students marched in the hallways in favor of the proposal, and settled in for a two-day-long sit-in at the auditorium and in the school lobby. Again the UFT reported incidents of violence and indiscipline in the school and accused parent activists of encouraging violence against teachers. Chapter chairman Irving Witkin noted in his "diary" that students were "roaming the hallways singing a song called 'Revolution,'" which he took as evidence of their extremism.[41] New York City School Board Member Isaiah Robinson, an ally of the school reform movement who was in the school supporting the parent table during some of the alleged unrest, disputed the reports of riots in the school.[42] Despite the accusations that they were agitators, parent allies, he argued, had "literally sat on" the student protesters to prevent "another Franklin K. Lane situation."[43] At Lane the conflict between students and teachers had devolved into violent confrontations.

On March 6, parents, school administrators, and representatives from the Board of Education finally agreed that the table should be set up under the supervision of the principal with appeals going to the assistant superintendent.[44] The UFT argued that the parents at the table usurped professional guidance responsibilities, disrupted the school, and violated the terms of the agreement. Citing concerns about teacher safety, the teachers joined UFT chapter leadership in a wildcat strike, leaving hallways and classrooms unsupervised. Faced with the threat of an extended teacher strike, the Board of Education reneged on its agreement with the Parent Table Committee.[45] Parent and student supporters of the table responded by sitting in at the principal's office. The UFT and the Board obtained a court order blocking further parent protest, and instructed acting principal Cherkis to have parents arrested if they continued in efforts to set up a complaint table.[46] School officials called police into the school to quell the protests. On March 16 police clashed with students. The pattern repeated in early April, with the table again put in place, again removed after action by the UFT, and a second major confrontation in the cafeteria between students and police, described by one policeman as like a "scene from a late show prison picture."[47]

The use of police to break up peaceful protests and provoke students into violence that could be used to discredit them was a harbinger of things to come. In the school year 1969–70, and again in the fall of 1970, the school was closed for weeks on end and police squads frequently entered the school to attack protesters and harass students. At the same time, teacher authority eroded almost completely. Student leaders willfully cut classes and disobeyed teacher directives, demonstrating their own power to confront hostile teachers on countless details of school life. Other students surely invested old habits of disobedience and confrontation, once fueled by vague feelings of resentment, with a new political content: support for the parent table. And some may have merely taken up the heady spirit of carnival as little by little the lobby, and especially the cafeteria, became liberated zones where students socialized, played cards, listened to music, smoked, and jeered (or ignored) attempts by school staff to reassert control. When teachers tried to clamp down on these liberties, students responded, "THE STUDENTS must have the POWER to make all rules and regulations pertaining to students. For example, the students should set SMOKING RULES, GYM REQUIREMENTS, LUNCH REGULATIONS, LOUNGE RULES, etc."[48] The United Federation of Teachers mocked the notion that student disobedience was a form of legitimate protest. And despite the already existing problem of violence related to drug addiction and petty crime, teachers intimated that all violence and all disobedience in the school was the responsibility of student protesters and their adult allies.

Some of the protesters were probably guilty of the violations of which they stood accused. Some were probably even guilty of extreme rhetoric or threats against teachers. Security guards and police, however, responded to challenges to their authority with shocking brutality. In October 1969, two school security guards badly beat a black student named Johnny Kimble. A policeman then arrived and as the guards forced Kimble to the patrol car, swung his nightstick between Kimble's legs, striking his genitals.[49] In December of 1970, a pair of students met with principal Louis Simon about setting up student patrols to help maintain order in the cafeteria. Leaving his office, they brushed up against two security guards. "Words were exchanged," Simon wrote in his report, and "the guards then beat and badly injured both students."[50] Police also began to patrol the streets around the building, trawling for student victims. For instance, when police outside the school teased student activist Eugene Schwaier about his long hair, asking him if he was a boy or a girl, Eugene sassed back at them. When they came after him saying "What did you say, Sergeant Pepper?" he did not back down. They arrested him for "harassment."[51] In another incident, Russell Jacquet-Acea remembers, "they had dispersed us and we were just walking, minding our business. Three police cars stopped, pinned us against the wall, and started harassing my sister." When Jacquet-Acea defended her, they put him in the car and began beating him. He fought back, but was taken to the station house where police "sat me in the chair and wailed on me. I lost a tooth. There was a lot of hatred for the police at that time."[52] Soon the removal of security guards and police from the school was also added to the list of student demands. In addition to their abuses against students, student leaders accused, the guards helped drug pushers to get into the school. Student reformers pointedly asked the Central Board to "investigate the relation between the *34th Precinct and the Drug Pushers* in GWHS."[53]

Most reporting on the conflicts at the school focused on black student militants. Yet Dominicans and Puerto Ricans, beginning with the leaders of the Asociación, were also present in some of the confrontations. As one Dominican man who graduated from the college-bound program in 1971 remembers, "[I]f there was a protest I was in it. I got into everything at the school."[54] This included receiving harassment or beatings from police, and sometimes fighting back. In 1970, for instance, police arrested two Dominican boys for "disorderly conduct" during one of the many conflicts between students and police at George Washington. But a still more interesting case was Arismendis De la Cruz, a Dominican boy who was arrested and suspended for his role in the student unrest in the cafeteria on April 10, 1970, shortly after the parent table had been shut down for a second time by a UFT power play.[55] Among the more than fifty arrested that day, the UFT chapter made a special effort to have him permanently transferred out of the school, threatening to walk out if he was returned to class. They argued that Arismendis and about a dozen of the other students, mostly black, were repeated violent disrupters of the school and posed a threat to teachers. The ACLU and Parent Table Committee retorted that the suspended students were political leaders being targeted in order to silence dissent.[56]

Arismendis's story offers an interesting counterpoint to Nelsy's. While he also came from a middle-class background in the Dominican Republic, though one seemingly lower in status than hers, his trajectory at George Washington was of creeping academic failure, low motivation, and discipline problems. Out of this experience he apparently built a different kind of political alliance with a very different crowd of black activists. Arismendis De la Cruz emigrated to Washington Heights from the Dominican Republic in the late 1960s along with his mother, Nancy De la Cruz. Ms. De la Cruz was a practical nurse trained at the International Hospital School of Nursing, a school operated by a Protestant missionary group, the Board for Christian Work, in Santo Domingo. She worked as a clerk and bookkeeper in various facilities run by the Secretary of

Health until the end of the Trujillo regime. In 1968, she found work as a nurse's aide at St. Elizabeth's Hospital, where she worked for four years, earning $155 a week. Her supervisor wrote, "[S]he is of extremely fine character, practices good nursing technique, is very kind to patients, and most cooperative to co-workers and supervisory personnel."[57] Yet by 1970 her job was in jeopardy because she had difficulty with the New York State certification exam. In August of 1972, she resigned after failing the examination for a third time.[58] Contrary to the notion of progreso, migration was pushing her down a social ladder. There is no record of where she turned next for work, but language barriers and certification problems pushed many middle-class and professional Dominicans into factory work and unemployment in New York.[59]

Arismendis's career at George Washington ran ahead of his mother's downward mobility. There is evidence that Arismendis started assimilating into the "wrong" crowd in Upper Manhattan several years before the explosions at George Washington. His first semester at George Washington he was absent only three days and earned an 83 and a 90 in two periods of English, although he failed math and his English teacher gave him a "needs improvement" in "courtesy" and an "unsatisfactory" in "self-control." The following semester, he was absent fifty-seven days and his grades dropped dramatically. Then he was arrested for possession of a stolen car. In the spring of 1969, perhaps to stem the tide of this downward assimilation, his mother sent him back to the Dominican Republic, where he was sent to the Hatillo Training School in San Cristóbal for six months.[60] This was a common strategy among Dominican parents in New York. They sent children back to a place where adults had more social control over adolescents, where reigning social norms condoned severe corporal punishment, and where, to the minds of many Dominican parents, the environmental influences were more wholesome and innocent. Dominican parents often regarded New York as a drain on their authority and on discipline in their households. Fear of investigation by child welfare agencies also restrained many parents from implementing what they regarded as proper punishment of misbehavior. Sending children back to live with family was one way of enlisting the homeland to reassert control. Dominicans in New York often joked that on visits to Santo Domingo at Christmas, as soon as their children passed through customs at the Airport of the Americas, parents administered pent-up beatings for all the disobedience and misbehavior they tolerated during the year.[61]

Despite this perception, in the late 1960s high schools in the Dominican Republic boiled over as repression by police and the Banda Colorá met mass student resistance to the Balaguer regime.[62] Unfortunately, documents kept by the New York City Board of Education do not show what part, if any, Arismendis took in these conflicts. Was he a suspicious "weirdo" because of his adoption of New York City cultural artifacts or a natural ally of student radicalism because of his antagonism to police? Was he a celebrity because of his experience in the bigger city, his clothes, his dollars, or was he a "gringo" rendered suspicious by his affiliation with the imperial enemy? In any event when he returned to George Washington the following fall, he joined the growing student movement. In the spring of 1970, Arismendis aligned himself with the parent table and its student advocates. Perhaps he joined as part of a more generalized protest against U.S. imperialism, on the principle that the enemy of my enemy is my friend. Perhaps he joined to protest discrimination against himself and his family. Or perhaps he acted in mere rebellion against the wishes of his mother and teachers. Though teachers maintained an anecdotal record of his involvement in the struggle, unfortunately they used it as an instrument to discredit Arismendis and other students they saw as opponents. His voice comes through in this record only in the slogan, "Teachers are pieces of furniture," which he reportedly shouted in response to teacher demands that he leave the immediate vicinity of the parent table. If he also offered more subtle or reasoned arguments for reform in the school, they chose not to record them.[63]

Yet Arismendis's support for the parent table and his alliance with its advocates do provide an indication of his politics beyond sheer rebellion. In March 1970, Arismendis was one of the dozens of students who spent their days hanging out near the parent table, willfully and cleverly disobeying teacher directives to return to class. On April 10, after the table was, for a second time, shut down by teacher opposition, he marched in the halls in protest with what one teacher loyal to the UFT called a "mob" of students.[64] Later in the day, he was sitting together with two girls in the cafeteria, now occupied by police, when a fight broke out and quickly spread. Students stood on tables to get a better view, threw food, trays, and even chairs, and police quickly moved into action, heading straight for students known as protesters. According to his own account, Arismendis struggled free of their nightsticks and ran upstairs to his locker. When he came back downstairs to the lobby, police handcuffed and arrested him, beating him on the legs in the wagon on the way to the precinct.[65] Then, despite the demand by the UFT chapter that he be transferred out of the school, Arismendis reappeared at George Washington the following fall, enrolled in the night school, and ran as a candidate for student government on the ticket proposed by student reformers. In this fashion he became another of the very first Dominicans to run for public office in New York.[66]

Furthemore, according to what Arismendis told his advocates in the suspension case, when the riot started in the cafeteria, rather than seeking protection among Dominican students, Arismendis quickly made his way over to the table where Johnny Kimble, Armand Reeves, and other black student activists sat. Lurie and her allies had recruited Kimble, along with his mother, Juanita, into the reform movement after his beating by security guards in October 1969. He and his friends were, according to their parent allies in the movement, remarkably talented leaders and committed reformers despite their lack of academic success. Some, like Ken Hillsman, were also known as peacemakers in the halls of the school. But others were loose cannons, "semi-truant" and "forceful."[67] They were, in the eyes of parent allies, exactly the constituency that had the most to gain from reform in the school. The school was not working for them, and their futures were grim without a better education. But they were also the group that teachers and administrators saw as least deserving. They were hoodlums and troublemakers, the UFT argued. Extremist radicals used them, the union claimed, to intimidate professionals in the school.

Quite apart from these accusations, it is unusual that a Dominican would turn to these defenders of a vigorous black male identity when running for cover during an unfolding riot. The fact that Arismendis moved to their table in the lunchroom melee, when viewed alongside his academic trajectory, might support the view, proposed by some social scientists, that new immigrants experience downward mobility when they learn "negative attitudes towards success" from existing black and Latino students. Yet that conclusion would miss the *political* aspect of his alliance with these black students. When he shouted "Teachers are pieces of furniture" (if indeed he ever shouted this) or when he endured beatings from the police, it was in the cause of expanded educational opportunity. And though his trajectory was somewhat distinct from Nelsy's, his alliances with black classmates reveal anything but negative attitudes toward success. There were ample opportunities at George Washington for Dominicans to misbehave, with or without befriending "forceful" black students. Arismendis De la Cruz did not merely slide into delinquency—he made a common cause with Johnny Kimble and others in his group in order to demand something better for themselves and in order to strike out at a system that marginalized them. These were kids, some with checkered academic records, demanding the right to middle-class aspirations.[68]

ETHNIC WARFARE, MINORITY COALITIONS, AND DOMINICAN POWER

While the alliances that Arismendis De la Cruz and Nelsy Aldebot made with black students offer key insights into the ways Dominicans could fit into the local political landscape, these alliances were never-theless unusual. Arismendis especially seems to have been a rare case. Most of the toughest, least academically oriented Dominican boys in the school fought against black counterparts over territory, dating, and other symbols of ethnic competition. Indeed, interethnic violence be-tween black and Dominican gangs came so intensely to overwhelm the student movement at George Washington in the early 1970s, that by 1973 a student writing in a local paper remembered the upheavals at the school simply as "many fights between students of different na-tionalities" in the school cafeteria, making no mention of student calls for reform and teacher reprisals.[69] The main part of the protests dur-ing the spring and fall of 1969 and Nelsy's work with Umoja occurred before the advent of organized violence between black and Dominican youngsters, though gang violence among other groups was already on the rise. One Puerto Rican student from the class of 1971 remembers, "At first, the blacks & Puerto Ricans were getting into it. I was right there when a P.R. dude got his forehead slashed. But soon the blacks & the Ricans joined forces against the whites."[70] Then, during the fall and winter of 1970, the major ethnic battle lines shifted. Rising tensions between black and Dominican gangs began to preclude the possibility of interethnic friendship and political cooperation. In February 1971, for instance, several Dominican students were robbed at knife point by a group of African American girls. According to a report in the *New York Times*, when the incident was brought to the attention of school officials, the money was returned but no actions were taken to punish the assailants. Fights between "Spanish-speaking" students and black students broke out in the school cafeteria and later spilled out onto the street. Police estimated that perhaps a total of five hundred students were involved in the various melees, in which five were injured and another five were arrested. Then a group of students, presumably Do-minicans, angry that the administration had declined to punish the of-fenders, marched on the principal's office wielding baseball bats and legs torn off desks.[71]

In repeated encounters over the following months, Dominican and black gangs, often comprised of nonstudents, clashed in front of the building, on subways, and outside other city high schools. Throughout 1971 and 1972, in the midst of the great efflorescence of student culture and politics in city schools, these gangs were "basically at war." Con-trary to the adult political fault lines between Hispanos and African Americans, Puerto Rican gangs defended their own turf, but gener-ally sided with blacks.[72] In addition to generalized Dominican retali-ation against blacks for what they perceived as their victimization as newcomers, there "were certain rules and territory that were not to be violated."[73] And in defining the boundaries of ethnic belonging, the tortured gender ideals of both African American and Dominican youth culture (male and female) contributed greatly to the problem of interethnic violence. Dominican gang members told the *New York Times* in 1970 that part of the reason they fought black gangs was to impress girls, who they believed liked to "see you messed up with blood on your shirt."[74] Group honor, revenge, and violence in and of itself all played a part in the way young men defined their masculinity and attractiveness. Dominican boys, as newcomers, were somewhat disadvantaged in other competitions for female attention, based on style and savvy. Several sources point out that black students, in part because they had more resources and in part because their tastes drove the whole notion of hipness in New York City at the time, dressed and groomed themselves better than Dominican newcomers. Dominican gang members reflected on the problem, using the rhetoric of civilization to explain the differences of style that separated them from black gangs. Dominicans were "not as advanced," they told the *Times,* as black and Puerto Ricans who dressed the same and partied together.[75] One Puerto Rican boy recalls, "To a young Hispanic who barely speaks the language and things are not all good at home he couldn't be a flashy dresser . . . and of course the girls like dressers with a little money. . . . This brought conflicts."[76] In other words, this brought conflicts over who was dating Dominican girls. But the conflicts were not just between black and Dominican boys. One woman, who describes herself as "a light skin Dominican and beautiful" and who graduated from GWHS in 1970 recalls, "the Black men loved me the Black women hated us." As a result black girls beat her up several times, along with her sisters.[77]

A surge in violence by some black and Latino youth seemed, to many white residents of Washington Heights, to confirm a story of neighborhood decline that stemmed from a changing racial composition. Irish residents in particular pined for what they remembered as the good old days of peace and safety. Yet fond memories of bygone urban culture are often selective.[78] In those good old days Irish gangs under the sway of anti-Semitic radio priest Charles Coughlin had attacked Jews and clashed with Jewish youth at Highbridge Park. In the early 1960s the Youth Board still kept an eye on dozens of Irish, Puerto Rican, and black gangs, only some of which it saw as "anti-social." Yet youth workers noted that Irish gangs, in particular, indiscriminately harrassed Puerto Rican children. In short, ethnically motivated gang violence had been a periodic element of neighborhood youth culture for at least four decades, and was in no way restricted to black and Latino youngsters. And likewise, the idea that the neighborhood was awash in youth violence, and therefore going downhill, had been a main, episodic feature of neighborhood culture for forty years.[79]

Like those earlier instances of gang violence, the new wave of conflicts reflected broader confrontations among ethnic communities. Youth gangs were at the front lines of neighborhood conflicts. Student violence at George Washington and at nearby Junior High School 143 resonated with the angry rivalry between black and "Spanish" parents in Washington Heights schools. Ellen Lurie wrote despairingly in her journals, "The Sp.-Black fight is awful everywhere. The way the black paraprof[essionals] talk to Sp kids is full of hatred. At 143 Dominican-Black gang fights and beating up of kids is fierce. While the adults cut down each other verbally, the kids tear each other apart physically."[80] Whether parents expressly encouraged their children's violence, the anger and "hatred" that permeated the most active adults in the schools surely fanned the flames of student rivalry. And fighting among kids provided more fuel for the bickering among parents on both sides, who invariably saw their own children as victims and the "other" children as the attackers.

Interethnic violence in the school, inspired by robberies, defenses of male or female honor, and simultaneous conflicts among parents, made Dominican alliances with the African American protest movement extremely difficult. One shocking incident between a Dominican student and some members of a black student protest group called the Brotherhood sent a particular chill through the prospect of a minority coalition at the school. The members of the Brotherhood were supporters of the parent table who also physically intimidated students they identified as drug dealers and fought repeatedly with school security guards. One day in October 1970, school officials called Brotherhood leader Curtis Francheschi to the principal's office on a pretext. There, in an ambush, police subdued him and dragged him out of the school, accusing him of an alleged mugging off school grounds. With Curtis on his way to Riker's Island, his angry comrades stormed through the halls to collect bail, using what their parent allies admitted were "unorthodox methods." The UFT described it more plainly as extortion and intimidation. The situation between black and Dominican students in the school was tense. And the Brotherhood was, to say the least, careless in the way they presented their case to one Dominican boy they cornered in the halls. Believing that a gang of black students intended to rob him, the boy defended himself from the fundraisers with a knife, cutting four of the black militants. Soon, though, they overpowered him and began to "stomp" him. It was only the intervention of parents from the table committee that prevented the Dominican boy from being beaten to death. Juanita Kimble and another black parent literally threw themselves between the angry militants and their victim.[81]

The Brotherhood's questionable tactics in rousing support for Curtis, and word of the beating they administered to their victim, did little to help open lines of communication between black militants and average Dominican students in the school. Fear of indiscriminate attack often trumped the interethnic friendships and political alliances. Most students in the school, and especially most student leaders, had little role in the gang warfare between black and Dominican teenagers. But the spread of ethnic violence scared many George Washington students away from the protest movement. Any large gathering of students at George Washington was a dangerous and frightening place to be, and days of demonstrations or clashes with police were sometimes also days of chaotic violence. Students learned to huddle together in school offices. One Dominican graduate remembers, "No, I did not [participate in the student movement]. I can say I was a little scare[d]. [T]here were a lot of riots in the school. I believe there were more racial tensions than anything else."[82] Students were vulnerable to harrassment or attack despite friendships and political alliances across ethnic lines. Nelsy Aldebot recalls her dismay when, after a semester of intense collaboration with black student activists, on Senior Day in 1969 a group of black students attacked her with eggs, shaving cream, and water guns.[83]

It was in this general context that politically active Dominican students began demonstrating on their own, as Dominicans. In January 1971, a group of thirty to forty students staged a noisy, nonviolent protest at the school, chanting slogans against U.S. imperialism. A principal's report identified the students only as "Spanish speaking."[84] But there can be little doubt: if the theme of the rally was antiimperialism, the organizers were Dominican. The politics of exile, earlier practiced by the filósofos, grew into a larger movement as the numbers of Dominicans in the school began to swell. Unlike the filósofos, however, the new crop of antiimperialists at George Washington knew about the other student political groups in the school. The demonstrators in January 1971 called for an end to suspensions of students at George Washington, by then a major demand of parent table activists. Around the same time a group called the United Front of Progressive Dominican Students at George Washington High School published a bilingual flyer declaring, "We support the efforts of progressive parents, teachers, and students who want to reform our school."[85] The group denounced the "efforts of the racists to divide the black and Hispanic student body with the aim of confusing us" and pledged that Dominican revolutionaries "will never fight against black students nor against the whites."

These other students are not the enemy, they wrote. "The enemy is a racist educational system controlled by racist administrators."[86]

The Brotherhood, likewise, expressed public solidarity with the Dominican protesters who marched to the principal's office in February 1971 to protest black violence in the school. The Dominicans, they claimed, were "third world" brothers and sisters. Blacks in general, and the black movement in particular, they said, had no quarrel with Dominicans. Most of the new violence in the school was a conflict between the "junkies," including many who happened to be black, and their victims, including many who happened to be "Spanish." The February robbery, they said, was "just one of the many cases where sisters and brothers have been 'taken off' by junkies," another example of how the school failed to deal with the drug problem.[87] Both groups saw the ethnic violence around them as an obstacle to the kind of politics they wanted to build—a politics that identified a common enemy, if not always a shared social identity or a unified cause. Similarly the United Students Association, a multiethnic political group allied with the Parent Table Committee, made peace among students one of its key goals in the school.[88]

Nevertheless, even as tensions began to cool at George Washington, Dominican political organizations in the school began to assert their own messages and their own power rather than joining a generalized student movement. Their success in this effort owed largely to a regime of responsiveness to student demands initiated in 1971 by a new principal, Samuel Kostman. Kostman's attitude toward student involvement in school affairs was wholly opposite to that of his predecessors. He had a "hip" attitude, which he demonstrated in the December 1971 edition of the *Cherry Blossom*, calling the students in the school "beautiful."[89] He instituted rap sessions in the auditorium for students to air their grievances. He ate his lunch in the cafeteria with students. He encouraged publications and ensured fair elections for student government. He also called the police back into the school, but this time with the idea of cracking down on gang violence, not political dissent. And he invited members of key black and Dominican gangs to a series of weekend retreats in upstate New York, for ice skating, hot cocoa, snowball fights, and workshops designed to break down hostilities. Kostman complemented his personality and his faith in students with educational reforms funded by the Educational Development Council.[90] He created narcotics programs, summer programs for Spanish-speaking students, programs to help students plan for college, an informal annex for students at risk of dropping out, and a program in the George Washington tower that, according to one student, was "like the sweathogs in *Welcome Back Kotter*." One of those students started a gay student alliance at Washington.[91]

Almost universally, former students credit Kostman for restoring their feelings of safety in the school and for improving their chances for a decent education. But no group benefited more from his reforms than the growing cadre of Dominican political activists. Many of these students were veterans of the anti-Balaguerista student movement in the Dominican Republic. To them the school, even with its flaws, represented a treasured opportunity for progreso, and the student body represented fertile terrain for political organizing. Shortly after Kostman's arrival, a group of Dominicans, with one or two Cuban and Puerto Rican friends, revived the old Asociación de Estudiantes Hispano-Americanos, dormant for several years since its participation in the first student strikes. Under the guidance of Mr. Fraga, a Spaniard, the group now called itself the Club Pan-Americano. Unlike the earlier group, these students did not immediately join a reform movement led by black students. And unlike the earlier group, they found an administration that saw student activism and expression as a boon to the school, not as "total social disruption." Kostman allowed them to publish a Spanish-language school newspaper and to run their own voluntary assemblies, in Spanish, after school hours. The auditorium filled with Dominican students, attracted by the novelty of Spanish-language, student-run activities.[92]

The Club Pan-Americano overlapped considerably in its politics with the earlier United Front of Progressive Dominican Students and the filósofos. Pedro Rodríguez, a club organizer, had been a high school militant at the Instituto Evangélico in Santiago before coming to New York. He and his allies easily translated their antiimperialism to their new school. At the after-school assemblies the leadership speechified about human rights and social revolution in the Dominican Republic. They organized protests against imperialism and authoritarianism. They participated in vigils at the Dominican consulate and in antiwar rallies. They resembled the earlier Asociación de Estudiantes Hispanos in their attention to student concerns like counseling and Spanish-language assemblies. Like many Puerto Rican and Dominican adults in the neighborhood, they did not see the UFT as an absolute enemy. The Club Pan-Americano collaborated with the local UFT chapter on a solidarity campaign for striking Chicano farmworkers.[93]

The Club Pan-Americano also inherited, from the United Front of Progressive Dominicans, the spirit of solidarity for other social causes in the school and a repudiation of interethnic violence. Nevertheless, by 1972 members began to discuss the possibility of a takeover of the Student Government Organization (SGO) from the black officers who controlled it. Two years earlier, the United Student Movement had proposed a slate of reform candidates for SGO that included several white, several black, and one Dominican candidate, Arismendis De la Cruz.

Principal Sol Levine excluded the United Student Movement from the elections by fiat. By contrast, in the first year of Kostman's tenure, black candidates ran in and won the SGO elections, making no alliances. They then governed in a way that Dominicans in the Club Pan-Americano perceived to be exclusive and parochial. Club leader Pedro Rodríguez cannot recall, thirty years later, exactly what the differences between black and Dominican leadership in the school were. But he does remember, with some regret, that ethnic rivalries with blacks were the major inspiration for Dominicans to take control over local government. Though the leadership of the Club Pan-Americano was skeptical of elections—being avid readers of Fidel Castro and especially Juan Bosch on the matter of hollow parliamentary democracies—they built a campaign to put the leadership of the Pan-American Club into the key positions of student government. Their message to fellow Dominicans in the school, Rodríguez remembers, was, "We have to get the blacks out." Both shifting demographics and the popularity of the Spanish-language assemblies acted in their favor. In 1972 Pedro Rodríguez, formerly a leader in the student movement in Santiago, became student government president at George Washington High School.[94]

The Club Pan-Americano, now in control of the student government, maintained constant contact with a broad constituency through publications and regular assemblies. With help from some black football players and benefiting from the new administration, the new Dominican leadership exerted an unusual control over a territory that had, until recently, slipped treacherously into chaos. They confiscated weapons at the door to the school, keeping them in an apartment across the street until school was over. They confiscated drugs from Dominican students. While the new administration presided over a renaissance of George Washington's academic programs, the new student government created a sort of Pax Dominicana in the hallways. In this sense the group was the perfect embodiment of a social ideal that circulated among the cultural clubs and youth movements in the Dominican Republic. Organized youth should assert themselves not only to mobilize collective action, but also as an instrument of social control, as a barrier to corruption and in one sense to Americanization. For a brief moment, in the middle 1970s, Dominican activists managed to impose their notion of cultura at George Washington High School.

The Club Pan-Americano also deployed another aspect of cultura in mobilizing a Dominican constituency at George Washington, sponsoring performances of merengue and salsa. The two Quezada sisters, Milly and Jocelyn, who later led the first New York–based merengue band to break into the charts in Santo Domingo, were then students at George Washington, as was José Alberto, a Dominican singer later known as El Canario.[95] These students performed at the meetings of the Pan-American Club, luring Spanish-speaking students to their assemblies. Music, like language, served to mark the distinct ethnic communities that belonged in these settings. In Santo Domingo in the early 1970s, many perceived the opposition between merengue and rock to be a key battle in the defense of national identity, the distinction between us and them. But now the important difference was not between the United States and the Dominican Republic as abstract wholes; it was the practical difference between blacks and Spanish (and in only partially playful battles between salsa and merengue, between Puerto Ricans and Dominicans) in the halls of their school.

Outside the context of ethnic activism, however, even the most radical of Dominican antiimperialists began to give up their prejudices against the "modern" music and styles enjoyed by classmates. In their assemblies they deployed a cultural politics that blended the ideals and practices of the Dominican left with the neighborhood pressures for ethnic rivalry. But in everyday life they listened to rock and soul. Pedro Rodríguez, who after leading the Pan-American Club to victory at George Washington became a lifelong activist and a committed ally to black and Puerto Rican struggles, recalls, laughing, "when I arrived at George Washington I was 5 foot 6, and a year later I was six feet tall, because of my afro and platform shoes."[96]

SCHOOLS, CLASS, AND RACE

The failure of urban public schooling at the end of the century should not lead us to idealize earlier moments in the lives of these institutions. Segregated by race and class since their beginnings, they had always been democratic tools for social mobility only for some. Nor should the obvious failure of many schools lead us to ignore the ways that Dominican, black, Puerto Rican, and other immigrant children still rely on public schools and colleges to eke out their own social advancement. Nevertheless, these battles over turf inside the school, the valiant if sometimes erratic efforts to reform the school, and even the years of relative recovery in the middle of the 1970s all took place in the context of a broader shift. With the exception of a few magnet schools, many middle-class New Yorkers no longer felt that they could send their children to public schools in Manhattan. Teachers with the opportunity to work outside the city no longer chose to work at places like George Washington. Even as some students won a battle for peace and new programs at George Washington, the war to create equal opportunity through public schooling was lost. By 1975 the city budget would be in the red, and the White House would famously tell the city to "Drop Dead." The reshuffling of political priorities under the watchful gaze of the city's creditors would make disagreements within the school look trivial. Indeed, in the 1980s teachers and students would march *together* in Washington Heights against budget cuts. The story of urban decline and of the erosion of public life in the United States in the late twentieth century is easily and powerfully captured in the fate of the most public of institutions, schools.[97]

Little by little, George Washington changed from an institution "in transition" to a recognizably "inner-city" school, though one that was majority Dominican rather than African American. Here, the familiar story of urban crisis composed of desegregation, white flight, a shift of government to suburbs, and a declining industrial economy looks somewhat different, because it resulted in a new immigrant school and neighborhood rather than resegregated black spaces. Locally, at George Washington High School, and in the metropolitan region as a whole, the class, racial, and ethnic status of new Latin American immigrants (rather than long-standing Puerto Rican and Mexican American citizens) reflected the urban crisis into which they settled in ways that allied them with and distinguished them from black and Puerto Rican neighbors. Antiimmigrant forces, allied with labor groups, had structured the restrictive immigration legislation passed in 1965 with the hopes of preventing new Latin American immigration to cities in economic downturn. After 1968, the law required Dominicans, and other visa applicants from the Western Hemisphere, to obtain certification that a labor shortage existed in their field in the region they planned to settle. Certification from the U.S. Department of Labor was a nearly impossible bureaucratic hurdle for residents of Santo Domingo. Yet, even if the administrative task had been easy, jobs, not workers, grew scarce in New York after 1968. Between 1968 and 1977, when Congress stopped requiring labor certification for Canadian and Latin American immigrants, the city lost more than half a million jobs.

The restrictive legislation did not cut off the flow of U.S. visas granted in Santo Domingo, however. An exemption to the labor certification requirement for relatives of U.S. residents allowed the Visa Office in Santo Domingo to grant 110,394 immigrant visas to Dominicans in the decade after 1968, just as the bottom fell out of the New York economy.[98] This was surely a relief to the State Department and its local representatives, who felt the pressure of Dominican public opinion and sought to maintain a friendly image through relatively open borders. Visa officers tacitly colluded with Dominicans to undermine the immigration restrictions by granting 319,118 nonimmigrant visas in these years too. Such visas technically gave permission only to enter the United States for purposes of study or travel, and not legally for work. But it was hardly a secret that many Dominicans overstayed such visas and worked while in the United States.[99] Thousands of unskilled workers arriving in a city with a shrinking industrial economy did not face immediate unemployment, as might be expected. New migrants found jobs because ethnic whites fled factory work faster than factories closed. Facing competition from producers in low-wage regions of the globe, New York's small apparel, leather goods, and electronics factories turned to the pool of low-cost labor, especially women workers, arriving from Latin America and Asia. New migrants also drove taxis, cared for children and the elderly, worked as janitors and in construction. Some even bought small manufacturing firms and corner stores, sold off by third-generation white ethnics eager to leave both the city and the stress of small business. To compete in strapped industries, new migrant entrepreneurs tapped the pool of undocumented labor provided by coethnics and relied heavily on the unpaid or underpaid labor of family members.[100]

The recession therefore did not produce widespread unemployment among new arrivals from the Dominican Republic, as it did among Puerto Ricans and blacks. Most Dominicans were temporarily spared the ordeal of surviving on public assistance. Most nevertheless joined the ranks of the working poor. As they moved into jobs and businesses formerly occupied by the ethnic white working classes, Dominicans also moved into the apartment buildings that formerly housed those workers. In Washington Heights they moved especially into the walk-up tenement buildings east of Broadway, between 150th Street and 190th Street. Built shortly after public transportation reached the area in 1906, these buildings had once offered a welcome respite from the tenements of the Lower East Side. But seven decades later they were the oldest, most cramped housing in the neighborhood. Similar housing stock across the river in the South Bronx and in nearby parts of Harlem saw rapid patterns of white flight, abandonment, and arson in the 1960s and 1970s. As real estate values began to sink, property owners frequently paid to have their buildings set afire, took insurance claims, and washed their hands of their old communities, leaving the specter of burnt-out and empty buildings behind to low-income black and Puerto Rican families.[101] Even the most rundown sections of Washington Heights had not yet fallen off the precipice, but the buildings were in a state of severe deterioration. By 1978, the city took over more than one hundred neglected buildings and planned to seal up or demolish more than sixty-five abandoned buildings.[102] Dominicans increasingly came to occupy those rundown areas of the neighborhood, areas that had already been rundown for decades.

The new pool of highly exploitable labor, living doubled and tripled up in aging apartments, retarded the collapse of industry in New York without slowing the effects of this transition on black and Puerto Rican New Yorkers. Yet if Dominicans found employment, being part of the working poor in New York nevertheless meant living on one side of the widening gap between rich and poor. This economic gulf raised the stakes of educational opportunity. Dominican parents might find relative opportunity in the shrinking incomes provided by factories, hospitals, hotels, and bodegas. But Dominican children without college degrees would, in the 1980s, find mostly low-paid service work, progressively farther down in status from high-paid jobs downtown. So while Dominican student reformers at George Washington came from families with, on average, a slightly different relationship to the shifting economy of the city than black and Puerto Rican classmates, the eventual stakes of the struggle were equally high for all. Teachers may have been right that they should not take all the blame for social problems that extended well beyond the school. They may even have been right that the attitudes of some students (even some student radicals) made teaching them harder, not easier. But students were surely right that access to college was organized according to social class and race, and that the outcome of battles over that access would be decisive in their own standing in their city. Whatever personal failings students like Johnny Kimble or Arismendis De la Cruz may have had should not hide the political nature of their rebellions. They stood in protest against an institution set up to weed them out and cast them into the maw of the unemployed and working poor. In this context, given what was coming, even blind fury was a prescient politics.

The broader context of economic change helps highlight both the unique place Dominicans occupied and the broader process by which they joined the status of nonwhite minority in the city. As the idea of "inner-city" schools and children became a racial idea, Dominicans' memories of their immigrant cultura and of the Pax Dominicana stood in the face of a tide of public opinion that was unlikely to make the same distinctions between them and their black and Puerto Rican neighbors. At first this was mostly because white New Yorkers had trouble identifying differences among "Spanish" New Yorkers. But over the course of the 1970s, on the heels of the first experiments at George Washington, "Dominican" emerged as a readily understood kind of person one could be. Settlement by Dominicans became a primary neighborhood feature recognized by all. When other New Yorkers caught on to the fact that Dominican was a distinct kind of person someone could be, they drafted Dominicans into narratives of urban distress that made them out to be threats to the neighborhood and to the nation. It was not that George Washington became an "inner-city" school despite being a Dominican school; in the eyes of white New Yorkers it became an "inner-city" school *because* it was a Dominican school. These stories were shockingly opposite to the idea of progreso, the idea that broadly underwrote the project of migration. When they could, Dominicans responded directly, often at the expense of black and Puerto Rican New Yorkers. They proclaimed the honesty and hard work of their community to the neighborhood and city. But in the 1970s, as they sought to narrate their migration in a positive light, many came to rely heavily on a concept of home that was somewhere outside the neighborhood. Indeed, as they struggled to tell the story of making a new home in Washington Heights, they often seemed to speak only of the home they had left in the Dominican Republic.

SEVEN

Not How They Paint It

IN 1978, a Mayor's Task Force in Washington Heights reported that white residents complained about new Dominican immigrants who "were not being forced to assimilate as earlier immigrants had done." The story of the "old immigrants" who voluntarily assimilated into the politics and culture of the United States was, after midcentury, a central myth of liberal nationalism. In this view, the United States was a beacon to the world, drawing willing converts to Americanism like moths to a flame. In exchange for forsaking their homelands, immigrants got the benefits of freedom, democracy, and opportunity. This had never really been the experience of new arrivals. But liberal nationalists had promoted this story of immigrant assimilation to defend earlier immigrants against racial nativism, which saw newcomers as incapable of becoming American. Liberals thus saw any reluctance or ambivalence toward Americanization as a troubling novelty. This view resonated with culture-of-poverty arguments as well, which located the problem of African American and Latino poverty in obstacles that racial exclusion, and disorganized family life, placed in the way of their full assimilation into national culture. If new immigrants chose not to assimilate, that they posed a similar danger to "stable" neighborhoods was obvious. Thus as Dominicans settled in New York, the older traditions of nativism were transformed into a new, false distinction between the good old immigrants and the troublesome new ones. Not coincidentally, this transition took place at a time when the grandchildren of old immigrants asserted their power as middle-class whites in conflicts with the new immigrants in their neighborhoods.[1]

The idea that old immigrants fit in better than the new ones still largely constrains political debates about new immigration in the United States. Yet among Dominicans in Washington Heights in the 1960s and 1970s, a contrasting Dominican nationalist narrative tended to drown out the idea of dutiful Americanization and gradual social advancement. To be a deserving migrant, the most vocal of Dominican activists in New York asserted, one had to resist incorporation into the United States and remember the homeland. Assimilation was, after all, the same process that nationalists understood as cultural penetration back in Santo Domingo. And Dominican nationalists in both cities were not shy about saying as much to migrants. In 1974, a group of young radicals invited the musical group Expresión Jóven to New York. The musicians told reporters that they hoped, in their performance, to convince Dominicans in New York that the United States was the enemy. They believed that "our compatriots should begin to take the Dominican Republic into account, they should start to form a consciousnesses about their distant, and perhaps forgotten, homeland."[2] Yet Dominican nationalists had their own set of class and color prejudices, their own unreasonable cultural expectations, and their own evolving vision of New York's ethnic ghettoes. So when Dominican New Yorkers turned home seeking a refuge from their low social status in New York, they found an ambivalent welcome. Dominican New Yorkers thus faced the question of their belonging in the Dominican Republic simultaneously with the question of their racial and class status in New York.

The Attractions of Home

Nationalist messages of the sort offered by Expresión Jóven often sounded much like rebukes, reflecting a generalized skepticism about migration on the part of the Dominican left. But home offered attractions along with the demand for loyalty. Dominican Minister of Tourism Angel Miolán, himself a former exile and New Yorker, led a commission to New York around 1970. There he attended a series of house parties pleading with migrants to "come to their home, Santo Domingo, to eat roast pork and all the fixings, and to experience the great joy of family, a Dominican Christmas." Miolán and his commission also distributed photographs of a Dominican beauty queen, presumably that year's "Miss Tourism Dominican Republic," with the caption "Dominican, your land awaits you at Christmas."[3] The promotional tour in New York was part of a broader effort to sell trips to the island to the growing population of Dominicans abroad, through a complex metaphor of nation, family, food, and gender. A high-profile member of the opposition, Miolán had justified his defection and alliance with Balaguer by promising that tourism would bring industry to the republic "without smokestacks." Yet the flow of tourism was anemic at best, and Miolán's missing tourists became a public joke. ¡Ahora!'s editors quipped that tourism was in fact "all smoke and no industry."[4] In this context Miolán, a former New Yorker, initiated official gestures toward Dominican New Yorkers that described an idealized relationship with home, mediated through vacations. During the holiday season, the Santo Domingo city government and Miolán's Turismo hosted a music festival in Santo Domingo for returning New Yorkers. As Dominican New Yorkers passed through customs, Miolán recalled, "[T]here was always a *perico ripiao* [a folkloric merengue group], cocktails, and attentive and elegant female 'receptionists' to assist and to welcome them."[5]

While Miolán took credit for the success of his "Dominican Christmas" project, most likely Turismo merely capitalized on a process that was already under way. Trips home were something Dominicans shared with almost all Latin Americans in New York, and especially with Puerto Ricans, who referred to plane flights between New York and San Juan as "jumping over the pond." As early as 1949, airlines flying to San Juan reported that "in about October the flow just about reverses itself with the bulk of it going southward. The southbound traffic hits its peak just before the Christmas holidays."[6] As the immediate risk of political violence in Santo Domingo diminished in the early 1970s, the seasonal flow to Santo Domingo grew as well. According to official statistics, in 1967, five thousand Dominicans with permanent residence abroad arrived as tourists at Dominican airports. In 1971 the number was twenty thousand, and by 1975, forty-five thousand. The actual number of visitors from the United States was probably higher, since many Dominicans were living abroad without the legal status of permanent residence. Many of those counted as Dominican tourists returning from holiday in New York were probably actually part-time or full-time New Yorkers returning to Santo Domingo for vacation.[7]

Despite the sometimes blurred boundary between who was a Dominican New Yorker vacationing on the island and who was an islander visiting New York, in the 1970s relatively settled Dominican New Yorkers did make vacations "home" to the Dominican Republic a central part of their lives. Juan Contreras, who moved to Queens with his mother in the 1960s, remembered that Dominicans "would go to work, go home, go to work, go home, and then take a three-week vacation and go to the Dominican Republic and spend everything that they made, in those three weeks vacation, that was the life they used to live, just that, those three weeks."[8] Miolán's efforts can hardly be credited with inspiring this pattern. But the language he employed in attempting to capitalize on it reflected the kinds of public rewards offered to Dominicans who invested in trips home. Like other wage workers in the United States and Europe, Dominican New Yorkers often saved relatively scarce resources to spend them in a tropical setting where dollars stretched much farther. But while the Dominican Tourism Ministry encouraged Europeans to escape to an exotic foreign land, to Dominican New Yorkers it suggested that migrants could confirm their national belonging through annual visits to the island. In this sense, Turismo not only articulated an image of the nation, through folklore, parades, and beauty contests, that migrants would appropriate for the purposes of ethnic assertion. It also articulated an idea about the nation as a welcoming *hogar* (hearth), a resource that migrants incorporated into their ideas of home.

Nationalists made demands on migrants and Turismo made appeals to migrants, but New Yorkers themselves often saw another reward in their communications with and visits to the island: the opportunity to claim social status, to perform and narrate tales of their own progreso.[9] In a small town outside Santiago, in 1968 and 1969, anthropologist Glenn Hendricks tracked the letters arriving from New York. These letters first complained about the cold, the harsh work regime, and other distasteful aspects of city living. But within a few months, Hendricks noted, migrants generally shifted their tales to celebrations of the opportunities to work in New York, describing with special detail the material comforts that their hard work afforded. Visits home served to elaborate these same stories of hard work and material triumph to family, neighbors, and even casual observers. Hendricks witnessed taxis from the airport honking their horns on the way to town, announcing the arrival of the visitors for the winter holidays. Drivers delivered passengers to the door of homes so all the neighbors could see who had returned and what they were wearing.[10] The gap between incomes in the United States and incomes in the Dominican Republic temporarily made humble factory workers into wealthy people of leisure. Flying home could turn the story of Dominican integration into New York around. The idea that New York represented an advanced stage in the ineluctable process of modernity and well-being placed Dominican migrants at a disadvantage in New York, making them seem like backward outsiders. Yet the same powerful idea of U.S. superiority could be put to advantage on visits back home, where it reinforced the migrant's claims to individual progreso. Juan Contreras, a Queens resident who was among the visitors to the Dominican Republic in 1975, remembered his happy surprise in the reception he received, especially from local girls. "In those days [if] you came from the United States and from New York and you went to any one of those rural areas, you were a god."[11]

Telling these stories of progreso at home made sense, since the stories other people told about Dominicans in New York reflected their more troubling incorporation as a working-class racial minority. As Dominicans moved into the dilapidated housing of Upper Manhattan, the white political alliance that took shape in the aftermath of the teacher strike incorporated Dominicans into a standard language of neighborhood decline. In 1978, Mayor Ed Koch appointed a Task Force to keep Washington Heights "stable" and "vital." The Task Force noted "pockets of blight" that had emerged in the neighborhood and "examples of some of the city's most troubling problems." In most neighborhoods, indeed in Washington Heights until the early 1970s, the coded racial language of revitalization and blight referred to shifting lines of black, Puerto Rican, and white settlement. Yet by the end of the 1970s, the Task Force described Dominicans as the primary motor of neighborhood "change." Washington Heights, it reported, was "moving from a strong and diverse base of varied ethnic origins (Jewish, Irish, Greek, black, Hispanic), an older population, to a predominantly Hispanic (Dominican), younger group."[12] As early as 1971, Dominican journalist Tirso Valdez, writing in the Santo Domingo newsmagazine ¡Ahora! reported that other New Yorkers saw the arrival of Dominicans as a signal of neighborhood decline. When this happens, he wrote, "there is something like an exodus of persons, who settle themselves into other buildings."[13]

Home had other meanings too. When Angel Miolán invited New Yorkers to return home, he specifically used the word *hogar*, meaning hearth, as well as national terms such as *land*, *people*, and *country*. It was relatively easy to slip between celebrations of a welcoming hearth, a space for private family reunion, and a national homeland because Latin Americans often imagined the differences between themselves and Anglo-America in terms of family relations. Responding to a 1980 *New York Times* survey of Latino New Yorkers, 40 percent of respondents cited "family unity" as a key cultural trait pertaining to Latinos. These Latin American immigrants saw in themselves a commitment to family, personal warmth, love, and "respect" for elders.[14] By contrast they frequently represented Anglo-Saxons as "cold" and unfeeling toward their families.[15] Many Dominicans understood the assault on Dominican family values to be one of the major drawbacks of settlement in New York. As Héctor Chacón explained, Dominican "moral values and family virtues are being eroded" by the corrupt influences in New York.[16]

As part of this erosion, Dominican parents particularly noted what they saw as a lack of respect for elders in Anglo-American families seeping into their own households. One Dominican mother told the *Times* in 1980, "The manner of rearing children is very different because for us, Hispanics, respect for adults is first and foremost."[17] Yet, in New York, children generally spoke more English and were more at ease with local culture and institutions than their parents, becoming mediators between the home and the society. Bearing the burden of translating for their parents at schools, hospitals, stores, and government offices, children also demanded greater freedoms and contested adult authority.[18] Girls, in particular, adapted quickly to the new freedoms available in New York City. Miguel Rodríguez O. wrote in horror that when "a fifteen year old girl" stayed out to all hours with a neighborhood boy, "her mother or father gets up to open the door with only a slight grumble."

Kids, he reported, went to movies or to parties without even asking permission. "Later there are sad and irreversible consequences."[19]

Migration to the United States also shifted the dynamics of gender relations in Dominican homes. Migrant women often had the freedom to work, travel unescorted, and make household and financial decisions for the first time. Sharing in the wage work, migrant men were often willing also to take an unusual share in household labor. One migrant woman remembered that the United States was "good for men because it teaches them to work as women do. They even have to work at home and help prepare meals, because if they don't cook, they might not eat."[20]

For men, women, and children, then, the idea of a return to a home-land described in the symbolic terms of a family or a hearth likely called up tensions around shifting gender and generational relations in their homes. Parents often saw a return to Santo Domingo as an opportunity to reassert authority over their children. For many migrant men, as well, the loss of status in the family was part of the nostalgia for home, the return to a "Dominican family." Migrant women told researchers in the 1980s that they resisted their husbands' plans to return to Santo Domingo because they did not relish a return to a traditional home life.[21] On the other hand, some Dominican women migrants to Boston reported that they liked the idea of home because it offered a return to female roles mediated by improved class status. "I couldn't wait to come home and live a life of leisure," one woman explained. "It was good working there, but now I am happy to live calmly back in Miraflores."[22] A returned migrant living in the Dominican Republic explained, "In the Dominican Republic it is so easy to have the maid you wouldn't even have dared dream of in the United States."[23] For her, being a middle-class housewife in the Dominican Republic was better than working double shifts in factories and households in the United States.

So while some women resisted the return home to maintain the transformations of their home life, others preferred to exchange inde-pendence for the "leisure" offered by improved class status back home. These gendered tensions over the relationship between the home, the homeland, and progreso were likely easier to manage on temporary vis-its to the island than permanent return. As vacationers, migrants could be women of leisure, if only temporarily. The "modern" role they had in their households in New York could even become a feminist variant on the tale of migrant progreso. One villager in the Dominican Republic reported, "On a visit to Juan Pablo, my cousin saw the way my husband made me wait on him hand and foot, and the way he'd yell if everything was not perfect. She said she didn't see such behavior in New York. She said, 'Wait till you get there. You'll have your own paycheck, and I tell you, he won't be pushing you around there the way he is here.'"[24]

The idea of a return to the homeland as a return to a Dominican family also reflected, quite practically, the fact that migration frequently split parents and children or husbands and wives for extended periods. And since U.S. immigration law tended to have a narrower view of what constituted family than Dominicans did, it was more difficult for migrants to reconstitute broad kinship networks than immediate families in New York.[25] This helps explain why vacations to the homeland often involved an elaborate ritual of gift giving to a wide range of kin. This distribution renewed migrant closeness to the homeland because it fulfilled obligations to relatives and kin, and it highlighted their distance from the homeland because the act of giving demonstrated a higher status derived from their place in the United States. The impulse to distribute gifts and assistance to kin left behind also perhaps reflected a kind of survivors' guilt for those fortunate enough to escape the economic disasters of the homeland.[26]

This simultaneous closeness and distance had pitfalls as well as pleasures. "Every time I go home," anthropologist Georges Fouron notes of his own trips to Haiti, "there is a certain tension because everyone imagines that Rolande and I are extremely wealthy."[27] Most accounts describe Dominican nonmigrants, in the 1970s, as similarly receptive to migrant tales of progreso and similarly apt at exerting pressure on migrant visitors in the form of inflated expectations. Dominican New Yorker Juan Contreras remembers feeling perplexed when one old friend in Bonao asked him if he was rich. "I said rich, no. He said, wait a minute, doesn't everybody that goes to New York get rich? I said no. He thought I was lying to him."[28] Migrants might enjoy the celebrity that their imagined wealth brought and the act of renewing family bonds. But they also ran the risk of sanction or criticism if they did not bring the requisite gifts, send sufficient assistance, or treat friends and relations to generous quantities of food and drink on their vacations. Already by the 1980s, migrants in New York complained that the cost of renewing relationships with home, the cost of performing both progreso and family obligation, was rising despite the increasing difficulty of earning a living in New York. A group of Dominican New Yorkers told a reporter that they felt "tied down" in New York because the cost of returning home in "triumph" was out of reach.[29]

The Boundaries of Home

If Dominican New Yorkers sometimes found themselves wishing that their poorer kinfolk at home would believe tales of migrant progreso a little less fervently, they encountered a different problem among the middle and upper classes in Santo Domingo. Residents of middle-class and elite neighborhoods often portrayed upwardly mobile migrants as untutored campesinos, weaklings, unable to survive in the harsh social realities of the Dominican Republic. In 1971 *El Caribe* flatly declared that "a vast majority of the Dominican colonia in New York" consisted of "peasants, workers without any trade, *marginados*, and political agitators."[30] This story was actually written for an English-language paper by a reporter in New York, then republished or commented on by all of the Spanish dailies. Nevertheless, it reflected a widespread idea that migrants were peasants and marginados. In this view, the relative ease of life in New York was the only thing that explained the dollars brought by returning migrants. As author Mario Emilio Pérez wrote in a nostalgic vignette about life in the capital in the 1960s, the neighborhood fool went to New York because "over there, even those who don't know how to do anything find work."[31]

Among intellectuals and activists on the left, this middle-class condescension toward migrants shaded heavily into political repudiation and personal resentment. Many in the opposition still smarted from what seemed like a capitulation by comrades who agreed to go into exile in "the land of the invaders."[32] Human rights activist Pedro Ubiera remembers more strongly feeling "perhaps a feeling of betrayal, a feeling of grief . . . 'this coward is leaving, this son of a bitch is leaving and leaving us here.'"[33] "It was assumed," radical seminarian and barrio activist Marcos Villamán explains, "that you had to sacrifice yourself in the country in order to change the regime." In Villamán's barrio, Simón Bolívar, in the early 1970s, "When people found out that someone was putting together the paperwork to get a visa, the youth responded with strong rejection. It was seen as a kind of submission, or sometimes even a moral failing."[34] And this failing was inseparable from the performances migrants made of their progreso when returning to the island. Steeped in the traditions of Dominican nationalism as well as Marxism, young leftists in Santo Domingo considered materialism to be a corrupting imperialist influence. As Juan Bolívar Díaz wrote in 1974, the generation of students that came of age under Balaguer perceived life as a choice between opposition and poverty or passivity and material pleasure. Faced with a choice "between political humiliation and unemployment, between selfishness and death or prison," he wrote, many began to opt for "consumerism and individual pleasures," distancing themselves little by little from "the pueblo that they used to love."[35] Radical nationalists thus doubly frowned on migrants who moved to the United States and returned to celebrate their material plenty. Open displays of consumption by migrants vacationing on the island proved that migrants had submitted to foreign influence, not that they had progressed.

Although only a small portion of Dominican society harbored these prejudices, it was a group with disproportionate influence. Most of the Dominican intellectuals who drove the evolution of the social sciences in Santo Domingo in the 1970s were both middle class and left-leaning. Those researchers began to study the villages and barrios of the Dominican Republic, yet they tended not to ask questions about migration to New York. The Jesuit priest and urban sociologist Jorge Cela remembers, "[W]e still thought that [international migration] was bad."[36] Nevertheless, in their scholarly writings social scientists tended to confirm the idea that international migrants were part of the marginal rural surplus population. The move to New York, in other words, served as a footnote to their central intellectual concerns: dependency, development, urbanization, and marginality. If the same rural poor who were forced tearfully into the abyss of Dominican cities were also forced into the brutal maw of the imperial monster, this was merely more evidence for their critique of the government's development strategies. And it was a source of profound melancholy. The nationalist writer María Ramos, for instance, described the line at the United States Visa Office as a collection of country folk dressed in their Sunday best, a "spectacle" that "while colorful, was nevertheless sad and depressing."[37]

If these young nationalists had investigated further they would have been surprised to find that desperately poor rural folk were a relatively small proportion of international migrants in those years. A 1974 survey showed a generalized urban bias to migration, and that migrant families tended to be better off and better educated than the average Dominican. On the 1980 Dominican census, 65 percent of Dominican women who reported children living abroad themselves lived in either Santo Domingo or Santiago. Thus, contrary to the presumptions of many in the Dominican Republic, scholarship since the early 1980s has described the pool of international migrants in the 1970s as predominantly urban and middle class. Still, there is an important difference between the finding that Dominican New Yorkers were not unemployed campesinos and seeing them as urban "middle classes." First of all, some of their above-average status in the surveys is likely due to their having family members living abroad and sending resources home. Second, the large urban expanses of Santo Domingo and Santiago were themselves recent constructions, populated by many people who while not technically campesinos were also not perceived as urban by the city's upper classes. In fact, marking someone as rural in Santo Domingo was a way of marking their lower-class status. The slightly better off, slightly better educated families living in the barrios (precisely the people who were apparently most likely to have relatives living abroad) often adopted these same distinctions of urban cultura in their own efforts to avoid exclusion. Thus while migrants were not generally rural marginados, from the perspective of Santo Domingo's upper crust, there was little to separate them from peasants.[38]

Santo Domingo elites also used the accusation of rurality as tool for containing the upward mobility of new middle classes. The problem with new middle classes, Melvin Mañón complained in a 1974 feature in ¡Ahora!, was that when such people gained enough wealth to aspire to middle-class neighborhoods in Santo Domingo, they retained their uncultured *rural* ways. They did not want to live in modern apartments because they needed patios in order to raise chickens and throw their coffee grounds out the window. But rural origins were worse still when combined with foreign cultural influence. Just as elites in Santo Domingo in the 1920s had rejected newly wealthy classes for their vulgar materialism, Mañón complained specifically about the consumer behavior of the new middle class. Their motto, he wrote, was "buy first, find out what it is good for later." They bought houses, electronics, and furniture but never invested in rational or productive activity. What is more, materialism was a trait imported, like the electric can openers and refrigerators themselves, from the United States. It was, as he put it, a kind of behavior that "belonged to other countries."[39]

Mañón did not write specifically about migrants. Still, his complaints offer a clear backdrop to the class biases migrants faced when they returned to the Dominican Republic, especially the idea that they were campesinos. Patricia Pessar and Sherri Grasmuck noted in their fieldwork in the early 1980s that many residents of Santiago were "fond of the stereotype of the rural dweller, the *campesino*, returning from New York with a lot of cash and little capacity for 'proper' urban consumption."[40] Former student activist Pedro Ubiera remembers this stereotype in Santo Domingo too: "A guy would come back bringing with him what he thought was the best up there, and he would bring it back here . . . maybe a jacket that was a bit too hot for the weather here . . . so people made fun of him, we said 'poor devil.'"[41] Journalist Bonaparte Gautreaux Piñeyro agrees that middle-class people in Santo Domingo saw the figure of the returning migrant "as an ostentatious character, as a show-off, as a clown."[42]

READING HOME, WRITING HOME

Most New Yorkers returning home for the holidays probably never came into direct contact with a representative from the Tourism Ministry. Most also never came into direct contact with people who openly rejected their stories of progreso for reasons of class condescension and nationalism. Still, like residents of Santo Domingo barrios, migrants imagined and practiced their relationships to home in the context of a social world shared unequally with Dominican elites and intellectuals. Newspapers and magazines published in the Dominican Republic provide the clearest documentary record of migrant attempts to assert themselves in this shared world. Indeed, newspapers from the homeland figured prominently in the lives of many Dominicans living in New York. Newsstands in Washington Heights were sites of daily gatherings, as migrants awaited the arrival of newspapers on morning flights from Santo Domingo. On street corners, on subways, and in cafés, Dominican New Yorkers read and vociferously debated the news from home only a few hours after it was printed. This tradition originated in the late 1960s when Milagros Ortíz Bosch, who would later become vice president of the Dominican Republic, began distributing the daily newspaper El Nacional in New York. The newsmagazine ¡Ahora! and the newspapers El Sol, La Noticia, El Caribe, and Listín Diario all soon followed suit, setting up distribution networks in New York.[43]

Benedict Anderson argues that the rise of print culture in Europe and the Americas in the early modern period made it possible to "think the nation" as a community connected in the present by membership in a reading public. Daily papers constructed a notion of the simultaneous experience of current events, allowing readers to comprehend one another as a national community. The nearly instantaneous circulation of the homeland press in New York also made it possible for Dominicans to continue to "think the nation" even at a great distance. That is, reading the homeland press did not merely reflect a homeland orientation—it helped make such an orientation possible. At the same time, Santo Domingo's newspapers also became important venues for public expression in Dominican New York, at a time when New York's newspapers were mostly inaccessible. Rather than founding their own publications and, in them, defining new identities apart from the nation, Dominican New Yorkers formulated the written accounts of their lives within a national public sphere. Santo Domingo newspapers thus became a place to write home, both to constitute and to preserve a relationship to home through writing. In the process, Santo Domingo newspapers evolved into a sphere for debating the meaning of that relationship.[44]

Writing home, however, meant working within the limits imposed by editors in Santo Domingo. For if the distribution of Santo Domingo newspapers in New York was a fairly straightforward economic enterprise, the flow of information from New York back to editors in Santo Domingo was more idiosyncratic. Coverage of the colonia in Santo Domingo newspapers emerged slowly out of the earlier traditions of reporting on New York. Before the advent of mass migration to New York, the major Santo Domingo papers published regular chronicles from correspondents there. Xavier Montes, for instance, published "El Mundo desde Nueva York" (The World from New York) in *El Caribe* in the last days of the Trujillo regime. The title expressed the notion that the whole world was uniquely visible from New York, not Santo Domingo, and the reporting resembled the form of the famous dispatches of José Martí from New York and Alejo Carpentier from Paris, if not their literary merit. Correspondents in New York often doubled as sports reporters to cover the Dominican players in the major leagues, but they did not naturally turn into reporters on Dominican barrios in the city. Emilio Escalante, who wrote a regular column called "Entre los Rascacielos" (Among the Skyscrapers) for *El Nacional*, scrupulously avoided any mention of the growing Dominican presence in New York in the 1960s. Escalante twice wrote features on Latin American immigrants in New York, but in neither case did he mention that Dominicans lived among them. The point of reporting from New York, it seems, was to share the privileged gaze of a resident of a world capital, not to report on the lives of Dominican immigrants.[45]

In the last years of the 1960s, however, the reliance on one or two correspondents to report from New York gradually evolved into a system of reporting on and for the colonia. In February of 1965 a column called "Desde New York" (From New York) appeared for the first time in *¡Ahora!* announcing a dance held by the Miramar Social Club in celebration of national independence day. Over the next several years the column reported weddings, baptisms, and other society events from the colonia. In 1968, *¡Ahora!* established "En serio y en broma . . . Dominicanos en Nueva York" (Seriously and Kidding Around . . . Dominicans in New York), the first regular column published in Santo Domingo and ostensibly dedicated to Dominican New York. Yet the author of the column, the aging Puerto Rican–Dominican writer Miguel Rodríguez O., only sometimes sprinkled observations on the Dominican migrant experience among his philosophical meanderings and autobiographical anecdotes. The pronounced idiosyncrasy of this column suggests that while editors were starting to understand that there was a market for regular coverage of Dominican New York, they had few ideas as to how to carry it out.[46]

Still, by the end of the 1960s, readers of *El Nacional* and *¡Ahora!* in New York learned how to make use of the few designated correspondents to publicize their activities to both New York and Santo Domingo audiences. In the early 1970s, Tirso Valdez took over for Rodríguez O. at *¡Ahora!* publishing a regular page called "Mosaicos de Nueva York" (Mosaics of New York). In it he gradually shifted from entertainment and gossip reporting (mostly translated from the *Daily News*) to a loose mixture of social and political announcements, Dominican entertainment news, and even events like migrant birthdays or graduations. At the same time, a Colombian photographer named Héctor Chacón, who frequented Dominican parties and social events in Queens, began sending photographs and reports to *El Nacional*. In the early 1970s, Dominican New Yorkers with access to either Valdez or Chacón appeared almost daily in the Santo Domingo press, in smiling photographs of associations such as the Club Juan Pablo Duarte or the Johnny Ventura Fan Club. The job of Dominican journalists, and eventually of the Dominican columnists at each of the two major Spanish-language dailies in New York, was to receive invitations to social events, attend, take pictures, and then include a mention of these events in their regular columns. The República Dominicana Social Club held a dance, for instance, and a group of young women appeared in a photograph dressed in long paisley skirts. A group of young New Yorkers who had been part of the Club Enriquillo in Villa Francisca held a raffle in New York to raise funds for the club back home and also appeared in a short news item.[47]

This style of reporting proliferated so quickly that newspaper archives in Santo Domingo seem to document the flowering of dozens of community organizations, charitable societies, and service agencies in New York City under the leadership of Dominican professionals and politicians. Appearing in the newspapers, however, depended more on access to journalists or editors, on tenacity, or even on payment than on any easily identified demonstration of leadership or newsworthiness. The owners of the newspapers, New York–based writer Amín Cruz wrote bitterly, were unwilling to pay professional journalists. They hired "inept persons," he complained, who "interview the so-called community 'leaders' who really have very little interesting to say."[48] Instead of offering real coverage of the community, they published "publicity pieces for businessmen and paid political messages."[49] Dominican migrant Andrés Canto observed similarly in 1971 that the system of reporting tended to encourage the proliferation of groups that "only exist in the minds of those who claim to preside over them." This was, Canto added, a sort of *figureo periodístico*, self-promotion through the manipulation of news coverage.[50] Lawyer Víctor Espinal, who helped to incorporate dozens of Dominican organizations and associations in the 1970s, remembers that the only thing most of these groups did to warrant newspaper coverage was to pay kickbacks to journalists.[51]

From the point of view of frustrated, unemployed journalists and many local activists, the Santo Domingo press was woefully inattentive to the needs of the migrant community. Yet the purely economic motives that drove coverage of the colonia also caused newspaper editors to suspend, in part, their biases as members of the Dominican intellectual and middle classes. In fact, precisely because Dominican New Yorkers were recognized as a reading public and a source of advertising revenue before they were seen as a subject of relevant news reporting, some migrants enjoyed a unique opportunity to insert themselves into the Santo Domingo press in the early 1970s. It is easy to see how a wide range of Dominican journalists and activists in New York would have despised this system for the ways it favored particular visions of the community, promoted certain leaders, and provided work for only a few reporters. Still, it would be a mistake to ignore the self-representations that many migrants managed to produce through this system of exchange. It would also be a mistake to allow these observations about the nature of newspaper reporting, as frequently driven by a coalition of self-promoters and marketers, to diminish the importance of Dominican associational life in New York in these years. Reports of New York clubs and societies in Santo Domingo publications show, rather, that the homeland press played an important, and not entirely transparent, role in constructing claims to progreso, cultura, respectability, and community leadership. Seeking to appear in cultural reporting or in a society column distributed at home in the Dominican Republic was one way that many Dominicans in New York expressed their claims to admiration, both as individuals and as a collective. And the dozens of notices of "lyrical and cultural" events, beauty pageants, or dinner dances contained multiple layers of meaning that could help fill out the complicated relationships migrants constructed with their neighborhoods and their home.

Although reports on club events from New York reflected the particular political goals of those promoting the stories, in aggregate these announcements demonstrated, in the words of the short-lived New York–based newspaper *El Dominicano,* "The successes and triumphs of our vigorous community in the fields of the Economy, the Sciences, the Social, of *Cultura* and of *Progreso* in all of its manifestations."[52] In addition to the dozens of announcements about clubs and dinner dances, in 1971, *El Nacional* announced the formation of a special monthly section called "Dominicanos en New York," dedicated to paid messages by Dominican New Yorkers. Two enterprising Bronx Dominicans, Elías Lama and Pedro de León, came up with the scheme, which essentially offered access to "figureo periodístico" in the form of paid advertising. Lama and de León traveled door to door in Dominican business districts in New York selling space in their supplement. Almost immediately, they were swamped with requests for advertisements in their section, and they soon switched from a monthly to a weekly format. In 1971 and 1972, "Dominicanos en New York" published hundreds of advertisements for bodegas, furniture stores, nightclubs, and apparel factories in Corona, in Washington Heights, and along Amsterdam Avenue on the Upper West Side. These were in part actual advertisements for *El Nacional*'s many readers in New York. The insert, Lama and de León explained, highlighted "the Dominican merchants and Dominican persons who have gotten themselves started in this great city" so that patriotic Dominican readers in New York could identify Dominican businesses and patronize them.[53] Lama himself took the opportunity to advertise his Washington Heights photography studio in *El Nacional*, offering Dominican flags, shields, and music as well as color photographs of Duarte and other national heroes.[54]

But Lama and de León were clear that they had another purpose as well. "Dominicanos en New York" was a way to "bring to the readers of this newspaper announcements and reports, illustrated with photographs, of our compatriots who struggle to obtain a good future."[55] They advertised shopkeepers' accomplishments to readers back home who would never have an opportunity to patronize their businesses. Photographs of the owners and their families behind the counter accompanied most of these announcements. In some cases, an ad for the Hoe Avenue Laundry Service in the Bronx, for instance, added an actual story of the progreso of the proprietor. In "his twenty years of residence in the United Status," Hoe Avenue Laundry's owner, Mr. Martínez, "has succeeded in making a very comfortable position for himself." The biography of Martínez described his laundry, his supermarket, his rental properties, and also his home in Connecticut.[56] Another ad told the life story of Rafael Belisario Medina Méndez, who was born in Neiba in 1946, studied at the public Liceo Juan Pablo Duarte in Santo Domingo, then in 1968 moved to New York, where he learned English and took a course at H&R Block. Now he was a member of the Association of Public Accountants and had his own accounting firm on Amsterdam Avenue, the first Dominican "who has reached such a high rung on the ladder."[57]

Alongside these individual messages of progreso, journalists in New York and editors in Santo Domingo rewarded *bodegueros* (the thousands of Dominicans who invested in small corner stores, or bodegas, in these years) and other Dominicans in New York with more generalized narratives expressing a collective experience of progreso and respectability. Miguel Rodríguez O., for instance, explained to readers that the social, cultural, and patriotic activity of Dominicans in New York was in the "front row" among the "enthusiastic, hard working, and honest Spanish-American family." In another column he added, "You can be sure that everyone is working. And that thousands have *progresado*, becoming owners of bodegas, restaurants, barber shops, travel agencies, workshops, industries, etc. Many have their own house and car and live comfortably."[58] Similarly, at Christmas in 1971, *El Nacional* paid homage to Dominican professionals in New York, to whom they had sold a full page of paid advertisements. "Being Quisqueyanos, we feel proud of the position occupied by the Dominican colony within the Hispanic community, and proud of the many values the colonia has offered, from the hardworking factory employee, to the industrialist, the merchants, and most especially the professionals whose greetings we publish today."[59]

In Santo Domingo, pictures of Dominicans behind the counters of their bodegas illustrated a tale of migration and progreso. Among neighbors in New York the same shops and proprietors illustrated harsh tales of ethnic invasion and neighborhood decline. As white ethnics abandoned the drudgery of corner stores, selling out to Dominicans, the changing over of shop signs to Spanish became a measure of the shifting ethnic and racial landscape in Upper Manhattan. As an Irish resident of Inwood told oral historian Robert Snyder, "You wouldn't go to Dyckman Street for two weeks, and you'd go down there and there'd be a Spanish sign up there where an Irish deli used to be." This was a sign of the transformation and decline of the neighborhood.[60] Meanwhile, in African American and Puerto Rican neighborhoods, Dominicans inherited the role of ethnic outsider from the Jews who sold to them, experiencing some of the tensions that more famously structured Korean shopkeepers' relationships with black patrons. In 1979, for instance, a Dominican bodeguero on East Fourth Street in Brooklyn shot and killed a Puerto Rican man, who he alleged was attempting to rob the store at knifepoint. Angry Puerto Rican neighborhood residents first threatened to burn the store but eventually only looted the merchandise.[61] Although celebrations of the Dominican migrants as the "front row" in the "enthusiastic, hardworking, and honest Spanish-American family" do hint at the kinds of accusations leveled against immigrants in New York, there is no evidence that the advertisers in "Dominicanos en New York" sought specifically to counter such accusations. Still, the fact that the same image—a bodega counter with Dominicans behind the register—could evoke a narrative of progreso and triumph in one context and a narrative of decline or intrusion in another helps explain the importance of writing home in structuring Dominican ethnicity in New York.

The same can be said of the many notices of cultural and social club events. In 1978, police representatives to the Washington Heights–Inwood Task Force described "mostly Hispanic" social clubs as a threat to public safety and neighborhood revitalization. The police had only sketchy information on the clubs, and still identified some by their earlier names, such as "The Old Pig and Whistle," and "Old Red Barrel

Bar and Grill." These names suggest that the clubs were like bodegas; they occupied the spaces in the neighborhood that formerly housed Irish businesses and social life. Others they named as "Social Club" or "Cultural Club." The police admitted that criminal behavior had actually been documented at only one of these social clubs, a place called Bimboland. Yet they listed dozens of clubs as places "where drugs could very well be sold."[62] The police were not alone in their accusations. In an interview in the *New York Post,* Andrés Belén, a Dominican labor activist and exile from La Romana, described a string of "social clubs" along Columbus Avenue north of 104th Street where gambling, billiards, and prostitution were commonplace. Dominicans in Manhattan, he reported, referred to the stretch as Calle Barahona, referring to the street in Borojól, Santo Domingo, designated as a red light district under the U.S. occupation of 1916–1924.[63] That is, Dominicans in New York employed the geographical markers of indecency common in Santo Domingo to distance themselves from the rowdier social clubs. But the Washington Heights–Inwood Task Force was not particularly attuned to the distinctions between decent and corrupt Dominican clubs. Indeed, it identified the Club Recreativo 30 de Marzo as a locus of possible criminal activity in the neighborhood only a year after *El Nacional* published a report that the club had launched a new project, along with a dozen other clubs in New York, for the "development of cultural and sports programs for the children of Dominican parents."[64] Here again, the contrast between stories told about emerging Dominican spaces in Washington Heights and stories told about those same spaces in the homeland press is dramatic. Conversations in the transnational public sphere shared between New York and Santo Domingo often seem simultaneously, and with the same images or language, to address two separate questions of belonging: the matter of cultura and class status inherited from the barrios of Santo Domingo and the problematic narratives of urban decline encountered in Manhattan.

In some instances, writing home also allowed migrants specifically to enunciate their relationship with the national community in the Dominican Republic. In response to attitudes on the island, an exile named Miguel Andujar wrote to *El Nacional* in 1971, "sectors of our revolutionary left" mistakenly portrayed Dominican New Yorkers as "traitors," "sell-outs," "ingrates," "ignorant," "without principles," "etc.," a characterization that he flatly denied.[65] With slightly more subtlety, a report from New York in *El Nacional* argued that many Dominicans in New York celebrated the anniversary of the 1965 uprising "with more enthusiasm than those who sympathized with this cause and are still in the country."[66] In other words, migrants were *more* patriotic than nonmigrants. Along with frequent generalizations about the patriotism of migrants, *El Nacional* also provided ways for individual Dominican New Yorkers to demonstrate that, as a group, they had not forgotten their homeland or the hardships endured by those left behind. Santo Domingo editors published scores of articles about New Yorkers' anonymous acts of charity on behalf of helpless Dominican orphans, sick children, and desperate widows. The paper would report on needy cases, and Dominicans in New York would send checks directly to the editors. The paper then published photographs of *El Nacional* employees (usually attractive young women) handing over the money, and printed articles about the generosity of the donors, under headlines like "The Colonia in NY Helps the Poor."[67]

This collaboration between migrants and newspapers seems broadly parallel to the practices of distribution and gifting described by various anthropologists studying Caribbean migrations. New Yorkers could express both their closeness to, and their distance from, the poor in the Dominican Republic by sending help. Yet these public acts of giving differed from private exchanges since New Yorkers did not know the recipients of this help; they simply responded to reports in the newspaper. And unlike private gifting and most instances of "figureo," the donors were often anonymous. Rather than renewing specific ties of kinship, newspaper reports of charity expressed an abstract relationship between the colonia and the nation. As Rafael Antonio Suárez of Riverside Drive explained in a letter to *El Nacional*, New Yorkers had a responsibility to "let a grain of sand fall back to their Fatherland."[68] Here is perhaps the clearest example of how newspaper reading and writing mediated migrant relationships with the homeland. Migrants donated collectively and anonymously to needy cases identified in homeland newspapers. Together with editors they thus confirmed, in regular fashion, their participation in a national reading public as well as their responsibility and generosity toward the struggling nation. And, in exchange for both their avid readership and their generosity, editors in Santo Domingo rewarded them with open assertions that "the Dominicans who live in the United States remain concerned about those who are here."[69]

Like the idea of home itself, the practices of writing home also reflected a divide between male and female roles. All of the early correspondents from New York were men, and men were more prominent in the leadership of clubs and associations than women were. Women nevertheless occupied a marked, if circumscribed, prominence in the representations of cultural activities in homeland newspapers. Girls and women organized fashion shows, dances, and beauty pageants at Washington Heights social clubs, and male photographers, club leaders, and editors frequently published images of beauty queens in New York. It seems likely that the desire to publish accounts and photographs of beauty contests and contestants derived easily out of established social expectations in Santo Domingo, where beauty contests were as much a part of neighborhood life as national politics. As Dominican performance artist Josefina Báez explains, public recognition of these club activities was something that working-class, urban Dominicans had always wanted but never had until they came to New York. Indeed, Dominicans with access to journalists published similar accounts of their activities in the social pages of the same Santo Domingo publications.[70] In New York, however, representation of female bodies also blended smoothly with other elements of the stories of cultura, progreso, and loyalty to the homeland. The Centro Cívico Cultural Dominicano, led by Alfida Fernández, took up a collection of children's clothing for the poor, for instance. A young beauty queen elected at the Miramar Social Club then brought the clothes to Santo Domingo and San Pedro de Macorís when she returned to the Dominican Republic to spend the Christmas holiday.[71] Alfida Fernández had worked with the Tourism Office in New York to organize Dominican participation in New York's Columbus Day parade, where young beauty queens were part of the projection of the nation. ¡Ahora! reported on the participation of Dominican ladies in the 1967 parade that "Dominican beauty was on display."[72] Club leader Onésimo Guerrero likewise described the purpose of a beauty contest inside the Dominican social clubs as "bringing to light the beauty of the Dominican woman."

If beauty pageants in Santo Domingo made young women into symbols of neighborhood and national identity, and beauty pageants in New York expanded the symbolism to include ethnic pride, in reports to the homeland press the specifically Dominican beauty of migrant girls supported broader migrant claims to full belonging in the national community. This symbolism worked in tandem with the desire for individual recognition. Indeed, photographic depictions of young women sometimes stood in entirely for actual reporting on the colonia. Beginning in 1971, the Colombian photographer Héctor Chacón organized a regular section in ¡Ahora! comprised almost entirely of photographs of young Dominican women but titled, "Dominicans in the United States," suggesting a broader documentary account of the colonia. Although he seems to have recruited many of his subjects at club events and pageants, Chacón also placed an advertisement in ¡Ahora!. Female readers in New York wishing to appear in the magazine were directed to call his office or home. Chacón, or perhaps his editors, explained the unusual structure of his reporting with the aphorism "A woman is always news."[73] Some of Chacón's pictures were clearly intended as pinups, after the fashion of ¡Ahora!'s regular series featuring topless and swimsuited actresses from France and the United States. The notable difference was that these pinups were Dominicans whose access to the spotlight relied entirely on being in New York and having a connection to Chacón. The female subjects apparently sought to represent themselves as *vedettes* or "starlets." Editors seem simply to have been satisfying their male readers' prurience (and their own). Most of the women depicted in "Dominicanos en los Estados Unidos," however, were carefully dressed. Some appeared as demure migrant daughters, some as actresses or singers in stage costumes, or in party outfits. These seem to be migrant girls who, as Josefina Báez remembers, came from neighborhoods in the Dominican Republic where beauty contests and carnival dances would never receive publicity. And they were girls who, as they began to integrate into the world of youth culture in places like George Washington High School, occupied the lowest rung on the local scale of hipness. Yet in *¡Ahora!* their party costumes read as the "ultra modern fashions" common among Dominican youth in New York.[74]

As with visits home, which revealed tensions within migrant households along gender and generational lines, depictions of female bodies captured tensions about the sexuality and style of young migrant women. Indeed, some of the same adult men who took these photographs and judged beauty contests expressed profound ambivalence about the styles chosen by young women in New York. Miguel Rodríguez O. observed disapprovingly that women in New York "now go out in the street half naked" and that girls were allowed to socialize with boys unsupervised. In 1978, Chacón himself published a feature on hot pants—a new style, he explained to Dominican readers, designed to show off their "private parts" and "curves."[75] The result of this ambivalence, as Chiqui Vicioso observed in 1971, was that Dominican girls in New York who expressed independence or asserted their sexuality were considered "Americanized."[76] Paradoxically, in published photographs and beauty contests, migrant men appropriated the sexual allure of young women to express pride in their nation, club, or in the colonia. Chacón or his editors went so far as to publish a caption under a photograph of a nearly naked migrant woman describing her as "just as Creole as a real Dominican woman."[77] It is impossible to know just what Dominican girls imagined as they dressed and posed for Chacón's camera, knowing their images would circulate in Santo Domingo and New York. But, caught as they were between the pressure to be sexy and the pressure to be sexless, it seems reasonable to interpret these photographs at least partly as self-representations. These were opportunities to appear before a broad public, as an artist, as a hip dresser, as a young adult, and as a sexy woman. Posing was a means for telling yet another tale of progreso.

HOME AS A SPACE OF ETHNIC DEFINITION

The space afforded in the Santo Domingo press, like the celebrity offered on visits to the island, encouraged migrants to imagine home as an alternative to the low status imposed by their adopted city. In this sense, Chiqui Vicioso worried in 1971, dreams of home could serve as an instrument of denial, allowing migrants to drown out processes that were making Dominicans into a new racial minority in New York. If bodega owners or club leaders, for instance, wrote home in order to contradict the negative stories told about them by New Yorkers, they frequently did so without acknowledging such stories directly. They spoke much more directly to the ideas of class status reigning in Santo Domingo. Yet choosing home as a space to write one's own story did not always mean leaving out the parts of the story where one lived in a troubled city, faced discrimination, or suffered economic hardship. The homeland press also provided space for Dominicans directly to contest, and debate among themselves, the social prejudices they faced in New York. These conversations carried a risk: they undermined the messages of respectability and class advancement that many migrants hoped to send home. Indeed, the most vigorous early reporters on Dominicans' social ailments in New York, including Chiqui Vicioso herself, set out intentionally to debunk what they saw as the false image broadcast in tales of progreso. Such critics broadly succeeded in convincing middle-class readers in Santo Domingo that New York was teetering on the edge of crisis. The troubling question of how Dominicans fit in the decline of New York City confirmed old class prejudices on the island, gradually reshaping how newspapers covered migrants' relationship with home.[78]

The first, and most powerful, blow to migrant stories of cultura and progreso came with the return of antiimmigrant politics to the city. In September of 1971, the *Daily News* published the first of a five-part exposé on the "scandal" of "illegal aliens" in New York. Earlier that year, the House Subcommittee on Immigration and Naturalization had held hearings on "the problem" of illegal aliens, and the *Daily News* called on Congress to shift attention from the undefended border with Mexico to the flood of illegals into New York. By March 1972, Judiciary Chairman Peter Rodino responded with hearings on undocumented migration in New York City. Though the committee never adopted the extreme racial language of the "wetback crisis" of the 1950s, the hearings sent a chill through Dominican, Haitian, and other new immigrant settlements in New York. In theory, the focus on illegal aliens ratified the rights of legal immigrants, but talk of an illegal crisis was also a way of blaming social problems on immigrants who were universally understood as poor, dark-skinned Latin Americans. Arguments that undocumented workers were responsible for the distress of more deserving workers and for the depleted coffers of state agencies cast a broader web of suspicion and blame on immigrant and Latino workers in general.[79]

In New York, many Dominicans responded to the *Daily News* series and the congressional hearings by emphasizing distinctions between hardworking illegals and supposedly lazy native minorities. J. Velázquez wrote, in a letter to the editor of the *Daily News*, "As for putting Americans out of jobs, bunk. In most cases, the jobs these aliens take are refused by our needy citizens who prefer welfare."[80] Velázquez did not specify his national origin, but his message was a familiar refrain in Dominican circles. Officials in the Partido Revolucionario Dominicano, interviewed in a feature in the *New York Times* in the aftermath of the *News* piece, likewise rejected the notion that illegals were a threat to the United States. In fact, they argued, illegal Dominicans could not collect public benefits. They were therefore harder working and less likely to accept welfare than blacks and Puerto Ricans.[81] A group of Dominicans calling itself the Comité de la Cordialidad (Committee of Friendship) approached Rodino himself in 1971 and 1972 to "clarify some points," especially that the Dominican community deserved consideration since it is "very hardworking, honest, and has a very low level of public assistance."[82]

But the attacks on illegals were also a turning point in Dominican politics in New York, serving to redirect the attention of the Dominican left in New York toward the status of migrants. These activists tended to focus directly on the mistreatment of Dominican migrants instead of deploying stereotypes about other racial groups. By 1974, for instance, the Movimiento Popular Dominicano called for the "community to unite against the Rodino law" or see itself "PERSECUTED, IMPRISONED, DISCRIMINATED AGAINST, LOOKED ON WITH SUSPICION, [AND] HARASSED IN THE STREETS AND IN OUR OWN HOMES."[83] The PRD, the MPD, the 1J4, the Dominican-American Civic Association, and the Comité de Defensa, along with a scattering of other Dominican, Haitian, and Latin American groups, formed a Coalición Para la Defensa de Inmigrantes (Coalition for the Defense of Immigrants, CODI). Under this umbrella, the same party leaders and young radicals who had organized rallies against Balaguer's abuses now turned against INS abuses and the "Rodino Bill," but maintained a strong revolutionary undercurrent. CODI staged rallies outside the headquarters of the *Daily News*, threatening the paper with a boycott if it did not reverse its stance on undocumented workers and its generally negative coverage of "Hispanic peoples." In a letter to the *News*, CODI made familiar arguments that undocumented workers took jobs that citizens and legal residents did not want and that "our brothers and sisters have been forced to flee from underdevelopment and hunger caused by plundering multinational corporations which rob their nations' wealth."[84] At a rally at 112th Street and Amsterdam Avenue in September of 1974, the crowd chanted, "We are not illegals, we are not criminals, we are workers" but also carried signs reading "Dictatorships Supported by the U.S. Create the Latino Exodus." Although the PRD was not above shifting blame to Puerto Rican and black welfare cases, party leader José Ovalles also linked the fight for power in Santo Domingo to the question of immigrants' rights. "It is a shame," he declared to the crowd, "that while this is occurring, certain irresponsible governments, like that of Dr. Balaguer, lay out the finest carpets and age the finest wines to receive the managers and agents of the corporations."[85]

Thus, many Dominican radicals in New York managed to tie the question of INS abuses to what they regarded as the bigger picture, the continued fight against U.S. imperialism and the continued fight for power in Santo Domingo. Still, the energies organized by the attacks in the *Daily News* and the hearings in Congress also gave birth to a new generation of community organizations specifically focused on Dominicans as a local constituency. As part of the movement for immigrant rights, in 1971 Alfredo White, Diego Delgado, José Cabezas (a radical Cuban priest who had been deported by Balaguer), Porfirio Valdez, Chiqui Vicioso, and others created the Centro Dominicano de Asistencia (Dominican Assistance Center, CEDOAS) with federal funding and help from the Church of the Intercession and the Episcopal Church in Washington Heights. CEDOAS provided legal assistance to undocumented workers, English and high school equivalency classes, and help to political exiles. CEDOAS also maintained ties to the nationalist left in Santo Domingo, helping, for instance, to bring Expresión Jóven to New York in 1974. In 1974, when the initial funding for CEDOAS ran out, White formed a new community agency, proceeded to build ties to the Democratic Party, and secured funding from the Community Planning Board. A year later Nasry Michelen, Onésimo Guerrero, Cotubanamá Dipp and Rafael Trinidad created Asociaciones Dominicanas (Dominican Associations) to provide legal services and training to immigrants. Michelen was a doctor who had collaborated with Puerto Rican community leaders in the creation of Hostos Community College and had served as president of the college and of Lincoln Hospital before turning to Dominican community politics. This group of professionals, some of whom maintained active ties to the PRD, won a grant of $111,000 from the mayor's office in 1975.[86]

The flurry of new organizing produced a shift in the language used in the Santo Domingo press. Dominicans in New York were a "comunidad" (community) rather than a "colonia" (colony). The Dominican-American Civic Association sponsored an essay contest in February

1975, which showed the conscious nature of this transformation. Suggested essay topics included "The Dominican Community, what is it?" and "What are the biggest problems facing the Dominican Community?"[87] However, this shifting language did not necessarily mean giving up on Dominican politics. And the focus on immigrants and the community had little effect on the importance of the homeland press. CEDOAS, CODI, and Asociaciones Dominicanas all actively publicized their activities through connections at *La Noticia, El Nacional, El Sol,* and *El Caribe.* Indeed, the vaults of the newspaper *El Caribe,* now part of a private archive in Santo Domingo, contain evidence of photographs and typescript articles seemingly sent from activists in New York, including a carbon copy of the letter CODI sent to the *Daily News* threatening a boycott. Often this publicity looked nearly identical to other kinds of figureo, as when CODI announced a "lyrical cultural act" on behalf of undocumented immigrants with a performance of Normandía Maldonado's folkloric dance troupe. When the *Times* published its feature on the PRD, a rare moment when Dominicans managed to answer charges in the U.S. media, *El Caribe* published a translation of the entire piece and *El Nacional* published a story on the story under the headline, "Publicity in *Times* Is Judged Favorable." Even when Alfredo White announced his retirement from homeland political activity and called for Dominicans to focus on their exploitation and persecution at the hands of the Immigration and Naturalization Service, he did so in the Santo Domingo magazine ¡*Ahora!.* This gesture expressed the idea that Dominicans were permanent fixtures in New York, yet it was possible only in the public sphere centered in Santo Domingo.[88]

New Yorkers also wrote home about the question of illegal immigration because the hubbub in the U.S. press had quickly seeped across the border, and editors in Santo Domingo had developed a keen interest in the topic. Generally, coverage was slanted against the INS. Throughout the early 1970s, visa policy remained a hot button issue in Santo Domingo, and accusations of mistreatment against Dominican citizens elicited nationalist outcries, like an editorial in *La Noticia* that objected that calling Latin Americans "illegals" was ironic since no country is more prolific than the United States in its propensity to "illegally invade sovereign territories." The United States had despoiled Latin America, the editors argued, then imprisoned Latin Americans as criminals for the "'crime' of wanting to work."[89] Politicians in the opposition pounced on the issue, arguing that President Balaguer was guilty of abandoning Dominican citizens faced with persecution. For their part, officials in the government promised to intervene on behalf of illegals. In the wake of the *Daily News* series, Reformista Consul Federico Antún told *El Nacional* that Dominicans only broke immigration laws in order to support their families. "Almost all come here to work and with one goal, to *progresar*."[90] Several years later his replacement, Carmen Rosa Hernández Balaguer, opined that "now is not the moment for . . . persecution against those who honorably try to work."[91]

Yet it was easy for the Dominican press to deplore the crackdown on illegals while still confirming many of the prejudices expressed in the crackdown. The Santo Domingo press translated and republished articles about the illegal alien crisis from the U.S. press, beginning with Tirso Valdez's uncritical summary of the *Daily News* series in 1971.[92] This had the effect of focusing coverage of the colonia (or community) abroad around the question of illegality. Editors in Santo Domingo had a particular penchant for coverage of document forgery and illegal boat trips. Such stories tended to portray migrants as hapless dupes in the hands of unscrupulous smugglers and counterfeiters, as in a report on "a known delinquent, a swindler who takes advantage of the ignorance of the campesinos."[93] Editors in Santo Domingo also avidly reproduced reports of the decline of New York. In this context, police reports suggesting that Dominicans were increasingly involved in common criminal activity in New York seeped into the press in Santo Domingo in the early 1970s. *Última Hora*, for instance, told readers, "It seems that the Dominican immigrants in New York have not been able to avoid the contagion of the growing wave of delinquency that is striking North American society." The paper added, "[C]rime statistics in New York reveal that the previously peaceful Dominican community is now reporting more than one homicide per month."[94] In 1975, *El Caribe* reported a Dominican in New York "figured among the most notorious traffickers" of drugs.[95]

In the face of reporting that linked Dominicans with rising crime in New York, some Dominican New Yorkers simply repeated the refrain that the Dominican colony distinguished itself by its honesty and work ethic. As the short-lived newspaper *El Dominicano* put it, Dominicans had "never traveled down the harsh and tortuous paths of crime or degeneration; of vice or corruption."[96] Revolutionary activist Freddy Gómez wrote to *¡Ahora!* that North Americans had invented the idea that Dominicans were delinquent as an excuse to crack down on undocumented migrants.[97] But others in New York accepted the reports of Dominican misbehavior and delinquency as unfortunate facts. They defended their own good names, the good name of the colonia, and the good name of the Republic by distinguishing between the long-established, honorable Dominican settlement and the few bad apples that had recently begun spoiling its good reputation. Dominicans were suffering a declining group reputation in New York, Tirso Valdez reported, for which "not all are to blame."[98] Reginaldo Atanay, the lone Dominican columnist in the New York Spanish-language daily *Diario-La Prensa*, also sided with the antiimmigrant sentiments of the *Daily News*. He did not call into question the possible injustice behind other New Yorkers' stereotypes about Dominicans. He saw the problem as evidence that the whole ethnic group, the whole Dominican nation, suffered as a result of a few illiterate peasants, car thieves, and "self-proclaimed revolutionaries."[99] Valdez reprinted Atanay's complaint, as well as the opinion of a reader named Carlos Morel who argued simply that he hoped the U.S. authorities would "throw out the back door all those Dominicans who have come to discredit our country since the year 1960."[100]

For these authors, the lack of basic cultura lay at the heart of the divide between the majority of honest Dominicans in New York and a handful of newer arrivals. Their accounts were reminiscent of the complaints of neighborhood decency groups in Santo Domingo who objected to the behavior of their neighbors. Atanay complained of "characters who need to read and assimilate an instruction book on urbanity to be able to behave like decent people and not as they have until now, as delinquents."[101] Valdez wrote that neighbors shunned Dominicans in New York because they "usually put their record players on at full volume, and also frequently speak at the top of their lungs and noisily joke around."[102] Similar complaints about loud music were commonplace in Santo Domingo. But in New York, noisy neighbors not only disturbed Dominicans, Valdez complained; they paraded their lack of cultura in front of North American audiences, giving all Dominicans a bad reputation.

Atanay and Valdez saw an influx of uncultured campesinos as the problem, but other authors attributed the worst behavior to "newer" migrants from Dominican cities. Here again the tension between disdain for rural Dominicans and idealization of their simple, virtuous lives is clear. A group of Corona residents, originally from the countryside outside Santiago, explained to a *New York Post* reporter in 1975 that the stereotype of young Dominican men listening to music on a street corner was not typical of their neighborhood, which had been settled by campesinos in the 1960s. The problem, they said, was a more recent, more desperate, more urban immigration. A group of urban toughs "travel back and forth," they believed, creating problems in both New York and Santo Domingo.[103] In a similar vein, a Dominican social worker named Ubi Rivas argued in *¡Ahora!* in 1971 that their mostly rural origins protected Dominicans in New York from degeneracy because, as campesinos, they were "characterized by a healthier lifestyle."[104]

Meanwhile, a third group of authors criticized the repeated celebrations of the established Dominican settlement (whether urban or rural) as the most honest community in New York. These writers, many of whom participated in the creation of CEDOAS in the early 1970s, saw reports of dinner dances and corner stores as a dangerous façade hiding the facts from view. The problem was not that a few delinquents were besmirching the otherwise pristine reputation of the community, they argued, but rather that most Dominicans in New York lived in ghettos, worked in oppressive factories, and suffered widespread discrimination. New York, radical-nationalist-turned-immigrant-rights-worker Alfredo White wrote in ¡Ahora! in 1974, "is not how they paint it."[105] Activists in New York first put out this message in the Santo Domingo Catholic magazine Amigo del Hogar. Calling for more attention to the needs of migrants on the part of Dominican authorities, a priest named Juan Oleaga wrote in 1968, "You who have seen youngsters dressed in pretty suits and dollars still warm, telling of the marvels in New York . . . you should know that behind this many other things are hidden, many trials that they don't show, many ruined souls and also many lives cut down by violence."[106] Another priest, Porfirio Valdez, spiritual adviser to student activist Nelsy Aldebot, wrote his own story of the Dominican settlement shortly after the Daily News raised the alarm of the illegal alien crisis in 1971. His story was less about the false images INS officials disseminated about Dominicans than about the false image Dominicans presented about their own lives in New York. In reality, "They live in apartments that suffocate because the buildings are so old and narrow," he wrote. In the factories where they work, "not infrequently they are subject to a slave driver."[107]

Social Catholics in New York thus attempted to undermine narratives of progreso in order to identify social injustice and inspire political action. In this cause, the writers at Amigo del Hogar were not squeamish about discussing what they saw as the social degeneracy of Dominican migrants in terms reminiscent of the culture of poverty arguments popular in the United States. The only difference was that they saw this noxious culture as the result of too much assimilation in New York, rather than too little. At the same time their critiques resonated with the view of cultura promoted by left-wing, religious, and middle-class nationalists in Santo Domingo. Juan Oleaga described the social "derailment" of Dominicans in New York, including family disintegration, alcoholism, and "gambling, with all of its derivative vices."[108] Following suit, in the Santo Domingo News in 1971, journalist Danilo Vicioso used crime statistics in New York to criticize the "negligence" of the Balaguer regime and call for a center for the orientation of immigrants, offering employment, medical, educational, and legal services. Unscrupulous gangsters, he argued, provided forged visas and then required "campesinos to enter into vice rings, turning them into drug dealers and prostitutes, etc." In his defense of these exploited workers, he confirmed the suspicions of many in Santo Domingo that "a vast majority of the Dominican colonia in New York" was "made up of peasants, workers without any trade, *marginados*, and political agitators."[109]

Not only was New York turning Dominican settlers into delinquents, the young writers in *Amigo del Hogar* argued; it was turning them more broadly into materialists. Chiqui Vicioso, for instance, wrote that in their alienation Dominican migrants turned to material objects; "pretty clothes and cars become the longed-for objects and the CLIMAX of these youths' aspirations."[110] Similarly, in her 1974 memoir, María Ramos mixed her tales of cruel bosses and overcrowded, filthy living conditions with sharp disdain for the materialism of Dominican migrants. In New York, "happiness means having things, surrounding yourself with things, even becoming a thing yourself."[111] Like cultural nationalists in Santo Domingo, in other words, social activists in New York saw the material progress that Dominican New Yorkers often celebrated as signs of a shallow, alienated, and un-Dominican culture.

These critics did not bemoan the bad reputation ascribed to the bulk of honorable Dominicans as the result of a few troublemakers. To the contrary, they emphasized that the disasters of Dominican settlement were widespread and that successes were few. The whole narrative of progreso represented a perversion of national values and was, anyway, a sham. But perhaps more important, they argued that the responsibility for Dominican degeneracy lay with an unfriendly imperial system and inattentive Dominican religious and secular authorities. "In a word," another author in *Amigo del Hogar* wrote, Dominicans in New York "have been objects of exploitation."[112] To this claim that Dominican migrants were victims of their environment, Tirso Valdez and Reginaldo Atanay wryly retorted that just the opposite was true. New Dominican arrivals brought their lack of culture (whether urban or rural) with them. The environment in New York was "a victim of them."[113] New York journalists who sought to maintain their own status and reputation blamed the incultura of Dominican newcomers for the racial injustices of U.S. society. On the other hand, the activists who set out to defend Dominican migrants from the oppressions of the imperial system and the indifference of Dominican authorities perpetuated emerging stereotypes of migrants as lower-class weaklings in Santo Domingo and the idea of the culture of poverty in the United States.

DREAMING OF HOME

The articles in *Amigo del Hogar*, Vicioso's piece in the *Santo Domingo News*, and the work of other radical critics in New York found a ready audience among allies on the island who spread their message. Activists Porfirio Valdez and Alfredo White helped organize a trip by Santiago archbishop Monsignor Roque Adames in 1971, for instance. The archbishop then returned to the island and took up the task of challenging popular impressions of migrant triumph. He wrote a pastoral letter warning of the disintegration of Dominican families, the alienation of Dominican parents, who dream only of a return to the island, and the derailment of Dominican children, who "choose outlets like rebellion, drugs, delinquency, and the formation of gangs." Adames also ratified suspicions about the migrants' class pretensions, declaring that New York was like a rural province of the Dominican Republic and that the "progreso of the New York Dominican is limited to work, food, and clothing." [114] Several years later Monsignor Agripino Núñez Collado and Archbishop Polanco Brito returned from a trip to New York with similar conclusions. "Man does not live by bread alone," Núñez Collado told the press, yet Dominican New Yorkers were perilously careless about "education, religion, and cultural matters." Some did not even know about "the values of their country, or its history."[115] Thus the generalized nationalist and class prejudices against migrants seamlessly incorporated stories immigrant rights activists told about the urban crisis in New York.

Soon, New York–based and Santo Domingo–based journalists and activists alike began to suggest that migrants were communicating the materialism and corruption they acquired in New York back to the Dominican Republic. Víctor Grimaldi, who had until then promoted positive images of migrants, warned in 1973 that despite their expressed antiimperialism, Dominican migrants were no longer really resisting incorporation into U.S. culture and were becoming responsible for "the transmission of anti-values" to the island, "like success, money, comfort, and excessive consumption."[116] In 1976, Chiqui Vicioso argued that consumer-oriented Dominican New Yorkers had become a dangerous source of "cultural penetration" on the island.[117] Coming from intellectuals in both New York and Santo Domingo, this message undercut the notion that migrants' visits to the island enacted their deep ties to home. Marxist historian Franklin Franco told *El Caribe* in 1976 that "far from the happy return to the beloved country," most returning migrants were "young people raised in New York" who "bring a series of maladjustments" and "abberant deviations" such as drug use.[118] In 1975, *Listín Diario* published a report under the headline "Dominicans in New York Have No Social Life." The piece began as a profile of a successful migrant, a man from the shantytown of Los Alcarrizos who returned "a respectable merchant . . . purchased a gas station, and is now a businessman." It then expressly subverted the tale of progreso. Such cases were rare, the reporter explained. Most migrants return home "with two or three thousand dollars, a few suitcases of last-year's clothes, a bunch of strange *costumbres* and the heavy yoke of frustration."[119]

This blending of bleak descriptions of crisis and social dislocation with well-developed hostility to migrants and their cultures began to multiply on the island by the second half of the 1970s. In 1975, for instance, a reporter in *¡Ahora!* depicted New York's crisis as "an insufferable pestilence" while condemning Dominicans in New York as illegal, delinquent, captivated by "the dollar sign," and "unmoved by and insensitive to the penury of others."[120] Two years later Frank Canelo, recently returned from a ten-year residence in New York, published a serialized sociological analysis of Dominican settlements in New York, San Juan, and Miami in *¡Ahora!*. He later republished these essays in a book called *Where, How, and Why Dominicans Live Abroad*. Canelo captured the emerging consensus among Dominican intellectuals. He saw Dominican migration as a tool designed by an imperial hand to calm social conflict in Santo Domingo and prevent national attempts to resolve development problems.

But if earlier critics had sympathized, at least superficially, with the plight of hapless migrants at the mercy of imperial capitalism, Canelo mostly slandered migrants. He incorporated a conservative middle-class disdain for migrants' lack of cultura with the revolutionary nationalist outcry that migrant degeneracy threatened to engulf the nation. Three-fourths of Dominicans in New York were welfare cases, he asserted. Many of them had lied and cheated in order to collect public assistance, and still others were simply delinquents. Personally, he saw this use of welfare as a combination of creeping degeneracy among Dominican New Yorkers and clever conspiracy by imperialists to trap Dominicans into dependency and thereby prevent national liberation. Relying on old oppositions between technological, modern, but alienated North American cultures and underdeveloped but spiritually rich Dominican cultures, he argued that Dominicans were ill-suited for acculturation into New York society. Yet he saw them also as increasingly divorced from what he thought were their own natural cultural expressions. Their illiterate rural origins and the moral contagion of the black and Puerto Rican ghettos in which they lived meant an inevitable degeneration of migrant popular culture. Worse still, in the public schools Dominican children learned all of the corruptions of their native classmates, with the result that "Dominicans have become very deeply involved in the sale and use of narcotic drugs."[121] While he advocated a small measure of charity on behalf of migrants who "need to be partly excused for having been uprooted," he thought there was no excuse for islanders who chose to imitate their cousins in New York.[122] Migration, he worried, served as a vector for the infection of national culture with external influences. "With the migratory connection our internal *cultura* is deformed and deteriorates."[123]

Critics seeking to debunk the myths of migrant progreso, whether in New York or in Santo Domingo, often saw themselves as the allies of the great bulk of exploited Dominicans in New York. Their efforts to undermine a false image of honesty and progress were a radical alternative to the pronouncements of conservative professionals and business leaders, who would whitewash the dire needs of Dominican New Yorkers. Yet such messages, tinged with accusation and prejudice, had limited appeal to the great bulk of New Yorkers themselves. This gap between poor migrants and those who would defend poor migrants is nowhere clearer than in the sociology thesis of Vilma Weisz, a student at the private Pedro Henríquez Ureña National University in Santo Domingo. Weisz read the articles published by Valdez and Chiqui Vicioso in *Amigo del Hogar* and relied on the organizers at CEDOAS to help her set up fieldwork among migrants on the Lower East Side in New York. Yet, as she interviewed residents there, she was troubled by the gap between her vision of migrant lives as destroyed and corrupted by too-close contact with the United States and migrants' visions of their own lives. Fully 82 percent of the Dominican New Yorkers she interviewed told her that they believed settlement in New York had been good for the country since it provided work and allowed them to support their families. Unable to accept that they might have insight into this question, Weisz concluded that Dominican New Yorkers either did not "understand why it is so grievous for our country that so many people are leaving"[124] or were hiding "the reality of their lives in the metropolis."[125]

BODEGUEROS AND THE URBAN CRISIS

For activists, publicizing the growing social crisis in New York, even perpetuating prejudices against Dominicans living there, seemed a matter of conscience. But for the bodegueros, who were the paying clients of Dominican newspaper editors, representing a crisis in New York and the hardships it brought to their own lives without undermining their own claims to respectability and progreso involved a delicate balance. They contributed stories that showed the colony suffering because of an economic collapse and an urban crisis, but resisted the idea that Dominican progreso was shallow and marred by cultural perversion. This balance is evident in a special supplement published in *La Noticia* in 1979, "Dominicans in New York: A City in Crisis." In it, Juan Deláncer wrote that Dominicans were a "minority among minorities" suffering the ravages of unemployment, failing schools, and decaying housing. Deláncer even went so far as to adopt the now obligatory posture of myth debunker. New York looked little like "the color photographs" most readers had probably been sent by relatives. He extensively quoted from interviews with Víctor Espinal, who ran for school board in 1975 as part of the Parent Association coalition but with a platform emphasizing Latino unity, and Nasry Michelen, who had helped to found Asociaciones Dominicanas. Through Deláncer, they argued that only increased local political involvement could solve the problems facing the "community."[126]

Deláncer's account of the troubles haunting Dominican New Yorkers was restrained, however, seemingly because he funded his supplement with advertisements placed by Dominican businessespeople in New York. Santo Domingo newspapers traditionally rewarded such advertising with paeans to the honesty and patriotism of the colonia, not with stories that undermined the idea of migrant progreso. Deláncer, though, took another message from his encounter with bodegueros. Through him, they sent the message that "things are not as good as they used to be."[127] Through Deláncer, and through their old ally Héctor V. Chacón, shopkeepers and restaurant owners presented a picture of honest migrants, struggling mightily to get ahead, to get educations, to practice their professions in the face of widespread discrimination and inhabiting neighborhoods, a city, and a world capitalist system in decline. At times, they used stories of the crisis to combat the inflated expectations for migrant success prevalent in Santo Domingo. "If you in Santo Domingo only knew the suffering," Chacón wrote in 1978, "the quantities of sweat and even tears the ones who punctually send your money orders have dried, perhaps you would better appreciate these remittances."[128] Chacón also took pains to represent Dominican New Yorkers as untainted by contact with the United States. "Neither the attacks of cultural penetration, nor *travoltismo* [the popularity of John Travolta was then causing a major uproar among cultural nationalists in Santo Domingo], nor consumerism have succeeded in preventing the Dominicans from remaining just as Dominican as when they left Santo Domingo years ago."[129]

Generally, by the second half of the 1970s, Chacón's interviews and profiles of Dominican migrants were broadly reminiscent of the kinds of stories of urban decline that Jewish and Irish residents of Washington Heights told. That is, they recognized the crisis and highlighted its effects on their attempts at decent lives. Yet they blamed others for the crisis itself, especially black and Puerto Rican "welfare" cases who increasingly encroached on respectable Dominican communities.[130]

This perspective, which conformed in many ways to the old booster-ism that distinguished Dominicans as "honest" and "hardworking," served especially as a way to interpret the explosion of reporting in Santo Domingo on crime and violence in New York. Reporters writing on behalf of the bodegueros mirrored tales of crime and violence in the city told by many of the Jews and Irish of Upper Manhattan, among whom store robberies were the "fearful stuff of everyday conversation" in the 1970s.[131] Though many Jews and Irish saw the coming of Domini-cans, heralded by the coming of Dominican shopkeepers, as the source of neighborhood decline, Dominican shopkeepers often saw things from the perspective of white ethnics. After the 1977 blackout, Rafael Lantigua described how "the wise vigilance of Dominican merchants prevented vandals from sacking or destroying their stores." Although other reports on the blackout highlighted the Dominicans who were apprehended and deported for looting, Lantigua referred only to riot-ing in black and Puerto Rican neighborhoods.[132]

This same perspective emerged within the broader trend of detailed reporting, in Santo Domingo, about crime in New York City. While many newspapers reported meticulously on the rise of crime among migrants in that city, and critics from New York emphasized the derail-ment of Dominican youth, Chacón and two other reporters in El Na-cional found a niche reporting on murders or other attacks committed against Dominicans in New York. El Nacional published as many as five stories a month on murders in New York between 1978 and 1983. These accounts tended to emphasize Dominicans' role as victims, not perpe-trators. Chacón explained: "Dominican merchants who labor honestly and honorably in New York" owned 70 percent of bodegas above 80th Street. Their businesses, he wrote, were targets for "the 'blacks' who lurk in those sectors."[133] Among the scores of accounts of Dominican deaths, Chacón also described some instances in which Dominican business owners, defending their businesses, killed black or Puerto Ri-can assailants.[134]

TRANSNATIONAL TIES

In 1980, the New York Times reported a survey showing that five out of every six Dominican New Yorkers considered their "home" to be in the Dominican Republic. At the time, popular versions of immigration history generally obscured earlier European immigrants' deep attach-ments to foreign lands. By comparison, Latin American immigrants' at-tachments to home seemed strange and troubling. Times reporter David Vidal recognized that some earlier immigrants had looked homeward.

But they had, he wrote, "eventually loosen[ed] or cut those ties." The question of whether the new Latin American immigrants would do the same thing, Vidal told readers, "was unresolved."[135]

Vidal's concern about whether the new immigrants would ever become Americans like the old immigrants had done was based on a faulty comparison. The process by which New York's Jews and Italians became American, so often remembered as the voluntary and natural stripping away of foreign traditions by immigrants in pursuit of an American dream, took place in a unique period of immigration restriction after 1924. With new arrivals no longer renewing the ties between immigrant neighborhoods and the old country, the U.S.-born second generation did create predominantly ethnic-American identities during the Great Depression and World War II. But the liberal narrative of assimilation made the experience of this second generation, uniquely severed from the old country by legal restriction, into an imagined model of "normal" immigrant incorporation. To hold Dominican settlements, where the second generation lived surrounded by ever-growing numbers of new arrivals, to such an ideal unfairly made the new immigrants seem anomalous.

Within a few years of the *Times* survey, social scientists studying immigration, most of whom were sympathetic to immigrants, turned these worries on their heads. Dominican dreams of home were not deviant, they argued. They were an example of a new kind of immigrant incorporation: transnationalism. In a world where airplanes, wire transfers, televisions, and telephones regularly and rapidly moved goods, money, ideas, and people across national boundaries, migrants could permanently belong to two national communities. There was something fitting, the early proponents of transnationalism added, in the fact that immigrant workers were becoming transnational given the increasing power of transnational corporations. If capital had no national allegiance, why should labor? Although at first proponents of transnationalism sometimes focused a bit too intently on the supposed novelty of homeland ties, the observation that migrants did not simply leave behind their foreignness, that they became *simultaneously* incorporated into two national communities, was quite useful. For Dominicans, ties to home were part of the process of becoming New Yorkers, and the process of becoming New Yorkers helped constitute ties to home.[136]

Dominicans' notions of home, that is, were often a response to the reception they encountered in New York, especially as the city's industrial base contracted in the 1970s. In this context, turning wages from a garment factory into reliable middle-class status inside the United States was, as one scholar punned, like passing through "the eye of a needle." Like earlier generations of immigrant workers in previous economic downturns, Latin American migrants in New York turned to home as a resource, both imagined and practical, in the recession of the 1970s. But rather than simply returning home, as others had frequently done, Dominicans and other newer migrant groups made regular transactions with home into a strategy for coping with economic constriction. Factory and service work might not provide a clear path to the U.S. middle class, but remitted wages could support family members, purchase real estate, and subsidize small businesses back in Santo Domingo. Migrants thus capitalized on the ability to ship goods, wire money, place phone calls, and vacation back across the border in order to translate their migration into improvements in status.[137]

At the same time, home offered a respite from the jarring social prejudices Dominicans faced in the city, as they went from being simply invisible or seen as "other Spanish" to being recognized as a distinct racial minority. Complaints about the "illegals" and the new neighborhood invaders highlighted their homeward orientation and their failure to assimilate—as the older "legal" immigrants were imagined to have done. But ironically, many Latin Americans saw the defense of their national cultures as a response to the cultural prejudices they faced in the United States.[138] The celebration of homeland values, journalist Héctor Chacón wrote to explain the *Times* survey, was a defense against the forced assimilation of the "melting pot." He explained that the "ideal of many North Americans is that everyone has to melt in the great forge of their way of life, and leave behind the 'scum' of their own traditions and experiences." This was "precisely the battle," he argued, of the cultural groups in New York that sought to preserve the "nationalist spirit and cultural wealth of the Latin world."[139] Dominican cultural nationalism—like black nationalism and Chicano nationalism—thus rejected assimilation narratives that made certain kinds of cultural differences out to be deficiencies.

Dominican cultural nationalists, though, did not have to imagine a future homeland or a homeland in the precolonial past. They had government officials from the Dominican Republic inviting them back to Santo Domingo for joyful holidays. A story of migration punctuated by returns "home," where one belonged, where one's color was interpreted in familiar terms and one's humble origins were mitigated by new spending power, could offer a contrast to stories that made migrants into outsiders, invaders, and the racialized cause of pockets of blight.

Not all migrants had equal access to home in their efforts to resist, or compensate for, social prejudice in New York. Nor, for that matter, did all Dominicans have equal access to New York City. In fact, despite the increased mobility made possible by airplanes, faxes, and money transfers, widespread experiences of exclusion, dislocation, and immobility still characterized life for many in the Dominican barrios of New York

198 · Chapter Seven

and Santo Domingo. What is more, creating a relationship with New York or maintaining a relationship with home did not always offer a reliable solution to the problem of social prejudice. Migration, return migration, and transnational transactions did not undo the social inequalities that marked Santo Domingo, New York, and U.S.-Dominican relations. They merely shifted the terrain in which Dominicans worked to avoid exclusion to an urban social space that encompassed both New York and Santo Domingo. This new landscape is what theorists call the "transnational social space." Not everyone in the Dominican Republic or Dominican New York regularly participated in transactions across the national boundaries. Yet even those who never moved across a national border, or rarely left their barrios, lived within a world of shared relationships and expectations that spanned the border.[140]

As the story of Dominican New Yorkers in the 1970s makes clear, these relationships and expectations represented no easy consensus. They were more often a series of debates or of conversations transposed, translated, and altered in their meanings as they moved between New York and Santo Domingo. When they chose to engage in this conversation with Dominicans in Santo Domingo, Dominican migrants faced many of the old barriers of class, race, and culture that permeated that city's social geography. Nationalist ideas about the cultures of the United States and spreading stories about Dominicans' involvement in an urban crisis in New York served only to reinforce those barriers.[141] By the end of the 1970s, migrants simultaneously negotiated U.S. ideas about them as illegal, delinquent slum invaders and the idea in Santo Domingo that migrants were poor Dominican peasants, infected by the vices of a degenerate and consumerist U.S. society, returning to the Dominican Republic laden with the trappings of foreign materialism. Yet even this did not stop migrants from using home, both the idea and the place, to make claims for respectability, to offer their own interpretations of the urban crisis, to air disagreements among themselves, or to contest prejudices against them.[142]

In short, the attachment to home that the *Times* saw as a strange new attitude among migrants—that antiimmigrant forces saw as a challenge to "American" national identity, that proponents of transnationalism saw as a bottom-up response to global capitalism and the pressures of assimilation—was actually the tip of a very large and complicated iceberg. Ties to home reflected the broader evolution of a social sphere of ideas and expectations shared between Dominicans in New York and Dominicans in Santo Domingo. But these expectations and ideas were never shared equally or completely. Rather than belonging easily and equally in two national communities, Dominican New Yorkers often faced simultaneous and overlapping exclusions in both. In 1975, when

Juan Contreras flew home to the Dominican Republic, he found that living in New York made him a hero in his hometown and that no matter how hard he tried he could not convince his old friends that he was not rich. Ten years later, Dominican New Yorkers returning to Santo Domingo might still be heroes to their families, but they contended with a Dominican public awash in suspicion.

EIGHT

Strange Costumbres

IN NEW YORK, by the middle of the 1970s, thirty years of expanding programs for the poor ran aground against a shrinking tax base, a deep economic recession, and increasing pressure from creditors. In 1975, the city declared bankruptcy. Ed Koch, who won the race for mayor in 1977 and held the office until 1989, set about restoring the faith of lenders by cutting spending across the board. With a solid electoral base among white ethnics in the outer boroughs, he gradually loosened the purse strings for investment in housing, real estate development and some city services, but did not restore spending in public health, welfare, and social services for the (mostly black and Latino) poor. After 1981, President Ronald Reagan compounded these cuts by reducing federal spending on welfare, jobs, housing, and education. Blaming black and Latino pathologies and lavish government spending for the decline of cities in the United States played well with the electorate in the 1980s. Koch fought publicly with black leaders over cuts to social services, calling them "welfare pimps." Reagan painted inner cities as hopeless, burnt-out shells, populated by drug addicts, teen mothers, and "welfare queens." The shift in priorities from redistribution to the poor to pleasing creditors, developers, and other constituencies helped create a recovery in the New York economy based on a boom in financial services, real estate, and insurance. However, instead of lifting all boats, as Reagan promised, this rising economic tide widened the gap between rich and poor in the city.[1]

The neighborhood known as Soho, an area of abandoned factory buildings settled by artists and bohemians as manufacturers moved out in the 1960s and 1970s, became a symbol of this transformation. In the 1980s, as economic life returned to the city, wealthy stockbrokers, bankers, and advertisers priced the artists out of the neighborhood. The abandoned factories of a bygone industrial age became luxury condominiums for the new service elite. In Soho, the postindustrial city ceased to be a place where people made things and moved into a new phase of urban succession as a place to live for people made wealthy by the new service economy. The neighborhood went from edgy to funky to hip and to chic before finally becoming a luxurious cliché. But Washington Heights, home to many of the workers who moved into low-wage service work as downtown factories closed, was also a symbol of a city transformed by the political economy of the 1980s. When Koch was first elected, his appointed Washington Heights Task Force still imagined a mostly white neighborhood seeking to prevent the encroachment of slums. By the middle of the decade, the city's politicians and news media all saw the neighborhood as a distressed "inner-city" area marked by crime and poverty. During the 1980s, seven of the eight hospitals in Washington Heights closed. Between 1980 and 1990, the proportion of neighborhood residents receiving public assistance rose from 23 to 32 percent. Dominicans, who settled in every corner of Washington Heights during the decade, fared worse than anyone in the neighborhood. Their per capita income was half of the neighborhood average and less than a third of the average for whites (excluding white Latinos). In 1990, 40 percent of Dominicans in Washington Heights lived below the poverty line. Twenty percent had no telephone.[2]

One of the running jokes about New York in the 1980s was the importance of cocaine in local culture, from the all-night parties at Studio 54 to the high-paced lives of the city's "Yuppies." But again, cocaine played quite differently in the playgrounds of the elite service class and in the neighborhoods left behind by the boom. Residents of Washington Heights felt this difference sharply as the neighborhood took on a new economic role as a drugs distribution hub. At a "speakout" organized by a group of Dominican politicians in 1988, a neighborhood parent named Ramona Andujar complained, "At the bus stops there are more drug dealers than passengers," and along Amsterdam Avenue there were "14 and 15 year old girls working as prostitutes and addicted to drugs."[3] But if neighborhood residents complained about the drug dealers, they also suffered the effects of the War on Drugs, declared by President Reagan in 1982. Politicians eager to appear "tough" on crime and to deflect responsibility for the urban crisis onto poor black and Latino residents depicted Washington Heights as the center of a "crack epidemic." In July 1986, for instance, then-prosecutor Rudolph Giuliani donned a sleeveless Hell's Angels jacket seized from a criminal defendant and traveled to Washington Heights, news cameras in tow, to buy a vial of crack. Accompanied by Senator Alfonse D'Amato, he easily accomplished the task, "looking," as the *Washington Post* put it, "like a paunchy middle-aged version of T.V.'s Crockett and Tubbs." Giuliani and D'Amato argued that their stunt proved the need for mandatory prison sentences for even small amounts of crack cocaine.[4] That they went to Washington Heights for the buy, rather than raiding the loft condominiums of Soho or office buildings on Wall Street, was not a casual choice. Indeed, the federal sentencing laws that D'Amato helped to pass disproportionately imprisoned (and deported to Santo Domingo) low-level Dominican retailers from Washington Heights, while leaving suburban and downtown consumers unmolested.[5] And the focus on Washington Heights residents as the source of the "crack epidemic" took its toll on the reputations of all Dominicans. As parent activist Ramona Andujar complained in 1988, "[T]hey accuse Dominicans of being responsible for the drugs."[6] That accusation became a central aspect of the incorporation of Dominicans, now recognizable as distinct from African Americans and Puerto Ricans, into narratives of "inner-city" pathologies in the United States.

Despite the deeply divided city and the growing prejudices that awaited them, Dominicans still crowded onto airplanes to reach New York in the 1980s. Although historically net immigration has often slowed, or even reversed direction, in times of economic distress, the number of documented Dominican immigrants admitted to the United States rose from an average of 13,900 in the 1970s to 22,600 per year in the 1980s, to more than 40,000 per year in the early 1990s.[7] Dominicans also increasingly set out in small open vessels called *yolas*, in an attempt to cross to Puerto Rico. Some settled in San Juan barrios. Others made Puerto Rico a stopover, blending into the great stream of Puerto Ricans "jumping over the pond." Dominican yolas received little attention in the mainland U.S. news media, especially when compared with the uproars over Cuban and Haitian boat people. But in the Puerto Rican press, the problem of undocumented Dominicans grew to a shrill din. It is difficult to judge, from these reports, exactly how many Dominicans attempted yola voyages in these years. But researchers studying the phenomenon in the early 1990s concluded that undocumented migration by boat picked up dramatically in the middle of the 1980s. A long-standing practice of contraband between coastal towns in the Dominican Republic and Puerto Rico grew into a lucrative network of human smuggling. Boat captains charged migrants thousands of dollars and filled boats beyond their safe capacity. The INS in Puerto Rico estimated between one thousand and fifteen hundred arrivals a month at the end of the decade.[8]

The Dominican press meanwhile published repeated tragic accounts of shipwrecks, shark attacks, and drownings. Freddy Sandoval, writing in 1986, described "an avalanche of people" who set out "ignorant of the distance, the shark infested waters, and an extremely dangerous route." To explain why thousands risked everything to reach the harshest of New York neighborhoods, Sandoval turned to the familiar refrain that New York was a false paradise. Yoleros took their chances in the search for well-being, "real or fictitious."[9] However, it was not necessarily true that Dominicans were unaware of the dangers at sea or deceived as to the situation in the northernmost of Dominican barrios.

The transnational media and informal oral networks in Dominican society effectively diffused tales of sharks and tales of the urban crisis in New York. It seems, rather, that the economic and urban crises in the Dominican Republic, beginning around 1982 and lasting through the early 1990s, made the urban crisis in New York seem attractive by comparison. A popular refrain puts it directly: "Allí las piñas son agrias, pero aquí ni hay piña." (Over there the pineapples are sour, but here there are no pineapples at all.)

Like the crisis in New York, a high-profile bankruptcy (in this case the national government) augured the urban crisis in Santo Domingo. But also like New York, the crisis actually reflected a long-term transformation of the national economy. And, as in New York, the influence of a new group of ideologues in Washington severely constrained the possibilities for a political response to economic transformation that might have reduced the impact on the poor. Latin American public debt had long provided opportunities for the exercise of U.S. power in the region. In 1905, Roosevelt took over the Dominican customs house to make Dominicans repay their debts. Now in the 1980s, the Reagan administration pushed for the virtual abolition of the customs house in Santo Domingo, as in all of Latin America, demanding elimination of trade restrictions and tariffs in the region. Washington pushed the Dominican government to shift resources from factories producing for local consumption to export processing zones producing for consumption in the United States. These processing zones, encouraged by provisions in Reagan's Caribbean Basin Initiative, attracted U.S. manufacturers of clothing and electronics, further eroding the industrial economy of New York City without alleviating the inequalities of Dominican society. At the same time, Washington demanded the end of a system of governmental supports to the urban poor in Santo Domingo. Indeed, the simultaneous erosion of incomes in the barrios of New York and Santo Domingo can be seen as part of a new phase in the imperial relationship between the United States and the Dominican Republic, built on two pillars: a reorganization of the hemispheric division of labor and a transnational politics hostile to spending on the poor.[10]

The crises in the two largest Dominican cities were parallel in another sense as well. In Santo Domingo, cuts in social spending compounded the deep recession, leading to an urban subsistence crisis in a country that, by 1981, was majority urban. Just as inner-city U.S. neighborhoods bore the double blow of poverty and prejudice, the barrios of Santo Domingo also became the objects of political attacks and sensationalist journalism. The Partido Revolucionario Dominicano won the presidency in 1978 with strong support from the barrios, putting an end to the authoritarian regime in place since the U.S. invasion. But by 1984, the PRD decided to swallow the economic medicine prescribed by Washington, cutting back on price controls on food and other basic necessities. The barrios of the Zona Norte led the country in five days of protest over the "reforms." The government blamed the outburst on "gangs of evil-doers" and marched the army into the barrios, killing more than one hundred and wounding more than four hundred.[11] Joaquín Balaguer returned to office in 1986, bringing back a repressive politics of urban renewal. Balaguer's urbanism centered on the construction of an expressway, lined with multistory buildings, three hundred meters wide and two kilometers long, through the middle of Villa Juana and Villa Consuelo. The construction, proponents argued, would turn slums into "a beautiful area, an area where progreso will always be present," and would turn marginal neighborhoods into the "center of the city."[12]

In this project—and also in other plans, like the construction of Avenida Paseo de los Reyes Católicos through El Caliche and the eviction of El Hoyo de Chulín to build a housing complex—Balaguer claimed to be helping families who lived in "shocking promiscuity."[13] But as developers and the national government wrested urban territory from barrio residents in order to convert it into commercial property, they played up barrios as dangerous and plagued by delinquency. Balaguer delegated the task of removing two thousand families and building the V Centenario Expressway to an engineer named Ramón Pérez Martínez, known as Macorís. Macorís had been, in the earlier decade, the head of the Banda Colorá, which had terrorized barrios and had famously killed young activists in the Club Héctor J. Díaz near the site of the new expressway. The dismantling of the Banda Colorá in the late 1970s had opened the door to the successful political campaign by the PRD. But the decline of the Banda Colorá also shifted the nature of neighborhood violence, as independent youth gangs emerged to terrorize neighborhoods in their own way. The state, in turn, promoted the idea of neighborhood delinquency in order to justify its violent evictions. "These are neighborhoods with high levels of delinquency," Macorís told reporters in 1987: "Yes we have had to use a heavy hand, that is true. But we are talking about *barrios* where if you don't take care they will eat you alive."[14]

While in the United States inner-city residents saw their exclusion primarily in racial terms, in Santo Domingo most barrio residents perceived their exclusion in terms of class and geography. This is not, as we have seen, because color prejudice was absent in Dominican society. Ideas about color permeated the descriptions of barrios as dangerous spaces and representations of elite neighborhoods as civilized spaces. But neighborhood residents reported that they were evicted from their homes, beaten by police, or turned down for employment on the basis of where they lived. Neither the high degree of segregation nor the structural rewards that contributed so powerfully to defining neighbor-hood politics in racial and ethnic terms in New York existed in Santo Domingo. Neighborhood movements therefore mobilized around class and geographically based barrio identities, not racial communities.[15]

At the same time, Dominican politicians, like their counterparts who inveighed against "criminal aliens" in the United States, shifted some of the blame for the sagging economy and social dislocation in the Dominican Republic onto immigrants. Beginning in 1978, right-wing nationalists claimed that Haitians were illegally voting in Dominican elections, and that the governing PRD was permitting the "pacific inva-sion" of the country by illegal Haitians. In targeting Haitians, Balaguer again took the lead, attacking in 1986 and 1987 his principal politi-cal opponent for supposed Haitian ancestry and sympathies. He was joined by right-wing intellectuals Luis Julián Pérez, Manuel Núñez, and Mariano Vinicio Castillo, who in the early 1990s espoused the fantasy that the United States was working on a plot to reunify Haiti and the Dominican Republic into a single, blended nation. The politics predicated on an idea that Haitians were a racial and cultural threat to Dominican national identity culminated, in 1991, in massive roundups and deportations. An estimated half of the deportees were Domini-can citizens suspected of Haitian ancestry. These anti-Haitian projects likely contributed to a barrio politics that understood racial differences in terms of the divide between Dominicans and Haitians, not along strict lines of color.[16]

In this context of a changing hemispheric division of labor and si-multaneous and intertwined urban crises, politicians, journalists, and neighborhood activists in Santo Domingo turned again to the problem of cultura. Televisions, nightclubs, and outdoor gathering places pro-viding loud music and liquor spread rapidly through rich and poor neighborhoods in Santo Domingo even in the midst of the economic collapse and social upheavals. Imported goods such as music, clothing, and television programs acquired a double meaning as international agencies pressured the Dominican government to reduce trade barriers. They were part of an age-old threat of cultural penetration and sym-bolic of a new powerful threat to economic nationalism. While right-wing nationalists sounded the alarm of the Haitian threat, nationalists on the right and the left worried about the corrosive effects of cultures from the United States. The idea developed by a few left-wing intellec-tuals in the 1970s, that migrants in particular were vectors of cultural perversion, grew into widespread prejudices against "dominicanyork" and "cadenuses," a nickname for migrants referring to the heavy gold jewelry some wore on their trips to the island. Interpreting the parallel urban crises of poverty and violence in Santo Domingo, New York, and the changing global context, Dominicans focused particularly on the problem of costumbres.

The Crisis

In May 1978, Antonio Guzmán of the PRD faced Joaquín Balaguer in the first contested elections since the withdrawal of U.S. troops from Santo Domingo in 1966. Obviously losing the elections, Balaguer and the Dominican armed forces accused their opponents of fraud, took control of ballot boxes, and threatened to end the elections. Balaguer eventually agreed to step down in exchange for control of several key seats in the Senate. The pact ensured that instead of facing a truth and reconciliation commission, he continued to be the most powerful player in national political life for two more decades.[17] As in many parts of Latin America, high expectations for the end of authoritarian rule crumbled as democratic elections and pacts brought little institutional change. The PRD stumbled badly in its eight years in power, falling easily into established patterns of governance in the Dominican Republic. Holding office was as much about personal enrichment and distribution of favors as about ideology or public service. Meanwhile, a growth model established in the twelve years of Balaguer's authoritarianism collapsed, thrusting the Dominican Republic into an economic crisis. For both political and economic reasons, social inequality and poverty would get worse, not better, under democratic rule.[18]

From the withdrawal of U.S. troops in 1966 to the democratic elections of 1978, government spending had been the key to growth. On top of the massive investments in urban construction, Balaguer distributed subsidies, incentives, and contracts to fledgling industrial concerns, in an attempt to stimulate local production of basic consumer goods from macaroni and cooking oil to concrete. The government also offered trade protections to local industrialists who otherwise could not compete with foreign competitors. Finally, the state absorbed part of the cost of feeding, however meagerly, growing urban populations. The basic consumption needs of the new urban workforce surpassed the capabilities of new industries to supply jobs and surpassed the ability of the Dominican countryside to produce surplus food for market. In the interest of modernization and political stability, the Dominican state responded with price controls on products shipped in from the countryside. The state also imported foodstuffs, petroleum, and other staples and distributed them, along with electricity, to the urban populace at fixed prices. By the end of the 1970s, the Dominican state was the largest importer of food and basic commodities in the Dominican economy. While price controls were hardly a solution to urban poverty, they were a boon to urban employers, and they were essential to the basic social fabric of urban barrios. Poor Dominicans, displaced to the city, could no longer produce their own food. They depended heavily on the dozens of small colmados that distributed food in the neighborhoods on credit or in increments of one or two cheles. Those colmados bought the food wholesale from warehouses run by the Institute for Price Stabilization (INESPRE).[19]

The complicated system of state spending in Santo Domingo, on which most economic growth and political legitimacy rested, thus depended on the government's solvency. This in turn depended on exports of sugar produced by the monopoly that the state had inherited from the Trujillo family. Throughout the 1970s, a sugar quota guaranteed by the United States and temporarily high prices helped to fund Balaguer's urban growth machine. But at the end of the decade, world sugar prices fell in response to farm subsidies in wealthy countries. Just as North American and European agricultural subsidies would eviscerate the agricultural sectors in Mexico and Africa in the 1990s, around 1980 sugar subsidies in the United States, Europe, China, and India left the sugar economies of the Caribbean in ruins. In the decade that followed, instead of providing the income for state spending on urban growth, sugar enterprises began to lose money, draining resources from government coffers. To make matters worse, oil-producing countries colluded, in the 1970s, to keep the cost of energy high. Inflation in the United States drove up the cost of other imports. Suddenly, dramatically, as had happened so many times before, the things that the Dominican Republic sold to the world were almost worthless and the things that it bought from the world were very expensive.[20]

In the short run the new democratic government made up for the gap between state income and state expenses with loans from foreign banks. Oil producers, flush with windfall profits, were eager to lend as much money as Latin Americans wanted to borrow. But in the early 1980s, the U.S. Federal Reserve pushed interest rates up, and Mexico and other larger Latin American economies warned that they might default on their loans. When it became clear that the Dominican Republic would probably default on its loans too, credit to Santo Domingo dried up altogether. With neither sugar profits nor bank loans available, Antonio Guzmán's successor, Salvador Jorge Blanco, had no way of getting dollars to pay for the government jobs, contracts, food, energy, and other imports on which the entire system of politics in Santo Domingo depended, and it had no way of paying back the money previous administrations had borrowed. This was the arrival in the Dominican Republic of a cataclysm that shook the entire region, an event that Latin Americans refer to as the debt crisis.[21]

Taking a long view, the onset of the debt crisis in 1982 was a death blow to the old political economy of sugar, urban growth, and state spending. The debt crisis was an opportunity for a group of economic ideologues, who took control of the major institutions of the international financial order in the early 1980s, to enforce their vision of trade and social reform on weakened Latin American states. Led by William Clausen and Ann Kreuger, the International Monetary Fund and World Bank used their control over the flow of money into the paralyzed Dominican economy to attempt to enforce major transformations in Dominican society. They particularly sought to dismantle the established mechanisms of state spending. They pushed for a reduction in trade barriers, for floating interest and exchange rates, for cuts in public employment, price controls, and industrial subsidies, and for creation of export processing zones exempt from taxation, labor laws, and environmental protection. Eventually the Dominican political class, like its counterparts in most of Latin America, would adopt these economic policies, participating in what came to be known as the "Washington Consensus." From 1990 to 1995, the Dominican Republic gradually toed the line on exchange rates, banking and trade deregulation, and state spending. But in 1982 the death of the old system was merely foretold. Dominican politicians would hold on to their systems of distribution and extraction for more than a decade, alternating between the bitter medicine prescribed by the IMF and ostensibly nationalist economic policies that were of dubious value to anyone outside the ruling coalitions.[22]

The political pendulum in Santo Domingo swung between austerity packages and efforts to renew the politics of patronage and urban construction. In 1984, PRD president Salvador Jorge Blanco accepted the terms of an IMF restructuring plan, and cut price supports to the poor drastically. Then in the elections of 1986, Balaguer returned to power. Through the early 1990s, Balaguer accepted some of the dictates of international financial institutions and ignored others. He fostered the development of tourism and free trade zones. But to raise money for his patronage machine, he also printed money, enforced dual exchange rates, imposed fuel taxes, and preserved trade barriers. Friends of the president received exonerations from import or export duties in exchange for political contributions. In the ten years after he returned to office, Balaguer personally controlled more than half of all state expenditures, with no congressional oversight. He spent more than 90 percent of that on construction projects. The barrios thus suffered in multiple ways from the evolving political economy of the 1980s. The high unemployment of the economic slump, cuts to basic subsidies and public employment, and high inflation produced a subsistence crisis in

Santo Domingo in the 1980s. And the poorest barrios suffered too from aggressive urban renewal campaigns.[23]

The Barrios

Santo Domingo was no longer a city, as it had been up until the 1960s, where rich and poor alike clustered within walking distance of the old colonial walls. In 1981, two-thirds of the city's residents lived in the congested barrios *populares* and *marginales* of the old Zona Norte (and in a few newer outlying barrios). They occupied about 19 percent of the city's land mass, including much of what was now the geographic center of the city. Meanwhile, a privileged third of the city lived in neighborhoods that had spread to occupy almost 130 square kilometers. Middle-class residents moved freely on roads and in public spaces downtown and in the expansive western developments, and many barrio residents could scarcely afford the cost of transportation to travel to the commercial and industrial sectors or public spaces of their own city. The frequent injuries to pedestrians struck by automobiles along the Avenida Padre Castellanos (known colloquially as Avenida 17) eloquently, if tragically, symbolized the relationship between the motorized city and the crowded barrios at its core. Motorists sped along the route to quickly bypass the Zona Norte, while local residents crossed it on foot to get from one barrio to the next. And, of course, the relationship of the city to the barrios played out in the eviction of poor urban citizens to make room for more roads and expressways.[24]

Although few who did not live there cared to venture off the main roadways into the dense maze of alleys and canyons of the barrios, Santo Domingo's middle classes increasingly got information about the heart of their own city from broadcast images.[25] In the 1980s, the seven broadcast channels in the Dominican Republic began producing local reporting, allowing residents of the sprawling ensanches and urbanizaciones to consume images of barrios where they would never dream of setting foot. It is telling, for instance, that when Bonaparte Gautreaux Piñeyro reported in ¡Ahora! in 1984 on riots in the barrios, he relied on his maid (who lived near Avenida Ovando) for some of his insights and "on the T.V. screen" for the rest.[26] Although it is difficult to document exactly how newscasts depicted the barrios to middle-class viewers, television reporting likely resembled contemporary newspaper coverage of the barrios in its almost exclusive focus on stories of violence and chaos. Frequently these reports highlighted protests or complaints by neighborhood activists hoping to draw attention to local problems. But more often they were variations on a theme that first burst into the national press around 1983 and was expressed par excellence by Juan Francisco Martínez Almanzar in 1989. He described the "tear-out-your-liver" gang and the "finish-you-off-quickly" gang and other groups that rode around the barrios of the Zona Norte on motorbikes, snatching jewelry or extorting local businesspeople. Among the many sins these youngsters committed, he singled out their "exotic clothes and hairstyles" and their "slang full of badly formed Anglicisms."[27] A neighborhood group in Gualey actually kept track of all the reporting on their neighborhood in daily newspapers over a span of four years in the 1990s. They found that 100 percent of the articles dealt with violence.[28]

Television and newspapers thus helped to widen the divide between the city and the barrios, even as they transmitted images between the two spaces. Sensationalist crime reporting created, in the words of scholar-activist Rita Ceballos, a generalized notion that "the impoverished *barrios* are violent, uninhabitable spaces, where you cannot go without risking robbery or death."[29] Barrio residents and activists like Ceballos agreed that violence and delinquency were problems. Indeed, a survey conducted in 1990 found that nearly 90 percent of city residents—in both middle-class and marginal barrios—thought that violence had gotten worse in the decade of the 1980s (although in this regard the poor may have been nearly as influenced by news media as the rich). Yet the boom in reporting on crime led to an extremely skewed image of barrios like Capotillo, Gualey, and Cristo Rey. The idea that the barrios were sites of extreme violence proved useful to developers and contractors like Macorís, who made the danger of the neighborhoods an excuse for violently displacing residents. Images of barrio degeneracy and violence also made it exceedingly difficult for the majority of neighborhood residents to avoid exclusion in a city where geography was a key marker of social place.[30]

BARRIO POLITICS

In the transition to democracy and the ensuing economic chaos, old neighborhood leaders who had survived the authoritarianism of the 1960s and 1970s reemerged to negotiate with the state for local development and to promote ideas of progreso and cultura among their neighbors. These activists led the formation of dozens of neighborhood groups in the 1980s, similar to the "new social movements" that sprang up across Latin America during transitions to democratic rule. New social movements were new in the sense that they operated outside the boundaries of "old" party politics, guerrilla movements, or union militancy.[31] Yet in the barrios of Santo Domingo, they were also a return to a well-established local politics of progreso and cultura. The first sign of these new movements among Santo Domingo's poor came in 1979, when the Vicinis, one of the wealthiest families in the Dominican Republic, claimed legal ownership over neighborhood lands in the Zona Norte. Church organizations in the progressive parishes of Simón Bolívar, Gualey, and Guachupita successfully mobilized to protect the settlements from the claims of the Vicinis. This organizing also led to a formalized association of local neighborhood groups, known as the Committee for the Defense of Barrio Rights (COPADEBA). Despite its origins in the struggle for land rights, this diffuse network of local groups dedicated itself mostly to familiar demands for urban services and modernization.[32] In El Caliche, the continuity between the new social movements and the old struggle for neighborhood progreso was particularly marked. Ramona Báez, the leader who in the 1960s had helped to organize the movement that brought electricity and water, returned to the project of neighborhood organizing. Taking advantage of ties between the governing PRD and the Socialist International, Báez and her allies won a grant from the Social Democratic government of West Germany to form the Sociedad para el Desarrollo del Caliche (Society for the Development of El Caliche, SODECA), establishing a clinic, school, and other services.[33]

Neighborhood groups had high hopes for the populist government that came to power in 1978 with resounding electoral support from the barrios. The leadership of the Club S. E. Díaz went so far in 1978 as to address the minister of the interior as "distinguished comrade" in an appeal for help fighting immoral establishments in Villas Agrícolas. Yet despite the promise of friendship between the neighborhoods and the government they had elected, a series of violent confrontations in the early 1980s radically reshaped the political relationship between the barrios and the state. Barrio groups participated in a nationwide general strike called by transportation workers in 1980 over the price of gasoline. Next they joined in a highly contentious strike by employees of the state-run telephone company in 1982.[34] Then, in April 1984, President Salvador Jorge Blanco returned from Washington to announce a reduction in government subsidies of flour, powdered milk, cooking oil, sugar, and a dozen other basic goods. Residents of Capotillo and Simón Bolívar called for a general strike against the price hikes, inaugurating the protest by burning a government bus outside the Moscoso Puello Hospital. Within hours, the strike had swept through the Upper Barrios, then the capital, and then the entire country.[35]

This was a revolt over consumption, over the provision of basic services and the prices of basic goods. Across the city and around the country, crowds of protesters attacked government offices and sacked local warehouses, pharmacies, and colmados. These were the local sites of articulation with state power and private enterprise, particularly as they related to basic consumption. They were also places where food could be seized and distributed. In Los Alcarrizos, for instance, protesters sacked and destroyed a municipal mortuary, then moved on to the local offices of the governing PRD and the Institute for Price Control distribution center. The social Catholics who formed the core of COPADEBA and other neighborhood social movements were exhilarated by the riots in 1984, and rightfully indignant at the violent repression practiced by a government that was supposed to represent the barrios. The uprising, as they understood it, had been a "cry of the barrio subject": a demand to be heard, a rejection of marginal and invisible status in their own city.[36] Together with the increasingly splintered left, neighborhood activists mobilized new neighborhood associations called the Committees of the Popular Struggle (CLP). Based on territorial affinities, just like the neighborhood councils of COPADEBA, these groups coordinated what was now generally referred to as "popular protest." A centralized leadership, the Coordinators of Popular Struggle, convoked barrio strikes as a means for joining in negotiations with the other major sectors of society in the social pacts that increasingly defined the experiment in democracy in Santo Domingo. At crucial moments over the next half decade, the organizers of "popular struggles" joined business groups, government, the church, peasant groups, students, professional associations, and unions in negotiations. Barrio protests continued at a rate of one strike every four months for the next decade, picking up especial fervor in the context of double-digit inflation in 1988 and 1989 and after the contested elections of 1990.[37]

But if the uprising in 1984 inspired neighborhood activists to new political projects, it also revealed some of the complications they would face in organizing the popular movement. That they could unleash the fury of a popular uprising earned neighborhood representatives a seat at the table of power, but politicians quickly learned that neighborhood protest could be bought and sold like other political commodities. For if in April 1984 the barrios had demonstrated a high degree of cohesion, they remained extremely diverse in their social and political composition. The key participants in the local social movements that worked to get roads paved and electricity installed in the barrios were young activists formed in the cultural clubs of the 1970s, often students and church workers. The key participants in the strikes, the young people who burned tires and fought the police, were neighborhood tígueres. As Rita Ceballos puts it, the neighborhood strikes evolved from a moment of spontaneous eruption in 1984 into a regularized form of "social protest with a delinquent element."[38] This meant that neighborhood groups could keep calling strikes and use the fear of strikes to support their negotiation with the state, but also that they were not in control of social protests in the neighborhoods. To complicate matters further, other political actors began to turn to the resource of angry neighborhood youth in their search for political advantage. Business groups angry with Balaguer in the late 1980s, for instance, gave encouragement to barrio protests that were beginning to destabilize his government. When Joaquín Balaguer fraudulently snatched victory from Juan Bosch in the 1990 election, Bosch's Partido de la Liberación Dominicana (Party of Dominican Liberation, PLD) encouraged neighborhood strikes.[39] Balaguer and the Reformista Party responded by paying street toughs in some neighborhoods and towns to threaten local activists or prevent strikes. The Dominican political class slowly incorporated barrio protest into its growing repertoire of electoral strategies. By the end of the 1990s, some neighborhood strikes seemed to be organized by the tígueres themselves, as cover, neighborhood residents suspected, for drug shipments. Because strikes were the only reliable way to bring news cameras into the neighborhoods, the proliferation of social protest and violence also contributed to the general impression of the barrios as exceedingly violent spaces.[40]

COMMUNITY POLITICS

The transition to democracy in 1978 marked a dramatic change in the relationship between Dominican New York and political life in Santo Domingo. While an authoritarian government had ruled in Santo Domingo, the leaders of the opposition in New York—many of the most eloquent and active Dominican migrants—strove to shape the colonia into their image of an exiled revolutionary force. This produced a strong pull on public life in Dominican New York toward projects for human rights and social transformation on the island, often at the expense of local engagement with neighborhood and city politics. The electoral victory of the PRD was, in effect, the high-water mark of this kind of homeland politics. The political demonstrations, denunciations, and vigils, familiar in Washington Heights since the late 1960s, reached a climax in May 1978 when Balaguer began to signal that he intended to hold power despite losing the election. Groups like the Citizens' Committee for Democracy in Santo Domingo, the Comité de Defensa, and the newly formed Asociación Nacional de Dominicanos Ausentes (National Association of Absent Dominicans, ANDA), all based in New York, sprang into action. They made use of their relative freedom from repression, their deft facility for public relations, and their close allies

FIGURE 8-1. Youth activists from the Centro Juvenil at the Cristo Rey Parish march with Padre Rogelio Cruz in National Youth Day, ca. 2000. This was one of many efforts by barrio groups to contradict the general view of the neighborhood as violent and delinquent. (Courtesy of *Listín Diario*)

in the U.S. left to push for a smooth transition in Santo Domingo. When the aging tyrant seized the ballot boxes in the Dominican Republic, they kept demonstrators and cars in the streets of Washington Heights at all hours and made many phone calls to the Democratic leadership in Washington.[41]

If the transition was a high point for mobilized opposition to authoritarianism in New York, it was also a final parenthesis on the powerful idea that international migration was primarily a form of exile. The very success of the 1978 campaign eroded the monopoly that exile identity, and political parties, held on public life in the barrios of Manhattan. After 1978, and especially as the PRD proved disastrously corrupt and inept in power, more and more of the Dominicans left in New York followed the turn toward community politics begun in the middle 1970s. Rafael Lantigua and Moisés Pérez formed Alianza Dominicana, a service agency. Alianza's leadership eventually supported David Dinkins in his successful run for mayor in 1989, and several members of the group served in his administration. A group of disaffected members of the Línea Roja, a Marxist group, formed the Asociación Comunal de Dominicanos Progresistas (Community Association of Dominican

Progressives, ACDP). At the head of the ACDP, a City College educated bilingual teacher named Guillermo Linares led the effort to wrest control of the school board from the Jewish bloc. In 1983, he was elected to the District Six Community School Board and continued to rally Dominican voters around school politics. In 1989 the courts ordered New York to redraw districts to facilitate the election of more Latino and Asian candidates to local government. Dominican activists in northern Manhattan vigorously and successfully campaigned for the creation of a Dominican City Council district, encompassing most of Washington Heights and Inwood east of Broadway. In 1991 Linares became the first Dominican member of the City Council. Linares was known for his alliance with Puerto Ricans and other minority politicians. Still, he campaigned on a platform of Dominican power, not coalition politics, distributing Dominican flags with his campaign materials.[42]

While some leaders in Washington Heights moved toward a more vigorous politics of community mobilization around racial and social injustices in New York, others took 1978 as a moment to demand political rights for migrants as citizens of the Dominican Republic. The most prominent exponent of this call was ANDA, formed by lawyer and former candidate for the community school board Víctor Espinal just prior to the elections of May 1978. Espinal and his allies launched a call for permanent representation of Dominican New Yorkers in the Dominican Congress, the right to vote in national elections, and the establishment of local elections in New York to appoint consular officials.[43] A group called the Dominican Patriotic Congress, led by Rafael Méndez Cuello, Rodolfo de la Cruz, and Luis Peralta in New York, actually called for a remittance strike in October of 1987 to protest the government's resistance to political rights for the colonia.[44] A New York business group similarly threatened that the "tradition of the massive return of *criollos* [Dominicans] for Christmas will disappear in a few years because of the coldness with which they are received in the country."[45] Their interventions into Dominican public life relied heavily on the emerging consensus that Dominican New Yorkers had "contributed in avoiding economic catastrophes in Santo Domingo."[46]

In the new era of political competition in Santo Domingo, New Yorkers were a key base for political fundraising. Much of the PRD leadership had lived in exile and knew the economic resources available in the New York settlements. But both major political parties sought to raise funds in New York, and both quickly responded to calls for migrant political rights. Reformista leaders promised New Yorkers the right to vote early in their 1978 campaign.[47] Luis Cruz Sánchez, a veteran PRD loyalist in New York appointed consul general in New York by the Guzmán government, began his tenure by convening a full spectrum of social and political leadership in September to promise that he would back them in their demand for extending "the right to vote in New York to the residents of this city." [48] Salvador Jorge Blanco, the Dominican president from 1982 to 1986, also made strong overtures to the New York constituency, presenting bills in favor of voting rights for Dominicanos Ausentes while in Congress and as president.[49] The promise of political rights became a common currency in Dominican politics in the 1980s, but never materialized. Víctor Espinal wearily recalls that Dominican politicians quickly learned the importance of figureo in the New York colonia. They could, he sighs, win the support of New Yorkers with symbolic gestures. A bodeguero in New York who supported a candidate might then receive an invitation to the presidential palace or a plaque recognizing contributions to national progreso.[50] When Joaquín Balaguer's nephew, Joaquín Ricardo, arrived in New York after being named consul in 1986, he promised to set up an office to help undocumented migrants, to build stronger cultural ties between the colonia and the island, and to intervene against mistreatment by customs officials in Santo Domingo. Pedro Familia, a Dominican journalist in New York, wrote doubtfully in *El Sol*, "[W]e are very used to 'political demagoguery.' We will wait and see."[51]

Dominican leaders in New York learned to accept patronage when it was offered and to be as skeptical of the promises of electoral politics as their counterparts in Santo Domingo. Some maintained their calls for rights as dominicanos ausentes, but many also invested increasingly in the projects of Dominican power in New York politics. Since the constituents that leaders sought to mobilize into a Dominican political bloc in New York were highly attentive to the symbolic value of the homeland, the two projects were largely compatible. In the weeks before his election to City Council, Guillermo Linares traveled to his hometown of Cabrera to donate an ambulance and to meet with political leaders of the three major parties, as well as the archbishops of Santo Domingo and San Francisco de Macorís.[52]

The True Riches of the Nation

The politicians were not alone in their friendly gestures toward New Yorkers in the 1980s. As the national economy ground to a halt, Dominicans depended ever more on the possibility of relocating to New York and on the Dominicans already living there. If during the first two decades of mass Dominican migration to New York, the population of migrants was still skewed toward the upper echelon of the working classes in Santo Domingo and toward relatively well-off small farmers from the countryside, by the end of the 1980s, migration seems to have spread to all sectors of Dominican society. Migration spread, for instance, ever deeper into the fabric of everyday life among the rapidly multiplying urban poor. In the 1980s, as the government withdrew its supports and prices climbed, migration became a common strategy for basic household subsistence in the barrios. In a survey conducted at the end of the decade, fully 76 percent of households in Gualey, Buenos Aires, Ensanche Luperón, and Villa Juana reported a family member living abroad. Twenty-seven percent reported receiving money at least once a month from relatives living outside the country, money that many depended on for basic survival. Another study several years later put this figure as high as 40 percent in the Zona Norte, with 30 percent of residents reporting their own plans to emigrate in the future.[53]

In some ways, the crisis years of the 1980s began to reshape social reality to conform to the old image that portrayed migrants as the desperate poor. According to residents of Cristo Rey, in the 1980s young people in the neighborhood increasingly attempted to reach the United States in small open boats called yolas. Doña Blanca, a resident of the housing projects in Cristo Rey, recalls that in 1984 her fourteen-year-old son decided to try his luck migrating by sea. "He took two gallons of water and a box of chocolates and he went as a stowaway." Dominican police twice imprisoned the boy before he finally made it to the United States. Several of his companions drowned in the attempt.[54] Sebastián Colón rattles off the names of eight or nine families, living in the muddy cañada behind his Cristo Rey funeral home, with teenagers who decided to "go as stowaways" in the 1980s, including at least one who drowned off the coast of Puerto Rico.[55]

Yet the poor were not the only ones in Santo Domingo to turn to migration during the economic collapse. In May of 1991, Dominican authorities arrested five medical doctors trying to flee to Puerto Rico in a small boat to start over as undocumented laborers and someday reach New York. Professionals and businesspeople had, of course, always been a part of the Dominican settlement in New York, especially among those who fled in the late 1950s and early 1960s, when emigration was difficult and expensive. The new influx of professionals into New York in the 1980s, however, owed in large part to the tremendous growth of Santo Domingo's educated middle class during the 1970s. This was, in turn, a mark of the success of the student movement of the 1960s and 1970s in opening universities to the children of rural and urban lower-middle classes. In 1970, for instance, there were three medical schools in the Dominican Republic producing 2,400 doctors. In 1983, there were thirteen medical schools producing 13,895 doctors. The dramatic increase in the number of doctors in the country, without a corresponding growth in paying demand for medical care, led to a devaluation of the economic and social status of graduates. At the same time, the middle 1980s and early 1990s saw deep cuts in public spending on health care. By 1991 physicians' salaries in Santo Domingo ranged from $116 to $220 a month.[56] One result of this squeeze was the active participation by Dominican professional associations, especially doctors and teachers, in the growing wave of social protest in Santo Domingo in the 1980s. The student protesters of a decade earlier continued angrily to demonstrate, demanding a chance at a stable professional livelihood. Another result was the steady "brain drain" as Dominican professionals made their way to Puerto Rico and New York to join the immigrant working class.

The growing number and diverse origins of migrants and their families were not the only sign of the increasing importance of New York in the Dominican economy. As export revenues and international credit dried up, the dollars earned by taxi drivers, bodegueros, waiters, and factory workers in New York caught the eyes of the wealthy and powerful in Santo Domingo. The Dominican Central Bank, for instance, under pressure to close the gap in the balance of payments, began to track the macroeconomic role of remittances, discovering that the flow of dollars from New York was a key resource in balancing the country's books. Bernardo Vega, who had served as chief economist at the Central Bank, estimated in 1984 that 40 percent of the Dominican Republic's foreign exchange came from migrant remittances.[57] The conclusion that migrant remittances were the lifeline of the national economy became an instant consensus among journalists, financiers, real estate agents, and construction contractors. At the peak of the crisis in 1984, for instance, the president of the Dominican Chamber of Construction, Diego de Moya Canaán, told reporters that Dominican New Yorkers accounted for between 65 and 70 percent of on-the-books new home purchases in the Dominican Republic. Moya Canaán attributed the rise to the declining value of the peso, which allowed New Yorkers to get more for their dollars. María Mora, president of the Association of Dominican Realtors, remembers that the collapse of the local systems of finance and the paralysis of the local economy also suddenly made New Yorkers' cash purchases into a lifeline for the Dominican housing industry.[58]

Alejandro Grullón, president of the Banco Popular and one of the most important financial capitalists in the capital, similarly picked up the scent of dollars from New York around 1984, announcing his conviction that remittances were "one of the true riches of the country."[59] And he moved quickly to bring migrant dollars into his banking operations. New Yorkers had complained bitterly about the problem of sending money orders through the Dominican mail system since the 1960s. Their calls for a Dominican bank in Upper Manhattan, however, had never elicited much interest from financiers or politicians. Now, with his bank deprived of traditional capital markets, Grullón took a detour uptown on one of his frequent visits to Wall Street to find political backing for the formation of Remesas Populares, a branch of the Banco Popular that would transfer money from New York to the island. He enlisted Víctor Espinal, leader of ANDA, to help present a case to the city's Banking Committee that Remesas Populares was desperately needed by the Dominican "community." Eventually, Espinal was able to broker the support of Democratic Party leader Herman Farrell. Remesas Populares became the commercial operation that would gird the success of the Banco Popular through the worst of the economic crisis in Santo Domingo.[60]

Dominican business and political elites seeking to cash in on the economic power of the Dominican diaspora turned to several new Dominican business groups in New York, especially the Federación de Comerciantes e Industriales Dominicanos en Nueva York (Federation of Dominican Merchants and Industrialists in New York). The Federación organized a series of visits to Santo Domingo, press conferences, and symposiums announcing their projects and advocating for an improved investment climate for dominicanos ausentes in Santo Domingo. At the same time, the major business associations in the Dominican Republic, newly vigorous elements of civil society with the transition to democratic rule, responded to the initiative. Santiago merchants and industrialists led the way, collaborating with the Federación and other New York associations to organize seminars for Dominicans in New York on how to invest in the Dominican Republic.[61] Struggling to make up for the dramatic decline in export revenues with the collapse of sugar, the government-supported Dominican Center for Export Promotion (CEDOPEX) identified Dominicans living abroad as a fertile "export" market. Selling Dominican plantains, Dominican yucca, Dominican rum, Dominican insecticides, and other familiar products in bodegas in Washington Heights was yet another way to capture some of the wages earned by migrants. CEDOPEX therefore also forged links with Dominican business groups in New York, beginning a program to train Dominican retailers in New York to import Dominican products.[62]

When traditional centers of economic power began to look to migrant dollars and New York business groups as a source of survival, Dominican politicians did not lag far behind. As Balaguer printed money in the late 1980s and as inflation radically devalued the Dominican peso, the president literally claimed the wages of Dominican New Yorkers as part of the national patrimony. While Balaguer used the police and military to crack down on money changers and exporters in Santo Domingo, forcing them to sell their dollars to the state at a discount, Dominican New Yorkers escaped the enforced conversion rate by changing their dollars for pesos at informal exchange houses in

New York. The government and allied journalists attacked this practice vociferously, pointing angry fingers at the "dollar seekers" in New York, as one reporter put it, who "in an unpatriotic fashion leave the foreign exchange in foreign banks and send the money to our country in national currency."[63] This accusation elided the interests of the ruling faction with those of the Dominican people, calling on New Yorkers to help the government "defend" the national currency, when in fact the government was engaged in no such project. Balaguer's attacks on the "dollar seekers" in New York probably had little influence on the practices of Dominican New Yorkers. But they were a convenient way to deflect anger away from inflationary policies that enriched cronies while wreaking havoc on household incomes in Santo Domingo.[64]

Powerful ruling elites' sudden interest in Dominican New Yorkers' incomes marked a profound transformation in the basic relationship between the Dominican Republic and the world economy. The Dominican Republic had long been trapped by a system of exchange common in colonial societies: it exported cheap primary products like sugar to the United States and relied on income from sugar to pay for imports of almost everything else. Even attempts at import substitution industrialization had not been able to escape the basic dependence on sugar. But in the 1980s, when sugar no longer provided significant income, every sector of Dominican society scrambled to find a new stream of dollars that could support the continued consumption of imported goods. By the 1990s, tourism had largely replaced sugar as the primary product the Dominican Republic offered the world. Yet at the same time, in a much more widely diffused fashion, the Dominican Republic began to offer the world a supply of cheap labor, in the form of assembly plant workers and international migrants. By the middle of the 1980s, migrant remittances had surpassed agricultural and mining exports as the leading source of foreign exchange in the national economy. Dominicans no longer exported sugar in exchange for the consumer products they imported—they exported workers. Rather than leveling the economic playing field between the United States and the Dominican Republic, as classical economic theory predicted, migration simply reconfigured the unequal international division of labor. However, while the old model of exports (and the new investments in tourism and export processing zones) allowed large corporate interests or state cronies to control the exchanges between the Dominican Republic and the United States, migration and remittances filtered this exchange through hundreds of thousands of individual and family transactions. And it allowed for the rise of newly powerful economic actors, in the form of New York–based entrepreneurs, many of whom did not come from the traditional elite of the Dominican Republic. It is small wonder that business leaders and government officials began chasing after the thousands of small transactions carried out by Dominican New Yorkers, and began chasing furiously after the smaller number of successful businesspeople in New York.[65]

COCAINE CAPITALISTS

The new dependence on New York, and more broadly on selling cheap labor to the world, reflected the demise of the old model of exporting agricultural products from Latin America to the United States. Yet ironically, one of the significant economic niches Dominicans carved out in New York, and one of the key ways that Dominican banks and politicians profited from the new economic context, was tied to a major boom in demand for one particular Latin American agricultural export in the 1980s: coca. Except for its clandestine nature, the international trade in coca followed a model very much like earlier booms in bananas, coffee, or sugar: export elites, politicians, and financiers became fabulously wealthy by connecting farmers in South America with consumers in the United States. Although the Dominicans were neither producers of coca (which does not grow in the Caribbean climate) nor major exporters or consumers of cocaine, the Dominican Republic, with its weak institutions and porous border with the United States, was a convenient stopover point for transshipment. At the same time, Dominican New York was positioned at the intersection of Latin American suppliers of cocaine and the insatiable demand for the drug in the United States. As changing economic relations in the hemisphere shifted industrial work out of New York and ended the sugar industry in the Dominican Republic, the proceeds of cocaine capitalism trickled down into the Dominican barrio in Washington Heights. From there, some of this money then flowed into the centers of power in the Dominican Republic, so eager to attract migrant dollars. By the end of the 1980s, the combination of the cocaine trade and the War on Drugs had left a heavy footprint in the social space shared by Dominican New York and Santo Domingo. Dominicans interpreting the relationship between Washington Heights and the homeland increasingly saw, or thought they saw, the stain of cocaine on migrants who made claims to progreso.[66]

The recruitment of Dominicans into the cocaine trade began around 1980, when a group of Colombian tycoons known as the Cali Cartel consolidated control over cocaine shipments from South America to New York. These exporters contracted with Dominicans to set up the business of retail distribution in New York. The relationship proved highly successful, in large part because Washington Heights was a Latin American neighborhood strategically located to provide cocaine to consumers and dealers in the suburbs of New Jersey, upstate New York, and Connecticut, as well as major urban markets in Harlem and the South Bronx. Dominican settlements there clustered around the entrances to the George Washington Bridge and Interstates 80, 95, and 87 (see map 5). The neighborhood was also poorly patrolled by a corrupt police force little trusted by area residents. By the end of the 1980s, the Colombian importers had yielded not only the retail trade in Manhattan, but most regional wholesale distribution in the northeastern United States to Dominican subcontractors. Soon, Dominican entrepreneurs (most famously a cartel rumored to originate in the left-wing revolutionary movements in San Francisco de Macorís) also began shipping cocaine through the Dominican Republic.[67]

Despite the rhetoric of depravity and moral decline that both Dominican and U.S. commentators used when discussing cocaine in the 1980s, drug selling was a form of informal capitalism among a portion of Dominican society. Many officials and bankers replaced the flow of sugar proceeds with the influx of cocaine dollars. And a street-level trade flourished too as the capitalist order increasingly turned its back on poor urban Dominicans. One young dealer, interviewed by anthropologist Terry Williams in the 1980s, pointedly made the connection between the institutions of global finance and commerce. "Cocaine is our World Bank, it is our product."[68] In this sense, cocaine dealing was little different from the many forms of economic adaptation Dominicans practiced in order to survive and consume in the 1980s. Indeed, the active creativity and innovation of the first Dominican cocaine retailers helped transform the accidental geography that put Dominican neighborhoods at the intersection of supply and demand into an active drug market in Upper Manhattan. The greatest revolution came from a young migrant named Santiago Luis Polanco Rodríguez, or Yayo, who around 1985 invented a system for mass production and distribution of a smokeable form of cocaine known as crack. While police in New York emphasized the violence practiced by Yayo and other Dominican entrepreneurs as they pushed competitors out of the market, there is no mistaking their relationship to capitalism. They consolidated production, distribution, and sales while also introducing a range of marketing strategies for crack, such as branding and special discount offers. They even used focus groups to maintain quality control.[69]

The extent to which drug selling resembled other kinds of Dominican immigrant enterprise can be seen in the fact that Dominican drug dealers in Washington Heights did not in the 1980s and 1990s set up the complex, diversified organizations typical of many other immigrant and ethnic crime rings. They rather lived out the dream of other Dominican migrants from humble backgrounds, quickly amassing fortunes, then returning to the Dominican Republic to build luxurious homes, send their children to private schools, and invest in local enterprises.[70] Yayo himself returned to the Dominican Republic in 1986 or 1987, where, protected from extradition by Dominican law, he invested in nightclubs and sent his children to private school. Drug dealing was further confused with other forms of migrant capitalism because bodegas, beauty shops, and investments in the Dominican Republic were sometimes a way to recycle drug profits. Drug capitalists, even when they did not buy these businesses, often lent money to small businesspeople, extorted them for protection, and otherwise blurred lines between legitimate and illicit enterprise. The difference between drug dealing and other kinds of informal capitalism in Santo Domingo and New York was that drugs were highly profitable and offered room for quick expansion and career advancement. Selling peeled oranges or fried pork did not. Even running a corner store, as bodegueros and their journalist friends had begun to complain by the end of the 1970s, required a slow period of saving and investment, marked by long hours of work and fear of holdups. Drug capitalism also allowed for immediate participation in consumer society, in the form of clothing, jewelry, nightlife, and automobiles.

In some cases, drug profits underwote the new coalitions between "commercial" leaders from New York, political parties, and the national government. In the 1980s and 1990s, Vincho Castillo and Freddy Beras Goico, both right-wing political figures in Santo Domingo, published a steady stream of accusations that Jorge Blanco's government and national financial sectors were laundering money, accepting bribes from drug dealers, and allowing "secret airstrips."[71] Although such denunciations were part of a political strategy to discredit the PRD, they were not wholly without merit. Luis Cruz Sánchez, the long-time PRD activist in New York who received the post of consul general there in 1978, was arrested in 1999 and sentenced to life in prison on charges of cocaine smuggling.[72] And Erasmo Taveras, the vice president of the Federación in New York, pled guilty in 1990 to money laundering and loan sharking after he was caught transmitting more than $70 million to the Dominican Republic. In an interview granted after his plea, Taveras claimed that the merchants' group in New York was basically a collaboration between the Dominican government and a handful of New Yorkers for the purposes of smuggling and money laundering.[73]

CRACK CAPITAL OF THE U.S.A

Critics of the cocaine trade in Santo Domingo blamed corrupt politicians, but they nevertheless tended to see the origins of the problem in the unquenchable demand for the drug in the United States. In the United States, however, Drug Warriors preferred to present the "enemy" as suppliers of drugs from Colombia and the Dominican Republic and street-level dealers. In the middle of the 1980s, prosecutors and politicians used crack as a tool for discrediting the poor and racial minorities. Politicians, prosecutors, and reporters generally made crack addicts and crack dealers out to be the vectors of an infectious disease within inner-city neighborhoods, and made the neighborhoods out to be gangrenous tissue in the social body of United States.[74] In New York, fingers pointed especially toward black and Puerto Rican addicts and Dominican dealers. Several months after Giuliani and D'Amato made their costumed drug purchase in Washington Heights, police spokesman James McGlaughlin told the press that one out of every five Dominicans between the ages of nineteen and thirty-five was involved in the crack trade. The police could do nothing about it, because every time they arrested one Dominican dealer, another Dominican took his place.[75] In 1986 and 1987, as crack became a national media phenomenon, newspapers reported on police efforts to break up and convict Dominican crack rings operating out of Washington Heights, describing it as "among the neighborhoods hit first and most powerfully by the spread of crack."[76] Readers living outside New York, in other words, first heard that there was a predominantly Dominican neighborhood in New York at the same time they learned that crack was a new urban epidemic.

Community activists in Washington Heights generally agreed that crack dealing had become a scourge on the neighborhood. Dominican politics in Washington Heights, which had begun with marches in defense of immigrant rights in the 1970s and grown with marches for better schools in the early 1980s, turned toward the drug problem by the summer of 1986. A broad coalition of the emerging Dominican community groups, including the ACDP, the Dominican Women's Development Center, and the Club María Trinidad Sánchez, organized a march against drugs in Washington Heights, noting that drugs were "destroying the youth" of the neighborhood.[77] Barrio kids were drawn to the economic opportunities of the street-level trade, and as a result the barrio endured shockingly high levels of street violence and the highest murder rate in the city in the late 1980s. In the 1980s, Washington Heights earned the reputation of murder capital of the city, with between fifty and one hundred murders reported each year.[78] As sentencing laws targeted offenders caught with even small amounts of crack, Dominicans grew into one of the largest foreign-born populations in both New York State and federal prisons.[79]

New York–based activists produced a variety of explanations for the crisis of Dominican childhood in New York. Rodolfo de la Cruz, who ran something called the Movement for Immigrant Orientation, with close ties to the Koch administration, told a reporter from *Última Hora* that the problem was the new influx of undocumented migrants from the Dominican Republic who, unlike the traditionally honorable Dominican population, were involved in drugs and crime.[80] Others pointed fingers at the Dominican government or local leadership for failing to teach national customs and values to immigrant children. The problem was that Dominican cultura was fading in the face of assimilation into U.S. cultures, they said, yet the cultural clubs and politicians were standing by as "day by day the Dominican youth in New York is deteriorating."[81] Rafael Lantigua, a leader of the new community service agency Alianza Dominicana, told readers in Santo Domingo that the stresses on Dominican family life produced by the erosion of paternal authority were responsible for the rise in drug sales. Guillermo Linares, then a member of the Community School Board, argued that the drug problem in Washington Heights was the result of scarce resources for education. The solution was to organize to take control of the local school district.[82]

Despite the willingness of the Dominican leadership, in some contexts, to blame cultural deterioration for the spread of drug selling, they also sought to combat negative depictions of Dominican ethnicity and Washington Heights. Rafael Lantigua told *New York Times* reporters in 1992, "It is very easy to label Washington Heights the crack capital of New York. There are maybe seven or eight blocks that have a real drug problem, but the rest of the neighborhood is calm and quiet."[83] Like activists in the 1970s and like the community leadership in Santo Domingo barrios, these community leaders were torn between the duty to call out the problems in the neighborhood and the concern that descriptions of violence and delinquency would strengthen discrimination against Dominicans, excuse government neglect in the neighborhood, and justify police abuses.

Such concerns proved well-founded in 1988, when Washington Heights and its Dominican residents were pushed even further into the center of New York's politics of public order. A Dominican named Daniel Mirambeaux allegedly shot and killed police officer John Michael Buzcek during a botched robbery of drug profits. Mirambeaux fled to the Dominican Republic, where the law protected him from extradition. New York Senator Alfonse D'Amato threatened to cut off aid to the Dominican Republic and impose economic sanctions if the Dominican government did not hand over the accused cop killer.[84] In a move well practiced by governments across Latin America during the Cold War, Balaguer instead produced Mirambeaux's dead body. The police reported that the suspect had committed suicide while in custody by throwing himself down a flight of stairs.[85]

After the shooting, New York and national media outlets echoed the police in their descriptions of Washington Heights as a dangerous badlands, dominated by cocaine and violence. A *New York Times* reporter in 1989 described the neighborhood as an

American nightmare. On side streets in the 150's and 160's, clusters of tough teen-agers wearing beepers, four-finger gold rings and $95 Nikes offer $3 vials of crack, the high-octane, smokeable derivative of cocaine. On every block there are four or five different "crews," or gangs, each touting its own brand of the drug. . . . So much business is transacted on these streets that Washington Heights has gained a reputation as the crack capital of America.[86]

Although the 50 murders and 570 assaults per 100,000 residents reported in Washington Heights in 1990 were unacceptably high, the evening news and print media reported little else about the neighborhood. Stories about "Dominican drug dealers" focused on kingpins, some of whom were guilty of multiple gangland assassinations. But such stories did not mention that the vast majority of the kids who worked in entry-level jobs in the drug retail industry were not murderers. And the vast majority of Dominicans were not drug dealers. Newspaper reports about crack, and about the problem of "Dominican" drug dealers, mark a significant stage in the process by which Dominicans became a racial minority in the United States. Though these reports never explicitly mentioned that Dominicans were Afro-Caribbean, they communicated plenty about race, and helped to confirm Dominicans as a distinct ethnic group to a mainstream U.S. readership. Readers of the *New York Times*, many of whom lived outside of the city itself, did not need to know exactly what color Dominicans were. Four finger rings, Nikes, and crack were expressive enough symbols of racial difference. This American nightmare was not white.[87]

By 1989 and 1990, Dominicans were fully integrated into the complex public politics of race and crime in New York. Riding a wave of political sentiment against the neighborhood after the Buczek murder, INS officer Joseph Occhipinti began a series of raids against Dominican groceries in Manhattan called Operation Bodega, arresting twenty-five people and deporting forty-three more. He claimed to have uncovered an underbelly of drug dealing, document falsification, and gambling among Dominican businesspeople in New York. In response, bodegueros took their case to the newspapers, claiming that blanket accusations against Dominicans and their neighborhoods were racist, unfair, and corrupt. The Federación, the group that had figured so prominently in the boom in investments on the island, also hired lawyers to sue Occhipinti for civil rights violations. The courts found that the searches, conducted without warrants, were impermissible; the evidence gathered in them was thrown out, and Occhipinti was eventually jailed for conducting illegal searches and then falsifying warrants after the fact.[88]

Occhipinti's supporters, including Congressman Guy Molinari, Cuban American journalist Manuel de Dios, and *New York Post* columnist Mike McAlary, unleashed a barrage of accusations against Dominican leaders and businesspeople in Washington Heights. The Federación, they said, was a front group for a cartel of drug dealers from the city of San Francisco de Macorís. The case against Occhipinti was a setup, cynically orchestrated by this cartel in the name of civil rights. Some of the accusations against the Federación, individual bodegueros, and the Dominican government were probably accurate (although some sound suspiciously like the accusations of the PRD's political opponents in Santo Domingo). It was certainly possible to search bodegas and find undocumented workers, unlicensed firearms, and unreported cash. The line between cocaine capitalism and more or less legitimate (though frequently "off the books") enterprises was blurry. But evasion of government record keepers, and other kinds of informality, was not necessarily tantamount to being "enemies" in an all-out drug war. Nor did the existence of drug-trafficking networks in the neighborhood justify the suspension of civil rights for bodegueros. To excuse Occhipinti's trampling on these rights, as well as other abuses by law enforcement officials, allies painted a picture of Washington Heights in which honest cops were determined to weed out unspeakable evildoers in an "urban badlands." Ultimately, these accounts presented Dominicans' traditions of evading the state, their "cultura cimarrona," as proof of their status as undesirable aliens.[89]

Generalized accusations against the neighborhood and against Dominicans may have convinced some New Yorkers, but they did not help in breeding trust among neighborhood residents. While police imagined themselves as honest crime fighters in enemy territory, residents had a different view. In 1994 and 1996, independent investigations confirmed neighborhood suspicions that police from the Thirtieth Precinct stole from, extorted, and protected drug dealers in the southern portions of Washington Heights. Police also frequently lied in court, manufactured evidence, and covered up mistreatment of suspects. Most of the police in Washington Heights were not corrupt, just as most Dominicans were not drug dealers. But even honest cops maintained a "blue wall of silence," protecting fellow officers at the expense of the neighborhood.[90] Tensions ran high on both sides until, in July 1992, an undercover police officer named Michael O'Keefe shot and killed a young Dominican man named José García and the mutual resentments between police and the community in Washington Heights broke into open conflict. García's friends and family described him as lawful, respectful, and kind, an employee at a bodega in the Bronx. Witnesses claimed that García was unarmed and was already subdued by the officer when he was shot in the back. Residents also reported that O'Keefe was known in the neighborhood for his violence and racism. The Police Department circled around its own, suggesting that García was a drug dealer who, "high on cocaine and slick with sweat," had threatened O'Keefe with a gun. Police and journalists supported the allegation that García dealt drugs by pointing out that he was from San Francisco de Macorís and that he lived on 162nd Street, sites "known for" their heavy involvement in cocaine capitalism. The alleged witnesses against O'Keefe, they claimed, were yet another example of perjury orchestrated by drug dealers to "get" honest cops. Three days later a Dominican man named Dagoberto Pichardo fell to his death during a rooftop confrontation with police. Again the officers accused the man of drug dealing and attacking an officer. Again rumors spread in the neighborhood that the attack had been an unprovoked assault by police.[91]

As word spread of the two killings, outrage over police brutality and over the police strategy of accusation and insinuation against García swept through the neighborhood. Now it was not drugs themselves that brought Dominicans to the streets—it was the ways that police used drugs as an excuse to brutalize the neighborhood. Residents set up a shrine to García on 162nd Street, with candles and street murals. Newly elected city councilman Guillermo Linares led a demonstration to demand a civil trial for Officer O'Keefe (who was later acquitted by a grand jury). But the march was overwhelmed by confrontations between the police and neighborhood tígueres, some with their faces covered by bandanas. Apologists for the police argued that the entire demonstration was the work of organized drug gangs. Yet community leaders saw the protests as an expression of pent-up outrage. *Diario-La Prensa* quoted Fredesbinda Guerrero, who called the protests "simply a reflection of the outrage we feel over the mistreatment of the community." Groups of young men threw stones, burned trash cans, and fought with police. Neighborhood residents marched chanting "policía asesinos" (the police are murderers) and calling for justice.[92]

In July 1992, Dominican politics in New York were emblematic of the urban politics of race in the United States. Over the span of a week, Washington Heights acted out a reprise of the more famous riots in Los Angeles only a few months earlier. The circumstances around the death of Kiko García will never be as clear as the videotaped beating of Rodney King. But the rebellion in Washington Heights was about the same broad pattern of racially biased police brutality. The riots were also reminiscent of the repeated uprisings in the barrios of Santo Domingo, part of a transnational experience of urban exclusion particular to New York and the Dominican Republic. As the protests proceeded in Washington Heights, José García's family held a wake in their home in San Francisco de Macorís. In the barrio where his parents lived, the *New York Times* reported, "Dominicans who had lived in New York and friends of Mr. García gathered under a hot sun. The crowd began clapping, waving protest signs and chanting '¡La policía neoyorquina una banda asesina!' or 'The police of New York are a band of murderers!' Signs, written in English, read 'Stop the Killing' and 'We Want Justice.'"[93]

CADENUSES

In Santo Domingo in the 1980s, rumor and reporting on Dominican drug dealing in New York ranged from the complaints of migrant community activists to translations of *Times* articles about crack and San Francisco de Macorís drug "mansions," to the clamor of self-proclaimed moralists in Santo Domingo. Dominicans in Santo Domingo also saw with their own eyes a stream of migrants returning in "triumph" after suspiciously brief stays in New York. Together, these reports and impressions helped to deepen the prejudices against migrants first expressed by nationalists and intellectuals in the 1970s. By 1986, a group of New York merchants visiting Santo Domingo complained that "there exists the widespread belief that everyone who has made his fortune in New York has made it from drug selling and other illegal activities."[94] As in the case of earlier prejudices, the suspicion that New Yorkers were delinquent or involved in drugs reflected both nationalist sentiments and resistance to the class pretensions of upwardly mobile migrants. Drugs fit the category of modern degeneracy, and the international drug trade was largely driven by demand in the United States. Thus the presumed delinquency of New Yorkers could be expressed as part of a general outrage about how U.S. society corrupted the Caribbean.

New York businesspeople and professionals, well practiced at inserting their voices into the Santo Domingo press, launched antidefamation efforts in response to the seeping prejudices.[95] In a typical instance of these efforts, in 1989 a Brooklyn man responded to a report that Catholic prelate Monsignor Núñez Collado had used the word *dominicanyork* with a paid advertisement in *Listín Diario*. "It appears that for Mr. Núñez," he wrote, "to have lived in the United States is a very contagious social disease, a 'Social Leprosy' that must be isolated and thrown out."[96] The next day, the priest responded, denying that he had ever used the word *dominicanyork*.[97] Increasingly, although the term remained in frequent usage, it was considered impolite to use it in public discourse. In 1989, the editors of *El Nacional* referred to the "now discredited term *dominicanyork*."[98]

Yet if, as these fragments suggest, migrants were sometimes able to shame public figures into apologizing for the use of derogatory terms, they still encountered an underlying trend of social discrimination. Most migrant businesspeople who returned "home" from New York in the late 1980s lived segregated in a few Santo Domingo neighborhoods. María Mora, president of the Dominican Association of Realtors, freely admits that she and other agents tried to push Dominican New Yorkers away from certain neighborhoods, because their most exclusive clients would not buy anywhere "a *Domínican* lives." Unfortunately, she recalls, the disorganized nature of the Dominican housing market made it impossible to fully protect elite neighborhoods from New Yorkers or other undesirables. The most discriminating buyers therefore began moving into gated condominiums, which were easier to control. Residents of elite neighborhoods also relied on social ostracism to achieve the exclusion that real estate restrictions could not. Mora remembers that neighborhood social clubs excluded undesirable neighbors, including those identified as dominicanyork. Some private schools, including the Evangelical Institute in Santiago, began to deny admission to the children of returning migrants.[99] One returned migrant living in a traditionally elite neighborhood told researchers, "[M]y neighbors don't even return my greetings."[100]

Many of those who practiced such exclusion were happy to make theoretical distinctions between the good and the bad New Yorkers. In a sense, the other derogatory expression for New Yorkers, *cadenú*, captures this distinction. *Dominicanyork* referred to a suspect place, and in its shortened version *domínican*, to the English language pronunciation of the national marker, dominicano. But cadenú referred specifically to cultural artifacts, to symbols of consumer power. Gold chains stood in for the accusation of drug dealing, and more broadly for the foreign-inspired class pretensions of Dominicans with no real cultura. César Ramos, for instance, wrote in *Listín Diario* that some Dominican New Yorkers were honorable, hardworking, and patriotic, while others were obviously drug dealers and criminals. But there were others who, although they were not delinquents, were "big braggarts" who came to Santo Domingo "showing off their wealth with extravagant finery, and radios on their shoulders, like they want to demonstrate their superiority over us."[101] Realtor María Mora likewise highlighted that it was behavior or cultura related to New York that should be kept out of elite neighborhoods. Buyers in Santo Domingo had no prejudice against New Yorkers, she explained, but rather against the "*costumbres* that they might bring."[102] When pressed as to what costumbres elite

Dominicans attributed to returning migrants, Mora discussed the lack of respect children showed to parents and the open sexuality of young women. But like Ramos, she especially highlighted "those who put on adornments." In a sense Mora was right to see no special discrimination against New Yorkers. In a city where coming from a disreputable barrio meant facing discrimination in employment and elite social institutions, Washington Heights was merely another suspect barrio. At times Dominican nationalists explicitly described New York as a site where Dominicans learned modern corruptions. At other times, however, the problem with New York was simply that it provided economic power to people who never had any cultura to begin with. Responsible real estate agents, Mora reported, tried to steer "persons [who had] acquired money but not *costumbres*" away from the best neighborhoods.[103] Gold chains were such emphatic expressions of economic advancement that they became easy symbols of how New York was blurring the boundaries of social distinction.

CUSTOMS

If some Dominicans sought to keep generic "North American" cultural imports or generic Dominican lower-class costumbres out of elite neighborhoods, others worried about cadenuses' role in transmitting culture between New York's racialized inner city and the "worst neighborhoods" in Santo Domingo. Here again, the story is eerily parallel to New York itself. Advocates of law and order in New York saw the easy circulation of people, goods, money, and ideas between urban ghettos in the north and troubled barrios of the south as a contributing factor to their urban crisis. Criminal aliens, complained politicians, journalists, and law enforcement agencies, smuggled drugs, evaded laws, and then fled back to the Dominican Republic to live out their days.[104] For their part, Dominican nationalists had, since the beginning of the twentieth century, harbored grave reservations about the communication of modern ills from the United States. Now the treacherous path to modernity seemed not only to be leading Dominican campesinos to the city, but also teaching them to behave like the urban poor of the United States. The barrios of Santo Domingo looked more and more like the ghettos of New York, and despite the local crises, much of the culture of modern urban delinquency seemed to be coming from abroad. As author Juan Francisco Martínez Almanzar complained, barrio youths "assimilate the influences that they receive through the television and from the Dominicans that return from New York."[105] Nor was this concern limited to writers on the left, who had long been suspicious of New Yorkers' role in imperial cultural penetration. Balaguer, for instance, blamed drug abuse in the Dominican Republic on the "customs and resources" brought to the island by Dominicans living overseas.[106] That same year, Sócrates Baudilio, an official in Balaguer's government, proclaimed that "directly and indirectly 'cadenuses' incite the youth in the marginal barrios to the practice of gang violence."[107]

Barrio activists and allied cultural nationalists worried too about the broader transformation of barrio cultures by imperial penetration, and the resulting alienation and maladaption of barrio youth. They often held cadenuses responsible for corruption in the Zona Norte. The combination of the ways cadenuses made their fortunes and the ways they spent them, activists believed, had a dangerous effect on the morale of neighborhood youth. "Why does the cadenú come back?" barrio leader and COPADEBA founder José Ceballos asks. "For two reasons: first, to enjoy himself, which for Dominicans of that sort means women, and more than anything creating another view of himself, what we call here 'llenando los ojos.'"[108] Llenando los ojos literally means "filling the eyes," or in more general terms, showing off. In Cristo Rey, residents remember the gold chains of the 1980s. Doña Melliza, a resident of the multifamiliares of Cristo Rey and longtime participant in church groups, recalls that a nephew who returned from New York in the middle of the 1980s drove her around in his car, treated her to luxuries, and gave her a present of a gold chain with a medallion of the Virgin of Altagracia. She wore it happily, as gold chains were fast becoming a popular style in the neighborhood.[109]

Still, according to those same barrio activists and residents, neighborhood residents were hardly innocent about consumption or delinquency when the cadenuses began to arrive. From the very beginning of the democratic transition in Santo Domingo, barrio activists had begun to notice a generalized culture of consumption linked to foreign movies and television and to complain that these cultural influences were the cause of gang violence. The problem of youth gangs, Germán Santiago wrote in 1983, "is rooted in social decay, aggravated by foreign models imported through music, film, television, and the 'latest cry of fashion.'"[110] Indeed, a decade before the uproar over returning cadenuses in the barrios, most barrio activists directed their ire at another strange figure whose imitators seemed to lurk on every street corner: the movie actor John Travolta. The release of Travolta's *Grease* (1978) offered seemingly direct evidence of the link among foreign films, foreign music, and gang violence. *Grease* was a nostalgic musical about 1950s street gangs who dressed and groomed alike, held dance competitions, had sex, and engaged in dangerous car races. Several years later, the release of Michael Jackson's *Beat It* offered a second piece of evidence that U.S. media encouraged delinquency in Santo Domingo. The music video, though intended as a critique of gang violence, included an extended, choreographed confrontation between two groups of dancers dressed in exotic gang paraphernalia, culminating in a stylized knife fight. Barrio activists complained that neighborhood kids copied the gang behaviors in *Grease,* and cultural commentators of various stripes complained of look-alike competitions and re-creations of Jackson's dance routines on local television programming as well as in neighborhood dance competitions. This was evidence, critics clamored, that the U.S. media was teaching gang violence to Dominican teenagers. The "growth of drug addiction and gang violence" in the Dominican Republic, the leaders of the Club Cayo Báez wrote to *El Nacional,* were the result of "repeated presentations of this false idol," Michael Jackson, on national television.[111]

From the perspective of the United States, where neither Travolta nor Jackson fit into the fearsome mold of inner-city gangster, the idea that these performers caused the rash of delinquency in Santo Domingo barrios seems a stretch. But critics in Santo Domingo did not limit their complaints to the problem of direct emulation of *Grease* or "Beat It." Travolta, in particular, stood in for the broader transformation of Dominican urban culture in the 1970s and early 1980s as it came to include mass media, party life, commercial fashion, and discotheques. Nightlife in Santo Domingo had historically been restricted by the brutal social control of repeated dictatorships. Just as the end of the Trujillo regime in 1961 had spurred the boom in rock music and pop merengue, the transition to democracy in 1978 brought a new modern import: disco. For the first time in decades, young people began to venture out into the city at night. By the beginning of the 1980s, new commercial venues for leisure activities, dance clubs, and beer halls began to appear downtown. By one account, twenty-seven new nightclubs opened in Santiago between 1983 and 1988. Formal discos were, however, out of reach for the majority of the population in Santo Domingo.[112] The middle classes began to gather in public parks, parking lots, and along the oceanfront, where vendors sold cold drinks and snacks. By 1984, journalist Augusto Socías claimed that "[w]ithout a doubt, nightlife has picked up, maybe because in the middle of an economic crisis, many are looking to have fun as a kind of 'escapism.'"[113] In the barrios, residents reproduced these nightspots on a local scale. In Cristo Rey, several dozen dance spots opened on the Avenida Ovando in the early 1980s, but Juana Rosario and her friends could not afford these fancier spots. They began to go out dancing, she recalls, in rustic "centers" in Agustinita and Las Palmas, "where you went to get together, to drink your beer, and to dance."[114]

This was what barrio activists called Travoltismo. Travolta was their target because he was the first widely popular foreign screen star of the democratic era, because the soundtrack to the film *Saturday Night Fever* permeated the airwaves, and because his screen persona in the film glorified nightlife as a release from the boredom of working-class life. Travolta played a young man whose only joy in life was dancing at a Brooklyn nightclub, surrounded by drugs and aggressive sexuality. This film exalted exactly the kind of shallow, corrupt values that neighborhood activists hoped to block from the barrios: in short, it promoted Travoltismo. One critic described the movie as yet another example of how working-class youth in the United States and its colonial dependencies were "managed by consumer society."[115] The movie, José Ceballos recalls, allowed for a whole world of teenage sociability, including drinking, dancing, sexuality, and drug use, to come aboveground in the neighborhoods.[116] José Enrique Trinidad, a barrio cultural activist and former member of Convite, laughs when recalling Travoltismo. He has friends from the movement who invested so much political energy in the figure of John Travolta that even twenty-five years later they will still not watch movies starring the seventies icon.[117]

In the traditions of barrio proponents of cultura, the local councils that made up COPADEBA and the Committees of the Popular Struggle made the eradication of the beer joints and other sources of corruption in the barrios part of their renewed political efforts in the 1980s. In Cristo Rey, the newly founded Sociedad para el Desarrollo del Caliche, led by veteran activist Ramona Báez, complained of nightspots where prostitutes and delinquents gathered and where patrons openly played games of chance. These places, the activists argued, "tarnish[ed] the reputation and obstructed the development" of the neighborhood.[118] In Villas Agrícolas the Comités de Lucha Popular and the Club S. E. Díaz attacked the "brothels, games of chance, family bars that in reality are not for families, discotheques, Boites, etc.," in their neighborhood, arguing in a letter to the minister of the interior that "not only do they corrupt the youth—they have become a source of environmental pollution and moral degeneration."[119] As with earlier groups, the petitioners expressed a concern over the girls in the neighborhood; in this case, a sixteen-year-old who had been drugged and raped by a group of boys who frequented one of the *discotecas*. The fight against Travoltismo was, in these terms, a continuation of the fight against ye ye music and hippies in the barrios, and a precursor to stories about cadenuses. Strange hairstyles, foreign music, drugs, drinking, female sexuality, and noise all blended into the general category of "corruption." And though the 1980s provided new opportunities to present barrio protest as the politics of the pueblo or the *lucha popular*, the relaxation of state repression paradoxically made it progressively harder for activists to police barrio cultura from within. Neighborhood activists who cut off the ponytails of local hippies in the late 1960s found themselves relatively powerless against the appearance of polyester shirts, cream-colored leisure suits, and even attempts to coax kinky hair into imitations of Travolta's styles by the 1970s.[120] "I dressed very strangely back then," remembers Congressman Alfredo Pacheco, a teenager in Cristo Rey at the time. "[W]e wore those hats that they use over there [in New York] for the cold. Here they were all the rage even though it is a hot country. . . . [T]hose wool hats, they were really hip, and lots of polyester pants and shirts. . . . [I]t was terrible, but I remember it as a very beautiful time." He recalls that "a man named Chicho" in the club Pedro Bonó "was always watching how we were dressed and that sort of thing." But, he laughs, "no one paid attention to him—you went to the club and acted serious, then once you left the club . . . ha, ha, ha."[121]

Barrio activists also saw Travoltismo as evidence of the success of mass media as an instrument for cultural penetration. The rise of television viewing, combined with the spread of North American commercial music, seemed an immensely powerful weapon for erasing national culture and replacing it with imperial culture. In the 1970s and 1980s an extraordinary boom of electronic media brought the barrios into contact with the world of style, leisure, and consumption. That is, just as television brought images of the barrios to viewers in elite Santo Domingo neighborhoods, it brought the barrios in daily contact with a distant world of material plenty. Although televisions were luxury items in the 1960s and early 1970s, by the end of the 1980s, there were 670,000 sets in the Dominican Republic—65 percent of households owned one.[122] Although televisions arrived first in the homes of the wealthy and upper-middle classes, in the 1980s they appeared in the barrios as well. A 1983 neighborhood survey of Los Guandules found that despite continued problems with drinking water, open waste lines, and malnutrition, 51 percent of homes owned a television.[123] The spread of televisions in neighborhood households was part of a general spread of electrical appliances in the barrios. When they could, residents still put a premium on shelter, light, and water. But once these basics were secure, or when they were hopelessly out of reach, barrio residents began turning extra income into radios, televisions, furniture, refrigerators, and gas stoves. Televisions and other home appliances also served as informal savings accounts: they could always be pawned in times of economic emergency. As objects, these items grew to define progreso in the interior space of barrio dwellers' concrete homes.[124] But like the sound trucks that broadcast messages about household detergents and cooking oil in the barrios in the 1970s,

FIGURE 8-2. A color television occupies a prominent place in a home in Cristo Rey, 2005. In the 1980s and 1990s televisions became common household furnishings in barrios where electricity was still irregular and running water was still scarce. (Photo by John Paul Gallagher)

televisions also helped to communicate the idea that progreso could be measured in an array of consumer products.

Television production required such high degrees of technical sophistication and such large capital investments that it was difficult to imagine, in 1980, that Dominicans would ever be able to compete with production in the United States. So the link among mass media, consumption, and foreign culture seemed airtight. Televisions seemed to be the final nail in the coffin of national cultura. Yet within a few years, Dominican artists and producers responded with their own commercial music and television, which, though Dominican, was as dedicated to party life, discotecas, style, and consumption as *Saturday Night Fever*. Merengue performers and producers incorporated elements of disco, especially the flashy costumes, electronic instruments, and bass drum, to make their own highly successful commercial art form. By 1987, the evolving merengue genre constituted 70 percent of radio airplay in the Dominican Republic and 20 percent of television airtime.[125] As the cost of video recording and editing equipment came down, and as the expense of imported programming rose, Dominican television stations also developed local programming. Dominican audiences, especially popular audiences, generally preferred local programs or those imported from Mexico, Venezuela, and Brazil, to shows from the United

States. Dominican producers and advertisers shifted to local production and national programming between 1984 and 1987. By the end of the 1980s, the most popular shows were the locally produced variety shows and live musical performances. These variety shows, especially the marathon shows hosted by entertainer/politicians Rafael Corporán and Freddy Beras Goico, became essential pillars of mass culture and marketing in the Dominican Republic.[126]

Barrio activists were not wrong to argue that there was a problem, that mass media changed local ideas about consumption in barrios that were progressively excluded from participation in economic life. Barrio residents became sophisticated consumers even as national and international planners gave up on ever incorporating them into systems of economic production. However, calling this problem Travoltismo and relying on old ideas of a materialist other contaminating a spiritual self underestimated the extent to which Dominican capitalism could generate its own nationalized version of mass consumer society. Dominican television stations showed an average of two minutes of advertising for every three minutes of programming. This advertising, much of it also locally produced, sought expressly to promote the consumption of household appliances, Dominican brands of rum, beer, and cigarettes, as well as the national lottery. By 1994, Dominican television advertising grew into a $136 million industry.[127] Often, beer or rum manufacturers also endorsed specific merengue bands or paid bands to write and perform jingles. This meant that there was little boundary between the programming and the music and images broadcast during commercial breaks. This blending of advertising with music helped a process already under way, as the lyrics of commercial merengue increasingly celebrated leisure consumption. Merengue lyrics described beer, rum, music, and the body parts of women in a new kind of commercial populism. The most impressive practitioners of party merengue, Pochy Familia y su Cocoband, celebrated the young men of the barrios of Santo Domingo and New York, whose common Dominican identity was built around *el vacilón*, the party.[128] Nightlife, fancy clothing, open sexuality, drinking, and drugs, all of the components of Travoltismo, spread widely in the barrios in the form of locally produced television and national dance music.

One result of this changing neighborhood culture, Jorge Cela writes, was that residents grew to see their incorporation into the city in terms of the ownership "of the goods that are the symbols of citizenship, but which they cannot afford."[129] By the end of the 1980s, when reports began to emerge that the cadenuses were "filling up the eyes" of other neighborhood youth, the common language of progreso in the barrios had long since begun to incorporate this kind of consumption. So we should be wary of attributing too much of the cultural change in Santo Domingo in the 1980s to the influence of returning New Yorkers. Nevertheless, New Yorkers undeniably occupied a prominent place in the emergence of Dominican consumer culture, both because many Dominicans imagined them to be sources of consumer information and because they actually did sometimes contribute to the diffusion of new products, styles, or desires. Televisions, for instance, even when they showed Dominican programming, were frequently a by-product of family strategies of migration. In a rural community in the Cibao, 64 percent of households with one or more members living abroad owned a television in 1980, as opposed to 19 percent of nonmigrant families. In the city of Santiago, 89 percent of migrant households had a television, as compared to 64 percent of nonmigrant households.[130] Similar research does not exist for the barrios of Santo Domingo. Yet the story of the Pacheco family, living in the Las Flores section of Cristo Rey, is probably not unique. The family earned seven pesos a week from Mr. Pacheco's job at La Manicera, a subsidized cooking oil factory. But in 1970, when Mrs. Pacheco returned home from a year of wage work in New York, she brought a television with her. The whole neighborhood began gathering at the house to watch *Batman*, *Bonanza*, and the local variety shows.[131]

The merengue bands that increasingly dominated these televisions in the 1980s also owed much of their success to the growing settlement in New York. In New York, as merengue grew into a key symbol of Dominican ethnic identity, bands from Santo Domingo were able to earn big paychecks. Because airplay in the Dominican Republic depended on payola, merengue bands and recording companies with success in New York dollars were then able to push most competitors off the air in Santo Domingo in the lean years of the 1980s. With its foothold in New York, commercial merengue had a clear advantage over bachata, a style popular mainly in barrio dives.[132]

The importance of merengue in the ethnic terrain of Latino New York indirectly aided both the rise of Dominican music on Dominican airwaves and the commercialization of that music. Dominican musicians, who performed within a growing international Latin American pop circuit, publicly mediated between the hip fashion scene created by Dominicans, blacks, and other Latinos in New York and the markets of Santo Domingo. Two popular Dominican musicians, Wilfredo Vargas and Fausto Rey, adopted afros and the cool look of New York soul and boogaloo musicians early in the 1970s, when such styles still elicited scorn from both the left and the right in Santo Domingo.[133] By the 1980s, all merengue stars were expected to dress up as part of their performance. A return from a tour in New York in expensive and up-to-date styles was a sign of a band's "triumph."[134] Such styles were on display both on television screens and in the emerging Santo Domingo night-club scene. And like the music and the televisions, the nightclubs of the Dominican Republic also seem to have had important ties to the Dominican settlements of New York. The famous cases of Yayo and other drug capitalists returning to legitimate life by moving to the Dominican Republic and investing in nightclubs are well known. But according to a report in 1988, it was dominicanos ausentes, and not necessarily drug dealers, who were the major investors in nightclubs. Radhy Montero and three other Dominican businessmen from New York made use of contacts at the magazine ¡Ahora! to advertise a nightclub with "a modern design to match the lifestyle of the moment." An article in ¡Ahora! included a photograph of Montero wearing two gold chains around his neck, a big gold bracelet, and a ring.[135]

At the same time, money from New York or the gifts of visitors from New York became crucial supports to the consumption of all social groups in the Dominican Republic. The crises of the 1980s were expressly about the shortage of dollars in the Dominican Republic to import consumer items, and the government responded by placing barriers to imports in the hopes of reducing the trade deficit. Neighborhood women responded in turn bringing large suitcases full of clothing to the barrios on their return visits from New York. Some distributed clothing as gifts to friends and relations, others sold some of what they brought to help pay for the expense of plane tickets and gifts to friends and relations. Some even set up regular, under-the-table import businesses. This flood of clothing inevitably reflected the styles prevalent in New York City, although not necessarily the most costly or up-to-date of those styles.[136] But with John Travolta, Michael Jackson, Wilfredo Vargas, and Johnny Ventura appearing on Dominican television screens and with Dominican advertisers selling the party life, kids in Santo Domingo did not remain innocent audiences for migrant performances of cool for long.

A long line of activists and intellectuals, including some of the most committed defenders of the barrios, propose that the frustrations generated by contact with styles that were hopelessly out of reach led to risky attempts at migration, aggression, violence, and criminality.[137] And there does seem to be good evidence that Santo Domingo youth gangs were enthusiastic participants in a broader trend toward commercialized and consumerist culture, including new styles, nightlife, and gold jewelry. A group of psychology students from the UASD interviewed teenagers at the Liceo Panamá and the Preparatory Institute (a state-funded reform school) in 1981, to inquire about gangs in their neighborhoods. Most of the teenagers answered that gang activities in their neighborhoods were widespread but fairly mundane. Those who admitted belonging to gangs described their main activities as sports and parties.[138] Another study, an ethnography of gang life from the late 1970s, similarly discovered that being in a gang principally involved hanging out on a corner in the neighborhood after work or school, drinking rum and beer, discussing fighting and sexual conquests, and making plans for weekend excursions to brothels and nightclubs. Gang members, young researchers from the university reported, also increasingly paid attention to physical adornments. Although researchers chose the pseudonym *los capellanes* for the gang in their report, the gang referred to itself by the brand name of the tennis shoes members all wore. Another gang in the study had matching sneakers as well as a full uniform including black sweaters, berets, rings, necklaces, and bracelets.[139] Researchers concluded that the transformation of gangs in the barrios in the early years of democracy owed to "North American cultural penetration by way of the media, film, T.V. and people who have been in contact with the ways gangs operate in the United States."[140]

Yet there are other ways of reading the process of cultural diffusion between New York and Santo Domingo. In 1981, Frank Moya Pons argued that returning migrants should be seen as "new social agents of modernity, capitalism, and racial emancipation." Consumer styles that seemed troubling to some because they reflected the cultures of racialized ghettos in the north seemed to him a sign that "the urban ghettoes of New York made them aware of their real racial constitution." Migrants, he said, then communicated this discovery to residents of Santo Domingo through their afro hairstyles, "their thoughts, their clothes, their feelings, their language, and their music."[141] Moya Pons called for more research on the subject, and as we have seen, the notion that Dominicans are racially self-deluded and that the process of ethnic definition in New York was one of racial discovery does not hold up to scrutiny. Nor is there much evidence that New Yorkers vigorously adopted black identities or sent revised ideas of race back to the island.[142] Still, as Moya Pons observed, nationalist perspectives on the cultures of Dominican New Yorkers are exceedingly limited. Whether in intellectual work, fine arts, popular music, or "urban" styles, the creative gestures Dominicans invented in the contexts of barrios in New York could be useful, not simply destructive, when brought back to the barrios of Santo Domingo. Rather than derailment or imperial penetration, "customs acquired abroad" should be seen, in Juan Flores's words, as possible "cultural remittances," contributing like economic remittances to the resources of the nation. Flores also describes the transmission of these customs as a process of "globalization from below," an undercurrent (if not necessarily a countercurrent) to the commercial cultural and ideological diffusion controlled by large global corporations.[143] Styles and consumer postures adopted by New Yorkers on their trips to Santo Domingo did not "awaken" Dominicans to their "real racial identities." But these styles did reflect responses to the social realities of their New York neighborhoods, social realities that included racial as well as class oppression. Gestures of consumer defiance invented in the U.S. urban crisis could, sometimes, translate seamlessly into the parallel urban crisis in Santo Domingo.

Nevertheless, there is reason to be cautious about this model of cultural remittance as a simple transmission akin to wire transfers and money orders. For cultures are not as easily convertible as money. As we have seen, conversations between New York and Santo Domingo often operated in multiple, largely untranslatable, registers. So while a gold chain or a Nike sneaker communicated a racialized meaning in a *New York Times* article or in a New York City public school, the same objects meant something different in elite Dominican neighborhoods and something different again in the barrios of Santo Domingo. Many residents of Cristo Rey for instance describe dominicanyorks not as uncultured delinquents, but as *gente grande*, "important people."[144] Migrants returned not with changed or distorted cultures but with more "cultura," dressed in fine clothing and with their pockets full of dollars. Some barrio residents even add that migrants returned from New York "whiter." Most likely this idea of whitening has an intentional double meaning. Actual physical lightening could be the result of living in a cold climate, in the confines of apartment buildings. But to say that Dominican New Yorkers returned to the barrios whiter, despite (or because of) their four finger rings, gold chains, and hundred-dollar Nikes, is to use skin color and dress as overlapping metaphors for social advancement. Cultural remittances that reclaimed consumption, from below, reflected the process of racialization Dominicans had experienced in New York. Awareness of this process certainly crossed back over the border. But barrio residents easily incorporated them and invested them with their own localized meanings.

Indeed, the importance barrio residents in Santo Domingo placed on certain consumer symbols that had originated in New York was sometimes more important to their continued use than the lives migrants actually lived in New York. Some migrants consciously gave up wearing chains on their visits to the island, in order to avoid the presumption that they were drug dealers and to avoid social exclusion in the middle-class neighborhoods of the capital.[145] In other parts of Santo Domingo though, by the end of the 1980s, gold chains became an expectation for New Yorkers returning to the barrios. Even migrants who rarely wore gold jewelry in New York felt obliged to bring some of it to Santo Domingo, in order to show their triumph. One man in Cristo Rey tells of a

242 · Chapter Eight

relative who operated a business in the departures lounge at Kennedy Airport, renting gold jewelry to migrants for their trips home. Likewise, pawnshops in Santo Domingo reported that most of the gold chains they sold were to visitors from New York, who apparently purchased these foreign artifacts in Santo Domingo, not in New York.[146] This is not to say that New Yorkers never brought new ideas to the barrios or that barrio residents never just imitated what they saw migrants doing. But if returning migrants brought new ideas of luxury and well-being to the barrios, the barrios also seem to have imposed their own idea of luxury on returning migrants.

Despite the many ways that new systems of commercial exchange (including the elimination of the customs house) aided in their oppression, barrio residents learned to use the new language of consumption for their own purposes. To consume, as cultural critic Néstor García Canclini writes, is to "participate in an arena of competing claims for what society produces and ways of using it."[147] Other critics add that mass culture, style, and consumption—including the exaggerated and conspicuous consumption often adopted by poor urban youth—can sometimes be modes of creative expression, even resistance.[148] But despite the undeniable role that New York played in the ways Dominicans thought about consumption, and in the strategies they adopted in order to consume, we should not presume that such cultural change and invention always moved in a single direction, from the modern, dynamic United States to the traditional, static Dominican Republic. Living through parallel and interconnected urban crises, Dominicans in New York and Santo Domingo invented new customs simultaneously. As they took on new identities as consumers, residents of barrios in these two cities conversed back and forth, using shared symbols with distinct local meanings.[149]

Conclusion

In 2005, I returned to Cristo Rey, five years after my first visit and a decade into the experiment of neoliberalism in the Dominican Republic. Leonel Fernández, raised in New York in a family of bodegueros, was again in power. Fernández was a man of cultura, whose dark skin and tightly curled hair went generally unremarked in public discourse in Santo Domingo. His *educación* and buenas costumbres stood in marked contrast to the man he replaced, Hipólito Mejía. Mejía, though white, was widely regarded as a barely literate cretin and a public embarrassment. Fernández was a darling of the international investment community, an ardent modernizer who depicted modernization as the emulation of the United States. Political opponents nevertheless encouraged a whisper campaign calling him by the nickname "el Dominicanyork."

Increasing cooperation with global financial institutions and the World Trade Organization, however, had done little to improve things in Cristo Rey. In the 1990s, the neighborhood had a reputation as a relatively peaceful barrio. But since then, the Roman Catholic hierarchy had removed Padre Rogelio, the most famous radical priest in the city, and had forced many of the lay activists out of the local church. The social projects that had sustained my initial research, especially the youth groups, had moved out of the church into more diffused spaces. Activists blamed the demise of these social projects for the rise of *naciones*, or street gangs, in the barrio. During the long night time blackouts, residents no longer sat easily outside. They were afraid of youngsters who fired weapons in the air and at each other. Periodically the police mounted high-profile raids, roundups, and shootouts with gangs in the barrios. Friends warned me not to walk in the barrio as I used to, worrying that I might fall into the hands of tígueres who would steal my shoes, despite the fact that they were off-brand. I consistently heard two metaphors for the transformation of their part of the city; it was like the "Wild West"; and, more consistently, it was like New York. In fact, residents had renamed one of the original crowded settlements of Cristo Rey "The Bronx," in reference to its reputation for street violence.

This was not the first time Dominicans had transposed geographic markers of danger or respectability from one city to the other. In the 1970s, according to Andrés Belén, a Dominican New Yorker interviewed in the *New York Post*, Dominicans in New York assigned the name Calle Barahona to a segment of Amsterdam Avenue near 110th Street. In

FIGURE C-1. Children play with a toy gun in a cañada in Cristo Rey, 2005. Because of frequent shootings adults described the area as like the "Wild West." (Photo by John Paul Gallagher)

1917, the U.S. military government had designated the street as a "tolerance zone" in Santo Domingo. It had retained its reputation for scandal for the rest of the century. Renaming a block in New York after the iconic red-light district in Santo Domingo was a way for migrants like Belén to separate themselves from the worst stereotypes about Dominicans in New York. Indeed, Belén made an explicit contrast between the unlicensed social clubs on Amsterdam Avenue and the quiet decency of Dominicans in his own neighborhood, Corona, Queens. As it happened, Dominicans living in Corona used yet another Dominican place name for their own neighborhood, Sabana Church. Sabana Church was a partial translation of Sabana Iglesias, the rural town near Santiago where many of the first Dominican settlers in Corona originated. Naming one's own neighborhood after a town in the Cibao, the geographical place identified since the 1920s as the heartland of a rural, and whitened, national culture, was the inverse of naming someone else's block after Calle Barahona.

These stories provide a fitting end to this tale of two cities. They show how spaces in these cities, and cities themselves, became concrete symbols for the key experiences of modern life in a country rapidly moving from a rural to an urban majority. When this tale began, in the 1950s, foreign invasion and homegrown dictatorship had only recently trans-formed the Dominican Republic, a country of independent peasants, into an integrated national community composed of rural citizens. De-spite their interest in controlling urban space through regulation of mi-gration and public decency, the U.S. occupation and the Trujillo regime set in motion the precipitous, and largely uncontrollable, displacement of the rural citizenry to the margins of growing cities. By the 1960s, residents of the burgeoning popular and marginal barrios of the Do-minican capital grew into a potent social force, joining demonstrations in the center city and eventually an armed uprising. Meanwhile, hop-ing to stabilize Dominican politics and faced with Dominican demands for freedom of travel, a new generation of liberal imperialists in Wash-ington unwittingly opened the door to a second massive movement of Dominican citizens: to the city of New York. By the end of the century, the center of Dominican social, cultural, and political life had shifted from rural villages and plantations to barrios in these twin Dominican cities. These barrios, though interconnected in countless ways, never-theless grew in dramatically different contexts. In the midst of New York's economic restructuring and racial conflict, Dominican settlers engaged in a process of ethnic definition that made them a new racial minority, part of the emerging "inner city" of low-paid service work, failing schools, and the War on Drugs. In Santo Domingo, barrio resi-dents lived through a U.S.-sponsored "cleanup" operation and twelve years of authoritarianism, only to find that democracy and the debt cri-sis would thrust them farther to the margins.

The exchange of people and popular culture between these two kinds of barrios tested the limits of nationalist imaginations and narratives in both the United States and the Dominican Republic. New arrivals with dark skin, foreign cultures, and ties to "home" offended those in the United States who believed in the mythology of immigrant assimi-lation. And urban people, making claims to upward mobility and in-terested in mass media and consumer products, offended those who imagined a Dominican Republic pure of external influence, spiritual in its values, fixed in its class hierarchies, and rural in its culture. To those with high hopes for global capitalism, economic growth would eventu-ally incorporate and domesticate these troublesome people and spaces. To others, such barrios were explicit enemies of order and growth. They should be targets in wars on public expenditure, crime, and illegal mi-gration, and in campaigns to reclaim urban space. At the same time, many of the traditional defenders of the poor were often wary of, or hostile to, a populace that did not look like their visions of the "popu-lar": people who were neither rural peasants, self-conscious racial or indigenous communities, nor industrial working classes.

Barrios like Cristo Rey and Washington Heights, however, were neither odd exceptions to the otherwise exemplary experience of global capitalism, nor were they unfortunate deformations of Latin American identity in the face of empire. At the end of the twentieth century the modal experience of contemporary global capitalism was the tropical slum, whether Manila, Lagos, Mumbai, or Santo Domingo. More and more of these slums, at the end of the century, were on the road to deep entanglement with ethnic ghettos located in the cities of Europe and North America.[1] Although poor urban Dominicans in Santo Domingo and New York have been marginalized by the stories both societies tell about themselves, they are not marginal to the history of the Dominican Republic and United States. And the Dominican Republic, with its large, unruly slums and its tightly woven, though contested, relationship with New York, is hardly an exceptional case at the margins of Latin American history. Each barrio and city has its own particular history. But slums, international migrants, televisions, and controversial popular styles are as archetypal of twentieth-century Caribbean and Latin American history as sugar plantations, the emergence of peasantries, and the problems of freedom and citizenship were in earlier centuries.

Nevertheless, contemporary transformations in the Caribbean and Latin America, and even in the United States "inner city," are best understood not as radical novelties, but as social formations with deep roots in earlier history. Imperialism, cultural mixture, mobility, and international economic exchange in the region all predate the advent of late-twentieth-century "transnationalism" or "globalization" by nearly five centuries.[2] But perhaps more important for this study, the ideas driving contemporary migrations and the ideas governing contemporary renegotiations of Dominican national identity, class relations, racial identification, and social mobility are all artifacts passed down from earlier historical moments. Dominicans faced with new social arrangements, and new cultural predicaments, turned to ideas inherited from older social arrangements: to geographical symbols such as Calle Barahona and the Bronx and basic social concepts such as progreso, cultura, Dominican, North American, white, black, and Hispanic. In short, all of the categories Dominicans employed in attempts to define themselves and others had complicated histories. As urban and international migrants began to use such terms in new contexts, they inevitably took on new meanings. Hispanic, or Dominican, for instance, came to mean something different in Washington Heights than it had in Santo Domingo. Progreso meant something different among the poor of the Zona Norte in the 1980s or factory workers in New York in the 1970s than it had among liberal intellectuals in the 1880s. But these meanings changed reluctantly and unevenly.

This tale of two cities is a tale of conversations among Dominicans about who belongs and who does not belong in a rapidly changing society. It is about neighborhood residents faced with hostile political and economic institutions, and a dominant ideology that assigns them almost no value. These people sometimes fought mightily and openly for sovereignty, liberation, and justice through trade unions, peasant groups, guerrilla movements, ethnic activism, neighborhood strikes, and church groups. Yet even when they did not resist the tides of global power in ways we can easily identify as heroic, they did not simply drown or wash up on foreign shores. They learned to judge the dangerous waters and stayed afloat. They lived inside the nation-states and the imperial system that they could not abolish. They adopted ideas that had been invented to oppress them, turned them around, and made them part of their claims for respectability and belonging. They labored and sacrificed to move to the cities that excluded them. Above all they learned how to tell new stories about themselves, stories that challenged or reworked standard nationalist frames. Listening to their stories, the ones they lived and the ones they told, is a central challenge for our understanding of contemporary Latin America and the United States, and of contemporary urban life. For historians, this challenge can only be met by telling tales of cities both north and south of the border.

Population Change in the Dominican Republic

Year	Population of Dominican Republic	% Urban Population	Population of Santo Domingo	Dominicans in U.S.[†]
1920	894,665	16.6	30,943	—
1950	2,135,872	23.8	181,553	—
1960	3,047,070	30.2	367,053	11,883
1970	4,009,458	39.7	668,507	61,228
1981	5,584,681	51.3	1,313,172	169,147
1993	7,293,390	55.2	1,609,966	537,120
2002	8,562,541	63.6	2,115,916	1,121,257

Population estimates for the Dominican Republic are based on 1920, 1950, 1960, 1970, 1981, 1993, and 2002 censuses. Population statistics for the United States are from the nearest decennial censuses.

[†]Before 1990 the United States census did not identify "Dominican" as an ethnic group inside the United States. The figures listed for those years represent those born in the Dominican Republic and counted in the fifty United States. *Source*: Campbell and Lennon, "Historical Census Statistics on the Foreign-Born."

Beginning in 1990 the U.S. census allowed "Other Hispanic" persons to write in their own classification in the question on Hispanic ethnicity. The question, as designed, undercounted Dominicans as well as some other Latin American groups. The numbers included here are estimates produced by the Mumford Institute that seek to correct for this problem on the census form. They do not correct for the certain undercount of undocumented Dominicans. *Source*: Logan, "The New Latinos."

Notes

BIBLIOGRAPHIC ABBREVIATIONS

Newspapers
EC: *El Caribe*
EN: *El Nacional*
ES: *El Sol*
LN: *La Noticia*
Listín: *Listín Diario*
NYT: *The New York Times*

Archival Source Material
AGN: Archivo General de la Nación, Santo Domingo.

AGN-SEIP: Archivo General de la Nación papers of the Secretario de lo Interior y Policia, Santo Domingo.

AGN-CND: Archivo General de la Nación papers of the Comisión Nacional del Desarrollo, Santo Domingo.

CACD: Casa Abierta Centro de Documentación, Santo Domingo.

DDRS: Declassified Document Reference System. Reproduced online by Primary Source Media, Gale Group. All documents last referenced on October 11, 2006.

ELP: Ellen Lurie Papers. Special Collections, Teachers College Library, Columbia University, New York, NY.

GWHS Survey: A qualitative survey of George Washington High School alumni identified through online registries and conducted by the author via e-mail.

IRP: Isaiah Robinson Papers. Special Collections, Teachers College Library, Columbia University, New York, NY.

NACLA Collection: Dominican Republic in The North American Congress on Latin America Archive of Latin Americana. Wilmington, DE: Scholarly Reources 1998.

NARA: National Archives and Records Administration, College Park, MD.

NOTES TO FOREWORD

1. For one version of the critique of nationalism in historical practice, Prasenjit Duara, *Rescuing History from the Nation* (Chicago, 1995); as related to U.S. exceptionalism, Michael Geyer and Charles Bright, "World History in a Global Age," *American Historical Review* 100 (1995); Ian Tyrell, "American Exceptionalism in an Age of International History," *American Historical Review* 96 (1991). For important examples of nonnational or international history see Fernand Braudel, *The Mediterranean and the Mediterranean World in the Age of Philip II* (New York, 1972); Sidney Wilfred Mintz, *Sweetness and Power* (New York, 1985); Daniel T. Rodgers, *Atlantic Crossings* (Cambridge, MA, 1998); Rebecca J. Scott, *Degrees of Freedom: Louisiana and Cuba after Slavery* (Cambridge, MA, 2005); Jeremy I. Adelman, *Sovereignty and Revolution in the Iberian Atlantic* (Princeton, 2007).

2. There are examples of dependency school authors who also concerned themselves with the agency of nonelites. Stanley J. Stein, *Vassouras: A Brazilian Coffee County, 1850–1900* (Cambridge, MA, 1957), for instance, became a model for a groundbreaking work on agency, Rebecca J. Scott, *Slave Emancipation in Cuba* (Princeton, 1985). For more recent works addressing the role of popular sectors in constructing social meaning see for instance Laurent Dubois, *Avengers of the New World* (Cambridge, 2004); Peter Guardino, *The Time of Liberty: Popular Political Culture in Oaxaca* (Durham, NC, 2005).

3. Benedict Anderson, *Imagined Communities* (London, 1983); Partha Chatterjee, *Nationalist Thought and the Colonial World* (London, 1986); Gilbert M. Joseph, "Close Encounters: Toward a New Cultural History of U.S.–Latin American Relations," in *Close Encounters of Empire*, ed. Gilbert M. Joseph, Catherine C. Legrand, and Ricardo D. Salvatore (Durham, NC, 1998); Louis A. Pérez, *On Becoming Cuban* (Chapel Hill, NC, 1999).

4. In a sense this merely applies the insights of cultural Marxists regarding hegemony to international relations, see Stuart Hall, "Gramsci's Relevance for the Study of Race and Ethnicity, " *Journal of Communication Inquiry* 10 (1986); Raymond Williams, *Marxism and Literature* (Oxford, 1977).

5. For instance, Frank Moya Pons, *Dominican National Identity and Return Migration* (Gainesville, FL, 1981); Pérez, *On Becoming Cuban*.

6. Walter LaFeber, *The American Age* (New York, 1989); Immanuel Maurice Wallerstein, *The Modern World-System* (New York, 1974); William Appleman Williams, *From Colony to Empire* (New York, 1972).

7. For the origins of the more recent wave of scholarship on empire and culture see the widely cited Amy Kaplan and Donald E. Pease, *Cultures of United States Imperialism* (Durham, NC, 1993); George Lipsitz, *American Studies in a Moment of Danger* (Minneapolis, MN, 2001).

8. Thomas Bender, ed., *Rethinking American History in a Global Age* (Berkeley and Los Angeles, 2002); Louis A. Pérez, "We Are the World: Internationalizing the National, Nationalizing the International," *Jounal of American History* 89 (2002).

9. Two important sources for the history of this legislation are Mae Ngai, *Impossible Subjects* (Princeton 2004); David M. Reimers, *Still the Golden Door* (New York, 1985). Notable exceptions that focus on new Latin American immigration after

World War II are María Cristina García, *Havana, USA* (Berkeley and Los Angeles, 1996); David Gutiérrez, *Walls and Mirrors* (Berkeley and Los Angeles, 1995).

10. I am not the first to make this argument. See Christopher Mitchell, "U.S. Foreign Policy and Dominican Migration," in *Western Hemisphere Immigration and U.S. Foreign Policy*, ed. Christopher Mitchell (University Park, PA, 1992).

11. Sherrie Baver, "Including Migration in the Development Calculus," *Latin American Research Review* 30 (1995); Alejandro Portes and John Walton, *Labor, Class, and the International System* (New York, 1981). For the argument that gender and family relations conditioned international class relations see Sherri Grasmuck and Patricia Pessar, *Between Two Islands* (Berkeley and Los Angeles, 1991); and for the "social embeddedness" of migration see Pessar's introduction in Patricia Pessar, ed., *Caribbean Currents* (New York, 1997), 1–11.

12. For arguments about long-distance nationalism see Nina Glick Schiller and Georges Fouron, *Georges Woke Up Laughing* (Durham, NC, 2001). For transnational social fields see Peter Kivisto, "Theorizing Transnational Immigration," *Ethnic and Racial Studies* 24 (2001); Alejandro Portes, Luis Guarnizo, and Patricia Landolt, "Transnational Communities: Pitfalls and Promise," *Ethnic and Racial Studies* 22 (1999).

13. See for instance Arnold R. Hirsch, *Making the Second Ghetto* (Cambridge, 1983); Kenneth T. Jackson, *Crabgrass Frontier* (New York, 1985); Thomas J. Sugrue, *The Origins of the Urban Crisis* (Princeton, 1996); Martha Biondi, *To Stand and Fight* (Cambridge, MA, 2003); Robert O. Self, *American Babylon* (Princeton, 2003); Lizbeth Cohen, *A Consumer's Republic* (New York, 2004); Matthew Countryman, *Up South* (Philadelphia, PA, 2006); Matthew Lassiter, *The Silent Majority* (Princeton, 2006). For accounts that focus on Latinos and the transformation of urban space see Ana Y. Ramos-Zayas, *National Performances* (Chicago, 2003); Arlene Dávila, *Barrio Dreams: Puerto Ricans and the Neoliberal City* (Berkeley and Los Angeles, 2004); Nicholas De Genova, *Racial Transformations* (Durham, NC, 2006). On transformations and tensions of Caribbean-Latino racial identity, see Juan Flores, "'Qué assimilated, brother, yo soy asimilao': The Structuring of Puerto Rican Ethnicity in the U.S.," in *Challenging Fronteras*, ed. Mary Romero, Pierrette Hondagneu-Sotelo, and Vilma Ortiz (New York, 1997); Anani Dzidzienyo and Suzanne Oboler, *Neither Enemies nor Friends: Latinos, Blacks, Afro-Latinos* (New York, 2005).

14. On the need to break down the idea of national racial systems without losing the possibility of comparison see Peter Fry, *A persistência da raça* (Rio de Janeiro, 2005); Scott, *Degrees of Freedom*. On Dominican racial formation see especially Silvio Torres-Saillant, "The Tribulations of Blackness: Stages in Dominican Racial Identity," *Callaloo* 23 (2000); Richard Lee Turits, *Race, Slavery, and Freedom beyond the Plantation* (Forthcoming).

NOTES TO CHAPTER ONE

1. Raymundo González, "Ideología del progreso y campesinado en el siglo XIX," *Ecos* 1 (1993); Richard Lee Turits, *Foundations of Despotism* (Palo Alto, CA, 2003).

2. Manuel A. Peña Batlle, *Política de Trujillo* (Ciudad Trujillo, 1954).

3. Lauren Derby, "The Magic of Modernity" (Ph.D. diss., University of Chicago, 1998).

4. United Nations Population Division, "World Urbanization Prospects: The 2005 Revision Population Database," http://esa.un.org/unup. The Dominican Census, reported that 63.6 percent of the population was urban in 2002. Oficina Nacional de Estadística, *VIII Censo de Población y Vivienda, República Dominicana* (Santo Domingo, 2002), available from http://www.one.gob.do/index.php.

5. Centro Latinoamericano y Caribeño de Demografía—División de Población, "Boletín demográfico: Urbanización y evolución de la población urbana de América Latina, 1950–1990" (Santiago de Chile, 2001).

6. Precise figures are difficult to obtain. The 2002 Dominican Census reported 2,148,261 urban residents in the National District. Of these, 93,745 lived in the outlying towns of La Victoria, San Antonio de Guerra, Pedro Brand, and Boca Chica; the rest (2,054,516) lived in the contiguous urban areas of Santo Domingo. Not counted in this number, however, are the 61,400 urban dwellers in Bajos de Haina. Though part of the province of San Cristobal, Haina is contiguous with Santo Domingo and should be considered part of greater Santo Domingo. Oficina Nacional de Estadística, *VIII Censo de Población y Vivienda*. For a consideration of the rural and urban populations of the National District in 1993 see Nelson Ramírez, "El censo del 93," (Santo Domingo, 1997).

7. Joaquín Balaguer, opening remarks published in Centro Latinoamericano de Población y Familia, *Seminario de desarrollo población y família* (Santo Domingo, 1968); see too the other papers presented at this conference: Juan Ulíses García Bonnelly, *Sobrepoblación, subdesarrollo y sus consecuencias socioeconómicas* (Santo Domingo, 1971); Isis Duarte, *Capitalismo y superpoblación en Santo Domingo* (Santo Domingo, 1980); cf. Janice Perlman, *The Myth of Marginality* (Berkeley and Los Angeles, 1976).

8. Domingo A. Rodríguez Creus, *Don Cibaíto en la capital, diario cómico de un cibaeño, sin rumbo fijo, en los "vericuetos" de la gran ciudad.* (Santo Domingo, 1973), 25.

9. Ibid., 213.

10. For an overview, G. Pope Atkins and Larman C. Wilson, *The Dominican Republic and the United States: From Imperialism to Transnationalism* (Athens, GA, 1998); on the late nineteenth century, Cyrus Veeser, *A World Safe for Capitalism* (New York, 2002); on the first U.S. occupation, Bruce Calder, *The Impact of Intervention* (Austin, TX, 1984); the Trujillo years, Eric Paul Roorda, *The Dictator Next Door* (Durham, NC, 1998); the 1965 intervention, Piero Gleijeses, *The Dominican Crisis* (Baltimore, MD, 1978); and its aftermath, Frank Moya Pons, "Quid Pro Quo: Dominican-American Economic Relations, 1966–1974," *SAIS Review* 19 (1975).

11. David Scobey, *Empire City: The Making and Meaning of the New York City Landscape* (Philadelphia, 2002), 33.

12. Mercedes Sagredo, *Mi vida, mi Quisqueya* (Santo Domingo, 1994), 184–88.

13. The Ancestry.com digital index of the *1930 United States Federal Census* lists 340 Dominican-born New Yorkers. Sagredo and several family members, while recorded on the census itself, are not counted by this index. This suggests that the 340 figure is an undercount.

14. The census bureau estimated 11,883 Dominican-born persons residing in the United States in 1960 based on a 25 percent sample. Most had probably arrived in the preceding decade when about 9,000 Dominicans were admitted as immigrants. About 3,000 more Dominican immigrants were admitted in 1961. That would make the Dominican population of the United States about 15,000 at the beginning of 1962, not including U.S.-born Dominicans. The number was perhaps a bit higher since more than a third of Caribbean-born persons reported by the census had no enumerated country of origin. Given later demographic trends, it seems likely that a substantial majority lived in New York City. J. Gibson Campbell and Emily Lennon, "Historical Census Statistics on the Foreign-Born Population of the United States: 1850–1990," (Washington, DC, 1999).

15. John R. Logan, "The New Latinos" (Lewis Mumford Center for Comparative Urban and Regional Research, September 10, 2001), available from http://mumford1.dyndns.org/cen2000/HispanicPop/HspReport/HspReportPage1.html. For population of Dominican Republic see U.N. Common Statistical Database, http://unstats.un.org/unsd/cdb/ (code 15070). The nearest Dominican census is 2002, which counted 8.56 million residents. Oficina Nacional de Estadística, VIII Censo de Población y Vivienda.

16. Estimates based on the 1980 U.S. Federal Census and Logan, "The New Latinos."

17. Santiago de los Caballeros (622,101 in 2002) was a close third. Oficina Nacional de Estadística, VIII Censo de Población y Vivienda.

18. Francisco Rodríguez de León, El furioso merengue del norte (New York, 1998), 240–42.

19. Ramona Hernández, The Mobility of Labor under Advanced Capitalism: Dominican Migration to the United States (New York, 2002).

20. Arun Peter Lobo, Ronald J. O. Flores, and Joseph J. Salvo, "The Impact of Hispanic Growth on the Racial/Ethnic Composition of New York City Neighborhoods," Urban Affairs Review 37 (May 2002).

21. Inter-American Development Bank Multilateral Investment Fund, "Remittances to Latin America and the Caribbean" (2001), available from http://www.iadb.org/mif/v2/remittancesstudies.html.

22. For the concept of the social remittance see Peggy Levitt, Transnational Villagers (Berkeley and Los Angeles, 2001).

23. Moya Pons, National Identity and Return; Frank Moya Pons, El pasado dominicano (Santo Domingo, 1986), 360.

24. For a left-wing version of this prejudice see Juan De Frank Canelo, Dónde, por qué, de qué, cómo viven los dominicanos en el extranjero (Santo Domingo, 1982); for a right-wing version see Manuel Núñez, El ocaso de la nación dominicana (Santo Domingo, 2001), 563–65.

25. Alfonso (Pochy Familia) Vázquez, "El hombre llegó parao" (Santo Domingo, 1995).

26. Cohen, Consumer's Republic; Victoria de Grazia, Irresistible Empire (Cambridge, 2005); Herman Van Der Wee, Prosperity and Upheaval (Berkeley and Los Angeles, 1983); Reinhold Wagnleitner, Coca-colonization and the Cold War, trans. Diana M. Wolf (Chapel Hill, NC, 1994).

27. Interview with María Mora (Santo Domingo, 2000).

28. Torres-Saillant, "Tribulations," 1091.

29. For quote, Torres-Saillant, "Tribulations," 1089. For more on race and color in the Dominican Republic, Harry Hoetink, "'Race' and Color in the Caribbean," in *Caribbean Contours*, ed. Sydney W. Mintz and Sally Price (Baltimore, 1985); Mendiert Fennema and Troetje Loewenthal, *La construcción de raza y nación en la República Dominicana* (Santo Domingo, 1987); David Howard, *Coloring the Nation: Race and Ethnicity in the Dominican Republic* (Oxford, 2001); Ernesto Sagás, *Race and Politics in the Dominican Republic* (Gainsville, FL, 2000); Turits, *Race, Slavery, and Freedom.*

NOTES TO CHAPTER TWO

1. René Martínez Lemoine, "The Classical Model of the Spanish-American Colonial City," *Journal of Architecture* 8 (Autumn 2003).

2. Frank Moya Pons, *Después de Colón: Trabajo, sociedad y política en la economía del Oro* (Madrid, 1987); Genaro Rodríguez Morel, "Esclavitud y vida rural en las plantaciones azucareras de Santo Domingo. Siglo XVI," *Anuario de Estudios Americanos* 49 (1992).

3. Noble David Cook, "Disease and the Depopulation of Hispaniola, 1492–1518," *Colonial Latin American Review* 2 (1993); Frank Moya Pons, *The Dominican Republic: A National History* (New Rochelle, NY, 1995), 29–89.

4. Angel Quintero Rivera, *Salsa, sabor y control* (Madrid, 1998), 201–51; Antonio Benítez Rojo, *La isla que se repite* (Barcelona, 1998), 15–26. For the concept of reconstituted peasantries, Sidney W. Mintz, *Caribbean Transformations* (New York 1989), 131–56. For the peasantry in colonial Santo Domingo, see Turits, *Foundations,* 25–39. For a nineteenth-century description of mobile slash-and-burn agriculture see José Ramón López, "La caña de azúcar en San Pedro de Macorís," in *Ensayos y artículos* (Santo Domingo, 1991), 76–77.

5. Wendalina Rodríguez Vélez, *El turbante blanco* (Santo Domingo, 1982); Dagoberto Tejeda Ortíz, *Cultura popular e identidad popular* (Santo Domingo, 1998). For the indigenous role in this cultural evolution see Lynne Guitar, "Cultural Genesis: Relationships among Indians, Africans and Spaniards in Rural Hispaniola, Sixteenth Century" (Ph.D. diss., Vanderbilt University, 1998).

6. For a critique of the older idea of racial democracy see Ruben Silie, *Economía, esclavitud, y población* (Santo Domingo, 1976).

7. Dubois, *Avengers of the New World*; Moya Pons, *The Dominican Republic,* 91–164.

8. Sumner Wells, *Naboth's Vineyard, 1844–1924* (New York, 1928).

9. Teresita Martínez-Vergne, *Nation and Citizen in the Dominican Republic* (Chapel Hill, NC, 2005), 2–6.

10. José Ramón López, "La alimentación y las razas," in *Ensayos y artículos.*

11. Michiel Baud, "Ideología y campsinado: El pensamiento de José Ramón López," *Estudios Sociales* 19 (April–June 1986); Roberto Cassá, "Eugenio Deschamps ante la edad de oro del liberalismo," in *Política, identidad y pensamiento social en la República Dominicana, Siglos XIX y XX.*, ed. Raymundo González et al. (Madrid, 1999); González, "Ideología"; López, "Caña de azúcar," 77–82.

12. Veeser, *World Safe for Capitalism*, 66–70.

13. For an articulation of this ontology see Michel-Rolph Trouillot, *Silencing the Past* (Boston, 1995), 70–107.

14. Américo Lugo cited in Ernesto Sagás, *Race and Politics*, 40.

15. Martínez-Vergne, *Nation and Citizen*, 82–93.

16. Raymundo González, "Hostos y la conciencia moderna en la República Dominicana," in *Política, identidad y pensamiento social en la República Dominicana, Siglos XIX y XX*, ed. Raymundo González et al. (Madrid, 1999).

17. Pedro San Miguel, *La isla imaginada* (San Juan, 1997); Jeremy I. Adelman, "The Problem of Persistence in Latin American History," in *Colonial Legacies*, ed. Jeremy I. Adelman (New York, 1999).

18. Américo Lugo, *A punto largo* (Santo Domingo, 1901), 144–45.

19. Derby, "Gringo Chickens"; Turits, *Foundations*, 65–66.

20. For instance, Eileen J. Suarez Findlay, *Imposing Decency: The Politics of Sexuality and Race in Puerto Rico, 1870–1920* (Durham, NC, 1999); Gerstle, *American Crucible*, 14–43.

21. Calder, *Impact*; Veeser, *World Safe for Capitalism*.

22. They were avid readers of both José Enrique Rodó, *Ariel*, trans. Margaret Sayares Pueden (Austin, TX, 1988) and Oswald Spengler, *La decadencia de occidente*, trans. Manuel García Morente (Madrid, 1923). See Derby, "Magic," 157–81; Andrés L. Mateo, *Mito y cultura en la era de Trujillo* (Santo Domingo, 1993), 58–60.

23. "Raza y cultura" (1933) reprinted in Pedro Henríquez Ureña, *La utopía de América* (Caracas, 1978), 13; Torres-Saillant, "Tribulations," 1102.

24. Arcadio Díaz-Quiñones, "Pedro Henríquez Ureña," *Revista de Crítica Literaria Latinoamericana* 17 (1991); Pedro Henríquez Ureña, *La cultura y las letras coloniales en Santo Domingo* (Buenos Aires, 1936), 13.

25. Derby, "Magic," 86–128, 157–81.

26. For this idea as expressed in the United States, John J. Johnson, *Latin America in Caricature* (Austin, TX, 1980); Matthew Frye Jacobson, *Barbarian Virtues* (New York, 2000), 139–78, 221–60.

27. The idea of "performing civilization" comes from Ada Ferrer, *Insurgent Cuba* (Chapel Hill, NC, 1999), 191. For the argument that encounters with the United States as imperial power were a "stage" of Dominican blackness, Torres-Saillant, "Tribulations," 1087–90.

28. See "Negro tras las orejas" in Juan Antonio Alix, *Décimas* (Santo Domingo, 1969), 28–30.

29. Torres-Saillant, "Tribulations," 1091. Cf. Fennema and Loewenthal, *Construcción*; Sagás, *Race and Politics*.

30. Cited in Sagás, *Race and Politics*, 32–33.

31. Dubois, *Avengers of the New World*, 60–90.

32. Pedro San Miguel, "Discurso racial e identidad nacional en la República Dominicana," *Op. Cit.: Revista del Centro de Investigaciones Históricas* 7 (1992): 87–97.

33. Roberto Cassá, "Nación y estado en el pensamiento de Américo Lugo," in *Politica, identidad, y pensamiento social en la República Dominicana, Siglos XIX y XX*, ed. Raymundo González and Michiel Baud (Madrid, 1999).

34. Paul Austerlitz, *Merengue: Dominican Music and Dominican Identity* (Philadelphia, 1997), 30–51. Cf. Lillian Guerra, *Popular Expression and National Identity in Puerto Rico* (Gainesville, FL, 1998).

35. Martínez-Vergne, *Nation and Citizen in the Dominican Republic*, 53–81.

36. Eduardo Matos Díaz cited in Derby, "Magic," 176–77, also 86–128, 157–81.

37. "Esas ceremonias africanizantes deben terminar," *La Opinon*, September 27, 1930. Cited in Derby, "Magic," 200–201.

38. Calder, *Impact*, 49–62; Moya Pons, *The Dominican Republic*, 255–63.

39. Duarte, *Capitalismo*, 190–211.

40. Robert Crassweller, *Trujillo: The Life and Times of a Caribbean Dictator* (New York, 1966), 39–86.

41. G. Pope Atkins and Larman C. Wilson, *The United States and the Trujillo Regime* (New Brunswick, NJ, 1972); Roorda, *Dictator Next Door*.

42. Turits, *Foundations*, 10.

43. Peña Batlle, *Política*, 192.

44. Austerlitz, *Merengue*, 52–77; Turits, *Foundations*, 1.

45. Joaquín Balaguer, *Dominican Reality: Biographical Sketch of a Country and a Regime*, trans. Mary Gilland (Mexico City, 1949); Richard Lee Turits, "A World Destroyed, a Nation Imposed," *Hispanic American Historical Review* 82 (August 2002).

46. For examples of identity cards see Sagás, *Race and Politics*, 130–31; for merengue as a Spanish folkdance, Flérida de Nolasco, *La música en Santo Domingo y otros ensayos* (Ciudad Trujillo, 1939); on a similar process of cultural camouflage in Puerto Rico, Quintero Rivera, *Salsa*.

47. Derby, "Magic," 144–209; Juan Ulíses García Bonnelly, *Las obras públicas en la era de Trujillo* (Ciudad Trujillo, 1955), 43–120; Mateo, *Mito*, 107–23.

48. Lauren Derby, "The Dictator's Seduction," *Callaloo* 23 (2000): 1119.

49. J. D. Cerón and Toño Abreu (1930), "El Ciclón," in *Antología musical de la Era de Trujillo*, ed. Luis Rivera Gonzáles (Ciudad Trujillo, 1960[?]), 2:8.

50. For hundreds of newspaper articles announcing ribbon cuttings and inaugurations of public projects, see Archivo General de la Nación, ed., *Obras de Trujillo* (Ciudad Trujillo, 1956). For the language of progreso see Bienvenido Bustamante and Alfonso Asenjo (1958), "La epopeya," 1:28; Luis Rivera and Sergio de la Mota (1956), "El progreso no se detiene," 1:78; Bienvenido Bustamante and Felix López (1959), "Trujillo el gran arquitecto" 1:206. There are literally scores of other merengues celebrating bridges, roads, and the Feria de Paz y Fraternidad. See, for instance, Vito Castorina and Luis Alberti (1936), "Los dos puentes," 1:28 and J. D. Cerón and Alejandro Camacho García (1955), "Vamos a la feria" 1:28. All are reprinted in Rivera Gonzáles, *Antología*.

51. Derby, "Magic," 220–30. For popular expressions of this discourse of presidential construction, I rely on fieldwork in 1999 and 2000.

52. Derby, "Magic," 264.

53. Ibid. 144-209; García Bonnelly, *Obras públicas*, 43–120.

54. This speech was cited in Universidad de Santo Domingo, *Acta final del primer simposio para la evaluación y defensa de los recursos naturales de la República Dominicana, 24 al 29 de octubre de 1958* (Ciudad Trujillo, 1959), 167.

55. Decreto 9563, December 5, 1953, cited ibid., 168.

56. Interview with Don Marcelino (Cristo Rey, Santo Domingo, 2000).

57. Rafael Francisco Moya Pons, "Industrial Incentives in the Dominican Republic, 1880–1983" (Ph.D. diss., Columbia University, 1987).

58. On the construction of working-class neighborhoods see Amparo Chantada, *Del proceso de urbanización a la planificación urbana de Santo Domingo* (Santo Domingo, 1998), 152–65; García Bonnelly, *Obras públicas*, 130–37; Ramón Vargas Mera, "Evolución urbanística de Ciudad Trujillo" (Ciudad Trujillo, 1956).

59. Luis Rivera and Sergio de la Mota (1956), "El progreso no se detiene," in Rivera Gonzáles, *Antología*, 1:78.

60. O. Herrera Bornia, *Construcción de viviendas en la República Dominicana* (Ciudad Trujillo, 1958).This phrase is also cited in Derby, "Magic," 256.

61. Rafael Trujillo, Speech given in the inauguration of the neighborhood of Mejoramiento Social in Santo Domingo, January 1946. Reprinted in García Bonnelly, *Obras públicas*, 215–18.

62. Minerva Breton, Nelson Ramírez, and Pablo Tactuk, *La migración interna en la República Dominicana* (Santo Domingo, 1977).

63. Crassweller, *Trujillo*, 251–59; Turits, *Foundations*, 232–47.

64. On the effects of Trujillo's "Primitive Accumulation" on internal migration to the capital, see Duarte, *Capitalismo*, 139–45.

65. Neighborhood histories for Simón Bolívar and Guachupita interview with Jorge Cela (Santo Domingo, 2000). For a similar story in nearby Los Guandules, see Los Guandules, *Un barrio estudia a si mismo: Los Guandules* (Santo Domingo, 1983).

66. García Bonnelly, *Sobrepoblación*, 129.

67. Unversidad de Santo Domingo, *Acta Final*. For the survey see Pablo Tactuk, "Estudios sobre migración interna en la República Dominicana," in *La investigación demográfica en la República Dominicana* (Santo Domingo, 1977).

68. "Circular No. 1," January 10, 1960, AGN-SEIP, Leg. 5230 Exp. 4–9.

69. See data from the 1935 and 1960 Dominican censuses, Oficina Nacional de Estadística.

70. Bernard Diederich, *Trujillo: The Death of the Goat* (Boston, 1978); Howard Wiarda, "The United States and the Dominican Republic: Intervention, Dependency, and Tyrannicide," *Journal of Interamerican Studies and World Affairs* 22 (1980).

71. Stephen G. Rabe, *The Most Dangerous Area in the World: John F. Kennedy Confronts Communist Revolution in Latin America* (Chapel Hill, NC, 1999).

72. John Bartlow Martin, *Overtaken by Events* (Garden City, N.Y., 1966), 5–6, 65.

73. Gleijeses, *Dominican Crisis*, 256–81. For Gavilleros, Calder, *Impact*; Julie Franks, "The Gavilleros of the East: Social Banditry as Political Practice," *Journal of Historical Sociology* 8 (June 1995).

74. Wiarda, "The United States and the Dominican Republic," 247.

75. Alan McPherson, "Misled by Himself: What the Johnson Tapes Reveal about the Dominican Intervention of 1965," *Latin American Research Review* 38 (2003).

76. Gleijeses, *Dominican Crisis*, 114–15, 263–301, 369–70; José A. Moreno, *Barrios in Arms* (Pittsburgh, PA, 1970), 71, 94.

77. Moya Pons, "Quid Pro Quo."

78. Michael J. Kryzanek, "Diversion, Subversion, and Repression: The Strategies of Anti-opposition Politics in Balaguer's Dominican Republic," *Caribbean Studies* 17 (1978): 87, 89.

79. Roberto Cassá, *Los doce años* (Santo Domingo, 1991); Jonathan Hartlyn, *The Struggle for Democratic Politics in the Dominican Republic* (Chapel Hill, NC, 1998); Moya Pons, "Industrial Incentives."

80. Amparo Chantada, "Los mecanismos del crecimiento urbano de Santo Domingo, 1966–1978" (Ph.D. diss., University of Paris, 1982), 171–220; Thorson Sagawe, "Caudillismo and Urban Development," *Geographische Zeitschrift* 80 (1992).

81. Carlos Dore Cabral, *Reforma agraria y luchas sociales en la República Dominicana, 1966–1978* (Santo Domingo, 1981), 26–28, 58; Duarte, *Capitalismo*, 146–47; Turits, *Foundations*, 262–63; Rosemary Vargas-Lindius, *Peasants in Distress: Poverty and Unemployment in the Dominican Republic* (Boulder, CO, 1991), 162–81.

82. Joaquín Balaguer, *Mensajes presidenciales* (Barcelona, 1979), 84; Ildefonso Güemez, "Migración interna en la República Dominicana," in *Seminario sobre problemas de población en la República Dominicana* (Santo Domingo, 1975).

83. Centro Latinoamericano de Población y Familia, *Seminario de desarrollo*; Nelson Ramírez, "Demografía," in *Ciencias sociales en la República Dominicana*, ed. Wilfredo Lozano, Nelson Ramírez, and Bernardo Vega (Santo Domingo, 1989), 119–22.

84. For public housing projects in the 1970s see Chantada, "Mecanismos," 185. The construction of these early housing projects prefigured the mass evictions that Balaguer orchestrated when he returned to power in the 1980s. See Edmundo Morel and Manuel Mejía, "The Dominican Republic: Urban Renewal and Evictions in Santo Domingo, " in *Evictions and the Right to Housing*, ed. Antonio Azuela, Emilio Duhau, and Enrique Ortíz (Ottowa, 1998).

85. Tahira Vargas, *Las organizaciones de base en Santo Domingo* (Santo Domingo, 1994). On suspected political motivations behind certain evictions in the 1980s see Brada María Polonio and José R. Paulino G., "Renovación urbana y desalojos en Santo Domingo" (Licenciatura, Universidad Autónoma de Santo Domingo, 1992).

86. Consorcio Padco-Borrell, "Estudio sobre el desarrollo urbano de Santo Domingo" (Washington, DC, 1978), 102–15.

87. Derby, "Magic," 181–82; Nancie González, "Peasants' Progress: Dominicans in New York," *Caribbean Studies* 10 (1970).

88. For description of this "cuarteria y traspatio" housing type: Consorcio Padco-Borrell, "Estudio," 102–15. For intent of original architecture see Derby, "Magic," 258–62.

89. Consorcio Padco-Borrell, "Estudio," 102–15.

90. F. S. Ducoudray h., "La Ciénaga: Archipiélago de casas en mar de fango," ¡*Ahora!* June 13, 1984.

91. Consorcio Padco-Borrell, "Estudio," 93; Gregorio Lanz, "Servicio domestico, una esclavitud?" *Estudios Sociales* 2 (October–December 1969); Juan Almonte, Jesús Pino, and Ricardo Hurtado, "El chiripero: Realidad social y económica," *Estudios Sociales* 13 (January–March 1980).

92. Dagoberto Tejeda Ortíz, "Reflexiones sociológicas en torno a las eleccio-nes de la UASD" ¡Ahora! June 2, 1969; Doucodray h., "La Ciénaga."

NOTES TO CHAPTER THREE

1. Trujillo to the Congreso Nacional, February 27, 1937, reproduced in Un-versidad de Santo Domingo, *Acta Final*, 167. See also García Bonnelly, *Sobrepo-blación*.

2. Centro Latinoamericano de Población y Familia, *Seminario de desarrollo*; Ramírez, "Demografía," 116.

3. Duarte, *Capitalismo*, was the most important work by social scientists who came of age in opposition to the Balaguer regime. For an account of the generational shift away from modernization theory see Wilfredo Lozano and Ivette Sabbagh, "La sociología dominicana," in *Ciencias sociales en la República Dominicana*, ed. Wilfredo Lozano, Nelson Ramírez, and Bernardo Vega (Santo Domingo, 1989), 30–33.

4. Even sociologists who followed Oscar Lewis, arguing that elements of Do-minican popular culture stood in the way of political mobilization and social improvement in the barrios, saw cultures of poverty as outgrowths of unjust social relations. Culture was not, as in the United States, understood as an au-tonomous cause of poverty. See Jorge Cela, "Tengo un dolor en la cultura," *Estudios Sociales* 56 (1984).

5. Hernando de Soto, *The Other Path*, trans. June Abbott (New York, 1989).

6. Grasmuck and Pessar, *Between Two Islands*; Pessar, *Caribbean Currents*; Ale-jandro Portes, ed., *The Economic Sociology of Immigration* (New York, 1995).

7. Interview with Doña Pirín (Cristo Rey, Santo Domingo, 2000).

8. Interview with Marcelino.

9. Ibid. A member of another of the original agricultural families in Cristo Rey remembered similarly that migration eroded local subsistence practices. Interview with Marcelina Mejía (El Caliche, Santo Domingo, 2000).

10. Turits, *Foundations*, 19, 206–31.

11. Güemez, "Migración interna," 186–87.

12. Interview with Señora Polanco (Santo Domingo, 2000).

13. Güemez, "Migración interna," 178.

14. This was, for instance, the contention of Güemez, "Migración interna," 186, although the raw data do not support the conclusion very strongly.

15. Walter Cordero and Neici Zeller, "El desfile trujillista," in *Homenaje a Emilio Cordero Michel*, ed. Academia Dominicana de la Historia (Santo Do-mingo, 2004), 113–14.

16. Interview with Doña Francisca (Cristo Rey, Santo Domingo, 2000).

17. Ortíz, "Healers in the Storm," 240–50. Because my research there was built on friendship with the official church, I did not visit a *servidora* in Cristo Rey. I did attend a communal service to San Antonio organized by a servidora in Nigua, just west of Santo Domingo, in August 1998.

18. Interview with Juan Dagoberto Tejeda Ortíz (Santo Domingo, 1999).

19. On popular religiosity and migration, Ortíz, "Healers in the Storm," 241,

253, 279. Cristina Sánchez Carretero, "Santos y Misterios as Channels of Communication in the Diaspora: Afro-Dominican Religious Practices Abroad," *Journal of American Folklore* 118 (Summer, 2005). I attended one of these *horas santas* with Father Rogelio Cruz in the summer of 2000.

20. Oficio No. 13075, September 25, 1969, AGN-SEIP, Leg. 1262 Exp. 3-1.

21. Interview with Ramona Báez viuda de Reyes (El Caliche, Santo Domingo, 2000).

22. "Informe sobre desalojo de una propiedad del Ingeniero Manuel E. Tavarez Espalliat," September 8, 1964, AGN-SEIP.

23. Interview with Báez viuda de Reyes.

24. Interview with José Radhamés Polanco (Cristo Rey, Santo Domingo, 2000); interview with Señor Felix (Cristo Rey, Santo Domingo, 2000); interview with Doña Pirín.

25. Interview with Báez viuda de Reyes.

26. Interview with José Polanco.

27. José A. Moreno, "Precursores de la teología de la liberación en República Dominicana," *Revista Mexicana de Sociología* 48 (1986).

28. Hector Herrera, "El Caliche tiene ya agua" *Listín,* March 25, 1968.

29. Interview with Báez viuda de Reyes; Hector Herrera, "El Caliche ¡Tendrá agua!" *Listín,* October 14, 1967.

30. Interview with Báez viuda de Reyes. See also Moreno, "Precursores."

31. Oficio No. 13075, September 25, 1969, AGN-SEIP, Leg 1262 Exp. 3-1.

32. "Información acerca de desalojo en el Ingenio Consuelo," May 13, 1968, AGN-SEIP, Leg. 1082.

33. Oficio No. 13075, September 25, 1969, AGN-SEIP, Leg. 1262 Exp. 3-1.

34. Luis Rivera and Sergio de la Mota (1956), "El progreso no se detiene," in Rivera Gonzáles, *Antología,* 1:78.

35. Interview with Dominga Ogando (Cristo Rey, Santo Domingo, 2000).

36. Rafael Tomás Hernández, "La jornada de Chulín" (1987), reprinted in *Renovación urbana en Santo Domingo, 1986–1994,* ed. Juan de Dios Delance (Santo Domingo, 1993).

37. Rafael Tomás Hernández, "El puente que va a ninguna parte," *Listín,* August 2, 1983, reprinted in Delance, *Renovación urbana en Santo Domingo.*

38. Interview with Ogando.

39. Hernández, "El puente que va a ninguna parte"; Rosa Lockward de Lamelas, "Informe de actividades desarrolladas durante la ejecución del Proyecto de Renovación Urbana del Hoyo de Chulín, Febrero 1988," in Delance, *Renovación urbana en Santo Domingo.*

40. For an example of Balaguerista ideology about evictions see Freddy Sandoval, "De lo colonial a lo moderno," *¡Ahora!* September 1987, 3–5. For critique by barrio activists and advocates, "Padre Cela: Desalojos en parte norte de capital afectarán a medio millón de personas." *LN,* July 11, 1987, 23.

41. Oficio No. 13075, September 25, 1969, AGN-SEIP, Leg. 1262 Exp. 3-1. Cf. Amparo Chantada, "Crónica de una muerte por desalojo anunciado," *Perfil* (1992).

42. See photograph of a political message painted on a barracón in el Caliche, *Última Hora,* December 6, 1989, 2; "Los Farallones," *Hoy,* March 5, 1991, 5;

Margarita Brito, "Los desalojados de Cristo Rey amenazan con iniciar ocupación," *Listín,* July 30, 1996.

43. For stories of residents "buscando desalojo" I rely on informal interviews with residents in Pablo VI. For stories of the improvisation deployed to get apartments in the multis in Cristo Rey, interview with Doña Melliza (Cristo Rey, Santo Domingo, 2000); interwew with José Polanco. For the sale of apartments and investment in resources for survival, interview with Amparo Chantada (Santo Domingo, 2000).

44. For this popular usage I rely on conversations with residents, local scholars, and activists.

45. There was, of course, another presence in the conversation that may well account for such silence, a historian from the United States. Such silence was nearly universal in my interactions with people of varying status in Cristo Rey, in large part because I was based in the Catholic Church. Church activists, and the people they introduced me to, were likely the most avid practitioners of official Roman Catholic spirituality in the barrio. Also, my affiliation with the church shaped the kinds of questions that were comfortable to ask. Although I do not consider African Dominican religion to be shameful, I chose not to risk insulting people who invited me to their homes by asking them if they practiced rituals that they considered (or might have presumed that I considered) "witchcraft."

46. Interview with José Ceballos (Santo Domingo, 2000); interview with Nicolás Guevara (Santo Domingo, 2000). See Quintero Rivera, *Salsa.* The author describes this phenomenon of *minusvalía* as part of maroon culture in nonplantation societies. See also Carlos Esteban Deive, "Y tu abuela, dónde está?" *Boletín* 10 (1981); Silvio Torres-Saillant, "Hacia una identidad racial alternativa en la sociedad dominicana," *Op. Cit.: Revista del Centro de Investigaciones Históricas* 9 (1997).

47. Interviews in Cristo Rey (to avoid potential embarrassment, I have chosen to keep these conversations anonymous).

48. Deborah Pacini Hernández, *Bachata* (Philadelphia, PA, 1995).

49. For the spread of jukeboxes in Santo Domingo see ibid., 54. For complaints about popular music played on them see "Dialogando," *¡Ahora!* March 6, 1965.

50. C. M. De la Cruz, F. del Villar, et al., Letter to Miembros del Triumvirato que Gobierna la República, July 7, 1964; Santo Domingo, AGN-SEIP, Leg. 5718.

51. Residents of San Pablo, Letter to Rafael de Js. Checo, April 14, 1973, AGN-SEIP, Leg. 1950 Exp. 220.

52. Ibid.

53. Letter to Salvador Lluberes Montás and Report to Comandante Departamento División Radio Patrulla, August 13, 1973. Both in AGN-SEIP, Leg. 1950 Exp 220; Moradores de María Auxiliadora, Letter to General Belisario Peguero Guerrero, Jefe de la Policía Nacional, April 24, 1964; Santo Domingo, AGN-SEIP, Leg. 5648.

54. Secretaría de Estado de Salud Pública, Announcement, 1964, Santo Domingo, AGN-SEIP, Leg. 5718.

55. *Constitution of the Dominican Republic* (Washington, DC: Pan American Union, 1967). Both major political factions in Santo Domingo agreed that buenas costumbres were more important than freedom of speech and conscience. See for instance the Constitutionalists' "Proyecto de Acta Institucional," July 1965, Titulo III, Articulo 105, AGN. 342.02 R 426.

56. Report to Comendante División Radio Patrulla, Santo Domingo, November 19, 1973, AGN-SEIP, Leg. 1950 Exp. 220.

57. On the widespread acceptance in the barrios of an opposition between centers of culture and corruption in the 1970s, interview with Cela.

58. Pacini Hernández, *Bachata*.

59. Residents of Barahona Letter dated October 27, 1917. AGN-SEIP, Leg 2845. I am grateful to Melissa Madera for sharing this document with me. For a longer analysis of this material see Melissa Madera, "It is Better to Prevent than Remedy: Gender, Sexuality, and Social Hygiene in the Dominican Republic during the Trujillato (1930–61)" (Ph.D. diss., State University of New York, Binghamton, forthcoming).

60. Miguel Angel Moreno Hernández, "Mapas sociales de Villa Francisca y contexto neoliberal," *Ciencia y Sociedad* 27 (April–June 2002): 207; for the story of Las Honradas, interview with Iván Domínguez (New York, 2001).

61. Moreno, "Mapas sociales de Villa Francisca."

62. Many interviews with barrio residents and local intellectuals, Cristo Rey, April–June 2000.

63. Herrera, "El Caliche tiene ya agua"; interview with Domínguez.

NOTES TO CHAPTER FOUR

1. González, "Peasants' Progress."

2. Atkins and Wilson, *Dominican Republic*; Calder, *Impact*; Veeser, *World Safe for Capitalism*.

3. For Dominican ambivalence about the U.S. see Derby, "Gringo Chickens." Cf. Pérez, *On Becoming Cuban*.

4. Immigration and Naturalization Service, "1997 Statistical Yearbook of the Immigration and Naturalization Service" (Washington, DC, 1999).

5. Mitchell, "U.S. Foreign Policy," 106.

6. Ngai, *Impossible Subjects*, 239–48, 254–64; Reimers, *Still*, 77–81.

7. *República Dominicana en cifras* (Santo Domingo, 1969), 103.

8. Canelo, *Dónde*, 42, is the source for the much-cited statistic of 19,631 passport applications in 1959, of which 1,805 were granted. His claim is not footnoted and unfortunately the migration files for 1959 are missing at the AGN. Scholars generally accept and repeat the statistic (as I have on several occasions), most likely because it illustrates so dramatically a point confirmed by many sources: that Trujillo restricted travel. It remains to be explained, however, why such large numbers of Dominicans would apply repeatedly only to be turned down, especially given the cost and the evident hostility of the regime toward such applications.

9. Hernández, *Mobility*, 21–23.

10. "Línea aérea no transportará pasajeros dominicanos sin visas," May 22, 1961, AGN-SEIP, Leg. 5375 Exp. 533.

11. Pamela Graham, "Reimagining the Nation and Defining the District: Dominican Migration and Transnational Politics," in *Caribbean Circuits*, ed. Patricia Pessar (New York, 1997).

12. "El senado aprueba reducir pasaportes y otros impuestos," *EC*, July 5, 1961, 1.

13. "Dominicans Curb 2nd Anti-U.S. Riot," *NYT*, December 14, 1961.

14. Tomás Báez Diaz. "Asunto exposición relativa a la expedición de pasaportes," March 15, 1962, AGN-SEIP, Leg. 5490 Exp. 522.

15. "El senado aprueba reducir pasaportes y otros impuestos," *EC*, July 5, 1961, 1.

16. "Supresión de pasaportes provisionales," July 25, 1961, AGN-SEIP, Leg. 5375 Exp. 522.

17. Luciano Torres Letter to Foreign Ministry, July 18, 1961, AGN-SEIP, Leg. 5375 Exp. 522.

18. "Exposición relativa a la expedición de pasaportes," March 15, 1962, and daily logs for 1961 and 1962 in AGN-SEIP, Leg. 5490 Exp. 522, also Leg. 5491, 5493.

19. Increasingly embattled in 1963, the Bosch government cancelled the passports of the extended Trujillo clan to prevent their return to the island. Of the nearly two hundred passports listed, only twenty-nine had been granted while the dictator was still alive. The others were all granted between August and November 1961. "Nómina de personas a quienes se le cancelaron los pasaportes," July 3, 1963, AGN-SEIP, Leg. 5578 Exp. 522

20. For such requests in 1962 see AGN-SEIP, Leg. 5491. For 1963, see Leg. 5578 Exp 523.

21. Manuel Bianchi Gundian, *Misión cumplida* (Santiago de Chile, 1967).

22. Department of State, "Background Paper," Secret, October 12, 1961, available through the Declassified Document Reference System, Gale Group (DDRS). For a Dominican government document regarding the deportation of Dominican citizens accused of "subversion," including two prominent figures, Dr. Marcio Mejía Guzmán and Dr. Hugo Tolentino Dipp, see AGN-SEIP, Leg. 5489 Exp. 514.1; Martin, *Overtaken*, 99, 100.

23. Tomás Báez Díaz, "Asunto exposición relativa a la expedición de pasaportes," March 15, 1962, AGN-SEIP, Leg. 5490 Exp. 522.

24. For the economies surrounding travel documents in the 1960s see Glenn L. Hendricks, *The Dominican Diaspora* (New York, 1974), 55. For a typology of corruption in the Dominican Republic see José Rafael Abinader, *La corrupción administrativa en América Latina: El caso de la República Dominicana* (Santo Domingo, 1992), 23–33.

25. N. V. Elsevier, *Grote Elsevier Atlas Voor Buitenlandse Handel, Internationale Migratie, Toerisme, Waarin Opgenomen Tweehonderd Kaarten en Ruim Duizend Detailkaarten* (Amsterdam, 1950), 218–27; Richard Harrison, "The System of the Flying Clippers" (New York, 1947); "Dominican State Enjoying a Boom," *NYT*, March 17, 1958, 33; Diana Rice, "News Notes from the Field of Travel," *NYT*, December 11, 1949.

26. Letter from Dominican Consul to Lieutenant Governor of Curaçao, January 11, 1962, AGN-SEIP, Leg. 5489; "Autoridades Locales Tomarán Medidas para Restringir la Entrada a Curazao de Ciudadanos Dominicanos," September 29, 1961, AGN-SEIP, Leg. 5489. The bottleneck was temporary, however. Curaçao (a stopover to Venezuela and Europe) grew into a major and largely unremarked escape route for Dominicans over subsequent decades. By 1963, the Dutch colony was the third most common destination for air travelers from Santo Domingo (a total of 15,718 passengers). Dirección General de Estadística de la República Dominicana, *Movimiento marítimo y aéreo* (Santo Domingo, 1961–64, 1969, 1974–77).

27. Martin, *Overtaken*, 99–100. Department of State, Secret, Report from the Embassy in Santo Domingo, n.d., DDRS-U.S., fiche #: 1991-135.

28. "C.A.B. Aide Backs Dominican Flight," *NYT*, May 5, 1955, 67; "Airline of Brazil on First Hop Here," *NYT*, June 7, 1955, 66.

29. For flights in 1960 see AGN-SEIP, Leg. 5234 Exp. 516; "News Notes from the Field of Travel," *NYT*, April 5, 1959, 29.

30. Department of State, Secret, "Program of Action for the Dominican Republic," April 30, 1962, DDRS.

31. The best depiction of this period is the documentary film by Rene Fortunato, *La herencia del tirano* (Santo Domingo, 1998).

32. Martin, *Overtaken*, 98.

33. Ibid., 141.

34. National Security Action Memorandum, "Policy Statement on Dominican Republic," May 1, 1962, DDRS; Department of State, Secret, "Program of Action for the Dominican Republic," April 30, 1962, DDRS.

35. Mitchell, "U.S. Foreign Policy," 106.

36. Department of State, Secret, "Report from the Embassy in Santo Domingo," n.d., DDRS, fiche #: 1991-135; "Dominican Republic: Status of Plan of Action Approved by the President as of July 17, 1962," DDRS.

37. Immigration and Naturalization Service, "INS Yearbook (1997)."

38. Thomas Bailey and Roger Waldinger, "The Changing Ethnic/Racial Division of Labor," in *Dual City*, ed. John Mollenkopf and Manuel Castells (New York, 1991).

39. The refusal rates are combined from January and July 1962, as reported in "Dominican Republic: Status of Plan of Action Approved by the President as of July 17, 1962," DDRS.

40. Mitchell, "U.S. Foreign Policy," 100.

41. "Derogan ley impedía salida de dominicanos," *EC*, March 20, 1963; "Deportan de PR seis dominicanos," *EC*, October 12, 1963; Delfín Pérez y Pérez, "Tratan deportar de PR a once perredeistas," *EC*, November 28, 1963; "Cancelan visa lider 1J4," *EC*, September 21, 1963; "Regresan al país 37 dominicanos," *EC*, November 2, 1963; "68 Dominicanos llegan del exterior en 3 días," *EC*, November 7, 1963.

42. "Proyecto de Acta Institucional," July, 1965, Titulo III Articulos, 114, 121, AGN 342.02 R 426.

43. White House, "Memorandum for Mr. Bundy," September 7, 1965, Subject: Dominican Republic—Institutional Act," DDRS. Also Cable, Department

of State, Secret, June 28, 1965, DDRS, "We agree that OAS should stand firm against demands for no-deportation guarantee."

44. See, for instance, Cable, Department of State, Secret, August 4, 1965, DDRS; Cable, Department of State, Secret, August 5, 1965, DDRS.

45. Interview with Bonaparte Gautreaux Piñeyro (Santo Domingo, 2000). Gautreaux was a PRD activist who was personal secretary to Colonel Francisco Caamaño, the leader of the Constitutionalist forces. Documents in Santo Domingo indicate that police officers also used their influence to recommend family members and friends for preferential treatment by the Consul. For "recommendations" for visas see, for instance, AGN-SEIP, Leg. 1441 Exp. 1-3 (1970), Leg. 2779 (1982). For evidence of embassy efforts to "bolster" Balaguer in the late 1960s see White House, Secret, "Memorandum for the President, Subject: Dominican Situation," January 16, 1968, DDRS.

46. Interview with Rafael (Fafa) Taveras (Santo Domingo, 1999). For the pessimism of the CIA about Balaguer's chance to stay in power for more than a few months, see National Intelligence Estimate Number 86.2-66, "Prospects for Stability in the Dominican Republic," submitted by Director of Central Intelligence, April, 28, 1966, DDRS.

47. Martin, *Overtaken*, 125. In the early 1960s, the Fourteenth of June Movement (1J4) and other radical anti-Trujillo groups were made up predominantly of the children of the old Trujillo-allied middle class, professionals, administrators, and businessmen. For a somewhat derisive view of this middle-class family dynamic, see Juan Bosch, *The Unfinished Experiment: Democracy in the Dominican Republic* (New York, 1965), 11. See also the memoir by Manuel Matos Moquete, *Caamaño: La última esperanza armada* (Santo Domingo, 1999).

48. Interview with Sully Saneaux (Washington Heights, NY, 2001); interview with Leonardo Tapia (Washington Heights, NY, 2001).

49. Interview with Agustín Vargas-Saillant (Santo Domingo, 2000).

50. María Ramos, "Historia de una familia que emigró a New York," *Amigo del Hogar*, January 1974, 26–27.

51. María Ramos, "Historia . . . ," *Amigo del Hogar*, March 1974, 6–7.

52. As Graham points out, the increase in immigrant *visas* granted in the year after the 1965 invasion was only a few thousand. Immigrant *admissions* to the United States did spike by more than six thousand in 1966, falling thereafter, suggesting that many Dominicans who already had visas decided to leave the Dominican Republic during the conflict. Pamela M. Graham, "Re-imagining the Nation and Defining the District: The Simultaneous Political Incorporation of Dominican Transnational Migrants" (Ph.D. diss., University of North Carolina, 1996), 89–91.

53. Interview with José Enrique Trinidad (Santo Domingo, 2000).

54. On music see AGN-SEIP, Leg. 5096. Exp. "Espectáculos Públicos." On film see Foreign Service Dispatch, American Embassy, Ciudad Trujillo, "Censorship of Foreign Films," June 11, 1957, State Department Record Group 59, National Archives and Records Administration, College Park, MD (NARA).

55. Austerlitz, *Merengue*, 70–73; Pacini Hernández, *Bachata*, 35–63.

56. Pacini Hernández, *Bachata*, 77.

57. "Dial-ogando" ¡*Ahora!* February 20, 1965, April 3, 1965.

58. Luis Eduardo Lora, "Anteponen merengue a la nueva ola: Chicos ye ye culpan emisoras prefería go go," *EN*, August 4, 1967, 12.

59. Austerlitz, *Merengue*. 87; Johnny Ventura, *Un poco de mí* (Santo Domingo, 1998).

60. Miguel Alfonso, "Hippies desfilan por calles SPM," *EN*, July 18, 1968.

61. Discurso de Joaquín Balaguer ante el Congreso Nacional, 16 de Agosto, 1970, in Balaguer, *Mensajes Presidenciales*.

62. For the repression there are many sources. See Kryzanek, "Diversion, Subversion, and Repression"; César Pérez, "Introducción," in *Las organizaciones de base en Santo Domingo*, ed. Tahira Vargas (Santo Domingo, 1994).

63. Miguel Angel Brito Mata, "Una sociedad en decadencia," *¡Ahora!* July 14, 1969, 57–58.

64. Caribbean Research Limited, "Public Opinion Study, Dominican Republic," 1962; Lloyd Free, "Attitudes, Hopes, and Fears of the Dominican People," NARA, Record Group 306, Box 24.

65. Alan McPherson, *Yankee No!* (Cambridge, MA, 2003), 128–62.

66. Interview with Tony Estrella (Santo Domingo, 2000).

67. Ibid.

68. "La encuesta de la semana: La brujería en el país" *¡Ahora!* September 8, 1975, 9.

69. Eliás, *¡Ahora!* July 22, 1974, 17.

70. Mario Emilio Pérez, "Una juventud frustrada," *EN*, November 27, 1968, 10.

71. See three articles by Bolívar Díaz Gómez in *EN:* "Declinan comentar drogas," July 30, 1970, 6; "Libertan acusados por drogas," July 20, 1971, 3; "Someten dos acusados de consumir drogas," August 7, 1971, 3. For the case in Bella Vista, see "Someten mañana acusados de usar drogas," *EN*, October 20, 1970, 5.

72. Interview with Plácido Rodríguez (Philadelphia, 2001).

73. "UER y 1J4 critican grupos de hippies," *EN*, June 26, 1968, 13.

74. Altagracia Coiscou-Guzmán, quoted in "Movimiento liberación de la mujer," *Qué? La revista del pueblo* (Santo Domingo), October 30, 1971, 38–42; *Dominican Republic* in *The North American Congress on Latin America, Archive of Latin Americana*, Wilmington, DE: Scholarly Reources, 1998 (hereafter NACLA Collection). Cf. Deborah Pacini Hernández and Reebee Garofalo, "Between Rock and a Hard Place: Negotiating Rock in Revolutionary Cuba," in *Rockin' Las Américas*, ed. Deborah Pacini Hernández, Héctor Fernández L'Hoeste, and Eric Zolov (Pittsburgh, PA, 2004), 43–67; Maria Teresa Velez, *Drumming for the Gods* (Philadelphia, 2000), 71–85, 92–94.

75. Pacini Hernández, *Bachata*, 127–36; F. S. Ducoudray h., "Así fueron los 7 días con el pueblo," *¡Ahora!* December 9, 1974, 16–24. For a cogent presentation of the problem of penetración cultural in Mexico see Carlos Monsivais, "Penetración cultural y nacionalismo (El caso mexicano)," in *No intervención, autodeterminación y democracia en América Latina*, ed. Pablo González Casanova (Mexico City, 1982).

76. See José A. Moreno, "Intervention and Economic Penetration," *Summation* 5 (1975); interview with Cela.

77. Interviews with residents of Cristo Rey; Latin American Working Group, "La Banda" (Toronto, 1971), "Human Rights" and "Origenes de la Banda" ¿Que? La revista del pueblo 1:7 (1971) 4–6, both in NACLA Collection.

78. Angel Alsina and Juana Jourdain, Letter to Secretario de Estado de Interior y Policía, November 27, 1973, AGN-SEIP, Leg. 1910-180 Exp. 3-16; Consorcio Padcco-Borrell, "Estudio," 3:99; "MCU y clubes acuerdan programa para 1971," EN, January 17, 1971, 16.

79. "La Banda incendia club," EN, May 15, 1971, 9.

80. "Califica ideario Duarte de 'político y agitador,'" EC, January 9, 1971; "Cruzada Amor inicia labor cultural popular beneficio juventud barrios," EN, Febrary 8, 1978, 13.

81. For María Trinidad Sánchez, Angel Alsina and Juana Jourdain, Letter to Secretario de Estado de Interior y Policía, November 27, 1973; for Club Burmudez see Julio Rosa, Letter to Rafael de Jesús Checo, General de Brigada, September 14, 1973; for Villa Consuelo, Leónidas Martines Gabino Núñez, Letter, November 6, 1973, all in AGN-SEIP, Leg. 1910-180 Exp 3-16.

82. Bolívar A. Reynoso, "Club Deportivo-Cultural Mauricio Báez" ¿Qué? La revista del pueblo (Santo Domingo) 1:12, November, 1971, 8–10, NACLA Collection.

83. Interview with Isidro Torres (Santo Domingo, 2000).

84. "Dice ama la paz niega sea de Banda," EN, May 16, 1971, 4.

85. Interview with Señor Fania (Cristo Rey, Santo Domingo, 2000).

86. "La Banda no está borracha," EN, May 15, 1971; EN, May 17, 1971, 2; "Aseguran que crean otra Banda," EN, February 5, 1971, 9. Cf. Dick Hebdige, Subculture: The Meaning of Style (New York, 2002).

87. Ngai, Impossible Subjects, 254–64; Riemers, Still, 73–75, 81, 89.

88. Mexican and Jamaican applicants also benefited disproportionately from the combination of labor certification rules and family reunification exemptions, much to the dismay of Congress. "Western Hemisphere Immigration," in House Committee on the Judiciary (Washington, 1973). On family structures and migration law see Vivian Garrison and Carol Weiss, "Dominican Family Networks and United States Immigration Policy," in Caribbean Life in New York City: Sociocultural Dimensions, ed. Constance Sutton and Elsa Chaney (New York, 1987); José Labourt, "Para el niño Michael Díaz Cruz 'third grade' es 'teicei cuiso,'" EN, September 21, 1988; Eugenia Georges, The Making of a Transnational Community (New York, 1990). 93–97. Probably the most famous example of this family-centered process of migration was the Corona family, a tightly connected network of siblings, cousins, and compadres from the countryside near the small town of Sabana Iglesias, for which see José Labourt, "¡Se trabaja duro tanto en Sabana Iglesia como en Sabana Church!" EN, September 18, 1988; José Labourt, "Sabana Church: Nadie lleva dinero porque no se puede ahorrar ni un centavo," EN, September 19, 1988; Rodríguez de León, Furioso, 49.

89. See González, "Peasants' Progress."

90. Georges, Making, 82–92. For extensive press coverage of document forgery, see folders labeled "Falsificaciones de Visas" at OGM Base de Datos for the years 1972–78.

91. Reimers, Still, 200–240. Dominican responses to the threat of deportation are discussed in a subsequent chapter.

92. Jorge Duany, *The Puerto Rican Nation on the Move* (Chapel Hill, NC, 2002), 168–72; Richard Witkin, "Aviation: Puerto Rico," *NYT*, April 10, 1955, 21; William Kennedy, "Puerto Rico's Air Service Pops Its Buttons," *NYT*, January 18, 1959, 19.

93. "Doce mil criollos emigran a EU en 68," *EN*, January 6, 1969, 1, 8.

94. "Western Hemisphere Immigration," in *House Committee on the Judiciary* (Washington, DC, 1973), 23–24, 35–36.

95. Mitchell, "U.S. Foreign Policy," 110. For an example of the Dominican press pestering Hurwitch about visas see Carlos Luciano, "Facilitarán viajes a EUA durante 1976," *EC*, January 1, 1976, 1.

96. See for instance Barbara Fischkin, *Muddy Cup* (New York, 1997), 144–91.

97. Hendricks, *Dominican Diaspora*, 65.

98. "Norteamérica: éxodo de dominicanos," *¡Ahora!* March 3, 1969, 10.

99. Admissions totaled by Graham, "Re-imagining," (Ph.D. diss.), 107, 113; Dirección General de Estadística de la República Dominicana, *Estadística demográfica de la República Dominicana* (Santo Domingo, 1964–77).

100. For this concept see Ronald Robinson, John Gallagher, and Alice Denny, *Africa and the Victorians* (London, 1981).

101. Cable, Department of State, Secret, June 5, 1965, DDRS.

102. I am grateful to Frank Moya Pons for sharing the anecdote about this graffitti.

NOTES TO CHAPTER FIVE

1. Miguel Rodríguez O. "En serio y en broma . . . dominicanos en new york" *¡Ahora!* July 7, 1969.

2. J. D. Gould, "European Inter-Continental Emigration: The Road Home. Return Migration from the U.S.A.," *European Journal of Economic History* 9 (1980). On the Dominican ideology of return see especially Grasmuck and Pessar, *Between Two Islands*; Luis Guarnizo, "'Going Home': Class, Gender, and Household Transformation among Dominican Return Migrants," in *Caribbean Circuits*, ed. Patricia Pessar (New York, 1997).

3. Linda Basch, Nina Glick Schiller, and Cristina Szanton Blanc, *Nations Unbound: Transnational Projects, Post-colonial Predicaments, and De-territorialized Nation-States* (Langhorne, PA, 1994); Graham, "Re-imagining" (Ph.D. diss.); Luis Guarnizo, "One Country in Two: Dominican-Owned Firms in New York and in the Dominican Republic" (Ph.D. diss., Johns Hopkins University, 1992); Levitt, *Transnational Villagers*; Alejandro Portes, "Transnational Communites: Their Emergence and Significance in the Contemporary World System," in *Latin America in the World Economy*, ed. R. P. Korzeniewicz and W. C. Smith (Westport, CT, 1996).

4. For a critique of scholars of transnationalism on the grounds that they obscure Dominican attempts at local engagement see Torres-Saillant, *Diasporic Disquisitions* (New York, 2000).

5. GWHS Survey Response, Cruzer (see chapter 6, note 8); José Itzigsohn, et al., "Immigrant Incorporation and Racial Identity: Racial Self-Identification

among Dominican Immigrants," *Ethnic and Racial Studies* 28 (January 2005); Benjamin Bailey, "Dominican-American Ethnic/Racial Identities and United States Social Categories," *International Migration Review* 35 (2001); José Itzigsohn and Carlos Dore Cabral, "Competing Identities? Race, Ethnicity, and Panethnicity among Dominicans in the United States," *Sociological Forum* 15 (2000); Duany, "Reconstructing Racial Identity." On relationships among Latino groups and Latino racialization more generally, Dzidzienyo and Oboler, *Neither Enemies nor Friends*; Nicolás De Genova and Ana Ramos-Zayas, *Latino Crossings* (New York, 2003); Clara E. Rodríguez, *Changing Race* (New York, 2000); Felix M. Padilla, "On the Nature of Latino Ethnicity," *Social Science Quarterly* 65 (June 1984).

6. Lizbeth Cohen, *Making a New Deal* (New York, 1990); Gerstle, *American Crucible*; Matthew Frye Jacobson, *Whiteness of a Different Color* (Cambridge, MA, 1998).

7. For a summary of neighborhood construction and demographics see Ira Katznelson, *City Trenches* (New York, 1981), 65–89. For the economic status of black families in Washington Heights and Central Harlem and 1946 demographics, see Gerhart Saenger and Harry M. Schulman, "A Study of Intercultural Behavior and Attitudes among Residents of the Upper West Side" (City College Dept. of Sociology, 1946) in Schomburg Center for Research in Black Culture, General Reference Collection (New York, 1946). For African American residents' perceptions of Washington Heights as middle class, see Lee Lendt, "A Social History of Washington Heights to 1960," in *Urban Challenges to Psychiatry*, ed. Lawrence Kolb, Viola Bernard, and Bruce Dohrenwend (Boston, 1969), 42–43.

8. Katznelson, *City Trenches*, 65–89.

9. See Virginia E. Sánchez-Korrol, *From Colonia to Community* (Berkeley and Los Angeles, 1983), 59–62.

10. Protestant Council of the City of New York, "Upper Manhattan: A Community Study of Washington Heights" (New York, 1954), 9.

11. Survey response, anonymous GWHS graduate.

12. Lendt, "Social History," 42–43.

13. Katznelson, *City Trenches*; Saenger, Schulman, and 1946, "A Study." Jewish clergy told researchers that the process of receding north and west was already under way in the middle of the 1950s. Protestant Council of the City of New York, "Upper Manhattan," 10.

14. See notes from the Washington Heights Neighborhood Association (June 6, 1962 and June 20, 1962), Ellen Lurie Papers, White Box 23, Special Collections, Teachers College Library, Columbia University, New York, NY (hereafter ELP).

15. Protestant Council of the City of New York, "Upper Manhattan," 7. For other examples of "massive resistance" to integration in northern urban neighborhoods see Hirsch, *Making the Second Ghetto*; J. Anthony Lukas, *Common Ground* (New York, 1986).

16. Saenger and Schulman, "A Study of Intercultural Behavior."

17. For accounts of this covenant and another along St. Nicholas Avenue between 152d and 155th see papers of the National Association for the Advancement of Colored People, Part 5, Campaign against Residential Segregation,

1914–1955, Reel 2, Frames 0089-0138. On resistance to housing desegregation in Washington Heights, Lendt, "Social History," 52.

18. Biondi, *To Stand and Fight*, 90; cf. Matthew Countryman, *Up South: Civil Rights and Black Power in Philadelphia* (Philadelphia, 2006), 162–63.

19. Coverage of these events was extensive; see for instance "Picture of City Gang: The Dragons in Action," *NYT*, February 23, 1958, E6; "4 Youths Convicted in Boy's Murder; 3 Others Cleared," *NYT*, April 16, 1958.

20. Monserrat in Laura Briggs, *Reproducing Empire* (Berkeley and Los Angeles, 2002), 162.

21 Lendt, "Social History," 52–53; "Washington Hts. Parents Clash with Harlemites," *New York Amsterdam News*, November 2, 1963; "PA 187 Adopts Policy," *Upper Manhattan Frontier News*, November 7, 1963; "A Storm Is Gathering: Parents Gird for Fight on School Integration," *Upper Manhattan Frontier News*, October 10, 1963. See also ELP, Box 23, Folders "Harlem Parents' Committee," "Open Enrollment," and "Heights-Inwood Parents' Committee." Leonard Buder, "Boycott Cripples City Schools," *NYT*, February 4, 1964, 1; Ande Diaz and Sonia Lee, "'I Was the One Percenter': Manny Diaz and the Beginnings of a Black-Puerto Rican Coalition," *Journal of American Ethnic History* (Spring 2007).

22. Lurie's notes show a shift in local concerns from a generalized crisis in youth culture to a specific focus on danger from black and Spanish children. Notes from "Heights Neighborhood Association Meeting" in 1962 show that gangs were a major concern, but perceived as a problem of unemployment and insufficient social activities for young people of all backgrounds. ELP, Box 23. By the early 1970s, Lurie wrote about Jewish opposition to a new school near the Yeshiva school: "orthodox Jewish community has many fears which are legitimate. Their kids are hurt, etc." and "Jewish children on way home from Madison Ave Museum get beaten up and yarmulkes taken off." See "Notes on PS 48" and Red Notebook entry for January 1, 1973, ELP, Box 22.

23. Cited in Philip Kay, "Striking Differences: What Really Happened at Ocean Hill–Brownsville?" *City Limits*, April 2003. On the historical evolution of the ideals of integration and community control in African American politics see Countryman, *Up South*.

24. Herman Benson, "Failing the Test of Civil Liberties: A Commentary on *The Burden of Blame*," in *Civil Liberties in New York* (ACLU Newsletter), March, 1969. See also Jerald E. Podair, *The Strike that Changed New York* (New Haven, 2002); New York Civil Liberties Union, "The Burden of Blame: A Report on the Ocean Hill–Brownsville School Controversy" (New York, 1968); Diane Ravitch, *The Great School Wars* (New York, 1974).

25. See Arthur Vidich and Charles McReynolds, "A Report on High School Principals," *New York Herald Tribune*, April 1969, a study of attitudes of education professionals based on interviews with thirty-five New York high school principals, conducted by researchers at the New School for Social Research; Podair, *Strike*, 48–70, 153–82.

26. John O'Neill, Letter to the Editor of *Civil Liberties in New York*, March 1969.

27. Podair, *Strike*, 123–54, 207–10; Jonathan Rieder, *Canarsie* (Cambridge, MA, 1985).

28. Handwritten notes on ethnic composition in community districts (1968), Isaiah Robinson Papers, Box 15, Folder 31, Special Collections, Teachers College Libaray, Columbia University, New York (hereafter IRP).

29. For the creation of the local district see Katznelson, *City Trenches*. For the accusation of gerrymandering and controversy see folders on PS 48 and PS 187 in ELP, Box 22.

30. See for instance Jose A. Vásquez, "Census of Puerto Rican Student Populations in Community School Districts Proposed in Dec. 1, 1968 Decentralization Plan" (New York City: Office of Intergroup Education, Bilingual Program in School and Community Relations, Board of Education, 1969[?]), District 6 ethnic censuses in "Misc" folder, ELP, Box 22.

31. The replacement of machine politics by entitlement programs and neighborhood school politics as the main contexts structuring ethnic definition in the city is the main contention of Katznelson, *City Trenches*.

32. Lurie Blue Notebook, September 19, 1972, ELP, Box 22.

33. Lurie Blue Notebook, September 1972, ELP, Box 22.

34. Lurie Purple Notebook, October 16, 1972, ELP, Box 22.

35. See literature regarding the joint Concilio Hispano–Parents Association ticket in ELP, White Box 27/28. See short biographies of Rivera and other candidates in "George Washington Parent Association Ballot," IRP, Box 15, Folder 33; "Criollo sera candidato a junta escolar Manhattan," *EN*, May 6, 1975, 6.

36. See campaign literature for various factions in 1972 ELP, Box 35.

37. "Juana upset. Today is 3rd day this week PRCDP made her close agency to go to demonstration somewhere (an anti-Black control demonstration in Bronx)." Lurie Red Notebook, November 3, 1972, ELP, Box 22.

38. Lurie Diary, October 12, 1972, Purple Notebook, October 30, 1972, Red Notebook, ELP, Box 22. For biography of Nieves, ELP, White Box 27/28.

39. "Slowly they are realizing their destiny is with us. Pinter moved Ben Garcia out of his large office/Strauss wouldn't let Nieves into the picture of 186–153," Beige Notebook, March 15, 1973, ELP, Box 22.

40. For information on this slate see attachment to "George Washington Parent-Table Committee letter to Dr. Harvey Scribner," November 16, 1970, IRP, Box 15, Folder 33.

41. For Pedraza campaign statement see ELP, Box 35. Lurie wrote "The UFT told Pedraza that if he ran on their ticket he couldn't accept Concilio or Pres Council support—he would have to accept entire UFT slate—so he's gone their way." Beige Notebook Entry from March 15, 1973, ELP, Box 22. For more on Pedraza see Peg O'Brien, "Irregularities Mar School Election Here," *Heights Inwood*, October 26, 1972.

42. See the United Bronx Parents leadership training materials, including notes from more than fifty home visits and interviews with neighborhood parents in the summer of 1969. ELP, Box 24; Aida Álvarez, "New York's Latins: The Dominicans," *New York Post*, February 24, 1975, quotes a Dominican parent: "public schools are too risky . . . they'll lose respect for us. I've seen it happen."

43. Armando Almánzar, "Las nuevas epidemias" ¡*Ahora!* November 18, 1974, 56.

44. "Asesinan dominicana en Estados Unidos," *ES*, February 15, 1975, 17; Bailey, "Dominican-American Ethnic/Racial Identities," 700, found widespread negative stereotypes of U.S. blacks in interviews of nonmigrant youth in Santo Domingo in 1990.

45. Gloria Rodríguez, Letter to the Editor of *Heights Inwood*, April 24, 1975, reprinted and distributed by the UFT, ELP, Box 35.

46. ELP, Box 22, Notes on PS 48.

47. Lurie Diary, August 1, 1971, ELP, Box 22.

48. Lurie Diary, July 17, 1972; Report of conversation with PS 192, Blue Notebook; for Rodríguez's ties to UFT see Beige Notebook, March 15, 1973, all in ELP, Box 22.

49. Lurie Diary, July 15, 1972 and November 16, 1972, ELP, Box 22.

50. Mr. Aymot, Isabel M. Heredia, Felix Rodríguez, Emerita Wiscoritch, Ana Luisa Ortiz, Elsee Lozada, Letter to CSB 6, August 27, 1971; "Appeal from Mrs. Gwen Crenshaw, President, Parent Association, PS 128M to Chancellor Harvey Scribner, NYC Board of Education, against Community School Board # 6 Regarding the Assignment of a Principal to PS 128 Manhattan," April 20, 1972; and other documents in Lurie's file "P.S. 128" in ELP, Box 22.

51. Gareth Davies, "The Great Society after Johnson: The Case of Bilingual Education," *Journal of American History* 88 (March 2002). Davies for instance points out that this strategy was an attempt by Nixon's staff to respond to an *already existing* "considerable animosity among Americans of Mexican descent toward Blacks."

52. Moya Pons, "National Identity and Return," 32.

53. For an analysis of the 2000 census numbers see Logan, "The New Latinos." For 1990 census see Rodríguez, *Changing Race*. For the idea that race relations in the United States have a therapeutic racial effect on Dominicans, see Moya Pons, "National Identity and Return." For an opposing view suggesting Latinos should deploy nonwhiteness strategically (*invent* rather than *discover* it) see Torres-Saillant, "Inventing."

54. Purple Notebook entry on October 10, 1972, ELP, Box 22.

55. For an analysis of the homogenizing tendencies of the Hispanic category, see Oboler, *Ethnic Labels*. For arguments about how *Hispanic* and *Latino* take on specific meanings where more than one national origins group live in shared space, see Padilla, "On the Nature of Latino Ethnicity"; and De Genova and Ramos-Zayas, *Latino Crossings*.

56. Interview with Tapia.

57. Greta Gilbertson, Joseph Fitzpatrick, and Lijun Yang, "Hispanic Intermarriage in New York City," *International Migration Review* 30 (Summer 1996).

58. Lurie, "The Crisis at George Washington High School," ELP, Box 41.

59. Nancie L. González, "Patterns of Dominican Ethnicity," in *The New Ethnicity*, ed. John W. Bennet (St. Paul, MN, 1975).

60. Ubi Rivas, "Radiografía de una emigración," *¡Ahora!* December 13, 1971, 49–54.

61. "Illegal Status of Dominicans Shaping Their Lives in the City," *NYT*, November 9, 1971.

62. Vilma Weisz, "Causas de las migraciones dominicanas al exterior" (Licenciatura, Universidad Nacional Pedro Henriquez Ureña, 1973), 147. For a critical report on these prejudices see María Ramos, "Historia de una familia que emigró a Nueva York," *Amigo del Hogar*, April, July, and November 1974.

63. Yolanda Martínez-San Miguel, *Caribe Two Ways* (San Juan, 2003); Duany, "Reconstructing Racial Identity"; Milagros Iturrondo, "'San Ignacio de la Yola' . . . Y los dominicanos," *Homines* 17 (1994). For an exhaustive catalogue of stereotypes and insults toward blacks in Puerto Rico see Isabelo Zenon Cruz, *Narciso descubre su trasero* (Humacao, 1974).

64. Magaly García Ramis, "Retrato de un dominicano que paso por puertorriqueño y pudo pasar a una mejor vida," in *Las noches de rieles* (San Juan, 1995).

65. "Illegal Aliens: A Stopover in Puerto Rico," *Daily News*, September 28, 1971, 30.

66. De Genova and Ramos-Zayas, *Latino Crossings*.

67. Blue Notebook, August 1, 1972, ELP, Box 22.

68. Interview with Normandía Maldonado Budhai (Washington Heights, NY, 2001).

69. González, "Patterns."

70. Interview with Rafael Estévez (Washington Heights, NY, 2001).

71. Graham, "Reimagining."

72. Ibid.

73. Interview with Gautreaux Piñeyro.

74. *EN*, May 10, 1971, 9.

75. For more on the PRD idea of revolutionary exile see "Illegal Status of Dominicans Shaping Their Lives in the City," *NYT*, November 9, 1971.

76. Interview with Ramón Bodden (Washington Heights, NY, 2001).

77. Interview with Nelsy Aldebot (Santo Domingo, 2000); interview with Juan D. Balcácer (Santo Domingo, 2000); interview with Bodden; interview with Dinorah Cordero (Washington Heights, NY, 2001); interview with Luis Simó (Santo Domingo, 2000).

78. See, for instance, "Niegan en NY denuncia en contra de la migración," *ES*, February 14, 1975, 14.

79. Victor Grimaldi, "La vida de los dominicanos en Nueva York," *El Dominicano*, 1973, NACLA Collection.

80. See article about Father Francisco Sicard, who broke with PRD leadership in New York to support participation in the 1970 presidential elections in Santo Domingo. Tirso A. Valdez, "Mosaicos de Nueva York," *¡Ahora!* August 16, 1971.

81. Interview with Bodden; interview with Cordero; interview with Víctor Espinal (New York, 2001).

82. Miguel Adújar, Secretario General de la Juventud Revolucionaria Dominicana en los EEUU," Letter to the Editor, *EN*, January 24, 1971, 8.

83. Interview with Balcácer.

84. Lesley Jones, "GW Students Blame Drug Traffic for School Violence," *Amsterdam News*, February 27, 1971.

85. "Repudian gobierno," *EN*, April 25, 1971, 1, 6. This article, for instance, listed the Young Lords and North American pacifists as participants in the latest demonstration outside the PRD headquarters. See also paid advertisement, "Demandamos aministía a los presos políticos—desde New York," *EN*, December 10, 1971, 23, which provides a long list of groups in solidarity with Dominican activists. Copies of the newsletter *La Trinitaria* consulted in the personal collection of Juan Daniel Balcácer. Interview with Tapia; "U.S. Role in Dominican Republic spurs NACLA founding," *NACLA Report on the Americas* 36, no. 3 (November/December 2002), 14.

86. "Lucha estudiantil en Nueva York," *Lucha: Órgano del Movimiento Popular Dominicano* 4 (New York, 1973), 16, from NACLA Collection.

87. Interview with Simó.

88. For 1978 elections see Graham, "Re-imagining" (Ph.D. diss.). For Peña Gómez see José Francisco Peña Gómez, "El PRD en los Estados Unidos," *¡Ahora!* October 28, 1974, 24–31. For the emergence of a new kind of neighborhood politics in response to antiimmigrant rhetoric see, for instance, "Inmigrantes gritan: No somos ilegales somos trabajadores," *LN*, September 2, 1974, 5.

89. Ana Lucia Aparicio, "Developing Politics in Quisqueya Heights" (Ph.D. diss., City University of New York, 2004); Georges, *New Immigrants*.

90. Moya Pons, *The Dominican Republic*, 386–87.

91. For instance, see "Dice consulado NY aumenta impuestos," *EN*, September 7, 1969, 12; A. Espinal, "Dominicanos denuncian: Somos estafados en el consulado. Cónsul dice: Es una calumnia," *¡Ahora!* July 19, 1976, 10–13.

92. "La cónsul en NY dice oposición está desesperada," *EN*, May 9, 1970, 20.

93. Derby, "Magic."

94. See minutes of the Comisión Nacional de Desarrollo, AGN-CND, Santo Domingo.

95. "Las declaraciones de Stuart Sharpe," *EN*, August 5, 1969, 10.

96. "Ven vida dominicana en folklore," *EN*, November 16, 1971, 7; "Entregan premios desfile turismo," *EN*, August 10, 1969, 16; "Caretas de la farándula," *¡Ahora!* October 11, 1971, 73. While the University Cultural Movement and the barrio cultural clubs viewed themselves as a sort of cultural opposition, eventually the neighborhood dance groups they founded were incorporated as a talent pool for hotel entertainers.

97. See photos in *¡Ahora!* February 13, 1967, 52–53.

98. *El Tiempo* was founded in 1946 by a North American newspaperman who formerly ran Trujillo's offical newspaper, *El Caribe*. Leftist critics saw *El Tiempo* as merely a front established by Trujillo and his ally Batista to emit propaganda to New York audiences. Still, in the late 1960s, coverage of Dominicans living in New York was scant in the paper, and Belén, who knew the editor from his own work with *El Caribe*, proposed a column on Dominican activities, and then served as a regular society columnist for the consul and related groups.

99. Reprinted in José Jiménez Belén, *Nueva York es así* (Santo Domingo, 1977).

100. This, contrary to popular history, was a continuation of a trend from the last years of the Trujillo era, when official celebrations began to demand a racialized national folklore, which after all was something that all modern countries had. Holdovers from the official folklorists of the Trujillo regime, es-

pecially René Carrasco, continued to incorporate and present an African past, boiled down to a rhythm or a dance step, digested, and "elevated" into elaborate choreographies and stage shows. The Dirección Nacional del Turismo funded these presentations—one of them, a performance for executives of Caribbean Travels Association, presented Carrasco's "típicas originaria de los Minas." San Lorenzo de los Negros Minas, now the barrio Los Minas, was a community of free blacks founded by "Minas" slaves escaped from plantations in French San Domingue. "Ven vida dominicana en folklore," *EN*, November 16, 1971, 7.

101. "Consideran estatua de Duarte en NY será orgullo para los dominicanos," *EN*, January 15, 1978, 12; "Celebran en New York día de Duarte," *EN*, January 27, 1978, 10, among dozens of reports in Santo Domingo press about this project.

102. "Dominicanidad," *ES*, February 26, 1975, 4.

103. "Cruzada Amor inicia labor cultural popular beneficio juventud barrios," *EN*, February 8, 1978, 13.

104. Interview with Maldonado.

105. Interview with Yolanda Richardson (New York, 2001).

106. Joseph Cedeno, "Playboys Hold Block Party," *Newspaper of the Upper West Side Independent Youth Council*, August–September 1970, ELP, Box 12.

107. Interview with Estévez.

108. Bailey, "Dominican-American Ethnic/Racial Identities"; De Genova and Ramos-Zayas, *Latino Crossings*; Dzidzienyo and Oboler, *Neither Enemies nor Friends*; Flores, "Qué assimilated"; Itzigsohn and Dore Cabral, "Competing Identities?"; Oboler, *Ethnic Labels*; Padilla, "On the Nature of Latino Ethnicity"; Rodríguez, *Changing Race*; Torres-Saillant, "Inventing."

NOTES TO CHAPTER SIX

1. Hirsch, *Making the Second Ghetto*; Lassiter, *The Silent Majority*; Bryant Simon, *Boardwalk of Dreams* (New York, 2004); Sugrue, *Origins*.

2. Louis D. Brandeis, a mostly black school on the Upper West Side, had 11 percent "other Spanish," mostly Dominican. Newtown High School in Queens was a white high school where Dominicans from Corona and Colombians and Ecuadorians from Jackson Heights comprised 20 percent of the population. Board of Education of the City of New York, "Special Census of City Schools" (composition of register) as of October 31, 1970, ELP, White Box 2(2).

3. Henri A. Belfon, Division Supervisor, "Confidential Report on George Washington High School" (Bronx, NY, March 26, 1970), IRP, Box 15, Folder 33; New York Civil Liberties Union, "Report on George Washington High School," April 16, 1971, ELP, Box 12.

4. Lurie Diaries, Blue Notebook (September 1972), ELP, Box 22.

5. *The Urban High School Academy: Evaluation Report*, prepared for the New York City Board of Education Bureau of Educational Research by Urban Directions, Inc., August 31, 1971.

6. Quoted in Leonard Buder, "The Tragic Case of Washington High," *NYT*, October 23, 1970.

7. Telephone Interview with Jerry Berger, May 2001.

8. GWHS Survey Response, Miguel Franco, May 2001. I sent several hundred e-mail requests for information to Spanish-surnamed alumni of George Washington High from the early 1970s, registered on publicly available alumni registries. The initial request asked for memories of the strike, student conflicts, ethnic relations, and popular culture. I received about thirty responses. Although sometimes I followed the initial response with more questions, unless I later interviewed the respondent, all of these exchanges are cited as GWHS survey response. Unless they sent me personal information, the respondents are identified only by their screen names.

9. For the changing class composition and rapid growth of public schools in the Dominican Republic, see Juan Dagoberto Tejeda Ortíz, "Reflexiones sociológicas en torno a las elecciones de la UASD," ¡Ahora! June 2, 1969, 29–32; "Ha sido superada la crisis de la UASD?" ¡Ahora! October 14, 1968, 17–21.

10. This quote is from the survey response of a Dominican attorney who graduated from GWHS in 1971.

11. For the summer program see Elizabeth Miller, Chairman of Faculty-Parent Committee, "Report: October 1969, GWHS Special Summer Program, Part I, July 7–August 15, 1969," ELP, Box 12. For the incident at IS 143 see Lurie Diaries, Red Notebook, entry of November 2, 1972, ELP, Box 22.

12. "Report: October 1969, GWHS Special Summer Program Part I, July 7–August 15, 1969," ELP, Box 12.

13. R. A Martín Ferreira and F. A. Peña, "Apuntes para una historia del Movimiento Estudiantil Universitario, UASD, 1961–1979" (Licenciatura, Universidad Autónoma de Santo Domingo, 1979).

14. "School Was Open," New York City High School Free Press 1 (3), November 20–December 11, 1968, 7.

15. "Case of David Arroyo . . . ," ELP, White Box 24.

16. For one account of how this happened, see James Horelick (English teacher at Washington Irving High), Letter to the Editor of the NYT, April 6, 1969. For more on the Ocean Hill–Brownsville conflict and the teacher strike, see New York Civil Liberties Union, "The Burden of Blame"; Podair, Strike.

17. From an estimate released by the Board of Education, cited in Nicholas Pileggi, "Revolutionaries Who Have to Be Home by 7:30," NYT, March 16, 1969.

18. For accounts of student attempts to change dress codes, win the right of due process in suspension cases, and win the right to peaceful protests and freedom of expression in school publications, see "Hot Time in a Cold Town," Civil Liberties in New York (March 1968). See also Ira Glasser, "Teaching Civil Liberties," Civil Liberties in New York, March 30, 1969.

19. Joseph Lelyveld, "Racial Strife Undermines Schools in City and Nation," NYT, February 9, 1970.

20. High School Principals' Association, Committee on Student Unrest, Subcommittee on Confrontation and Response, Report on School Year 1968–69, reprinted by the United Bronx Parents, ELP, Box 12.

21. "The High Schools v. The Bill of Rights," Civil Liberties in New York, April 1969.

22. Interview with Russell Jacquet-Acea (Seattle, WA, by telephone, 2001).

23. This was the principal claim of Dissident Teachers at George Washington, Letter to Board President Monserrat, May 11, 1970, IRP, Box 15, Folder 33.

24. GWHS Survey Response, MCBIND.

25. Interview with Balcácer; interview with Simó.

26. Nelsy Aldebot Diary, Tuesday, March 25, 1969, Personal Collection of Nelsy Aldebot, Villa Mella, Dominican Republic.

27. Interview with Aldebot.

28. In the Dominican Republic, Catholic youth organizations began, in the wake of April 1965, to incorporate antiimperialism and liberation theology into their view of Christianity, becoming, in essence, an extension of the Dominican left. Moreno, "Precursores"; interview with Pedro Ubiera (Santo Domingo, 2000).

29. See Porfirio Ml. Valdez, "Dominicanos en New York," *Amigo del Hogar,* October 1971, 22–23.

30. Interview with Aldebot.

31. Ibid. See Aleyda Fernández, "La mujer en Nueva York," *Amigo del Hogar,* September, 1971, 30; Nelsy Aldebot, "Las mujeres y la Revolución dominicana" (1975), personal collection of Nelsy Aldebot.

32. Aldebot Diary, April 11, 1969.

33. Aldebot Diary, May 3, 1969.

34. Memorandum of Understanding between Student Groups at George Washington and Principal Simon, May 1969, ELP, Box 12. For the UFT's version of these events see Irving Witkin, *Diary of a Teacher: The Crisis at George Washington High School* (New York, 1970), 7, 8. Over subsequent months the UFT used "Where We Stand," a regular paid space on the editorial page of the *Times* (e.g., *NYT*, December 27, 1970, 7) as well as contacts with journalists there to broadcast its version of events. The local chapter also collected what it called "a carefully documented account of the unhappy developments of the school," and the union published this account as Witkin, *Diary.*

35. Memorandum of Understanding between Student Groups at George Washington and Principal Simon, May 1969, ELP, Box 12.

36. Aldebot Diary, May 8, 1969.

37. Interview with Aldebot.

38. See for example Thomas Brady, "Fires Set in Williamsburg School, Eastern District Erupts," *NYT*, March 12, 1969; "2 Schools in City Shut by Protests," *NYT*, April 22, 1969; "Task Force Acts to 'Cool' Schools," *NYT*, May 4, 1969; "Fires and Disturbances Close Washington and Wingate Highs," *NYT*, May 8, 1969; Joseph Lelyveld, "Racial Strife Undermines Schools in City and Nation," *NYT*, February 9, 1970.

39. Emanuel Perlmutter, "Procaccino Gives School Policy," *NYT*, October 30, 1969; The City of New York Office of the Comptroller, Research and Liaison Unit, "The New York City School System and Drug Addiction," July 1971, in IRP, Box 15, Folder 27; Lesley Jones, "GW Students Blame Drug Traffic for School Violence," *Amsterdam News*, February 27, 1971.

40. Interim Board Member Isaiah E. Robinson, Memo to Irving Anker, Acting Superintendent, March 3, 1970, IRP, Box 15, Folder 33.

41. Witkin, *Diary*, 10, 25.

42. Isaiah Robinson, Press Release, March 4, 1970, ELP, Box 12.

43. Interim Board Member Isaiah E. Robinson, Memos to Irving Anker, Acting Superintentent, March 3 and 4, 1970, IRP, Box 15, Folder 33; for more accounts sympathetic to the Parent Table see New York Civil Liberties Union, "Report on George Washington High School." For the UFT view see Witkin, *Diary*, 8–10.

44. Martin Arnold, "Head of George Washington High School Resigns," *NYT*, March 7, 1970.

45. "Disorders Close Washington High," *NYT*, March 17, 1970.

46. Arnold Lubasch, "Fires Close Washington High; Court Blocks Parents Protest," *NYT*, March 14, 1970.

47. Robert McFadden, "George Washington High Melee Results in Arrests of 13 Students," *NYT*, April 11, 1970; "Disorders Close Washington High," *NYT*, March 17, 1970.

48. The Students of George Washington High School, "List of Demands," 1970, IRP, Box 15, Folder 33.

49. Ms. Elizabeth Rich, teacher GWHS, Letter to Mr. McLean, GWHS, October 17, 1969, ELP, Box 12.

50. Acting principal at George Washington High School Louis Simon, Letter to James Boffman, Assistant Superintendent, December 2, 1970, IRP, Box 15, Folder 33.

51. Notes on Schwaier's suspension case, ELP, Box 12.

52. Interview with Jacquet-Acea.

53. For the accusation against the guards, see the comments of James Pelton in the "Minutes from George Washington High School Consultative Council Meeting," December 16, 1970, ELP, Box 12; against the thirty-fourth precinct, The Students of George Washington High School, "List of Demands," 1970, IRP, Box 15, Folder 33.

54. GWHS Survey response, José M. López.

55. Arismendis was a minor at the time. Although his school records and documents relating to the suspension case are available in public archives, I have chosen not to use his real name.

56. Edgar Walker, Counsel for the Suspended Students at George Washingon, Letter to Joseph Monserrat, May 12, 1970, IRP, Box 16, Folder 50. See also Jacob B. Zack, Letter to Irving Anker, May 13, 1970, and other documents in IRP, Box 16, Folder 51.

57. Dorothy Schrade, Director of Nurses, Letter to Whom It May Concern, October 30, 1970; official transcript for De la Cruz signed by Raymundo García; Notarized translation of National General Files and Police Certificate for Nancy De la Cruz, ELP, White Box 27–28.

58. Elizabeth O'Hanlon, Letter to Nancy De la Cruz, March 23, 1970; Lois F. Grierson, December 30, 1970; Mary Jane Ewart, March 28, 1972; Nancy De la Cruz, Letter to Dorothy Schrade, August 21, 1972, ELP, White Box 27/28.

59. Grasmuck and Pessar, *Between Two Islands*, 16.

60. De la Cruz, Student Record Card (Spring 1970), IRP, Box 16, Folder 51; Ellen Lurie's handwritten notes on Arismendis's arrest, April 1970, ELP, Box 12.

61. See Nancy De la Cruz, Letter to Whom It May Concern at GWHS (requesting that school records be sent to Santo Domingo); De la Cruz, Student Record Card (Spring 1970[?]), IRP, Box 16, Folder 51.

62. For instance, "Buscan solución en liceo," *EN*, April 1, 1968, 1, 7; Jesús de la Rosa, "Tumulto en liceo, expulsan a ocho," *EN*, December 3, 1968, 1.

63. Anecdotal Record for Arismendis De la Cruz, May 1970, IRP, Box 16, Folder 51.

64. Ibid.

65. Lurie's notes on Arismendis's arrest, April 1970, ELP, Box 12.

66. See *George Washington High School Free Press*, October 1970, IRP, Box 15, Folder 33.

67. Alfred and Ruth Gutmann, Letter to Dr. Harvey Scribner, November 19, 1970, IRP, Box 15, Folder 33.

68. On the "segmented assimilation" hypothesis see Charles Hirschman, "The Educational Enrollment of Immigrant Youth," *Demography* 38 (2001).

69. Pamela Mahabeer, "GW Notes: 1972 Was a Good Year for George Washington High School," *Heights-Inwood*, January 18, 1973.

70. GWHS Survey Response, Bsly.

71. C. Gerald Frasier, "5 Seized and 5 Hurt in Fights Inside George Washington High," *NYT*, February 20, 1970.

72. GWHS Survey Response, Bsly.

73. GWHS Survey Response, Anon.

74. "Illegal Status of Dominicans," *NYT*, November 9, 1971.

75. Ibid.

76. GWHS Survey Response, Cruzer.

77. GWHS Survey Response, Anon.

78. Simon, *Boardwalk of Dreams*.

79. Robert W. Snyder, "The Neighborhood Changed: The Irish of Washington Heights and Inwood since 1945," in *The New York Irish*, ed. Ronald Bayor and Timothy Meagher (Baltimore, 1996). See also chapter five, notes 14 and 19.

80. Lurie Diary, October 12, 1971, ELP, Box 22 (2).

81. For the parents' perspective see Lurie, Letter to Nat Hentoff, October, 1970, ELP, Box 12. For the UFT perspective see Witkin, *Diary*, 58–59.

82. GWHS Survey Response, Anon.

83. Interview with Aldebot. For a description of "general disorder and chaos in the school during senior day" see Sol Levine, Letter to Irving Anker, June 5, 1970, IRP, Box 15, Folder 33.

84. Leonard Buder, "School Rescinds Transfer Orders: George Washington Pupils May Stay, Board Rules," *NYT*, January 15, 1971.

85. Mimeograph statement from the Frente Unido de Estudiantes Progresistas Dominicanos de GWHS, ELP, Box 41.

86. Ibid.

87. Quoted by Lesley Jones, "GW Students Blame Drug Traffic for School Violence," *Amsterdam News*, February 27, 1971.

88. See Harriet Mannheim, "We've Only Got Each Other," *Cherry Blossom*, December 23, 1971, 3, ELP, Box 12; Interview with Jacquet-Acea.

89. *Cherry Blossom*, December 23, 1971, 1, ELP, Box 12.

90. GWHS consultative council meeting of March 24, 1971 and Harvey Scrib-ner, "RE: The Economic Development Council Partnerships," December 11, 1970, ELP, Box 12; "Weekend in Country Calms Washington H.S. Tempers," *NYT,* January 11, 1972, 39; "Washington High: From Riot to Hope," *NYT,* June 1, 1971, 41.

91. GWHS Survey Response, Bsly.

92. Interview with Rodríguez.

93. Ibid.

94. Ibid.

95. For biographical information on Quezada see Frank Natera, "Milly Quezada: Nos quieren destruir," *¡Ahora!* June 6, 1977, 74–76; for Alberto, Chacón, "Así es Nueva York" *¡Ahora!* May 30, 1983, 28–29.

96. Interview with Rodríguez.

97. Lynne A. Weikart, "Follow the Money: Mayoral Choice and Expenditure Policy," *American Review of Public Administration* 33 (June 2003).

98. Garrison and Weiss, "Dominican Family Networks and United States Im-migration Policy"; Mitchell, "U.S. Foreign Policy"; Reimers, *Still.*

99. Mitchell, "U.S. Foreign Policy."

100. Bailey and Waldinger, "The Changing Ethnic/Racial Division of Labor"; Roger Waldinger, "Immigration and Urban Change," *Annual Review of Sociol-ogy* 15 (1989); Roger Waldinger, *Through the Eye of the Needle* (New York, 1986).

101. Frank F. DeGiovanni and Lorraine C. Minnite, "Patterns of Neighbor-hood Change," in *Dual City: Restructuring New York,* ed. John Hull Mollenkopf and Manuel Castells (New York, 1991).

102. See "Buildings Sealed or Demolished: Washington Heights–Inwood," in James Capalino, "Update: Report of the Washington Heights-Inwood Task Force" (New York, 1979).

NOTES TO CHAPTER SEVEN

1. For the Task Force report see Capalino, "Update." For antiimmigrant argu-ments see Peter Brimelow, *Alien Nation* (New York, 1995); Patrick J. Buchanan, "What Will America be in 2050?" *Los Angeles Times,* September 12, 1994; Arthur Schlesinger, Jr., *The Disuniting of America* (New York, 1992); Samuel P. Hun-tington, *Who Are We? The Challenges to America's Identity* (New York, 2004). For the idea of assimilation see Russell Kazal, "Revisiting Assimilation," *American Historical Review* (1995).

2. "Expresión jóven: La canción y la poesía para el combate," *¡Ahora!* August 19, 1974, 54; Rodríguez de León, *Furioso,* 99–100. For the example of Mexican nationalism in L.A. in the 1920s see George Sánchez, *Becoming Mexican Ameri-can* (Oxford, 1993), 108–125.

3. Angel Miolán, *Datos para la historia del turismo de la República Dominicana* (Santo Domingo, 1998), 65–66.

4. Kryzanek, "Diversion, Subversion, and Repression"; Miolán, *Datos,* 23–26; "Turismo ¿industria sin humo o humo sin industria?" and "Golpe de estado contra la reina del merengue," *¡Ahora!* August 5, 1968, 4, 6–8.

5. Miolán, *Datos*, 66; "Esperan 20 Mil Dominicanos en Navidad," *EN*, December 6, 1970, 12. For other government activity encouraging tourism by Dominican New Yorkers see Minutes of the Comisión Nacional del Desarrollo from October 28, 1970, AGN-CND: José I. Cuello H, "Un vuelo a Nueva York que puede valer unos cinco millones de dólares," *EN*, July 18, 1971, 10.

6. Duany, *Puerto Rican Nation*, 32–35; Frederick Graham, "Puerto Rico Found Airline Gold Mine," *NYT*, June 10, 1949, 24.

7. Dirección General de Estadística de la República Dominicana, *Estadística demográfica de la República Dominicana*.

8. Interview with Juan Contreras (Queens, NY, 2001).

9. Luin Goldring, "The Power of Status in Transnational Social Fields," in *Transnationalism from Below*, ed. Michael P. Smith and Luis Guarnizo (New Brunswick, NJ, 1998).

10. Hendricks, *Dominican Diaspora*, 41–42, 44–47.

11. Interview with Contreras Diógenes Céspedes; and Silvio Torres-Saillant, "Entrevista con Junot Díaz: Los Estados Unidos borran los datos que les son intolerables en los inmigrantes," *El Siglo*, October 10, 1998.

12. Capalino, "Update."

13. Tirso Valdez, "Mosaicos de Nueva York" *¡Ahora!* November 15, 1971, 38–39.

14. David Vidal, "Hispanic Residents Find Some Gains amid Woes," *NYT*, May 12, 1980, A1.

15. David Vidal, "Hispanic Newcomers in City Cling to Values of Homeland," *NYT*, May 11, 1980, 1.

16. Chacón, "En Nueva York hay que ser agresivo para sobrevivir," *¡Ahora!* June 2, 1980, 17–19.

17. David Vidal, "Hispanic Residents Find Some Gains amid Woes," *NYT*, May 12, 1980, A1.

18. Levitt, *Transnational Villagers*, 74–83, Alejandro Portes and Ruben Rumbaut, *The New Second Generation* (Baltimore, 1996).

19. Miguel Rodríguez O. "'En serio y en broma . . . dominicanos en new york,'" *¡Ahora!* September 15, 1969.

20. Lourdes Bueno, "Dominican Women's Experiences of Return Migration," in *Caribbean Circuits*, ed. Patricia Pessar (New York, 1997), 73; Chacón, "Vistazos de Nueva York," *EN*, August 5, 1978, 7.

21. Grasmuck and Pessar, *Between Two Islands*, 156–58.

22. Levitt, *Transnational Villagers*, 103.

23. Bueno, "Dominican Women's Experiences," 73.

24. Grasmuck and Pessar, *Between Two Islands*, 147; Patricia Fernández-Kelly and Anna M. García, "Power Surrendered, Power Restored," in *Challenging Fronteras*, ed. Mary Romero, Pierrette Hondagneu-Sotelo, and Vilma Ortiz (New York, 1997).

25. Fischkin, *Muddy Cup*; Garrison and Weiss, "Dominican Family Networks and United States Immigration Policy."

26. Schiller and Fouron, *Georges Woke Up*, 38.

27. Ibid., 36.

28. Interview with Contreras.

29. Chacón, "Vistazos de Nueva York," *LN*, August 6, 1986. In my conversations with residents in Cristo Rey I found they often complained that migrants did not contribute enough to family survival.

30. "Crece en NY delincuencia de la colonia dominicana," *EC*, October 19, 1971. Also see commentary in *¡Ahora!* November 15, 1971, 38–39.

31. Mario Emilio Pérez, *Mujeriegos, chiviricas y pariguayos* (Santo Domingo, 1997), 112–15.

32. This phrase is from a short story by Dr. Rafael A. Cedeño Valdez, "El emigrante," published in *EN Suplemento Cultural*, August 16, 1970, A-6.

33. Interview with Ubiera.

34. Interview with Marcos Villaman (Santo Domingo, 2000).

35. Juan Bolívar Díaz S., "Aquí y allá: Decadencia," *Amigo del Hogar,* January 1974, 3.

36. Interview with Cela; interview with Isis Durate (Santo Domingo, 1999).

37. María Ramos, "Historia de una familia . . . ," *Amigo del Hogar*, February 1974, 10–11.

38. José del Castillo, "Balance de una migración," in *La migración dominicana en los Estados Unidos*, ed. José del Castillo and Christopher Mitchell (Santo Domingo, 1987), 19–73; Grasmuck and Pessar, *Between Two Islands*, 75–80; Eric Larson and Teresa Sullivan, "Conventional Numbers in Immigration Research: The Case of the Missing Dominicans," *International Migration Review* 21 (1987); Antonio Ugalde, Frank Bean, and Gilbert Cárdenas, "International Migration from the Dominican Republic," *International Migration Review* 13 (1979). For a dissenting voice on this matter, Hernández, *Mobility*, 26–39. González, "Peasants' Progress," comments on the tendency to describe poor urbanites as campesinos.

39. Melvin Mañón, "Carnaval de la clase media," *¡Ahora!* December 2, 1974, 2–10.

40. Grasmuck and Pessar, *Between Two Islands*, 82.

41. Interview with Ubiera.

42. Interview with Gautreaux Piñeyro.

43. Amín Concepción Cruz A., *Periodismo dominicano en New York* (New York, 1993), 34; Jorge Duany, *Quisqueya on the Hudson* (New York, 1994), 19; interview with Frank Moya Pons (Santo Domingo, 2000).

44. Anderson, *Imagined Communities*, 22, 44.

45. See for instance Montes in *EC*, June 5, 1961, 8, and June 12, 1961, 8; Emilio Escalante, "Entre rascacielos," *EN*, August 24, 1968, 10–11; *EN*, September 17, 1968, 10.

46. "Desde New York," *¡Ahora!* February 27, 1965; Miguel Rodríguez O. "En serio y en broma . . . ," *¡Ahora!* June 24, 1968, 17, 72.

47. "Agasajan a cantante," *EN*, October 11, 1971, 24; "Jóvenes cooperarán campaña del pupitre," *EN*, October 17, 1970, 14.

48. Cruz A., *Periodismo dominicano*, 37.

49. Ibid., 35.

50. "Mosaicos de Nueva York," *¡Ahora!* August 2, 1971, 34–35.

51. Interview with Espinal; José (Pappy) Lafontaine, *Peripecias de un locutor de tercera* (Santo Domingo, 1995), 16, made similar accusations.

52. *El Dominicano* (New York), June 1973, NACLA Collection.

53. *EN,* October 20, 1971, 12.

54. *EN,* July 30, 1971, 5. The beauty pageant thus served to adorn reportage on two of the basic narratives of home that Dominicans had begun to construct, home as a place for charitable donations and for Christmas holidays. The overlap with the politics of tourism promotion and national projection was especially pronounced.

55. *EN,* October 20, 1971, 12.

56. "Dominicanos en New York," *EN,* December 22, 1971, 12.

57. Ibid., 13.

58. Miguel Rodríguez O., "En serio y en broma . . . ," *¡Ahora!* September 15, 1969; July 15, 1968, 72.

59. "Los Quisqueyanos en EU y las navidades," *EN,* December 23, 1971.

60. Snyder, "Neighborhood Changed," 453.

61. Chacón, "Acusan a oficial de NY negligencia en saqueo de negocio dominicano," *EN,* May 2, 1979, 11.

62. Capalino, "Update."

63. Álvarez, "New York's Latins: The Dominicans."

64. "Forman en Nueva York asociación deportiva," *EN,* October 8, 1978, 8.

65. "Ausentes," *EN,* January 24, 1971, 8.

66. "Dominicanos se movilizan," *EN,* May 14, 1971, 17.

67. "Colonia en NY ayuda pobres," *EN,* February 3, 1972, 6.

68. "Piden colonia en NY dé pupitres," *EN,* October 3, 1970, 1, 2.

69. "Aportando," *EN,* August 14, 1971, 1, 6.

70. Interview with Joséfina Báez (Ann Arbor, MI, 2005). For social pages see for instance the series "Gráficas de sociedad" in *¡Ahora!* (monthly in 1967).

71. "Obsequiarán a niñas RD," *EN,* December, 23, 1971, 26; see also *EC,* May 29, 1972.

72. *¡Ahora!* February 6, 1967, 52–53.

73. See "Bellezas de todas partes," *¡Ahora!* February 7, 1972, 69.

74. "Dominicanos en Estados Unidos," *¡Ahora!* January 10, 1972.

75. Chacón, "Vistazos . . . ," *EN,* April 24, 1978, 15.

76. Scherezada Vicioso, "El Dominicano en EE UU," *Amigo del Hogar,* November 1971, 17–18.

77. "Bellezas de todas partes," *¡Ahora!* February 7, 1972, 69.

78. Vicioso, "El Dominicano en EE UU."

79. "Illegal Aliens: A Stopover in Puerto Rico," *Daily News,* September 28, 1971, 30. See also *Daily News,* September 27, 29, 30 and October 1, 2, 4, 1971; "N.Y. Flooded by Aliens Listed as Puerto Rican," *Washington Post,* October 19, 1971, A1; Hearings of the House Committee on the Judiciary, March 10–11, 1972, CIS-NO: 72-H521-19; "Illegal Aliens Here Called Public-Services Burden," *NYT,* March 11, 1972, 58; "Proposed Alien-Hiring Bill Opposed," *NYT,* March 12, 1972, 52. For the racialization of "wetbacks" see Ngai, *Impossible Subjects,* 147–52.

80. "Voice of the People," *Daily News,* October 2, 1971, 17.

81. "Estiman es ventajosa publicidad de *NY Times,*" *EN,* November 10, 1971, 1, 2.

82. Reginaldo Atanay, "Extienden oportunidad comunidad," *EC*, March 17, 1972; José Tejeda, "Piden EU buen trato a ilegales," *EN*, November 17, 1971, 23.

83. *Lucha: Organo del movimiento popular dominicano* (New York), September 1974, 1, 8; NACLA Collection.

84. United Front for the Defense of Immigrants, Letter to Board and Publishers of the *Daily News*, OGM Base de Datos, Santo Domingo.

85. María Castillo and Ramon A. Grullón, "No somos ilegales, somos trabajadores," *LN*, September 2, 1974, 5. See also "Dominicanos asumen liderazgo en Nueva York," *LN*, July 8, 1974, 5.

86. Rodríguez de León, *Furioso*, 99–100; Rafael Calderón, "Asociaciónes Dominicanas han gestionado cerca de 1,200 empleados en Nueva York," *Listín*, June 5, 1985; Rafael Lantigua, "Plan ayuda comunidad Dominicanos cuenta con fondos por 111 mil," *ES*, May 9, 1975, 11; Georges, *New Immigrants*, 24–25.

87. "Celebrarán en Nueva York reunión dominicanista," *ES*, January 25, 1975, 30. See also *ES*, January 28, 1975, 13.

88. "Comité NY clausura semana del emigrante," *ES*, January 4, 1975; "Estatus ilegal moldea vida dominicanos," *EC*, November 10, 1971; "Estiman es ventajosa publicidad de *NY Times*," *EN*, November 10, 1971, 1, 2; Alfredo White, "El inmigrante dominicano ante las próximas elecciones," *¡Ahora!* May 20, 1974, 14–16.

89. *La Noticia*, June 1, 1976, 6. See also *ES*, October 27, 1971.

90. Luis A. Rojas Durán, "Cónsul de RD trata evitar repatriación," *EN*, October 30, 1971, 1, 6.

91. "Estiman proyecto ley inmigrantes afectaría relaciones de RD y EU," *EN*, June 12, 1974, 5.

92. *¡Ahora!* October 25, 1971, 60–61.

93. "Mas de 300 personas han salido al exterior con pasaportes vendidos por un sujeto," *EN*, clipping from OGM file "Relaciones exteriores con Estados Unidos: Visados y falsificaciones," June 1972.

94. "Sube delincuencia RD en Nueva York," *Última Hora*, December 31, 1971. See also "Crece en NY delincuencia de la colonia dominicana," *EC*, October 19, 1971.

95. *EC*, December 10, 1975, 1, 16.

96. "Dominicanos en esta ciudad de New York orgullo para el pueblo dominicano," *El Dominicano*, June 1973, NACLA Collection.

97. Tirso Valdez, "Mosaicos de Nueva York," *¡Ahora!* December 6, 1971.

98. Tirso Valdez, "Mosaicos de Nueva York," *¡Ahora!* November 15, 1971, 38–39.

99. Atanay quoted in Tirso Valdez, "Mosaicos de Nueva York," *¡Ahora!* January 17, 1972.

100. Carlos F. Morel in *Diario-La Prensa*, October 22, 1971, quoted in Tirso Valdez, "Mosaicos de Nueva York," *¡Ahora!* November 15, 1971. This idea of a traditionally honorable ethnic community being undermined by new, socially undesireable migrants is reminscent of Cuban American responses to Mariel immigrants and *balseros* as well as Mexican American civil rights groups responding to "Operation Wetback." García, *Havana, USA*; Gutiérrez, *Walls and Mirrors*.

101. Atanay quoted in Tirso Valdez, "Mosaicos de Nueva York," *¡Ahora!* January 17, 1972.

102. Tirso Valdez, "Mosaicos de Nueva York," *¡Ahora!* January 17, 1972.

103. Álvarez, "New York's Latins: The Dominicans"; José Labourt, "Comprueban que en Estados Unidos los dólares no ruedan por el suelo," *EN*, September 21, 1988.

104. Ubi Rivas, "Radiografía de un éxodo," *¡Ahora!* December 13, 1971, 49–54.

105. Alfredo White, "El inmigrante dominicano ante las próximas elecciones," *¡Ahora!* May 20, 1974, 14–16.

106. Padre Juan Oleaga, "Ametrallan 5 dominicanos," *Amigo del Hogar*, July–August 1968, 24–25.

107. Porfirio Ml. Valdez, "Dominicanos en New York," *Amigo del Hogar*, September 16 and October 17, 1971, 22–23.

108. Padre Juan Oleaga, "Ametrallan 5 dominicanos," *Amigo del Hogar*; July–August, 1968, 24–25.

109. Reported in "Crece en NY delincuencia de la colonia dominicana," *EC*, October 19, 1971.

110. Scherezada Vicioso, "El dominicano en EE UU," *Amigo del Hogar*, November 1971, 17–18.

111. María Ramos, "Historia de una familia que emigró a New York, séptima parte," *Amigo del Hogar*, May 1974, 34–35.

112. Melquíades, "New York: Micro noticias y comentarios," *Amigo del Hogar*, November 1971, 40.

113. Atanay quoted in Tirso Valdez, "Mosaicos de Nueva York," *¡Ahora!* January 17, 1972.

114. "La vida en Nueva York desajusta a criollos," *EN*, February 1, 1972, 1, 2.

115. Maria Castillo, "Atribuye irresponsabilidad dominicanos en Nueva York," *ES*, January 5, 1974, 5.

116. Victor Grimaldi, "La vida de los Dominicanos en Nueva York," *El Dominicano*, June 1973, NACLA Collection.

117. Chiqui Vicioso, "Dominican Migration to the United States," *Migration Today*, 1976.

118. "Inmigrantes dominicanos aceleran regreso a su país," *EC*, June 5, 1976, 16.

119. Francisco Alvarez C., "Nativos en NY sin vida social," *Listín*, January 23, 1975, 1, 4.

120. Hugo Antonio Ysalguez, "Nueva York no es un paraíso (Los dominicanos lo han comprabado)," *¡Ahora!* September 29, 1975.

121. Canelo, *Dónde*, 154.

122. Ibid., 132.

123. Ibid., 128.

124. Weisz, "Causas de las migraciones," 127.

125. Ibid., 153.

126. Juan Deláncer, "Dominicanos en New York: Una ciudad en crisis," *LN*, December 23, 1979, 1B–30B; "Criollo será candidato a junta escolar manhattan," *EN*, May 6, 1975, 6.

127. Juan Deláncer, "Criollos instalan diversos negocios, banilejos y cibaeños abren pulperías," *LN*, December 23, 1979, 28B–29B.

128. Chacón, "Vistazos . . . ," *EN*, August 5, 1978, 7.

129. Chacón, "Vistazos . . . ," *EN*, November 19, 1978, 13.

130. Chacón, "Vistazos . . . ," *EN*, July 9, 1978, 5.

131. Snyder, "Neighborhood Changed," 452; Lurie Red Noteboook, December 11, 1972, ELP; Steven M. Lowenstein, *Frankfurt on the Hudson* (Detroit, 1989), 224–25.

132. Rafael Lantigua, "Comunidad dominicanos evitan les saquean," *ES*, July 15, 1975, 1.

133. Both quotations are from Chacón, "Vistazos . . . ," *EN*, November 26, 1978, 29.

134. Chacón, "Acusan a oficial de NY negligencia en saqueo de negocio dominicano," *EN*, May 2, 1979, 11.

135. "For Hispanic Migrants, 'Home' Is Elusive," *NYT*, May 14, 1980, B1.

136. Basch, Schiller, and Szanton Blanc, *Nations Unbound*; Cristina Szanton Blanc, Linda Basch, and Nina Glick Schiller, "Transnationalism, Nation-States, and Culture," *Current Anthropology* 36 (1995). The organizers of a star-studded 1995 international conference on transnationalism attributed to Catherine Hall, the lone historian in attendance, the observation that transnationalism was not new. Sidney W. Mintz, "The Localization of Anthropological Practice: From Area Studies to Transnationalism," *Critique of Anthropology* 18 (1998); Kivisto, "Theorizing"; Torres-Saillant, *Diasporic Disquisitions*.

137. Guarnizo, "One Country in Two"; Portes, "Transnational Communites"; Waldinger, *Through the Eye of the Needle*.

138. David Vidal, "Hispanic Newcomers in City Cling to Values of Homeland," *NYT*, May 11, 1980, 1.

139. Chacón, "En Nueva York hay que ser agresivo para sobrevivir," *¡Ahora!* June 2, 1980, 17–19.

140. José Itzigsohn et al., "Mapping Dominican Transnationalism," *Ethnic and Racial Studies* 22 (1999); Kivisto, "Theorizing"; Portes, Guarnizo, and Landolt, "Transnational Communities."

141. Guarnizo, "'Going Home'"; Jesse Hoffnung-Garskof, "The Prehistory of the Cadenú," in *Immigrants in America*, ed. Donna Gabaccia and Colin Wayne Leach (New York, 2003); Silvio Torres-Saillant, *El retorno de las yolas* (Santo Domingo, 1999).

142. Michael P. Smith, *Transnational Urbanism* (Malden, MA, 2001), 5. Fouron and Glick Schiller discuss this in their chapter, "Long Distance Nationalism as a Debate: Shared Symbols and Disparate Messages," in Schiller and Fouron, *Georges Woke Up*, 17–35, 238–73.

Notes to Chapter Eight

1. Martin Shefter, *Political Crisis, Fiscal Crisis* (New York, 1985); Katz, *Undeserving Poor*, 137–66, 195–235; John O'Connor, "U.S. Social Welfare Policy: The Reagan Record and Legacy," *Journal of Social Policy* 27 (January 1998); Saskia

Sassen, "Economic Restructuring and the American City," *Annual Review of Sociology* 16 (1990); Weikart, "Follow the Money."

2. On Soho see Sharon Zukin, *Loft Living* (Baltimore, 1982). On Washington Heights, Capalino, "Update"; Hernández, *Mobility*, 112–17; Nathan Leventhal, "Report of the Washington Heights-Inwood Task Force" (New York, 1978).

3. Rosita Romero, ed., *Hispanic Families Speak Out* (New York, 1988), 15–16.

4. *Washington Post*, July 10, 1986, A1.

5. On sentencing see Douglas McDonald and Kenneth Carlson, "Sentencing in the Federal Courts: Does Race Matter? The Transition to Sentencing Guidelines, 1986–1990," (1993); "One Out of Four Federal Prisoners Not a U.S. Citizen," *Washington Post*, November 25, 1994, A1; "Immigrants Face Deportation for Old Crimes under New Laws," *Chicago Tribune*, October 12, 1997, 3; Bernardo Vega and Roberto Desprandel, *Tendencias migratorias hacia los Estados Unidos de dominicanos* (Santo Domingo, 2000), 37–39; "Taking Back Our Streets Act," http://www.house.gov/house/Contract/CONTRACT.html.

6. Romero, *Hispanic Families*, 15–16.

7. INS Yearbooks for 1980, 1990, and 1997.

8. Jorge Duany, Luisa Hernández Angueira, and César A. Rey, *El barrio guandul* (Caracas, 1995), 108–9.

9. Freddy Sandoval, "Los viajes ilegales: Complicidad-maffia o indiferencia," *¡Ahora!* October 1987, 3–6.

10. Manuel Pastor, "Latin America, The Debt Crisis, and the International Monetary Fund," *Latin American Perspectives* 16 (Winter 1989); Robert Pastor, "Sinking in the Caribbean Basin," *Foreign Affairs* 60 (Summer 1982); Joseph E. Stiglitz, *Globalization and Its Discontents* (New York, 2003), 12–21.

11. Roberto Cassá, "Recent Popular Movements in the Dominican Republic," *Latin American Perspectives* 22 (1995); Centro Dominicano de Estudios de la Educación, "Otro abril de lucha popular" (Santo Domingo, 1984); Ismael Dávila Borges and Héctor Meléndez Lugo, *República Dominicana: Sangre y fuego en protestas por el alza de precios* (Río Piedras, Puerto Rico, 1985), 24; Vianna Ianni, *El territorio de las masas* (Santo Domingo, 1987).

12. Freddy Sandoval, "De lo colonial a lo moderno," *¡Ahora!* September 1987, 3–5.

13. Delance, *Renovación urbana en Santo Domingo*.

14. *LN*, July 30, 1987. Rita Ceballos, *Violencia y comunidad en un mundo globalizado* (Santo Domingo, 2004), 103–6; Polonio and Paulino G., "Renovación urbana."

15. For example, neighborhood youth widely reported geographical discrimination in Ceballos, *Violencia*.

16. Fausto Rosario Adames, *El reinado de Vincho Castillo: Droga y política en República Dominicana* (Dominican Republic, 1998), 177, 193–95; Freddy Sandoval, "La haitianización de R.D.: Un problema importado con características criollas," *¡Ahora!* November 1987, 3–5; Sarah A. DeCosse, *Expulsions of Haitians and Dominico-Haitians from the Dominican Republic* (New York, 1991); David Howard, *Coloring the Nation*, 167–81; Sagás, *Race and Politics*, 105–14. For an analysis of interethnic relations in Santo Domingo barrios, Franc Baéz Evertsz, *Vecinos y extraños* (Santo Domingo, 2001).

17. Hartlyn, *The Struggle for Democratic Politics*, 160–218, 231; Terri Shaw, "Ruling on Senate Curbs Power of Dominican Victor," *Washington Post*, July 11, 1978; Rosario Espinal, "Procesos electorales en la República Dominicana, 1978–1990," *Caribbean Studies* 24 (1991); Hartlyn, *The Struggle for Democratic Politics*, 114–28.

18. See for instance Rosario Espinal, "Economic Restructuring, Social Protest, and Democratization in the Dominican Republic," *Latin American Perspectives* 22 (1995); Terry Lynn Karl, "Dilemmas of Democratization in Latin America," *Comparative Politics* 23 (October 1990).

19. Wilfredo Lozano, *La urbanización de la pobreza* (Santo Domingo, 1997), 13–55; Moya Pons, "Industrial Incentives"; "Expedientes referentes a la zona industrial de Herrera, 1967–1969," AGN-CND, Leg C, E.; Gerald F. Murray, *El colmado* (Santo Domingo, 1996).

20. Scott B. MacDonald and F. Joseph Demetrius, "The Caribbean Sugar Crisis," *Journal of Interamerican Studies and World Affairs* 28 (1986); Moya Pons, "Quid Pro Quo"; Bernardo Vega, "Problemas sociales y políticos creados por la industria azucarera dominicana," in *En la década perdida* (Santo Domingo, 1991).

21. Miguel Ceara Hatton, *Tendencias estructurales y conyuntura de la economía dominicana, 1968–1983* (Santo Domingo, 1985); Moya Pons, *The Dominican Republic*, 405–21.

22. "IMF Staff Country Report: Dominican Republic" (Washington, DC, 1999); Pastor, "Latin America, Debt Crisis"; Stiglitz, *Globalization*, 3–22.

23. Andrés Dauhajre hijo, José Achécar Chupani, and Anne Swindale, *Estabilización, ajuste, y pobreza en República Dominicana, 1986–1992* (Santo Domingo, 1994), 59–81; Hartlyn, *The Struggle for Democratic Politics*, 193–202; Moya Pons, *The Dominican Republic*, 412–21. On IMF reforms and poverty in the rest of Latin America, Oscar Altimir, "Income Distribution and Poverty through Crisis and Adjustment," *CEPAL Review* 52 (1994); Albert Berry, "The Income Distribution Threat in Latin America," *Latin American Research Review* 32 (1997).

24. Wilfredo Lozano, "Dominican Republic: Informal Economy, the State, and the Urban Poor," in *The Urban Caribbean*, ed. Alejandro Portes et al. (Baltimore, 1997). For the way that barrio residents regarded the rest of the city see Jorge Cela, Isis Duarte, and Carmen Julia Gómez, *Población, crecimiento urbano y barrios marginados en Santo Domingo* (Santo Domingo, 1988), 31. For neighborhood density see Freddy Sandoval, "Terror en los barrios: La delincuencia juvenil, el pandillerismo y las bandas," *¡Ahora!* March 1987, 3–7. For efforts to get a streetlight on Avenida 17 see Isabel Rauber, *Construyendo poder desde abajo: COPADEBA* (Santo Domingo, 1995), 36–37.

25. Antonio Menéndez Alarcón, *Power and Television in Latin America: The Dominican Case* (Westport, CT, 1992), 22, 38.

26. Bonaparte Gautreaux Piñeyro, "Se desató la violencia,"*¡Ahora!* May 7, 1984, 3–9.

27. Juan Francisco Martínez Almanzar, "El pandillerismo en Santo Domingo," *¡Ahora!* June 1989, 3–6.

28. Ceballos, *Violencia*, 60.

29. Ibid., 28.

30. Ibid., 33.

31. Arturo Escobar and Sonia E. Alvarez, eds., *The Making of Social Movements in Latin America* (Boulder, CO, 1992); David Slater, *New Social Movements and the State in Latin America* (Cinnaminson, NJ, 1985).

32. Rauber, *Construyendo*, 36–37.

33. Interview with Báez viuda de Reyes.

34. Interview with Ignacio Soto (Santo Domingo, 2000); interview with Torres.

35. See Centro Dominicano de Estudios de la Educación, "Otro abril"; Dávila Borges and Meléndez Lugo, *República Dominicana: Sangre y fuego*. Moya Pons, *The Dominican Republic*, 414–15, shows how Jorge Blanco attacked the IMF publicly even as he negotiated a restructuring package.

36. Ceballos, *Violencia*, 32.

37. Cassá, "Recent Popular Movements"; José Ceballos, "Organización y movimientos barriales," *Estudios Sociales* 28 (1995), 64–67; Espinal, "Economic Restructuring"; Bernardo Matías, *El poder barrial-comunal* (Santo Domingo, 1991).

38. Ceballos, *Violencia*, 32; interview with Guevara.

39. Cassá, "Recent Popular Movements"; Espinal, "Economic Restructuring."

40. Ceballos, *Violencia*, 83–85.

41. "Pueblo dominicano, la comunidad dominicana de Nueva York protesta: Espacio pagado por el Comité de Ciudadanos para la Democracia en Santo Domingo," *EN*, May 23, 1978, 12. When I interviewed members of the PRD in 1999–2000, almost all remembered and celebrated the role of the New York *colonia* in pressuring for the transition.

42. Aparicio, "Developing politics in Quisqueya Heights," 120–51; Graham, "Reimagining"; Milagros Ricourt, *Dominicans in New York City* (New York, 2002), 63–85. For Linares's attempt to mobilize parent outrage against the abuses of the UFT, and to frame these abuses as racism against "the Dominican community" see Romero, *Hispanic Families*, 74–75.

43. Chacón, "Vistazos . . . ," *EN*, April 11, 1978, 5. For the activities of ANDA see Graham, "Reimagining." The idea of the dominicano ausente is similar to the earlier idea of Mexico "de afuera"; see Gilbert G. Gonzalez, *Mexican Consuls and Labor Organizing* (Austin, TX, 1999).

44. Nelson Sánchez, "Dominicanos en NY anuncian boicot," *Última Hora*, October 15, 1987.

45. Antonio Cáceres, "Creen dan poco estímulo a dominicanos EU," *EN*, December 19, 1989.

46. Rosanna Grullón, "Organizadores evento en Nueva York se quejan falta de apoyo gobierno," *ES*, July 22, 1986, 20.

47. "Lanzan volantes New York pidiendo reelección de Balaguer con Pichardo," *EN*, January 6, 1978, 10.

48. Chacón, "Nuevo cónsul RD en NY promete ayudar a la comunidad criolla," *EN*, September 17, 1978, 15. The added desire for dual citizenship responded to a change in U.S. immigration policy in 1977. The new policy shifted the system of preferences for family reunification. The immediate family of permanent residents no longer received the same preferential treatment as the family of United States citizens. This placed a new premium on naturalization among Dominicans in New York, spawning a demand for double citizenship.

49. Graham, "Re-imagining" (Ph.D. diss.), 237–42.

50. Interview with Espinal.

51. Pedro Familia, "Los Dominican York," *ES*, September 22, 1986.

52. Graham, "Reimagining," 115.

53. Lozano, *Urbanización*, 112–13; José Itzigsohn, "Migrant Remittances, Labor Markets, and Household Strategies," *Social Forces* 74 (December 1995).

54. Interview with Doña Blanca (Cristo Rey, Santo Domingo, June 2000).

55. Interview with Sebastián Colón (Cristo Rey, Santo Domingo, 2000).

56. For figures on social spending in the 1980s see Lozano, *Urbanización*, 189. For doctors, Ortíz, "Healers in the Storm," 224–26.

57. Bernardo Vega, "Convenientes e inconvenientes de la migración" in Bernardo Vega, *En la década perdida* (Santo Domingo, 1991), 259–70. Vega himself had first taken interest in the question of remittances in 1972, as reported in "Dominicanos en NY," *EN*, January 7, 1976, 11.

58. José Romero, "Ausentes compran mayoría viviendas," *Listín*, January 31, 1985. See also "Dominicanos radicados en Nueva York son mayores adquirentes viviendas R.D.," *Listín*, December 4, 1986; interview with Mora.

59. "Pondera valor remesas exterior," *Listín*, December 12, 1984.

60. For earlier calls for a bank in New York see, "Respaldan en NY sucursal de banco," *EN*, December 29, 1968, 1, 8; for Grullón's dealings, interview with Espinal. Frank Moya Pons, *Pioneros de la banca en la República Dominicana* (Santo Domingo, 1989). Also "Ejecutivos de Banco Inmobiliario Dominicano viajan a Nueva York," *EC*, August 18, 1984.

61. "ACIS celebrará banquete en NY," *Listín*, July 21,1984; "Celebraran seminario orientación NY para posible inversionistas en RD," *Listín*, June 6, 1984; "Propone unión empresarios lograr bienestar de la RD," *La Información*, October 25, 1989. For the role of these business groups in these years see Rosario Espinal, "Business and Politics in the Dominican Republic," in *Organized Business, Economic Change, and Democracy in Latin America*, ed. Francisco Durand and Eduardo Silva (Coral Gables, FL, 1998).

62. "Anuncia ofensiva comercial NY nativos consuman productos RD," *Listín*, April 7, 1989.

63. Rómulo Vallejo Pradel, "Remesas: Via Banco Central," *EN*, July 14, 1987.

64. "Balaguer recibe comerciantes dominicanos de NY," *Listín*, May 2, 1988. See, for instance, "JB exorta dominicanos en NY a defender el peso con remesas," *Última Hora*, August 4, 1989; "Balaguer pide 'ausentes' venden sus dolares a BC," *Hoy*, January 29, 1988. Cf. Miguel Gallastegui, "Envio divisas traba sistema monetario RD," *EC*, December 4, 1978, 1; Tulio Navarrete, "Bosch ve escape remesas dólares," *Listín*, August 27, 1984.

65. Grasmuck and Pessar, *Between Two Islands*, were the first to apply this historical structuralist model to Dominican migration. For the emergence of New York entrepreneurs see Guarnizo, "One Country in Two."

66. Joseph Michael Rogers, "Political Economy of Caribbean Drug Trafficking: The Case of the Dominican Republic" (Ph.D. diss., Florida International University, 1999); Miguel Angel Velázquez-Mainardi, *Narcotráfico y lavado de dólares en la República Dominicana* (Santo Domingo, 1992).

67. William Kleinknecht, *The New Ethnic Mobs* (New York, 1996), 250–70; Rogers, "Political Economy of Caribbean Drug Trafficking"; Select Committee on Narcotics Abuse and Control, "Dominican Drug Trafficking," U.S. Congress (Washington, DC, 1993).

68. Terry Williams, "Drugs, the Cocaine Capitalists: A World Bank for Inner-City Kids," *Los Angeles Times*, March 19, 1990, B7.

69. Kleinknecht, *New Ethnic Mobs*.

70. Terry Williams, *Cocaine Kids: The Inside Story of a Teenage Drug Ring* (Reading, MA, 1989). For comparison of Dominican and other ethnic crime organizations, see Kleinknecht, *New Ethnic Mobs*.

71. Rosario Adames, *Reinado*; Velázquez-Mainardi, *Narcotráfico*.

72. "Condenan ex cónsul RD por drogas," *Última Hora*, June 8, 1989.

73. Mike McAlary, "Cartel Used System to Bring Down Innocent Agent," *New York Post*, October 11, 1991.

74. D. M. Hartman and A. Golub, "The Social Construction of the Crack Epidemic in the Print Media," *Journal of Psychoactive Drugs* 31 (1999); Craig Rainarman and Harry G. Levine, "Crack in Context: Politics and Media in the Making of a Drug Scare," *Contemporary Drug Problems* 16 (1989).

75. Ruddy L. González, *Última Hora*, November 5, 1986.

76. "U.S. Breaks Up Major Crack Ring in New York," *NYT*, July 31, 1987, B1.

77. "Marcharán en calles preocupación por consumo de drogas dominicanos NY," *ES*, August 4, 1986.

78. "Murders Surge as Crack Spreads," *NYT*, March 29, 1987, E7; Hernández, *Mobility*, 117.

79. McDonald and Carlson, "Sentencing in the Federal Courts"; and "One out of Four Federal Prisoners Not a U.S. Citizen," *Washington Post*, November 25, 1994, A1.

80. Virginia Berges Rib, "Dice 65 por ciento nuevos ilegales NY se dedican al robo y drogas," *Última Hora*, July 22, 1986.

81. Pablo Aguilera, "Vicios corroen juventud dominicana," *ES*, December 5, 1986; Zunilda Fondeur, "Dicen organizaciones culturales desvían principales objectivos," *ES*, July 17, 1986; Rosanna Grullón, "Organizadores evento en Nueva York se quejan falta de apoyo gobierno," *ES*, July 22, 1986, 20.

82. Chacón, "Dominicanos en NY opinan sobre crack," *LN*, November 29, 1986.

83. "Talk in Washington Heights: Fear, Drugs, and Now Corruption," *NYT*, June 22, 1992, B1.

84. "D'Amato Targeting Dominican Aid," *New York Newsday*, June 20, 1989, 31.

85. "Conflicting Accounts Emerge of Suspect's Death," *NYT*, July 2, 1989, 24; "Suspect in Officer's Death Is Buried to Angry Protests," *NYT*, July 3, 1989, 24.

86. "Crack's Destructive Sprint across America," *NYT*, October 1, 1989, 6, 38.

87. For crime statistics, Hernández, *Mobility*. 117. According to a Proquest search, the *NYT* mentioned Washington Heights and Dominicans in 163 articles between 1986 and 1993. Of those 100 also mentioned drugs, crime, murder, or violence. For Dominican complaints about this, "It's an Injustice to Generalize," *NYT*, September 16, 1991, B6.

88. "Border Patrol in the Heights," *New York Newsday*, May 26, 1991, 43; "Immigration Raids on Bodegas Hit a Nerve in Washington Heights," *NYT*, April 10, 1990, B1.

89. Mike McAlary in the *New York Post*, October 9–11, 1991; Bill Berkeley, "Dead Right," *Columbia Journalism Review* 31, March/April 1993, 39–45; "Prepared Testimony of Joseph Occhipinti before the House Committee on the Judiciary Subcommittee on Commercial and Administrative Law," July 27, 2000, Subject: H.R. 4105—the Fair Justice Act of 2000, Lexis-Nexis. The Justice Department determined that much of the material submitted by Molinari to exonerate Occhipinti was fabricated. "Justice Dept. Is Critical of Molinari," *NYT*, December 23, 1992, B4.

90. Milton Mollen, "Commission Report" (1994), available from http://www.parc.info/reports/pdf/mollenreport.pdf; Amnesty International USA, "Police Brutality and Excessive Force in the New York City Police Department" (1996), available from http://web.amnesty.org/library/Index/engAMR510361996.

91. For the police department's perspective, including the description of García as "slick with sweat," see Edward Conlen, "The Pols, the Police, and the Gerry Curls," *American Spectator* 27, November 1994, 36.

92. "Upper Manhattan Block Erupts after a Man Is Killed in Struggle with a Policeman," *NYT*, July 5, 1992, 20; "Police Report on a Slaying Is Challenged; Police Report on Shooting Is Challenged," *NYT*, July 6, 1992, B1; "Stories Differ on Fatal Fall from Rooftop," *NYT*, July 7, 1992, B4; "Events Don't Surprise Dominican Residents; Police Harassment Said to Be Common," *NYT*, July 8, 1992; "Why Was José García Killed?" *Diario-La Prensa*, July 7, 1992; "Decimos basta, no queremos más golpes racistas," *Impacto*, July 14, 1992, 6.

93. "Another Native Son Returns in Coffin," *NYT*, July 10, 1992, B3. For criticism of the ways that being from San Francisco de Macorís was used to convict García in the press see Carlos Lithgow, a physician from San Francisco, de Macorís, Letter to the Editor, *NYT*, July 16, 1992, A24. For the distorted image of San Francisco's "opulent" drug mansions see Rogers, "Political Economy of Caribbean Drug Trafficking," 139–46.

94. Bolívar Díaz Gómez, "Preocupa imagen tienen en RD de dominicanos radicados NY," *EN*, December 9, 1986.

95. Ibid.

96. Espacio pagado, *Listín*, March 10, 1989.

97. "Monseñor Núñez desmiente cartas al *Listín*," *Listín*, March 11, 1989.

98. Sal Germán, "Maljuta rechaza imagen negativa tratan crear dominicanos," *ES*, November 8, 1988.

99. For residential segregation and social exclusion of return migrants see Guarnizo, "'Going Home,'" 45–51; interview with Morq; interview with Lourdes Bueno (Santo Domingo, 2000).

100. Guarnizo, "'Going Home,'" 49.

101. César Ramos, "Cortitos," *Listín*, May 2, 1988.

102. Interview with Mora.

103. Ibid.

104. Robert Jackall, *Wild Cowboys* (Cambridge, MA, 1997).

105. Juan Francisco Martínez Almanzar, "El pandillerismo en Santo Domingo," ¡Ahora! June 1989, 3–6.

106. Rafael Ovalles, "JB: Regreso criollos EU agrava drogadicción," EN, September 4, 1988.

107. "Culpa 'cadenuses' de delincuencia," EN, April 16, 1988.

108. Interview with Ceballos.

109. Interview with Melliza.

110. Germán Santiago, "De la delincuencia juvenil al bajo mundo," EN, March 28, 1983, 8.

111. "Cartas de los lectores: Michael Jackson," EN, March 16, 1984, 10.

112. Esteban Rosario, "Discotecas millonarias," ¡Ahora! January 1988, 54–56.

113. Augusto Socías, "La vida nocturna en Santo Domingo," ¡Ahora! December 1984, 40–41; Orión Mejía, "El malecón es principal centro de diversión de capitaleños," ¡Ahora! January 1987, 16.

114. For discotecas in Cristo Rey, interview with Polanco; interview with Juana Rosario (Santo Domingo, 2000).

115. EN, July 2, 1978, 12.

116. Interview with Ceballos.

117. Interview with Trinidad.

118. SODECA, Letter to Oscar Padilla Medrano, Secretario de Interior y Policía, August 12, 1983, AGN-SEIP, Leg. 2954 Exp. 4-18.

119. Ramón Emilio Jiménez, Secretario General de Club S. E. Díaz, Letter to Ministro de Interior y Policía, Santo Domingo, November 14, 1978, AGN-SEIP, Leg. 3274. Ianni, El territorio de las masas, 48.

120. Interview with Estrella.

121. Interview with Alfredo Pacheco (Cristo Rey, Santo Domingo, 2000).

122. Menéndez Alarcón, Power and Television, 22, 38.

123. Guandules, "Un barrio estudia a si mismo." The survey conducted by Isis Duarte, Jorge Cela, and others in 1976–77 revealed that 35–47 percent of households in selected barrios had televisions. TVs were more prevalent than electric fans. This data was shared with me by Padre Cela in 2000, interview.

124. Interview with Padre José R. Núñez Mármol (Santo Domingo, 2000). Núñez is a Jesuit priest and sociological researcher in Gualey and La Ciénaga.

125. Pacini Hernández, Bachata.

126. Menéndez Alarcón, Power and Television, 60–61; Joseph D. Straubhaar and Gloria M. Viscasillas, "Class, Genre, and the Regionalization of Television Programming in the Dominican Republic," Journal of Communication 41 (Winter 1991).

127. Menéndez Alarcón, Power and Television, 40, 68–73; Noel M. Murray and Sandra B. Murray, "Music and Lyrics in Commercials: A Cross-Cultural Comparison," Journal of Advertising 25 (Summer 1996).

128. Austerlitz, Merengue, 95, 105; Lafontaine, Peripecias de un locutor, 72–73.

129. Interview with Cela; Jorge Cela, La otra cara de la pobreza (Santo Domingo, 1997).

130. Georges, Making of a Transnational Community, 208; Grasmuck and Pessar, Between Two Islands, 73. See also Miguel de Jesus Parache and Javier Peña,

"Emigración a Nueva York de tres comunidades dominicanas: Jánico, Baitoa y Sabana Iglesias" (Licenciatura, Universidad Católica Madre y Maestra, 1971).

131. Interview with Pacheco.

132. Austerlitz, *Merengue*, 98–100; Pacini Hernández, *Bachata*, 29–31.

133. See photograph of Fausto Rey in ¡*Ahora!* January 25, 1971, 71.

134. Austerlitz, *Merengue*, 100–102.

135. Juan Flores, "Inaugurarán proximamente supernigh[T] club Dc-4," ¡*Ahora!* November 1984, 72–73; Esteban Rosario, "Discotecas millonarias," ¡*Ahora!* January 1988, 54–56. On Dominican New Yorkers and nightclubs, interview with Alejandro Paulino (Santo Domingo, 2000).

136. Interview with Pacheco.

137. See for instance Cela, *La otra cara de la pobreza*, 50–51.

138. José Juan Escobar Biaggi, Josefina Ivette Montolio Payan, and Sandra Zuleta Barichta, "Factores psico-sociales y conducta delictiva" (Licenciatura, Universidad Autónoma de Santo Domingo, 1981), CACD.

139. José R. Cruz et al., "Las pandillas juveniles" (paper presented at the VI Simposio de Psicología, Hotel Sheraton, Santo Domingo, 1983); Fernando José González, "Estudio exploratorio sobre pandillas juveniles en Santo Domingo" (Licenciatura, Universidad Autónoma de Santo Domingo, 1981), both in CACD.

140. González, "Estudio exploratorio," 143.

141. Moya Pons, *National Identity and Return*, 32–33.

142. David Howard, "Reappraising Race? Dominicans in New York City," *International Journal of Population Geography* 9; Levitt, *Transnational Villagers*, 107–12.

143. Juan Flores, *The Diaspora Strikes Back* (New York, 2007).

144. Interview with Melliza; interview with Margarita Monegro, Nicolasina Evangelista, and Margarita Arielo (Cristo Rey, Santo Domingo, 2000); interview with Ogando.

145. Pedro Familia, "Los Dominican York," *ES*, June 9, 1986.

146. Sara Pérez, "El tema de hoy: Los dominicanyorks veneran a San Lazaro," *Hoy*, January 21, 1991.

147. Néstor García Canclini, *Consumers and Citizens* (Minneapolis, MN, 2001), 39.

148. Dick Hebdige, *Subculture: The Meaning of Style*; Robin D. G. Kelley, *Race Rebels* (New York, 1994); George Lipsitz, *Time Passages* (Minneapolis, MN, 1990).

149. Livio Sansone, *Blackness without Ethnicity* (New York, 2003). Schiller and Fouron, *Georges Woke Up*, 238–57, call this "shared symbols and disparate messages."

NOTES TO THE CONCLUSION

1. Mike Davis, "Planet of the Slums," *New Left Review* 26 (2004).

2. Mintz, "Localization of Anthropological Practice."

Selected Bibliography

Aparicio, Ana Lucia. "Developing Politics in Quisqueya Heights." Ph.D. diss., CUNY, 2004.

Atkins, G. Pope, and Larman C. Wilson. *The Dominican Republic and the United States: From Imperialism to Transnationalism.* Athens: University of Georgia Press, 1998.

Austerlitz, Paul. *Merengue: Dominican Music and Dominican Identity.* Philadelphia: Temple University Press, 1997.

Baéz Evertsz, Franc. *Vecinos y extraños.* Santo Domingo: Sevicio Jesuíta de Refugiados, 2001.

Bailey, Benjamin. "Dominican-American Ethnic/Racial Identities and United States Social Categories." *International Migration Review* 35, no. 3 (2001): 677–708.

Bailey, Thomas, and Roger Waldinger. "The Changing Ethnic/Racial Division of Labor." In *Dual City,* edited by John Mollenkopf and Manuel Castells, 43–78. New York: Russell Sage Foundation, 1991.

Basch, Linda, Nina Glick Schiller, and Cristina Szanton Blanc. *Nations Unbound: Transnational Projects, Post-colonial Predicaments, and De-territorialized Nation-States.* Langhorne, PA.: Gordon and Breach, 1994.

Baud, Michiel. "Ideología y campsinado: El pensamiento de José Ramón López." *Estudios Sociales* 19, no. 64 (1986): 63–81.

Baver, Sherrie. "Including Migration in the Development Calculus." *Latin American Research Review* 30, no. 1 (1995): 191–202.

Bender, Thomas, ed. *Rethinking American History in a Global Age.* Berkeley and Los Angeles: University of California Press, 2002.

Benítez Rojo, Antonio. *La isla que se repite.* Barcelona: Editorial Casiopea, 1998.

Breton, Minerva, Nelson Ramírez, and Pablo Tactuk. *La migración interna en la República Dominicana.* Santo Domingo: Fondo para el Avance de las Ciencias Sociales, 1977.

Bueno, Lourdes. "Dominican Women's Experiences of Return Migration." In *Caribbean Circuits,* edited by Patricia Pessar, 61–90. New York: Center for Migration Studies, 1997.

Calder, Bruce. *The Impact of Intervention.* Austin: University of Texas Press, 1984.

Canelo, Juan De Frank. *Dónde, por qué, de qué, cómo viven los dominicanos en el extranjero.* Santo Domingo: Editora Alfa y Omega, 1982.

Capalino, James. "Update: Report of the Washington Heights–Inwood Task Force." New York, 1979.

Cassá, Roberto. *Los doce años.* Santo Domingo: Editora Búho, 1991.

——. "Recent Popular Movements in the Dominican Republic." *Latin American Perspectives* 22, no. 3 (1995): 81–93.

Ceara Hatton, Miguel. *Tendencias estructurales y conyuntura de la economía dominicana, 1968–1983*. Santo Domingo: Editora Nueva Ruta y Fundación Friedrich Ebert, 1985.

Ceballos, José. "Organización y movimientos barriales." *Estudios Sociales* 28, no. 102 (1995): 41–67.

Ceballos, Rita. *Violencia y comunidad en un mundo globalizado*. Santo Domingo: Centro Poveda, 2004.

Cela, Jorge. *La otra cara de la pobreza*. Santo Domingo: Centro de Estudios Sociales Padre Juan Montalvo, 1997.

———. "Tengo un dolor en la cultura." *Estudios Sociales* 56, April–June (1984): 23–36.

Cela, Jorge, Isis Duarte, and Carmen Julia Gómez. *Población, crecimiento urbano y barrios marginados en Santo Domingo*. Santo Domingo: Fundación Friedrich Ebert, 1988.

Centro Latinoamericano de Población y Familia. *Seminario de desarrollo, población y familia, Hotel Jaragua, December 4–6*. Santo Domingo: Arzobispado de Santo Domingo, CLPF, 1968.

Chantada, Amparo. *Del proceso de urbanización a la planificación urbana de Santo Domingo*. Santo Domingo: Editora San Juan, S.A., 1998.

———. "Los mecanismos del crecimiento urbano de Santo Domingo, 1966–1978." Ph.D. diss., University of Paris, 1982.

Consorcio Padco-Borrell. "Estudio sobre el desarrollo urbano de Santo Domingo." Washington, DC: Planning and Development Collaborative International, 1978.

Crassweller, Robert. *Trujillo: The Life and Times of a Caribbean Dictator*. New York: Macmillan Co., 1966.

Cruz A., Amín Concepción. *Periodismo dominicano en New York*. New York: Editorial Ace, 1993.

Cruz, José R., Fernando J. González, Casilda Ramos, José Rafael Peña, Sara Guilamo, and Luís Belliard. "Las pandillas juveniles." Paper presented at the VI Simposio de Psicología, Hotel Sheraton, Santo Domingo, 1983. CACD.

Dauhajre hijo, Andrés, José Achécar Chupani, and Anne Swindale. *Estabilización, ajuste, y pobreza en República Dominicana, 1986–1992*. Santo Domingo: Fundación Economía y Desarrollo, 1994.

Dávila Borges, Ismael, and Héctor Meléndez Lugo. *República Dominicana: Sangre y fuego en protestas por el alza de precios*. Río Piedras, Puerto Rico: Proyecto Caribeño de Justicia y Paz, 1985.

De Genova, Nicolás, and Ana Ramos-Zayas. *Latino Crossings*. New York: Routledge, 2003.

Delance, Juan de Dios, ed. *Renovación Urbana en Santo Domingo, 1986–1994*. Santo Domingo: Urbanizaciones Nacionales, 1993.

del Castillo, José. "Balance de una migración." In *La migración dominicana en los Estados Unidos*, edited by José del Castillo and Christopher Mitchell. Santo Domingo: Universidad APEC, 1987.

Derby, Lauren. "The Dictator's Seduction." *Callaloo* 23, no. 3 (2000): 1112–46.

———. "Gringo Chickens with Worms." In *Close Encounters of Empire*, edited by Gilbert Joseph, Catherine Legrand, and Ricardo Salvatore. Durham, NC: Duke University Press, 1997.

———. "The Magic of Modernity." Ph.D. diss., University of Chicago, 1998.

Diederich, Bernard. *Trujillo: The Death of the Goat*. Boston: Little, Brown, 1978.

Dirección General de Estadística de la República Dominicana. *Estadística demográfica de la República Dominicana*. Vols. 22–34. Santo Domingo: ONE, 1964–1977.

———. *Movimiento marítimo y aéreo*. Santo Domingo, 1961–1964, 1969, 1974–1977.

Dore Cabral, Carlos. *Reforma agraria y luchas sociales en la República Dominicana, 1966–1978*. Santo Domingo: Taller, 1981.

Duany, Jorge. *The Puerto Rican Nation on the Move*. Chapel Hill: University of North Carolina, 2002.

———. *Quisqueya on the Hudson, Dominican Research Monographs*. New York: City University of New York Dominican Studies Institute, 1994.

———. "Reconstructing Racial Identity." *Latin American Perspectives* 25, no. 3 (1998): 147–72.

Duany, Jorge, Luisa Hernández Angueira, and César A. Rey. *El Barrio Guandul*. Caracas: Editorial Nueva Sociedad, 1995.

Duarte, Isis. *Capitalismo y superpoblación en Santo Domingo*. Santo Domingo: CODIA, 1980.

Escobar Biaggi, José Juan, Josefina Ivette Montolio Payan, and Sandra Zuleta Barichta. "Factores psico-sociales y conducta delictiva." Licenciatura, Universidad Autónoma de Santo Domingo, 1981, CACD.

Espinal, Rosario. "Business and Politics in the Dominican Republic." In *Organized Business, Economic Change, and Democracy in Latin America*, edited by Francisco Durand and Eduardo Silva, 99–121. Coral Gables, FL: North-South Center Press, University of Miami, 1998.

———. "Economic Restructuring, Social Protest, and Democratization in the Dominican Republic." *Latin American Perspectives* 22, no. 3 (1995): 63–79.

———. "Procesos electorales en la República Dominicana, 1978–1990." *Caribbean Studies* 24 (July–December 1991): 45–53.

Fennema, Mendiert, and Troetje Loewenthal. *La construcción de raza y nación en la República Dominicana*. Santo Domingo: Editora Universitaria—UASD, 1987.

Fischkin, Barbara. *Muddy Cup*. New York: Scribner's, 1997.

Flores, Juan. "'Qué assimilated, brother, yo soy asimilao': The Structuring of Puerto Rican Ethnicity in the U.S." In *Challenging Fronteras*, edited by Mary Romero, Pierrette Hondagneu-Sotelo, and Vilma Ortiz, 175–86. New York: Routledge, 1997.

García Bonnelly, Juan Ulíses. *Las obras públicas en la era de Trujillo*. Ciudad Trujillo: Impresora Dominicana, 1955.

———. *Sobrepoblación, subdesarrollo y sus consecuencias socio-económicas*. Santo Domingo: Editora Cultural Dominicana, 1971.

Georges, Eugenia. *The Making of a Transnational Community*. New York: Columbia University Press, 1990.

———. *New Immigrants and the Political Process*. New York: New York Research Program in Interamerican Affairs, 1984.

Geyer, Michael, and Charles Bright. "World History in a Global Age." *American Historical Review* 100, no. 4 (1995): 1034–60.

Gleijeses, Piero. *The Dominican Crisis.* Baltimore: Johns Hopkins University Press, 1978.

González, Fernando José. "Estudio exploratorio sobre pandillas juveniles en Santo Domingo." Licenciatura, Universidad Autónoma de Santo Domingo, 1981, CACD.

González, Nancie. "Patterns of Dominican Ethnicity." In *The New Ethnicity*, edited by John W. Bennet, 110–24. St. Paul, MN, and New York: West Publishing Co., 1975.

———. "Peasants' Progress: Dominicans in New York." *Caribbean Studies* 10, no. 3 (1970): 154–71.

González, Raymundo. "Ideología del progreso y campesinado en el siglo XIX." *Ecos* 1, no. 2 (1993): 25–44.

González, Raymundo, Michiel Baud, Pedro San Miguel and Roberto Cassá, eds. *Política, identidad y pensamiento social en la República Dominicana. Siglos XIX y XX.* Madrid: Doce Calles, 1999.

Graham, Pamela. "Reimagining the Nation and Defining the District: Dominican Migration and Transnational Politics." In *Caribbean Circuits*, edited by Patricia Pessar, 91–125. New York: Center for Migration Studies, 1997.

———. "Re-imagining the Nation and Defining the District: The Simultaneous Political Incorporation of Dominican Transnational Migrants." Ph.D. diss., University of North Carolina, 1996.

Grasmuck, Sherri, and Patricia Pessar. *Between Two Islands.* Berkeley and Los Angeles: University of California Press, 1991.

Guarnizo, Luis. "'Going Home': Class, Gender, and Household Transformation among Dominican Return Migrants." In *Caribbean Circuits*, edited by Patricia Pessar, 13–60. New York: Center for Migration Studies, 1997.

———. "One Country in Two: Dominican-Owned Firms in New York and in the Dominican Republic." Ph.D. diss., Johns Hopkins University, 1992.

Güemez, Ildefonso. "Migración interna en la República Dominicana." In *Seminario sobre problemas de población en la República Dominicana*, 171–99. Santo Domingo: Universidad Autónoma de Santo Domingo, 1975.

Guitar, Lynne. "Cultural Genesis: Relationships among Indians, Africans and Spaniards in Rural Hispaniola, Sixteenth Century." Ph.D. diss., Vanderbilt University, 1998.

Hartlyn, Jonathan. *The Struggle for Democratic Politics in the Dominican Republic.* Chapel Hill: University of North Carolina Press, 1998.

Hartman, D. M., and A. Golub. "The Social Construction of the Crack Epidemic in the Print Media." *Journal of Psychoactive Drugs* 31, no. 4 (1999): 423–33.

Hendricks, Glenn L. *The Dominican Diaspora.* New York: Teachers College Press, Columbia University, 1974.

Hernández, Ramona. *The Mobility of Labor under Advanced Capitalism: Dominican Migration to the United States.* New York: Columbia University Press, 2002.

Herrera Bornia, O. *Construcción de viviendas en la República Dominicana.* Ciudad Trujillo: Editora El Caribe, 1958.

Hoetink, Harry. "'Race' and Color in the Caribbean." In *Caribbean Contours*, edited by Sydney W. Mintz and Sally Price, 55–84. Baltimore: Johns Hopkins University Press, 1985.

Howard, David. *Colouring the Nation: Race and Ethnicity in the Dominican Republic*. Oxford: Signal Books, 2001.

———. "Reappraising Race? Dominicans in New York City." *International Journal of Population Geography* 9 (2003): 337–50.

Iturrondo, Milagros. "'San Ignacio de la Yola' . . . y los dominicanos." *Homines* 17, no. 1–2 (1994): 234–40.

Itzigsohn, José. "Migrant Remittances, Labor Markets, and Household Strategies." *Social Forces* 74, no. 2 (1995): 633–55.

Itzigsohn, José, and Carlos Dore Cabral. "Competing Identities? Race, Ethnicity, and Panethnicity among Dominicans in the United States." *Sociological Forum* 15, no. 2 (2000): 225–47.

Itzigsohn, José, Carlos Dore Cabral, Esther Hernández Medina, and Obed Vázquez. "Mapping Dominican Transnationalism." *Ethnic and Racial Studies* 22, no. 2 (1999): 316–39.

Itzigsohn, José, Silvia Giorguli, and Obed Vazquez. "Immigrant Incorporation and Racial Identity: Racial Self-Identification among Dominican Immigrants." *Ethnic and Racial Studies* 28, no. 1 (2005): 50–78.

Jackall, Robert. *Wild Cowboys*. Cambridge: Harvard University Press, 1997.

Jiménez Belén, José. *Nueva York es así*. Santo Domingo: Editoria Taller, 1977.

Joseph, Gilbert M. "Close Encounters: Toward a New Cultural History of U.S.–Latin American Relations." In *Close Encounters of Empire*, edited by Gilbert M. Joseph, Catherine C. Legrand, and Ricardo D. Salvatore, 3–46. Durham: Duke University Press, 1998.

Katznelson, Ira. *City Trenches*. New York: Pantheon Books, 1981.

Kivisto, Peter. "Theorizing Transnational Immigration." *Ethnic and Racial Studies* 24, no. 4 (2001): 549–77.

Kryzanek, Michael J. "Diversion, Subversion, and Repression: The Strategies of Anti-opposition Politics in Balaguer's Dominican Republic." *Caribbean Studies* 17, no. 1–2 (1978): 83–108.

Lafontaine, José (Pappy). *Peripecias de un locutor de tercera*. Santo Domingo: Editora Taller, 1995.

Larson, Eric, and Teresa Sullivan. "Conventional Numbers in Immigration Research: The Case of the Missing Dominicans." *International Migration Review* 21 (1987): 1474–97.

Latin American Working Group. "La Banda." Toronto: NACLA Collection, 1971.

Lemoine, René Martínez. "The Classical Model of the Spanish-American Colonial City." *Journal of Architecture* 8 (2003): 355–68.

Lendt, Lee. "A Social History of Washington Heights to 1960." In *Urban Challenges to Psychiatry*, edited by Lawrence Kolb, Viola Bernard, and Bruce Dohrenwend, 39–62. Boston: Little, Brown, 1969.

Leventhal, Nathan. "Report of the Washington Heights–Inwood Task Force." New York: Department of Housing Preservation and Development, 1978.

Levitt, Peggy. *Transnational Villagers*. Berkeley and Los Angeles: University of California Press, 2001.

Lockward de Lamelas, Rosa. "Informe de actividades desarrolladas durante la ejecución del Proyecto de Renovación Urbana del Hoyo de Chulín, Febrero 1988." In *Renovación Urbana en Santo Domingo, 1986–1994*, edited by Juan de Dios Delance. Santo Domingo: Urbanizaciones Nacionales, 1993.

Logan, John R. *The New Latinos*. Lewis Mumford Center for Comparative Urban and Regional Research, September 10, 2001. Available from http://mumford1.dyndns.org/cen2000/HispanicPop/HspReport/HspReportPage1.html.

Los Guandules. *Un barrio estudia a si mismo: Los Guandules*. Santo Domingo: Ediciones Populares, 1983.

Lowenstein, Steven M. *Frankfurt on the Hudson*. Detroit: Wayne State University Press, 1989.

Lozano, Wilfredo. "Dominican Republic: Informal Economy, the State, and the Urban Poor." In *The Urban Caribbean*, edited by Alejandro Portes et al. Baltimore: Johns Hopkins University Press, 1997.

———. *La urbanización de la pobreza*. Santo Domingo: FLACSO, 1997.

Lozano, Wilfredo, Nelson Ramírez and Bernardo Vega, eds. *Ciencias sociales en la República Dominicana*. Santo Domingo: Fundacion Friedrich Ebert: Fondo Para el Avance de las Ciencias Sociales, 1989.

Lugo, Américo. *A punto largo*. Santo Domingo: Imprenta "La Cuna de América," 1901.

MacDonald, Scott B., and F. Joseph Demetrius. "The Caribbean Sugar Crisis." *Journal of Interamerican Studies and World Affairs* 28, no. 1 (1986): 35–58.

Martin, John Bartlow. *Overtaken by Events*. Garden City, NY: Doubleday, 1966.

Martínez-Vergne, Teresita. *Nation and Citizen in the Dominican Republic*. Chapel Hill: University of North Carolina Press, 2005.

Mateo, Andrés L. *Mito y cultura en la era de Trujillo*. Santo Domingo: Librería La Trinitaria, 1993.

Matías, Bernardo. *El poder barrial-comunal*. Santo Domingo, 1991.

McPherson, Alan. "Misled by Himself: What the Johnson Tapes Reveal about the Dominican Intervention of 1965" *Latin American Research Review* 38, no. 2 (2003): 127–46.

———. *Yankee No!* Cambridge: Harvard University Press, 2003.

McReynolds, Charles, and Arthur Vidich. "A Report on High School Principals." *New York Herald Tribune*, April 1969.

Menéndez Alarcón, Antonio. *Power and Television in Latin America: The Dominican Case*. Westport, CT: Praeger, 1992.

Mintz, Sidney W. *Caribbean Transformations*. New York: Columbia University Press, 1989.

———. "The Localization of Anthropological Practice: From Area Studies to Transnationalism." *Critique of Anthropology* 18, no. 2 (1998): 117–33.

Miolán, Angel. *Datos para la historia del turismo de la República Dominicana*. Santo Domingo: Editora de Colores, 1998.

Mitchell, Christopher. "U.S. Foreign Policy and Dominican Migration." In *Western Hemisphere Immigration and U.S. Foreign Policy*, edited by Christopher Mitchell. University Park: Pennsylvania State University Press, 1992.

Morel, Edmundo, and Manuel Mejía. "The Dominican Republic: Urban Renewal and Evictions in Santo Domingo. " In *Evictions and the Right to Housing*, edited by Antonio Azuela, Emilio Duhau, and Enrique Ortíz. Ottowa: International Development Research Centre, 1998.

Moreno Hernández, Miguel Angel. "Mapas sociales de Villa Francisca y contexto neoliberal." *Ciencia y sociedad* 27, no. 2 (2002): 194–223.

Moreno, José A. *Barrios in Arms*. Pittsburgh, PA: University of Pittsburgh Press, 1970.

———. "Intervention and Economic Penetration." *Summation* 5, no. 1–2 (1975): 65–85.

———. "Precursores de la teología de la liberación en República Dominicana." *Revista Mexicana de Sociología* 48, no. 3 (1986): 163–80.

Moya Pons, Frank. *Dominican National Identity and Return Migration*. Gainesville, FL: Center for Latin American Studies, University of Florida, 1981.

———. *The Dominican Republic: A National History*. New Rochelle, NY: Hispaniola Books Corporation, 1995.

———. "Quid Pro Quo: Dominican-American Economic Relations, 1966–1974." *SAIS Review* 19, no. 1 (1975): 32–38.

Ngai, Mae. *Impossible Subjects*. Princeton: Princeton University Press, 2004.

Ortíz, Ana Teresa. "Healers in the Storm: Dominican Health Practitioners Confront the Debt Crisis." Ph.D. diss., Harvard University, 1994.

Pacini Hernández, Deborah. *Bachata*. Philadelphia, PA: Temple University Press, 1995.

Padilla, Felix M. "On the Nature of Latino Ethnicity." *Social Science Quarterly* 65, no. 2 (1984): 651–54.

Parache, Miguel de Jesus, and Javier Peña. "Emigración a Nueva York de tres comunidades dominicanas: Jánico, Baitoa y Sabana Iglesias." Licenciatura, Universidad Católica Madre y Maestra, 1971.

Peña Batlle, Manuel A. *Política de Trujillo*. Ciudad Trujillo: Impresora Dominicana, 1954.

Pérez, Louis A. *On Becoming Cuban*. Chapel Hill: University of North Carolina Press, 1999.

———. "We Are the World: Internationalizing the National, Nationalizing the International." *Jounal of American History* 89, no. 2 (2002): 558–66.

Pessar, Patricia, ed. *Caribbean Currents*. New York: Center for Migration Studies, 1997.

Podair, Jerald E. *The Strike that Changed New York*. New Haven: Yale University Press, 2002.

Polonio, Brada María, and José R. Paulino G. "Renovación urbana y desalojos en Santo Domingo." Licenciatura, Universidad Autónoma de Santo Domingo, 1992.

Portes, Alejandro, ed. *The Economic Sociology of Immigration*. New York: Russell Sage Foundation, 1995.

———. "Transnational Communites: Their Emergence and Significance in the Contemporary World System." In *Latin America in the World Economy*, edited by R. P. Korzeniewicz and W. C. Smith. Westport, CT: Greenwood Press, 1996.

Portes, Alejandro, Luis Guarnizo, and Patricia Landolt. "Transnational Communities: Pitfalls and Promise." *Ethnic and Racial Studies* 22, no. 2 (1999): 217–37.
Portes, Alejandro, and John Walton. *Labor, Class, and the International System.* New York: Academic Press, 1981.
Protestant Council of the City of New York. "Upper Manhattan: A Community Study of Washington Heights." New York, 1954.
Quintero Rivera, Angel. *Salsa, sabor y control.* Madrid and Mexico City: Siglo Veintiuno, 1998.
Rainarman, Craig, and Harry G. Levine. "Crack in Context: Politics and Media in the Making of a Drug Scare." *Contemporary Drug Problems* 16, no. 4 (1989): 535–77.
Ramírez, Nelson. "El Censo del 93." Santo Domingo: Ayuntamiento del Distrito Nacional, 1997.
Rauber, Isabel. *Construyendo poder desde abajo: COPADEBA.* Santo Domingo: Centro Padre Juan Montalvo, 1995.
Reimers, David M. *Still the Golden Door.* New York: Columbia University Press, 1985.
Ricourt, Milagros. *Dominicans in New York City.* New York: Routledge, 2002.
Rivera Gonzáles, Luis. *Antología musical de la Era de Trujillo.* 5 vols. Ciudad Trujillo: Secretaría de Estado de Educación y Bellas Artes, 1960[?].
Rodríguez Creus, Domingo A. *Don Cibaíto en la capital, diario cómico de un cibaeño, sin rumbo fijo, en los "vericuetos" de la gran ciudad.* Santo Domingo: Ediciones Luminaria, 1973.
Rodríguez de León, Francisco. *El furioso merengue del norte.* New York: Rodríguez de León, 1998.
Rogers, Joseph Michael. "Political Economy of Caribbean Drug Trafficking: The Case of the Dominican Republic." Ph.D. diss., Florida International University, 1999.
Romero, Rosita, ed. *Hispanic Families Speak Out.* New York: Committee for Hispanic Children and Families, 1988.
Roorda, Eric Paul. *The Dictator Next Door.* Durham, NC: Duke University Press, 1998.
Rosario Adames, Fausto. *El Reinado de Vincho Castillo: Droga y política en República Dominicana.* Dominican Republic: Impresos Vargas, 1998.
Saenger, Gerhart, and Harry M. Schulman. "A Study of Intercultural Behavior and Attitudes among Residents of the Upper West Side." New York: City College Department of Sociology, 1946.
Sagás, Ernesto. *Race and Politics in the Dominican Republic.* Gainesville: University of Florida Press, 200.
San Miguel, Pedro. "Discurso racial e identidad nacional en la República Dominicana." *Op. Cit.: Revista del Centro de Investigaciones Históricas* 7 (1992): 67–120.
———. *La isla imaginada.* San Juan and Santo Domingo: Isla Negra and La Trinitaria, 1997.
Sassen, Saskia. "Economic Restructuring and the American City." *Annual Review of Sociology* 16 (1990): 465–90.

Schiller, Nina Click, and Georges Fouron. *Georges Woke Up Laughing*. Durham, NC: Duke University Press, 2001.

Shefter, Martin. *Political Crisis, Fiscal Crisis*. New York: Basic Books, 1985.

Snyder, Robert W. "The Neighborhood Changed: The Irish of Washington Heights and Inwood since 1945." In *The New York Irish*, edited by Ronald Bayor and Timothy Meagher, 439–60. Baltimore: Johns Hopkins University Press, 1996.

Szanton Blanc, Cristina, Linda Basch, and Nina Glick Schiller. "Transnationalism, Nation-States, and Culture." *Current Anthropology* 36, no. 4 (1995): 683–86.

Tactuk, Pablo. "Estudios sobre migración interna en la República Dominicana." In *La investigación demográfica en la República Dominicana*, 61–67. Santo Domingo: Asociación para el Desarrollo, 1977.

Tejeda Ortíz, Dagoberto. *Cultura popular e identidad popular*. Santo Domingo: Consejo Presidencial de Cultura: Instituto Dominicano de Folklore, 1998.

Torres-Saillant, Silvio. *Diasporic Disquisitions*. New York: CUNY Dominican Studies Institute, City College of New York, 2000.

———. *El retorno de las yolas*. Santo Domingo: Librería La Trinitaria y Editora Manatí, 1999.

———. "Hacia una identidad racial alternativa en la sociedad dominicana." *Op. Cit.: Revista del Centro de Investigaciones Históricas* 9 (1997): 235–52.

———. "Inventing the Race." *Latino Studies* 1 (2003): 123–51.

———. "The Tribulations of Blackness: Stages in Dominican Racial Identity." *Callaloo* 23, no. 3 (2000): 1086–1111.

Turits, Richard Lee. *Foundations of Despotism*. Palo Alto, CA: Stanford University Press, 2003.

———. "A World Destroyed, a Nation Imposed." *Hispanic American Historical Review* 82, no. 3 (2002): 589–639.

Ugalde, Antonio, Frank Bean, and Gilbert Cárdenas. "International Migration from the Dominican Republic." *International Migration Review* 13, no. 2 (1979): 235–54.

Universidad de Santo Domingo. *Acta final del Primer Simposio para la Evaluación y Defensa de los Recursos Naturales de la República Dominicana, 24 al 29 de Octubre de 1958*. Ciudad Trujillo: Librería Dominicana, 1959.

Vargas, Tahira. *Las organizaciones de base en Santo Domingo*. Santo Domingo: Centro de Estudios Sociales Padre Juan Montalvo, S.J., 1994.

Vargas-Lindius, Rosemary. *Peasants in Distress: Poverty and Unemployment in the Dominican Republic*. Boulder, CO: Westview Press, 1991.

Vargas Mera, Ramón. "Evolución urbanística de Ciudad Trujillo." Ciudad Trujillo: Consejo Administrativo del Distrito Nacional, República Dominicana, 1956.

Veeser, Cyrus. *A World Safe for Capitalism*. New York: Columbia University Press, 2002.

Vega, Bernardo. *En la década perdida*. Santo Domingo: Fundación Cultural Dominicana, 1991.

Vega, Bernardo, and Roberto Desprandel. *Tendencias migratorias hacia los Estados Unidos de dominicanos*. Santo Domingo: FLACSO, 2000.

Velázquez-Mainardi, Miguel Angel. *Narcotráfico y lavado de dólares en la República Dominicana*. Santo Domingo: Editora Corripio, 1992.

Vicioso, Chiqui. "Dominican Migration to the United States." *Migration Today* 1976, 59–72.

Waldinger, Roger. *Through the Eye of the Needle*. New York: New York University Press, 1986.

Weisz, Vilma. "Causas de las migraciones dominicanas al exterior." Licenciatura, Universidad Nacional Pedro Henriquez Ureña, 1973.

Wiarda, Howard. "The United States and the Dominican Republic: Intervention, Dependency, and Tyrannicide." *Journal of Interamerican Studies and World Affairs* 22, no. 2 (1980): 247–59.

Williams, Terry. *Cocaine Kids: The Inside Story of a Teenage Drug Ring*. Reading, MA: Addison-Wesley Publishing Co., 1989.

Witkin, Irving. *Diary of a Teacher: The Crisis at George Washington High School*. New York: United Federation of Teachers, 1970.

Index

Page numbers in italic type indicate illustrations.

category, 114; family as important to, 167; relations among, 114–16, 119
Hispaniola, xxv, 11, 16, 18
Hispanism, 27, 115, 119. *See also* cultura: Latin
historiography, xi–xvii; Latin American, xii–xiii; U.S., xiii–xiv
Ho Chi Minh, 123
Hoe Avenue Laundry Service, 177
"Hombre llegó parao, El" (song)
homosexuality, 64
Honduras (neighborhood), xxvi, 39
Hostos Community College, 185
housing, 32, 40–41, 57–58, 59. *See also* real estate sales; shantytowns
Hoyo de Chulín, 56, 204
human smuggling, 202
"Hurricane, The" (song), 28
Hurwitch, John, 92, 95

ideas, as migration factor, 44–45
identity: of Dominicans in New York, 80, 98–99, 106–7, 113–19, 130–31, 161–62; Hispanic, 114–16, 119
Ignacio, Father, 51–52, 86
Illidge, Eric, 115
immigrant optimism hypothesis, 135–36
immigration. *See* migration; post-war immigration
Immigration and Naturalization Service (INS), 91, 125, 184–86, 226
Immigration Reform Act (1965), 69
imperialism: cultura and, 80–86, 88; Dominicans in New York and, 116–17, 119–25; migration and, xiv–xv, 94–96, 185; nationalism and, xii; nonelites and, xiii; Spanish, 15–18; U.S., xiv, 3, 21, 80–86, 94–95, 203; U.S. scholarship on, xiii
incomes, 41–42
indio, 27
informal economy, 42
inner city: definition of, 132; George Washington High School and, 132, 159, 161–62
INS. *See* Immigration and Naturalization Service
Institute for Price Stabilization (IN-ESPRE), 207, 212
Institute for Social Promotion, 52
intellectuals: anti-U.S. sentiment of, 20–22; attitude of, toward migrants, 170–71;

and cultura, 21–24; and nationalism, 18–24; and rural population, 1, 19–20, 23–24, 26–27; and Trujillo regime, 26–27, 29; and urban beautification, 24–25. *See also* liberalism
International Monetary Fund, 208
Irish: gangs of, 152; immigration of, 196; in Washington Heights, 100–101, 152, 194–95

Jackson, Michael, 232–33, 239
Jackson State massacre, 137
Jacquet-Acea, Russell, 140, 146–47
Jamaica, 269n88
Jarro Sucio (settlement), 51
Jews: and education, 102–6, 272n22; immigration of, 196; and racial issues, 101–3, 105–6, 152, 272n22; in Washington Heights, 101–2, 194–95
Johnny Ventura Fan Club, 175
Johnson, Lyndon, 3, 35, 83, 90
journalism. *See* newspapers
jukeboxes, 62–63
Juventud Estudiantil Cristiana, 141
Juventud Obrera Católica, 51
Juventud Obrera Cristiana, 141

Kennedy, John F., 3, 34, 72, 77, 83
Kent State massacre, 137
Kimble, Johnny, 146, 150
Kimble, Juanita, 144, 150, 154
kinship networks, 91, 169
Koch, Ed, 166, 200–201, 225
Kostman, Samuel, 155–56
Kreuger, Ann, 208

labor migration, as economic exchange, xv
La Ciénaga (neighborhood), xxvii, 41, 42
La Cuadra (settlement), 51
La Cuarenta (settlement), xxix, 51–52
Lama, Elías, 176–77
landholdings, 38
language: children as translators, 167; of Dominicans versus Puerto Ricans, 116; shop signs in, 178; Spanish, in schools, 112–13, 143, 156
Lantigua, Rafael, 195, 214, 225
La Puya de Arroyo Hondo, 52
Las Americas (neighborhood), xxvii, 39
Las Honradas, 65, 66
"Last Stand, The" (Estrella), 83